M000200223

Revolutionary Contagion and International Politics

CHAD E. NELSON

UNIVERSITY PRESS

Oxford University Press is a department of the University of Oxford. It furthers
the University's objective of excellence in research, scholarship, and education
by publishing worldwide. Oxford is a registered trade mark of Oxford University
Press in the UK and certain other countries.

Published in the United States of America by Oxford University Press
198 Madison Avenue, New York, NY 10016, United States of America.

© Oxford University Press 2022

All rights reserved. No part of this publication may be reproduced, stored in
a retrieval system, or transmitted, in any form or by any means, without the
prior permission in writing of Oxford University Press, or as expressly permitted
by law, by license, or under terms agreed with the appropriate reproduction
rights organization. Inquiries concerning reproduction outside the scope of the
above should be sent to the Rights Department, Oxford University Press, at the
address above.

You must not circulate this work in any other form
and you must impose this same condition on any acquirer.

Library of Congress Control Number: 2022937830
ISBN 978-0-19-760193-8 (pbk.)
ISBN 978-0-19-760192-1 (hbk.)

DOI: 10.1093/oso/9780197601921.001.0001

1 3 5 7 9 8 6 4 2

Paperback printed by Lakeside Book Company, United States of America
Hardback printed by Bridgeport National Bindery, Inc., United States of America

Revolutionary Contagion and International Politics

LIBRARY OF
CONGRESS
SURPLUS
DUPLICATE

Contents

Acknowledgments   vii

1. Introduction: Ideologies and International Relations   1

2. A Theory of Domestic Contagion Effects   9

3. Democratic Revolutions and the Ancien Régime   32

4. Liberal Revolutions and the Concert of Europe   78

5. Communist and Fascist Revolutions in Europe   118

6. The Islamic Revolution and the Middle East   173

7. Conclusions, Extensions, and Implications   217

Bibliography   231
Index   261

Acknowledgments

This book is a product of me marinating in the subject for quite some time. It began as a dissertation at the University of California, Los Angeles and I want to thank my committee members: Art Stein, Marc Trachtenberg, Robert Trager, and Michael Mann. More than their help on this project, they taught me how to think about international politics. My graduate school compadres aided me through the process: Joslyn Barnhart, Eric Bordenkircher, Matt Gottfried, Ron Gurantz, Or Honig, Dov Levin, David Palkki, Leah Halverson Sievering, and Dane Swango. I appreciate receiving a Herbert F. York fellowship from the Institute for Global Conflict and Cooperation, which enabled me to finish the dissertation. At Brigham Young University I have been fortunate to have great colleagues. I appreciate the support of my chair, Sven Wilson, while I finished the book. I thank Celeste Beesley, Ray Christensen, Darren Hawkins, Kirk Hawkins, Quinn Mecham, Dan Nielson, and Ken Stiles, who read portions of the manuscript and provided great advice. I especially want to thank Josh Gubler, Scott Cooper, and above all Wade Jacoby. I am sorry my neighbor did not live to see the completion of this project. I also want to thank the BYU students who helped me by translating French, German, and Italian works and carrying out other tasks: Laura Wilde, Anika Argyle, Reilly Andreasen, Elizabeth Whatcott, Amanda Gach, and Emmanuel Reyes. I benefited from the feedback I got at conferences and other venues, especially from Mark Haas and John Owen. I also very much appreciate the constructive comments from the reviewers of the manuscript. A portion of Chapter 6 uses part of the material from my article "Revolution and War: Saddam's Decision to Invade Iran," published in *The Middle East Journal*, and I thank them for permission to reproduce some of the text. Finally, without the support and sacrifices of my wife, Kimber, this book would not exist. I dedicate it to her.

1

Introduction

Ideologies and International Relations

Do ideological differences between states affect their relations? Is there likely to be more conflict between states that have different ideologies to justify their right to rule? Are states that resemble each other ideologically more likely to get along? There has clearly been tremendous debate in the past several centuries over how to organize domestic politics. Monarchists have clashed with democrats, fascists with communists, Arab nationalists with Islamists, and so on. But do these struggles fundamentally affect how international politics has been conducted?

Some examples from history seem to suggest that they have. The Cold War seemed to divide the world into rival blocs of communist and democratic states. The French Revolutionary Wars pitted monarchs against democrats. The Arab Cold War at first pitted leftist Arab nationalists and conservative Arab monarchs against each other. The Three Emperors' League bound conservative monarchs together against liberal states.

On the other hand, there are many cases in international politics where states with drastically different domestic systems align and states with a similar ideology conflict. What followed the Three Emperors' League was an alliance between autocratic Russia and republican France. The Arab Cold War moved from a clash between monarchs and Arab nationalist republics to a clash within the Arab nationalist camp—Nasserist versus Baathist. The Cold War often had democracies siding with autocrats, and the major communist states—Russia and China—at loggerheads.

There is a long-standing tradition in international relations (IR) that argues that how states use ideologies to justify their rule matters for international politics, and that states similar in this regard are more likely to cooperate, while dissimilar states are more likely to conflict. Raymond Aron, for example, suggested that heterogeneous systems, "where the states are organized according to different principles and appeal to contradictory values," are more conflict-prone than homogeneous systems.[1] Likewise, Mark Haas argues that greater

---

[1] Raymond Aron, *Peace and War: A Theory of International Relations*, trans. Richard Howard and Annette Baker (Garden City: Fox, Doubleday and Company, Inc., 1966), 100.

Revolutionary Contagion and International Politics. Chad E. Nelson, Oxford University Press. © Oxford University Press 2022. DOI: 10.1093/oso/9780197601921.003.0001

ideological distance between states will increase threat perceptions and lead to conflict.[2]

Much of international relations scholarship, though, either implicitly or explicitly, disagrees with this "ideological" tradition. One prominent tradition in the study of international politics, the realist school, argues that international relations are driven by the distribution of capabilities in the international system, and that ideological differences are irrelevant.[3] Others simply ignore the notion that these ideological debates have been important—an implicit rejection. Most of the scholarship on how different regime types affect international politics divides those types into democratic and autocratic regimes and makes claims about how democratic regimes have certain domestic properties that make their foreign policy different, or about how democratic dyads are different from the alternatives.[4] Even the dichotomy of democratic and autocratic regimes masks much of the ideological struggle that has occurred between regimes grouped together as autocratic. This does not capture, for example, any differences between fascists and communists, or between conservative Arab monarchies and Arab secular nationalists.

If the "ideological" tradition makes too strong an assumption that ideological differences between states will always matter, those that reject the notion that ideological differences can be salient for international politics also go too far. One of the basic insights that drives this book is that ideological differences between states *do* matter, but they matter in certain times and certain places, for particular political reasons. Ideological differences between states do not always

[2] Mark L. Haas, *The Ideological Origins of Great Power Politics, 1789–1989* (Ithaca: Cornell University Press, 2005). For an overview of some of the thinkers in this tradition, see Fred Halliday, "International Society as Homogeneity: Burke, Marx, Fukuyama," *Millennium: Journal of International Studies* 21, no. 3 (1992).

[3] My use of "realism" in this book refers to the argument that, given anarchy, the distribution of capabilities shapes international politics, and domestic characteristics such as ideological regime types are irrelevant. This is characteristic of what is variously termed "structural realism" or "neorealism" or "balance-of-power realism." For representatives, see Kenneth Waltz, *Theory of International Politics* (Reading: Addison-Wesley, 1979); John J. Mearsheimer, *The Tragedy of Great Power Politics* (New York: W. W. Norton and Company, 2001).

[4] In addition to the vast literature on the democratic peace theory, see also the works on whether democracies are more likely to ally with each other than with non-democracies, e.g., Suzanne Werner and Douglas Lemke, "Opposites Do Not Attract: The Impact of Domestic Institutions, Power, and Prior Commitments on Alignment Choices," *International Studies Quarterly* 41 (1997): 529–46; Michael W. Simon and Erik Gartzke, "Political System Similarity and the Choice of Allies: Do Democracies Flock Together, or Do Opposites Attract?," *Journal of Conflict Resolution* 40, no. 4 (1996): 617–35; Brian Lai and Dan Reiter, "Democracy, Political Similarity, and International Alliances, 1816–1992," *Journal of Conflict Resolution* 44, no. 2 (2000): 203–27; Douglas M. Gibler and Scott Wolford, "Alliances, Then Democracy: An Examination of the Relationship Between Regime Type and Alliance Formation," *Journal of Conflict Resolution* 50, no. 1 (2006): 129–53. For more dynamic approaches, see John M. Owen IV, "When Do Ideologies Produce Alliances? The Holy Roman Empire, 1517–1555," *International Studies Quarterly* 49, no. 1 (2005): 73–99; Erik Gartzke and Alex Weisiger, "Fading Friendships: Alliances, Affinities and the Activation of International Identities," *British Journal of Political Science* 43, no. 1 (2013): 25–52.

prompt conflict, nor do similarities prompt cooperation. A better question than whether ideological differences matter in international politics is when, why, and how much they matter. Because ideological differences between states might matter at some times and not others, we need mechanisms that vary. A social identity mechanism, for example, asserts that states sort into in-groups and out-groups based on commonalities and differences. Such an approach would expect like states to universally gravitate toward each other and unlike states to repel each other. It cannot explain why such differences would be sometimes politically salient and sometimes not.

Is there a mechanism that explains why ideological differences between states become salient for international politics in some times and places and not in others? I propose that there is. One principal mechanism explaining why there could be conflict between ideologically different states is when rulers think an ideology is spreading. This is not something that is always salient across time and space. Ideologically different states can coexist. Some ideological differences between states might be irrelevant in terms of fear of contagion. The United States, for example, does not fear that the Islamic theocracy that is Saudi Arabia is a serious threat to its democratic order. But in certain circumstances, where there are fears that a rival way of organizing domestic politics is catching on, this can have a profound effect on international politics.

An examination of states' response to revolutions provides a particularly useful window into the question of the ideological differences between states. Revolutions are in some respects natural experiments. While certain attributes of the system, such as the distribution of power, often remain relatively constant, a stark change in the principles upon which one of the states is organized creates ideological differences between that state and others in the system. Revolutions are inherently transformations in the "political institutions and the justifications for political authority in a society."[5] The outcome of revolutions—that there is a

---

[5] Jack A. Goldstone, "Toward a Fourth Generation of Revolutionary Theory," *Annual Review of Political Science* 1 (2001): 142. Revolutions are defined as broadly as Charles Tilly's "a forcible transfer of power over a state in the course of which at least two distinct blocs of contenders make incompatible claims to control the state" and as narrowly as Theda Skocpol's "rapid basic transformations of a society's state and class structures . . . accompanied and in part carried through by class-based revolts from below." Jack Goldstone's four criteria accord more with the common usage of the term: (1) new ways to justify political authority, (2) accompanied by formal or informal mass mobilization, (3) accompanied by noninstitutionalized action (which encompasses both violent and nonviolent revolutions), and (4) existing authorities are undermined. Two of these involve the outcome and two involve the process. Scholars of the causes of revolutions, given their focus, often define revolution according to a particular process, but arguably what is most important in whether an event is commonly dubbed a revolution is the outcome. The old elites are removed and there is a new ideology justifying power. For example, the Free Officers' coup in Egypt in 1952 is often called a revolution because the officers displaced the monarchy with a new regime based on pan-Arabism. Charles Tilly, *European Revolutions, 1492–1992* (Cambridge: Wiley-Blackwell, 1996), 8; Theda Skocpol, *States and Social Revolutions: A Comparative Analysis of France, Russia, and China* (New York: Cambridge University Press, 1979), 4.

new regime that is based on a different legitimating ideology—is often what is most salient for the international effects of revolutions. Revolutions also point to a dynamic that helps to explain why ideological differences might be salient at particular times and not others. One reason heterogeneous systems—systems with different regime types—may at times be conflict-prone is that the different types fear the possibility of the other type spreading. This prospect is not something that is constant throughout time. It is salient in particular periods, when it is alternately hoped and feared that an ideology is on the march, and a revolution associated with the ideology is seen as the beginning of a larger wave that will sweep up other nations. This, however, is not consistent even across revolutions.

This book asks two main questions. First, if variations in fear of foreign revolutions cause variations in state reactions, then when exactly do leaders fear the domestic repercussions of revolutions abroad? To draw an analogy from the field of epidemiology (as leaders themselves do when discussing "revolutionary contagion"), I argue that the fear of contagion is derived not primarily from the infecting agent (the revolutionary state) but from the characteristics of the host (the established ruler). Whether the revolutionary state merely serves as a model for revolution or whether it also acts as a platform, attempting to spread revolution abroad, is not the crucial distinction. The fear of contagion is salient when rulers fear a foreign revolution will inspire movements within their country to subvert the existing order. I show that a useful proxy for the salience of this threat is the presence of significant opposition groups of the same character as the revolution. In short, I show that established leaders reason by analogy: they fear foreign revolutions when those events empower groups that they perceive to resemble their own existing opponents.

The second, more important question this book addresses is how and to what extent the prospect of a revolutionary wave affects international affairs. One possibility is that such fears do not have much of an effect—leaders of other states successfully repress their opposition while maintaining their usual geopolitical priorities. I assume, however, that when leaders have reason to fear that a revolution will spread, that fear will indeed affect patterns of cooperation and conflict in predictable ways: fearful leaders will align against the revolutionary state and with other states that face the same threat. These states are often of a similar regime type, though not necessarily so. Rather than engage the revolutionary state, they will try to destroy it or at least isolate it to prevent it from becoming a successful model and/or acting as a platform. Further, they will cooperate with states that face the same threat in order to coordinate both their policies against the revolutionary state and their efforts to suppress the transnational ideological movement. These priorities lead to policies that are otherwise puzzling, such as states shifting their alignments based on ideological changes rather than changes in the balance of power, policies of hostility toward countries that one might expect to be allies, and unexpectedly restrained relations with former rivals.

My argument, which I will call the domestic contagion effects theory, does not exhaust the ways in which ideologies can affect international politics. There are a variety of ways to define political ideology. Political scientists who are interested in explaining the behavior of individuals, such as voting behavior, often define ideology as a personal belief system that is relatively stable and coherent and that guides the individual's behavior.[6] One way ideology can impact international politics is through the belief systems of leaders. However, in the "ideological" tradition of international relations that I refer to, and here in this book, ideology is defined at a more macro level. An ideology is a particular vision "for ordering *domestic* politics."[7] In other words, an ideology can be a broad framework or set of principles that legitimizes rule. In practice, it refers to broad camps of regime types that have similar principles for legitimating rule, such as fascist, democratic, monarchical, Arab nationalist, or communist regimes. I focus on how leaders can fear the spread of an ideology to their own polity following a revolution elsewhere. There are other ways in which ideologies can spread as well. Seva Gunitsky, in his work on how hegemonic shocks have helped determine the nature of regimes, examines how hegemons that emerge apparently successful from such a shock, such as victors of a major war, can prompt emulation of their regime type, in addition to using coercion and inducements to spread their type.[8] Even given the fear of contagion from a revolution, there are two conceptually distinct reasons leaders could have such a fear. They may fear revolutionary contagion for geopolitical reasons—that is, they fear the wave will displace the regime of an ally. Or they may fear it for domestic reasons—that is, they fear the wave will envelop their own polity.[9] I focus on the latter—how fears of domestic disorder affect relations with other states. This is one of the main ways leaders find ideological differences between states politically alarming, and it is both theoretically interesting and neglected by scholars.

---

[6] John T. Jost, "The End of the End of Ideology," *American Psychologist* 61, no. 7 (2006): 653.

[7] Haas, *The Ideological Origins of Great Power Politics*, 5.

[8] Seva Gunitsky, *Aftershocks: Great Powers and Domestic Reforms in the Twentieth Century* (Princeton: Princeton University Press, 2017).

[9] During the Cold War, for example, with the partial exception of the late 1940s and 1950s, American policymakers feared states falling to communism more out of concern for the geopolitical contest than because they thought it would embolden domestic communists. For examinations of the domino theory, see Robert Jervis and Jack L. Snyder, *Dominoes and Bandwagons: Strategic Beliefs and Great Power Competition in Eurasian Rimland* (New York: Oxford University Press, 1991); Jerome Slater, "The Domino Theory and International Politics: The Case of Vietnam," *Security Studies* 3, no. 2 (1993): 186–224; Jerome Slater, "Dominos in Central America: Will They Fall? Does It Matter?," *International Security* 12, no. 2 (1987): 105–34; Robert Jervis, *System Effects: Complexity in Political and Social Life* (Princeton: Princeton University Press, 1997), 165–73; Betty Glad and Charles Taber, "Images, Learning and the Decision to Use Force: The Domino Theory of the United States," in *Psychological Dimensions of War*, ed. Betty Glad (Newbury Park: Sage, 1990), 56–81.

Leaders are faced with various challenges to their rule. Some challenges are direct, in the form of armed conflict, and some are indirect. Some indirect challenges emanate from abroad, and others come from within the state. The way indirect challenges to leaders' rule coming from abroad affect foreign affairs has not been extensively addressed in the study of international relations, but such an approach posits interesting ways in which international and domestic factors interact, causing outcomes that are anomalous from a geopolitical perspective. The focus of leaders is the interests of the political regime or the social order, which does not always coincide with the international interests of the state.[10]

Scholars have increasingly been aware that international factors can have domestic effects—the "second image reversed" effect.[11] The diffusion mechanism has received particular attention, especially regarding the spread of liberalism—free markets and democracy.[12] This has also reached the literature on revolutions and why they sometimes spread.[13] If leaders are cognizant of how international factors could affect their polity, one would expect that this awareness would affect not just their domestic policy but their foreign policy as well.[14] They would anticipate or experience such an effect and therefore pursue a foreign policy that shapes international politics in a way that benefits them domestically. In

[10] For some of the literature explaining international politics in terms of the security of regimes, or leaders, or social orders, see, for example, Giacomo Chiozza and H. E. Goemans, *Leaders and International Conflict* (New York: Cambridge University Press, 2011); Bruce Bueno de Mesquita et al., *The Logic of Political Survival* (Cambridge, MA: MIT Press, 2003); David Skidmore, ed., *Contested Social Orders and International Politics* (Nashville: Vanderbilt University Press, 1997).

[11] Peter Gourevitch, "The Second Image Reversed: International Sources of Domestic Politics," *International Organization* 32, no. 4 (1978): 881–912.

[12] See, for example, Kurt Weyland, *Making Waves: Democratic Contention in Europe and Latin America Since the Revolutions of 1848* (New York: Cambridge University Press, 2014); Beth A. Simmons and Zachary Elkins, "The Globalization of Liberalization: Policy Diffusion in the International Political Economy," *American Political Science Review* 98, no. 1 (2004): 171–89; Laurence Whitehead, *The International Dimensions of Democratization: Europe and the Americas* (New York: Oxford University Press, 2001).

[13] See, for example, Timur Kuran, "Now Out of Never: The Element of Surprise in the East European Revolution of 1989," *World Politics* 44, no. 1 (1991): 7–48; Mark R. Beissinger, "Structure and Example in Modular Political Phenomena: The Diffusion of Bulldozer/Rose/Orange/Tulip Revolutions," *Perspectives on Politics* 5, no. 2 (2007): 259–76; Kurt Weyland, "The Diffusion of Revolution: '1848' in Europe and Latin America," *International Organization* 63, no. 2 (2009): 391–423; Kurt Weyland, "The Arab Spring: Why the Surprising Similarities with the Revolutionary Wave of 1848?," *Perspectives on Politics* 10, no. 4 (2012): 917–34; Henry E. Hale, "Regime Change Cascades: What We Have Learned from the 1848 Revolutions to the 2011 Arab Uprisings," *Annual Review of Political Science* 16 (2013): 331–53. For work on the larger issue of revolutionary waves, see Mark N. Katz, *Revolutions and Revolutionary Waves* (New York: St. Martin's Press, 1997); Maridi Nahas, "State-Systems and Revolutionary Challenge: Nasser, Khomeini, and the Middle East," *International Journal of Middle East Studies* 17, no. 4 (1985): 507–27.

[14] For the domestic response to potential revolutionary contagion, see, for example, Karrie J. Koesel and Valerie Bunce, "Diffusion-Proofing: Russian and Chinese Responses to Waves of Popular Mobilizations Against Authoritarian Rulers," *Perspectives on Politics* 11, no. 3 (2013): 753–68; Nathan Danneman and Emily Hencken Ritter, "Contagious Rebellion and Preemptive Repression," *Journal of Conflict Resolution* 58, no. 2 (2014): 254–79; Rachel Vanderhill, "Active Resistance to Democratic Diffusion," *Communist and Post-Communist Studies* 50 no. 1 (2017): 41–51.

other words, if international factors play a role in preserving or eroding a re-gime, leaders have a strong incentive to shape those factors if they can. This second-image-reversed approach to the study of foreign policy provides a more interactive understanding of the relationship between domestic instability and international conflict than does the dominant narrative, the diversionary theory, which holds that the causal arrow runs only from the domestic independent var-iable to the international dependent variable. One reason scholars study the out-break of revolution is because it provides us with clues about what constitutes domestic order. The effects revolutions can have on international politics like-wise give us an insight into what constitutes international order, and how order at the domestic and international level interact.[15]

Beyond the theoretical insights, I aim to show that in certain periods in in-ternational relations, one simply cannot make sense of international politics—patterns of alliances and wars—without considering the fear of contagion. The contest over regime types has had a profound effect on international politics in certain times and places. The mechanism I examine is a principal way that this effect works.

In this book, I examine the major-power response to ten revolutions or revolts: the American Revolution; the Dutch Patriot Revolt of the 1780s; the 1820–21 revolutions in Spain, Portugal, Naples, Piedmont and Greece; the Russian communist revolution; the Italian fascist revolution; and the Iranian Revolution of 1979. Explaining the international response to these revolutions is important in explaining the outcome of the revolution in many cases. We would not have had a successful American Revolution, for example, without the sup-port of the French and the Spanish, and we would have had a successful demo-cratic revolution in the Netherlands in the 1780s if the Prussians had not crushed it. But it also gives us insights into international politics.

One of the main contributions of the book is that my theory helps us explain when ideological differences between states matter and when they do not. In some cases we see states acting in ways that the ideological theory would not predict; in other instances, we see states taking ideological differences very seriously. The do-mestic contagion effects theory explains why the French monarchy sought geopo-litical gain by aiding democratic revolutionaries in America and the Netherlands just prior to the French Revolution, yet forswore opportunities to aid revolution-aries to undermine their rivals when revolutions broke out in Italy. It explains why communism was viewed as a major threat in interwar Europe and fascism was not. Another contribution is demonstrating that a revolutionary state's policy about exporting revolution is usually not a large factor in prompting hostility

---

[15] A similar point is made by Nick Bisley, "Counter-Revolution, Order and International Politics," *Review of International Studies* 30, no. 1 (2004): 49–69.

toward the revolutionary state. Rather, hostility is based on contagion concerns, which are independent of the revolutionary state's policy. Finally, I show just how powerful the contagion effects are for international politics. The fear of contagion is essential in explaining such things as the transformation of European politics toward a more cooperative order in post-Napoleonic Europe, why interwar Europe had no strong balancing system against Germany, the origins of the Iran-Iraq War, and the sea change in alliance patterns in the Middle East ushered in by the Iranian Revolution. In Chapter 2, I elaborate the specific questions I am addressing, the domestic contagion effects theory, and my method for testing that theory.

2
A Theory of Domestic Contagion Effects

One key mechanism for how ideological differences between states can become salient for international politics is when states fear that a different regime
type, an alternative way of organizing domestic politics, will spread to their own
polity. That is the focus of this book. This prompts two questions. First, when will
leaders fear these contagion effects? Second, what are the international effects of
such contagion fears? This chapter will elaborate my answers to these questions,
which are interrelated. We need to know the answer to the first question because
I assume that the mere presence of an ideologically different state will not necessarily prompt fears of contagion, even in the context of the appearance of a new
regime due to a revolution. I use the answer to this question to get at the second,
and more important, question: how does the fear of ideology spreading affect international politics?

Question 1: When Do Leaders Fear Contagion from Abroad?

When do leaders anticipate contagion from revolutions? We can address this
question by considering how revolutionary states can encourage the spread of
other revolutions. They can do so in two ways: they can act as platforms and they
can be models. When a revolution acts as a platform, the revolutionary state directly acts to spread its revolutionary ideology abroad. When revolutions serve
as models, the cause is indirect—the appearance of a revolution in one place
inspires revolutionary movement in other places, without the direct action of the
revolutionary state.

I argue that leaders fear contagion when the revolutionary state serves as a
model and the leaders have their own significant revolutionary movement that
resembles the foreign revolution. The fear of contagion is primarily derived not
from the infecting (revolutionary) agent but from the characteristics of the (established ruler) host. In other words, contagion fears are not about what the revolutionary agent does, but what it is, when the established ruler has their own
opponents of the same character as the revolution. In those circumstances, the
model prompts contagion fears.

How can a revolution serve as a model for revolutions elsewhere? Why would
leaders fear models? What are the mechanisms? When revolutionary states serve

Revolutionary Contagion and International Politics. Chad E. Nelson, Oxford University Press. © Oxford University Press
2022. DOI: 10.1093/oso/9780197601921.003.0002

as a model for revolution abroad, contagion occurs due to a demonstration effect or diffusion of a revolutionary ideology. Both these terms are characterized by "uncoordinated interdependence": interdependence, because the effect of something happening somewhere changes the probability it will occur somewhere else, and uncoordinated, because it is specifically set apart as distinct from when there is direct coordination, by either cooperative or coercive means.[1]

There are a variety of mechanisms by which revolutions could diffuse that, to varying degrees, can fall under the terms "learning" and "inspiration," the inspiration mechanisms being particularly important in explaining leaders' contagion fears from a successful revolution. The first cluster of mechanisms is about emboldening a preexisting opposition. Opposition groups in other states can learn techniques or tactics from the experience of other revolutions that make it easier for them to revolt successfully. Of course, this narrow sense of learning can cut both ways—opposition groups can learn strategies of revolt, but states can learn strategies of repression from how the old regime fell and the tactics of the resistance, and more successfully stifle the opposition. More significantly, revolutions could cause opposition movements to reassess the plausibility of their regime toppling after seeing a similar regime crumble. Also, the occurrence of revolutions elsewhere can enable the opposition by providing something of a focal point in time—an opportunity for opposition to act simultaneously and overcome collective action problems.[2]

Revolutions elsewhere can cause not just the emboldening of existing opposition, but also the creation of new opposition. Enlarging the opposition further emboldens the existing opposition, as more actors decide the regime must go,

[1] Elkins and Simmons convincingly argue that "diffusion" should be used to describe a particular process that is uncoordinated, in contrast to mechanisms that involve coercion or cooperation. Zachary Elkins and Beth Simmons, "On Waves, Clusters, and Diffusion: A Conceptual Framework," *The Annals of the American Academy of Political and Social Science* 598, no. 1 (2005): 35. This is a process rather than outcome, because the process might not lead to an outcome of conversion, and an outcome of conversion could be the product of a different mechanism. Scholars often use "diffusion" in the broader sense of the "prior adoption of a trait or practice in a population alters the probability of adoption for remaining non-adopters." David Strang, "Adding Social Structure to Diffusion Models: An Event History Framework," *Sociological Methods and Research* 19, no. 3 (1991): 325. Diffusion in this sense could involve direct coordination in the form of cooperation or coercion. This direct coordination is sometimes referred to as vertical diffusion, as opposed to horizontal diffusion. For examples of the use of diffusion in this broader sense, see Gunitsky, *Aftershocks*, 55; Erin R. Graham, Charles R. Shipan, and Craig Volden, "The Diffusion of Policy Diffusion Research in Political Science," *British Journal of Political Science* 43, no. 3 (2013): 673–701; Beth A. Simmons, Frank Dobbin, and Geoffrey Garrett, "Introduction: The International Diffusion of Liberalism," *International Organization* 60, no. 4 (2006): 781–810. In the way I am using the term, "diffusion" and "demonstration effect" are interchangeable. The term "demonstration effect" originates from the economist James Duesenberry's discussion of how the dissatisfaction with one's habitual set of goods after observing higher consumptive patterns of one's neighbors drives consumption expenditures up. James Duesenberry, *Income, Saving and the Theory of Consumer Behavior* (Cambridge, MA: Harvard University Press, 1949), 27–32.

[2] The discussion of focal points in terms of coordination began with Thomas C. Schelling, *The Strategy of Conflict* (Cambridge, MA: Harvard University Press, 1960), 54–58.

and/or that they are going to do something about it. Opposition can mount as it becomes perceived as more probable that a regime will fall, but a prior cause of this may be that the regime is seen as increasingly illegitimate—the old ideology justifying the ruler's right to rule is increasingly discredited and new ideologies are seen as the wave of the future—powered by the example of a revolution somewhere else. Alternatively, it may be that actors that previously regarded the existing regime as illegitimate but were acquiescent are now inspired by another revolution to take action.[3]

It is the "inspiration" mechanisms that embolden and enlarge the opposition that are particularly salient if it is the case that rulers fear contagion from a revolution that has already succeeded. Much of the learning mechanisms take place when a regime falls. From this perspective, after the fall of the old regime, there is no new information that affects the fear of contagion. But the focus on the eroding legitimacy of the state and the inspiration of new opposition is affected by the continuing presence of the revolutionary state.

Rulers often face challenges to their rule, but the assumption here is that the frequency and nature of these challenges vary over time and space. In some periods and places the very basis of political authority is openly called into question. Rulers obviously have vested interests in seeing that these challenges do not arise, or at least remain contained. This involves crushing resistance and, more commonly, deterring those opposed to their rule from taking action. It also involves preserving their legitimacy among the population that accepts their rule. Rulers do not rely on coercion (or the threat of it) alone to provide order and preserve their rule. As one scholar has stated, Machiavelli "gave a misleading account of the choices open to rulers when he advised that it was better to be feared than to be loved. Certainly if rulers are not feared they cannot rule, for the law depends upon the ultimate sanction of enforcement. But fear works best when clothed in authority."[4] The more regimes lose even a veneer of legitimacy, the more they risk losing consent even by sources within the regime, the more governing becomes a risky and dangerous game.[5] Rulers thus go to great

---

[3] Inspiration involves emotions, which have been neglected in the study of revolutions. See, though, Wendy Pearlman, "Emotions and the Microfoundations of the Arab Uprisings," *Perspectives on Politics* 11, no. 2 (2013): 387–409. For a discussion of how revolutionaries becoming emboldened can create new structural facts, see Charles Kurzman, "Structural Opportunity and Perceived Opportunity in Social-Movement Theory," *American Sociological Review* 61, no. 1 (1996): 153–70.

[4] Rodney Barker, *Political Legitimacy and the State* (New York: Oxford University Press, 1990), 30.

[5] This may seem commonplace, but the concept of legitimacy has often been dismissed by scholars, including the scholarship on revolutions. Legitimacy has been characterized as amorphous and difficult to measure; it also assumes a type of political support that is grounded in shared moral evaluations, which does not fit with the assumptions of some scholars' models. Both structuralist and rationalist accounts of revolt assume actors are only waiting for their opportunity to pounce—they are not motivated by new goals or values. For an elaboration and critique on this point, see Jeffrey Berejikian, "Revolutionary Collective Action and the Agent-Structure Problem," *American Political Science Review* 86, no. 3 (1992): 647–57. Gilley makes an argument for a return to the concept; see Bruce Gilley, *The Right to Rule: How States Win and Lose Legitimacy* (New York: Columbia University

lengths to preserve their legitimacy and to prevent those who regard the regime as illegitimate from acting. They attempt to keep any contestation within certain bounds—not questioning the fundamental right of the rulers to rule. And part of preserving their rule is maintaining an international system that supports rather than casts doubt on their regime type. They want to snuff out sources of inspiration.

How can a revolutionary state act as a platform? Why might leaders fear revolutionary states acting as platforms? The most direct way a state can act as a platform is to invade other states and impose similar regimes. Less directly, it can engage in subversion to foment revolution in another state—organizing and aiding opposition groups, disseminating propaganda, even attempting to assassinate leaders in other states. Leaders will obviously fear revolutionary states that attempt to act as a platform in the strongest sense—invading them to impose their regime type. But that is uncommon. The instances of this occurring to a major regional power, which is the focus of this book, are limited to the most prominent case—the French Revolutionary Wars. Revolutionary states often desire that their regime type spreads, but they are not in a position to be the cause of the spread in such a matter. More common are revolutions acting as a platform in less direct ways. Revolutions always serve as models, and sometimes it is just that—doing little more to spread their regime type beyond their mere existence.

When will leaders fear contagion? One could argue that leaders fear contagion only when revolutionary states are directly fomenting revolution abroad. Leaders may be concerned only with what states do rather than with who they are: the indirect mechanisms outlined previously are simply too peripheral to have much of an effect. I will argue that while of course leaders will not be indifferent to the policies of the revolutionary state—they will not appreciate attempts of subversion, and such policies may increase their hostility toward the revolutionary state—their fears of contagion, and thus the international effects, are orthogonal to such policies.

The fear of contagion involves characteristics of the infecting agent and characteristics of the host. The infecting agent can be what the revolutionary state does (platform) or what the revolutionary state is (model). Regarding the latter, the "ideological" tradition in IR that argues ideological differences between states create antagonism supposes that the more difference there is, the more antagonism there is. The fear of contagion, though, does not necessarily increase with ideological distance. In fact, regimes of a completely different nature

Press, 2009). The loss of the legitimacy of a regime is often explicit or implicit in descriptive accounts of revolution, including the historiography of particular revolutions as well as an older scholarship on the causes of revolutions that focused more on describing the pattern of the revolutionary process— the "natural history" school. It has been understandably cast aside by scholarship that attempts to be more predictive, because the loss of legitimacy is obviously not a sufficient condition for revolution.

probably do not pose a serious threat of contagion, just as a Catholic may see Protestantism as more threatening than Hinduism. Ideological differences are not inherently threatening. At minimum, an ideology must make some claim to target some other state—for example, ideologies that are universal or based on religious/ ethnic "imagined communities" that spill across borders. This one factor alone explains a good deal of the variation of the international effects of revolutions rather than, say, whether revolutions are mass-based or elite-driven. For example, the 1952 Egyptian Revolution, which was a coup of army officers that subsequently mobilized the masses with their pan-Arabist ideology, had a much greater international impact than the Mexican Revolution, a mass-based social revolution, simply because Arab nationalism was more threatening to surrounding states than Mexican nationalism. All revolutions serve as models in the narrow "learning" sense—opposition movements can learn from the weaknesses of existing regimes and so forth. But only revolutions with transnational ideologies serve as models in the "inspiration" sense. However, even if ideologies potentially target other states, the threat will not necessarily be salient. One must examine characteristics of the host.

An ideological threat is salient when rulers fear it will inspire movements within their country to subvert the existing order. I argue it is not ideology per se that they fear, but how ideologies translate into social power when revolutions threaten to embolden and enlarge opposition groups. A useful, if imperfect, proxy for the salience of the ideological threat is the presence of significant opposition groups of a similar character as the revolution. To be of a similar character as the revolution does not mean that these groups are advocating for precisely the same system. Indeed, Kurt Weyland's work on revolutionary waves has shown that people use heuristics when they interpret events from abroad, and sometimes what they regard as an inspiring model is quite different from the one they want to implement.[6] Rather, it means that the revolutionary opposition movements share the same ideological family—Islamist, socialist/communist, fascist, liberal—as the revolutionary state. The presence of such groups captures characteristics of the revolutionary state as well as the established ruler's polity. It means the ideology legitimating the revolution is a transnational phenomenon, targeting other states. And it means that a state is already somewhat vulnerable— there is a level of organization and resistance that makes contagion plausibly threatening. Why there is a significant revolutionary opposition in the first place can be indicative of vulnerabilities in the regime. What lies outside the theory is the possibility that leaders might consider an ideological movement a salient threat and act to preempt such opposition from forming in their country in the first place. I suppose this level of threat remains too abstract for leaders to care.

---

[6] Kurt Weyland, *Making Waves: Democratic Contention in Europe and Latin America Since the Revolutions of 1848* (New York: Cambridge University Press, 2014).

I assume a soft rationality of leaders, or at least do not assume they are irrational. Just as leaders do not act on threats that are too abstract, I assume that when they have contagion concerns, those concerns are plausible. Sometimes leaders' fears of contagion are dismissed as irrational misperceptions perhaps due to their ideological blinders. For example, Stephen Walt assumes the fear of revolution spreading is a misperception, or myth, and thus mistakenly argued in the aftermath of the Tunisian Revolution in 2011 that there would be no contagion effects.[7] Michael Carley, in his historical analysis of the response to the Russian Revolution, assumes that the Western powers were foolish for thinking that communism would spread.[8] Revolutionary waves are admittedly rare events, but they might be rare events in part precisely because leaders take the necessary steps to prevent them from happening. In other words, there might be what Robert Jervis calls a "domino theory paradox": the mechanism is present, but its very anticipation provokes countervailing policies.[9] In addition, leaders have good reason to fear events such as revolutions that are rare but have severe consequences. Wars are also rare, and yet IR scholars often suppose that the fear of war drives behavior. Just because their fears of contagion do not come to fruition is not proof that their fears are irrational.

To summarize, I argue that rulers fear revolutionary threats to their regimes when revolutions are associated with existing opposition groups. Already challenged, the revolution threatens not just to embolden but greatly enlarge this opposition. I argue that this fear exists irrespective of the actual policies of the revolutionary state—that is, whether or not it seeks to actively promote its revolution abroad.

Question 2: What Are the International Effects of the Fear of Contagion?

Determining when leaders will fear contagion is a necessary part of this book, but even more important is what effect this fear has on international affairs. One possibility that runs counter to my domestic contagion effects theory is that it does not have much of an effect. First, there can be policy substitution. Leaders can repress opposition while maintaining their usual geopolitical priorities. Another possibility is that they can just switch sides. This seems to be a dubious strategy, because the goals of the revolutionaries and ruling class are usually

---

[7] Stephen M. Walt, *Revolution and War* (Ithaca: Cornell University Press, 1996), 40; Stephen M. Walt, "Why the Tunisian Revolution Won't Spread," *Foreign Policy*, January 16, 2011.
[8] Michael Jabara Carley, *Silent Conflict: A Hidden History of Early Soviet-Western Relations* (Lanham: Rowman & Littlefield, 2014).
[9] Robert Jervis, *System Effects: Complexity in Political and Social Life* (Princeton: Princeton University Press, 1997), 266–71.

incompatible, and the revolutionaries will not be content to leave the old elites in power. But certainly there can be a degree of co-option, whereby leaders use carrots along with sticks to concede to some of the demands of the opposition.

Leaders may increase their use of carrots and sticks toward their domestic opposition, but I assume that they will not consider this sufficient. I argue that ruling class strategies will extend to not just domestic but international affairs. When leaders fear revolution spreading, they will not be content with internal policies. It will have a discernable effect on patterns of cooperation and conflict: they will align against the revolutionary state and they will align with other states that face the same threat, which are often, but not necessarily, states that are of a similar regime type. The mechanism is political—leaders preserving their domestic regime—and it is not driven by ideological distance. Leaders of different regime types can face the same ideological threat and band together to defeat it. When leaders have a similar opposition, leaders will fear that revolutionary states will act as platforms and serve as models that will encourage the spread of revolutionary instability to their own polities. They will thus try to reverse or at least contain revolutions, which entail policies of hostility ranging from an invasion of the revolutionary state to diplomatic isolation.

Leaders' hostility toward revolutionary states follows from the discussion of revolutionary states as platforms and models. If it was just revolutionary states acting as platforms that leaders feared, then those states not acting as a platform, either because they are too weak to muster much of a threat or because they have chosen not to pursue such a policy, would not generate a hostile response. Even with those revolutionary states that did act as a platform, one could presumably bargain with such a state—attempt to cut a deal that involves the revolutionary state ceasing its exporting of the revolution in exchange for its survival. But if the problem is the revolutionary state acting as a model, then a bargain cannot be struck, because the issue is the revolutionary state's existence.[10] Henry Kissinger claimed that the "distinguishing feature" of a revolutionary state is that nothing can reassure it.[11] However, this is more characteristic of counterrevolutionary states. The hostility toward the revolutionary state is driven by a desire to "kill the baby in the crib"—to prevent a successful revolution or to reverse an already successful revolution. Even when leaders recognize that they will not be able to

---

[10] As Edmund Burke said about England's policy toward France, "we were at war not with its conduct, but with its existence." Edmund Burke, *Letters on a Regicide Peace* (Indianapolis: Liberty Fund, 1999 [1796]), 155.

[11] Henry A. Kissinger, *A World Restored: Metternich, Castlereagh and the Problems of Peace, 1812–1822* (Boston: Houghton Mifflin, 1957), 2. Kissinger considered revolutionary states as those who do not accept the international order. He was thinking of the French case, where there was both a revolution and a state that did not accept the international order, but these are conceptually different—not all states that reject the international order have had a domestic revolution, and not all states that have had a domestic revolution reject the international order.

suppress a revolution entirely, they are hostile as a means of isolating the state and preventing it from becoming a successful model and/or acting as a platform. Because the fear of contagion is not contingent on states acting as a platform, leaders' hostility will not be dependent on whether a state is acting as a platform. Certainly, leaders will not appreciate other states meddling in their affairs. That claim is unsurprising. My argument, though, is that the model drives contagion fears independent of the state acting as a platform.

When arrayed with the options of aligning with, remaining neutral toward, or aligning against states, leaders facing revolutionary contagion will not just engage in hostility toward the revolutionary state, but will align with states facing similar threats.[12] That is, they will have broadly cooperative security strategies. They will have similar aims and aid one another diplomatically and possibly materially, rather than exploit or undermine one another. Leaders will cooperate with states that face the same threat in order to coordinate their policies against the revolutionary state as well as coordinate their policies of suppressing the transnational ideological movement.[13] In these instances, I argue, it is not the balance of power or other pressures that determine patterns of cooperation and conflict, but the anticipation of revolutionary contagion. This creates policies that would otherwise be puzzling: states shifting their alignments based on ideological changes rather than changes in the balance of power, states intervening in revolutions they do not have much geopolitical interest in, or unexpectedly restrained relations with regimes of a similar nature. On the other hand, when leaders do not have revolutionary opposition movements and thus fear of contagion, other factors can come to the fore, such as realpolitik policies of using revolutions to exploit one's rivals, irrespective of ideological concerns.

The answers my domestic contagion effects theory gives to the questions of when leaders fear revolutionary contagion and what the international effects of that fear are is summarized in Table 2.1.

---

[12] I use "alignment" because the more formal written agreement, sometimes implied by the word "alliance," is not necessary to indicate a broadly cooperative relationship. The classic example is US-Israeli relations, where there is no formal alliance. Stephen M. Walt, *The Origins of Alliances* (Ithaca: Cornell University Press, 1987), 12

[13] The threat of revolution also encourages cooperation in general to prevent revolutions from erupting in the first place because war, and the preparation for war, can make regimes more vulnerable to upheaval. War can weaken the state to the point of breakdown, providing opportunities for revolutionary movements to strike. See Theda Skocpol, *States and Social Revolutions: A Comparative Analysis of France, Russia, and China* (New York: Cambridge University Press, 1979). Rulers, especially in the aftermath of major wars, are often aware of the strain interstate competition can place on the stability of the state. This has at times been a powerful factor in preventing conflicts between states. States also often face trade-offs of efficiency in whether their armed forces are structured to internally repress or to engage effectively in interstate war, which also promotes cooperation. See Stanislav Andreski, "On the Peaceful Disposition of Military Dictatorships," *Journal of Strategic Studies* 3, no. 3 (1980): 3–10. I touch on these issues, but do not systematically address them.

Table 2.1 Domestic Contagion Effects Theory

		Characteristics of Hosts	
		No Significant Revolutionary Opposition	Significant Revolutionary Opposition
Characteristics of Revolutionary State	Not Acting as a Platform	*Cell 1* No domestic contagion effects: often international politics as usual	*Cell 2* Domestic contagion effects: hostility toward revolutionary state, cooperation with states with similar movements
	Acting as a Platform	*Cell 3* No domestic contagion effects, but strong platform may still threaten weak states	*Cell 4* Domestic contagion effects: hostility toward revolutionary state, cooperation with states with similar movements

This table is an explanatory typology that maps the property space of the theory's two variables: whether the revolutionary state acts as a platform and whether other states have significant revolutionary movements or not.[14] Because I assume that all revolutionary states are models, being a model is not a variable and I do not include it in the table.[15] Cells 2 and 4 are situations where there are significant revolutionary movements and thus fears of contagion that lead to the pattern of conflict with the revolutionary state and cooperation with states that have similar movements and thus similar fears. As argued, I expect these patterns to exist whether the revolutionary state is acting as a platform or not, so there should not be variation in the outcome in Cell 2 and Cell 4 in terms of the basic patterns predicted. That is not to say that actions of the revolutionary state in spreading revolution will have no effect. They could further exacerbate the tensions with other states. But that does not alter the patterns of alignments and hostility. The fact that the basic outcome of these cells is the same is perhaps surprising, and highlighted by this table.

In Cell 1, where the revolutionary state is not acting as a platform (and is by implication only a model) and there are no significant revolutionary movements, there will be no domestic contagion effects. This could mean international politics as usual, and what that might mean is a realpolitik policy whereby ideological

---

[14] For explanatory typologies, see Colin Elman, "Explanatory Typologies in Qualitative Studies of International Politics," *International Organization* 59, no. 2 (2005): 293–326.

[15] Revolutions are all models in the sense that revolutionaries elsewhere can learn about how to overthrow a state; the revolutions I deal with in this book and that my theory applies to are also models in the sense that they represent a transnational ideology that can inspire others to take action.

differences between states are irrelevant and revolutions are exploited as a means to further a state's geopolitical position. I do not assume, though, that a realpolitik policy is necessarily the default position in international relations. The revolution could simply not disrupt existing patterns of cooperation and conflict. On the other hand, there could be non-domestic-contagion-related policy effects from the ideological change of the revolution. I argue that my mechanism will not be present, but others could be.

In Cell 3, states that are directly acting to foment revolution in these situations—that is to say, doing more than rhetorically denouncing other regimes— are likely to be rare in nature. If there is no significant opposition movement in a state, one option a revolutionary state has in spreading revolution is to invade that state and impose its regime type. This clearly requires a significant power disparity between the revolutionary state and its targets, one that we are unlikely to observe if we are considering only major regional powers, as this book is. As stated, the case of the French Revolutionary Wars is the only example in history. In this situation, there are obviously major international effects of the revolution. States will not take kindly to being invaded. If a foreign-imposed regime change is off the table, then the revolutionary state has the option of trying to organize from relative scratch a revolutionary opposition movement or aiding an insignificant movement, but this is the equivalent of trying to harvest a crop that is not ripe. If it does occur, it may be a source of irritation from the target state's perspective. But it will not fundamentally affect bilateral relations, given the insignificance of the movement and thus the lack of contagion concerns. This book has cases that fit in each of these cells, as I explain in what follows.

Testing the Theory

Based on my proposed answer to the questions given earlier, I need to assess the nature of the opposition in states and whether the revolutionary state tries to spread revolution abroad. I want to ascertain whether leaders fear contagion from a revolutionary state, to what extent that fear is driven by the policies of the revolutionary state acting as a platform, and to what extent it is driven by the presence of a revolutionary opposition at home. Then I want to see whether the fear of contagion leads to policies of hostility toward the revolutionary state and cooperation with states that have the same contagion fears.

I use qualitative methods in this book in two senses. The first is that I provide a qualitative description of the independent variables: I begin each case with a description of how the revolution acted as a platform and/or a model in spreading revolution, and the nature of the opposition within the major powers of the region. I then describe the relations between states before the revolution to provide a baseline to determine how the revolution affected international politics. I discuss the domestic contagion effects theory's predictions given those independent variables and alternate theories. Second, I use process tracing to determine the effect the independent variables had on the dependent variables: the patterns of cooperation and conflict between the major powers of the region.[16]

My answer to the questions about when leaders fear revolution spreading can be broken down into two specific hypotheses, as can my answers about the international effects of that fear. I will elucidate these four hypotheses and the evidence needed.

Hypothesis 1.1: Given a revolution, leaders anticipate revolutionary contagion affecting their own regime only when they perceive there is a significant revolutionary movement in their state of the same character as the revolution.

There are several things to unpack. First, what is "revolutionary"? Opposition groups are revolutionary *when they are bent on radically changing the nature of the regime*. In many cases, whether opposition groups are revolutionary is easy to determine because they are partaking in violent attempts to overthrow the regime, and the regime type advocated by the opposition movements is fundamentally inconsistent with the ruling regime. In other cases, differences may not necessarily be fundamental, but depend on the strategies of the opposition and ruling regime. For example, western European communist parties during the interwar period openly advocated the downfall of existing regimes (even while participating in elections), while those same parties during the Cold War accommodated themselves to democratic regimes. On the other side, the monarchies of France and Britain in the 1830s and 1840s accommodated themselves to liberal movements, whereas for the absolute monarchies of Austria, Prussia, and Russia these movements were revolutionary. To detail the strategic interaction between these players would be a book of its own. Instead, I focus on whether there was or was not a significant revolutionary movement.

What is a "significant movement"? Revolutionary *movements* suppose a certain level of organization dedicated to overthrowing the state, rather than isolated intellectuals haranguing against the regime. Revolutionary movements need not be vast to be significant. Indeed, most revolutions only involve a small minority of a state's citizens. But they need to be of sufficient size and/or placement to be a credible threat to the regime. It is difficult to postulate a clear dividing line between what is significant and not that cuts across a variety of

---

[16] For a discussion of process tracing, see, for example, James Mahoney, "Process Tracing and Historical Explanation," *Security Studies* 24, no. 4 (2015): 200–18; Andrew Bennett and Jeffrey T. Checkel, eds., *Process Tracing: From Metaphor to Analytic Tool* (New York: Cambridge University Press, 2015).

historical contexts. The ends of the spectrum are uncontroversial—historians concur that there was a significant segment of the population in France in 1820 that wanted to overthrow the Bourbon monarchy and there were people organizing to bring this about, just as they concur that there was no sizable constituency for overthrowing the monarchy prior to the French Revolution. But there can be borderline cases. Historians still debate the level of support for revolution in Britain in the 1790s.[17]

One clear marker for whether such movements are significant is whether there has been an uprising in the recent past. That supposes a movement with a significant following to make a bid for power. The Bourbon monarchy in 1820, for example, was well aware that it had been overthrown only a few years previously and was reinstalled by the great powers. Even so, a recent history of revolt is not the only indicator of the presence of a significant revolutionary movement. There could also be straightforward evidence of revolutionary parties garnering a significant percentage of the vote (say, 5 percent) or clear evidence of revolutionary organizations with sizable followings. The idea is simply to get at whether the movements exist and are not isolated and marginal—that is, whether they pose a potential threat. The domestic contagion effects theory is a threshold theory: that when there is a significant revolutionary movement, there will be fears of contagion and concordant international effects. Thus, I assess these movements in binary terms rather than comparative metrics. I also do not consider trends. Even if a significant movement has been recently successfully suppressed, I argue leaders will fear the possibility of it reconstituting itself.

Part of the strategy of the case selection elaborated in what follows is to choose cases where there clearly is or is not such opposition so that I can minimize ambiguous coding. In only one of the cases I deal with in this book is there a substantial historiographic debate over the significance of the revolutionary movement, and that is the French fascist case. This is due to discrepant views of what constitutes fascism, as I will discuss.

Judging a movement's level of support and thus significance can be difficult, for both the scholar and the ruler. Given that the opposition in question is revolutionary, these groups tend to be outlawed and heavily suppressed. If there are ambiguities about the strength of the movement and the nature of the movement—whether the groups are committed to overthrowing the current regime— I err on the side of classifying the movement as significant and revolutionary. If the size or nature of the movement is ambiguous, I assume rulers will err on the side of caution and think they have a significant revolutionary movement on their hands. This makes for a harder test of the theory, because I am assuming

---

[17] For a summary of this debate, see Edward Royle, *Revolutionary Britannia? Reflections on the Threat of Revolution in Britain* (Manchester: Manchester University Press, 2000), 1–10.

that even in cases with an ambiguously significant opposition movement there will be contagion effects that will have a decisive effect on foreign policy.

Regarding the perception of significant revolutionary movements, leaders' subjective judgments are of course what determine their policies. I pursue objective indicators as well as subjective judgments as a check on those subjective judgments. Because I assume a soft rationality for leaders, I assume their subjective assessments and objective indicators will be similar—they will usually correctly ascertain whether their countries have significant revolutionary movements. There could be reasons for a discrepancy between the two, some of which lie outside the theory and others within it. One possibility outside the theory is if leaders consistently claim the existence of a significant revolutionary movement when there is none. If this is the case, perhaps paranoia was at play, requiring a psychological explanation, or perhaps leaders were disingenuously claiming the presence of revolutionary movements for political purposes—to give them cover to crack down on their opposition, for example. Leaders might also underestimate the presence of significant revolutionary movements. This certainly can happen with a new revolutionary movement, and my theory would suppose that leaders would quickly update their beliefs and act accordingly. They may also play down a revolutionary movement when they fear there is another, greater revolutionary movement, which is what we will see regarding fascism and communism. In cases where there are multiple revolutionary threats, my theory does not have a means to determine ex ante which leaders will find more threatening. It assumes they will find all of them threatening.

I assume that leaders will be relatively prudent, so they will not fear contagion and thus base their foreign policy on such concerns when they do not perceive that there is no existing movement and thus the threat is too abstract. On the other hand, if, as I said, the significance of the revolutionary movement is ambiguous, I will assume that they will consider it to be significant. The same is true with leaders' perceptions of whether movements are revolutionary. Leaders have political reasons to portray potential reformers as revolutionaries that are in the same broad ideological camp as true revolutionaries, but it might not be just the motivation to discredit their domestic opponents that causes them to treat these movements as revolutionary. They may assume that the methods, and sometimes the aims, of these movements are fickle, and thus it is prudent to assume the worst. Things can get out of hand, even it is the intention of some reformers for it not to.

As discussed, what I mean by movements being the same character of the revolutionary state is simply that they are in the same broad ideological tent, pushing a similar agenda. Of course, there can be many divides within this tent. Infighting is endemic to ideological movements. Socialists will disagree with other socialists about the best way to pursue socialism, and so on. But these internal disagreements do not negate the fact that they are of the same movement and can be emboldened by other successes within that movement.

Whether the presence of revolutionary groups is a reliable predictor of the fear of revolutionary contagion given a revolution will be assessed by examining cases in which there were such groups and in cases where there were none. Evidence that regimes fear revolutionary contagion can be partially gleaned from private discussions of leaders. Their domestic policies are also indicators. When revolutions occur and a ruler's domestic opposition is significantly magnified, one can expect a ruler to fear revolutionary contagion. Increased visible resistance to the regime may be muted if the regime anticipates the threat and at least temporarily contains it. Evidence that is more reliable is a change in policy toward opposition groups: increased repression, sometimes in combination with concessions, depending on the strategy. There are also other indicators of a perception of threat to the regime, such as increased surveillance and censorship of the population at large, efforts to censor or distort reports of the revolution abroad, and a shift in public rhetoric.

Are there certain regime types that are more vulnerable to having significant revolutionary movements? This may be the case. Current political science puts great stress on the differences between democracies and autocracies, and it is plausible that, all else equal, significant revolutionary movements are more likely to emerge in autocracies when there is "no other way out" to address grievances.[18] My theory of domestic contagion effects does not get into the business of predicting which states will be vulnerable to revolutionary movements or revolution. I do not provide a theory of revolution or have a theory of the state. I simply argue that the presence of this movement will signal vulnerabilities and thus make leaders fear contagion effects. The regime's vulnerability could be about not just that revolutionary movement but what the movement says about the regime's vulnerabilities in general.[19] Although democracies may be less likely to have revolutionary movements, I do not assume it makes them invulnerable to these movements. My theory thus does not make a distinction between democracies and autocracies, and indeed this book has cases of democracies with significant revolutionary movements and leaders that feared contagion.

Hypothesis 1.2: If there is domestic opposition, as specified in Hypothesis 1.1, leaders will fear revolutionary contagion irrespective of the policy of the revolutionary state.

---

[18] The phrase is from Jeff Goodwin, *No Other Way Out: States and Revolutionary Movements, 1945–1991* (New York: Cambridge University Press, 2001).

[19] While perhaps democracies provide less motive for revolutionary movements to develop, they could provide more opportunity, because the authoritarian state might have greater tools of repression available to it.

There are three different ways I provide evidence of this assertion. First, the claim is most clearly evidenced in cases where revolutions do not attempt to export their movement to the state in question yet there are significant contagion concerns. Second, even in cases where the revolutionary state attempts to spread the revolution abroad, I assess whether the timing of the revolutionary state's attempts to spread revolution abroad corresponds with the fear of contagion. If fears of revolutionary contagion predate the revolutionary state's policies, or are greater in a period before the revolutionary state was acting as much of a platform, it suggests the power of the revolutionary state acting as a model, irrespective of platform concerns. Third, in cases where the revolutionary state attempts to spread revolution in some states but not others, or more in some states rather than others, I assess whether this corresponds with the fear of contagion. In other words, beyond temporal correlation, is the fear of contagion spatially correlated with states acting as a platform? If fear of contagion exists across the board irrespective of the extent to which the revolutionary state is acting as a platform, that also suggests the power of the model effect.

As mentioned, a revolutionary state acting as a platform to spread revolution means the state is taking direct action to spread revolution abroad, which can range from attempting regime change through invasion to more common, less costly efforts of subversion, such as aiding opposition movements. Often, revolutionary states will denounce the legitimacy of other regimes or even verbally encourage uprisings abroad. Mere rhetoric is somewhere on the borderline between acting as a platform and serving as a model. It is action, but it is not direct action. It is just making explicit what is at least implicit in a state's revolutionary ideology. The mere act of denouncing other regimes does not make a revolutionary state much of a platform if it is not materially aiding revolutions abroad. On the other hand, setting up radio stations to broadcast calls to neighboring countries or spreading propaganda to other regimes denouncing that regime and calling on the opposition to rise up is direct action to spread revolution.

Hypothesis 2.1: States that fear revolutionary contagion will engage in hostilities toward the revolutionary state.

The most direct international effect of the anticipation of revolutionary waves is the policy toward the revolutionary state. I hypothesize regimes with such fears will be hostile to that state, as opposed to taking a neutral position or actively cooperating. That hostility could include the initiation of war, some lighter form of intervention (such as aid to opposition groups), or a containment policy (economically or diplomatically isolating the state). Various factors will determine what form the hostility will take, and my theory does not attempt to predict these forms. Many of these are idiosyncratic.[20] I will examine instances where states anticipate revolutionary contagion and instances where they do not. In the latter case, my theory would not expect hostility toward the revolutionary state, but there might be unrelated reasons for a policy of hostility. In other words, my hypothesis is sufficient for hostility, but not necessary. I thus use process tracing to examine whether the hostility was the result of the mechanism I identified. The inverse case, however, when states anticipate revolutionary contagion and nevertheless align with those revolutionary states, is an anomaly for the domestic contagion effects theory, and indicates that other factors are overwhelming the factors I deem most salient. Again, I do not claim that, all else being equal, states will always be hostile to such revolutionary states; rather, I claim that the fear of revolutionary contagion will have a predominant influence on their foreign policy toward that state despite other countervailing factors. Other concerns can outweigh this factor, in contradiction to the prediction of the domestic contagion effects theory. Even in these cases, it is useful to assess to what extent contagion fears are salient.

> Hypothesis 2.2: States with similar oppositions and thus fear of revolutionary contagion will align with each other, despite other differences.

I argue that the anticipation of revolutionary waves not only initiates conflict, but also spurs cooperation—cooperation against the revolutionary state and against the revolutionary wave elsewhere. This cooperation can consist of formal alliances or of more informal alignments, indicated by military or economic aid, intelligence sharing, and other such coordination. I argue that cooperation, not mere neutrality or outright hostility, will exist between states that fear revolutionary contagion. They will forgo potential avenues to exploit these other states and instead look for ways to prop them up. There will usually be cooperation among like states, because like states usually face similar threats. But, in contrast to the "ideological" tradition that asserts like states cooperate and unlike states conflict, there can be cooperation between unlike states, because they might nevertheless share the same revolutionary threat.

I argue that when leaders fear revolutionary contagion, that factor will be their predominant foreign policy concern, prompting patterns of conflict and cooperation that would be otherwise difficult to explain. Several methods will be used to determine whether these patterns of conflict and cooperation are directly related to the possibility of revolutionary waves. The first of these is their private

---

[20] One critical factor determining whether there will be intervention is the assessment of the relative ease with which the revolution can be reversed. A protracted conflict may radicalize the revolution and increase the risk of unrest at home.

justifications for what they are doing. There is also timing—the onset of a revolution that inspires waves initiates cooperation and conflict that differ from cooperation and conflict in previous periods when the factor was absent. Another is whether the pressure for the policies of hostility toward the revolutionary state varies among states and within states to the extent that a state anticipates it will be a target of the revolutionary wave. Also, the extent to which states embark on foreign policies that seem to depart from their traditional geopolitical interests, such as mobilizing against states that pose no conceivable military threat, aligning with a traditional adversary, or refusing to align with a traditional ally, is an indication that other factors are at work.

The aim of this book is to assess when these ideological conflicts are likely to emerge, why, and how much of an effect they have on international relations. For the latter purpose, I make a strong assumption to draw into relief the extent to which these issues play a role in international politics. I argue that the anticipation of revolutionary contagion will have a large enough effect on the foreign policy behavior of other states to determine conflict and cooperation based on these regime security fears. Sometimes this factor will be overwhelmed by other factors. My claim is that even indirect domestic political threats have had a profound effect on international relations, creating interactions that are counterintuitive from a geopolitical perspective. Given the neglect of these issues in international relations theory, what might be surprising is not that the factors I identify are at times overwhelmed by other concerns, but that they have much explanatory power at all.

Situating This Book in the Literature

While the questions I address here have not been directly addressed by previous literature, there are several works that have dealt with similar dynamics. There are three books in particular I build upon. Stephen Walt's *Revolution and War* is the most comprehensive work on why revolutions sometimes cause interstate conflict.[21] There are several casual pathways in his explanation. He argues that revolutions cause wars of opportunism because revolutions weaken the state and prompt neighbors to invade in order to improve their relative position in the international system. Revolutions also create spirals of suspicions between the revolutionary state and its opponents because, given the uncertainty about the other side's intentions, they view the other through the prism of their ideology. Walt interprets the offense/defense balance not in terms of whether military conditions favor the offense or defense but in terms of how revolutions

---

[21] Walt, *Revolution and War*.

encourage both sides to exaggerate their own vulnerability as well as that of their opponents. Revolutions can lead to war because of "two parallel myths: the belief that the revolution will spread rapidly if it is not 'strangled in the crib' and the belief that such a reversal will be easy to accomplish."[22] My work is both broader and narrower than Walt's. It is broader because I consider how revolutions can lead to cooperation as well as conflict beyond war. It is narrower because I do not purport to account for the range of reasons revolutions can cause war or lesser hostilities between states. I focus on one mechanism and explain why it applies in some cases and not others.

Mark Haas's *Ideological Origins of Great Power Politics* asserts that ideological differences increase the perception of threat and thus conflict by three mechanisms.[23] One is a social identity theory: that states separate themselves into in-groups and out-groups based on similarities and differences, and mistrust those in the out-group. Another is similar to Walt's misperception mechanism: that ideological difference causes communication problems as states misperceive the hostile intentions of their ideological rival. His demonstration effects mechanism, that ideological differences will cause states to fear subversion at home, mirrors my own focus on the fear of contagion effects, though he uses the term in a broader sense than I do, one that encompasses both the model and platform effects I discuss. I depart from his assumption that ideological differences will necessarily increase the perception of threat.

John Owen's *The Clash of Ideas in World Politics* provides an account of the patterns of foreign-imposed regime change in a larger "ecological" framework.[24] In Owen's account, a mutation occurs in the international system in the form of radicals capturing a regime, which kicks off a transnational ideological struggle that does not end until one regime type has proven its superiority and spread throughout the system. I do not share this same ecological assumption, and for that reason, I view capturing a regime as neither necessary nor sufficient to initiate a transnational struggle, nor do I think the struggle only ends when there is one dominant regime type. I believe these ideological clashes are fundamentally about different ways to rule domestically. However, one of his reasons that states engage in foreign-imposed regime change is that in situations of transnational ideological polarization, they fear demonstration effects at home, which dovetails with the focus of this book.

Those works, then, are different in some ways from the project I take on here. But those works and this one all focus on a neglected aspect of international politics—how the clash of different ideologies that legitimate rule affects

---

[22] Ibid., 43.

[23] Mark L. Haas, *The Ideological Origins of Great Power Politics, 1789–1989* (Ithaca: Cornell University Press, 2005).

[24] John M. Owen, *The Clash of Ideas in World Politics: Transnational Networks, States, and Regime Change, 1510–2010* (Princeton: Princeton University Press, 2010).

international affairs. I hope to advance this literature with a detailed focus on a particular prominent mechanism: the fear of domestic contagion. My emphasis is on how ideological factors threaten leaders' political survival and how that prompts hostility toward different ideological regimes. In the instances I stipulate, I assume leaders are ideologically driven in the political sense—they are attempting to preserve their regime, which is associated with a particular ideology and faces a rival ideological threat. They are not ideologically driven in an abstract sense of opposing different ideologies, which is why mere ideological distance does not drive hostility. They are not ideologically driven to oppose different ideologies in circumstances when the ideological distance is not politically salient. In fact, I argue that ideologically distant regimes will cooperate with each other if they have similar revolutionary opposition movements and thus face a similar ideological threat.[25]

Case Selection and Overview of the Book

This book selects cases of revolution and revolt from the major ideological movements of the past two hundred years: liberalism, communism, fascism, and Islamism. These cases exhibit a range on the independent variables of interest: the fear of contagion based on the presence or absence of significant domestic revolutionary movements and the extent to which the revolutionary state acts as platforms to spread the revolution abroad.[26] The cases I select are not simply based on variation on the independent variable given the universe of cases of revolutions because I am not proposing a theory that applies to all cases of revolution. Revolutions can have a variety of effects. Instead, the strategy is to pick cases based on variation in the independent variable given a level of plausibility that leaders could fear revolutionary contagion.[27] This is the same logic behind selecting politically relevant dyads for quantitative testing of conflict, where politically relevant dyads are pairs that are contiguous or one of which is a great power. Here the relevant cases are revolutions that might credibly be a model to another state because the revolution espouses a universal ideology, or one based

---

[25] Walldorf has a somewhat similar emphasis on how domestic politics can create a political cost of deviating from a particular ideological line. He argues domestic agents create ideologically driven narrative discourses about foreign policy that constrains elites to following certain policies. C. William Walldorf Jr., *To Shape Our World for Good: Master Narratives and Regime Change in U.S. Foreign Policy, 1900–2001* (Ithaca: Cornell University Press, 2019).

[26] Although in qualitative methods researchers sometimes select cases based on the dependent variable to see the causal process at work, I select on the independent variables, to see it work and to see it not work.

[27] See James Mahoney and Gary Goertz, "The Possibility Principle: Choosing Negative Cases in Comparative Research," *American Political Science Review* 98, no. 4 (2004): 653–69.

on the religion or ethnicity shared by the other state.[28] I also do not just examine instances of successful revolution because, given the logic of the theory, one would expect rulers not only to be averse to revolutionary states but also to do what they could to prevent those revolutions from succeeding in the first place.[29] I focus on regions because that is where we would expect a contagion effect to be felt. I focus on primary regional powers as the players responding to these events because these are the states that dominate the region's international politics and are more in a position to be able to respond to revolutionary states. The cases are from different historical eras and places, which show that the dynamic I outline is not limited to the content of particular ideologies or specific historical eras.

I first examine two sets of democratic revolutions: the American Revolution and the Dutch Patriot Revolt of the 1780s in Chapter 3 and the wave of revolutions in the 1820s in Spain, Portugal, Italy, and Greece in Chapter 4. I examine the responses to these revolutions by the principal powers of the period: Prussia, Russia, Austria, France, Britain, and, in the case of the American Revolution, Spain. These cases of revolution/revolt provide for useful comparative case studies. They are roughly similar in that the revolutions occurred in relatively weak states that acted as models rather than platforms.[30] Thus, the variable of the revolutionary state acting as a platform is held constant, while the degree to which there were revolutionary opposition movements within the great powers varies. In the first set of cases, there were not; in the later set of cases, there were. In other words, cases in Chapter 3 are in Cell 1 of Table 2.1, whereas cases in Chapter 4 are in Cell 2. Whether rulers anticipated revolutionary contagion irrespective of the policy of the revolutionary state is evidenced if they are alarmed at potential revolutions in insignificant states or in states too distant to meaningfully act as a platform for spreading the revolution abroad.

The international reaction to the American Revolution and the Dutch Patriot Revolt provides a confirmation of the domestic contagion effects theory and establishes exactly why revolutions sometimes do not spark a strong reaction. Although I uncover some anxiety over the domestic spillover from the

---

[28] For politically relevant dyads, see Douglas Lemke and William Reed, "The Relevance of Politically Relevant Dyads," *Journal of Conflict Resolution* 45, no. 1 (2001): 126–44.

[29] The literature on the international effects of revolutions does not examine unsuccessful cases of revolution. Instances of states intervening in these revolts are a subset of the larger phenomenon of interventions in civil war. This large literature usually does not distinguish between different types of civil war, and usually has post–World War II, especially post–Cold War, ethnic civil wars in mind when they construct their theories. See, for example, Patrick M. Regan, *Civil Wars and Foreign Powers: Outside Intervention in Intrastate Conflict* (Ann Arbor: University of Michigan Press, 2000). The distinction between revolutionary and other types of civil wars is advocated by Nicholas Sambanis, "Do Ethnic and Non-Ethnic Civil Wars Have the Same Causes? A Theoretical and Empirical Inquiry (Part 1)," *Journal of Conflict Resolution* 45, no. 3 (2001): 259–82.

[30] The subsequent 1830 and 1848 revolutionary waves in Europe involved France, which was decidedly not a lesser power, and so those cases are less useful as a comparative case study.

revolutions, this concern remained too abstract, given the lack of significant revolutionary movements among the European countries at this time, to affect foreign policy. Although it was pointed out to the French king that there could be negative repercussions for supporting democratic revolutions, the extent of his concern was to suggest that French agents tone down their revolutionary rhetoric. Whether states supported these revolutions, were ambivalent, or were hostile was for the most part a product of their geopolitical aims. In France's case, they supported the revolutions to undermine their rival, Britain. Spain did have concerns about the American Revolution being a bad example, not because it was a democratic revolution, but because it was an anti-colonial revolt. They nevertheless supported the Americans.

The contrast between the response by the great powers to the revolutions in America and the Netherlands to the response to the revolutions in Spain, Italy, Portugal, and Greece is striking. But it is what the domestic contagion effects theory predicts. Because revolutionary movements existed in all the great powers, there was fear of contagion, and the powers were uniformly hostile toward these revolutions. There was an apprehension that the great powers would exploit these revolutions for geopolitical benefit, but that did not happen. Russia and France, for example, did not use the revolutions in Italy to undermine the Austrian sphere of influence there, even though France had been recently kicked off the Italian peninsula. Though the great powers had recently militarily resisted French influence in Spain, they welcomed French actions that successfully crushed a revolution there. Russia had previously been attempting to dismantle the Ottoman Empire and expand its influence, but the tsar refrained from intervening in the Greek Revolt out of monarchical solidarity. The transformation of European international politics from a war-prone environment to a remarkably peaceful one is undergirded by the fear of revolutionary contagion.

In Chapter 5, I examine two revolutions in a similar period, the communist revolution in Russia in 1917 and the fascist revolution in Italy in 1922.[31] I consider the responses to these revolutions by the principal powers of the region: Britain, France, Germany, Italy, and the Soviet Union. Among the non-Italian great powers, the only state where fascism was a significant movement was Germany. Communist/socialist movements were more widespread. All non-Soviet great powers had a significant socialist movement, though the case of Britain was somewhat ambiguous. Both the communist and fascist revolutionary states operated to varying degrees as platforms in spreading their ideology abroad. The Bolsheviks did not act as much of a platform abroad at first, but their attempts to

---

[31] Some have resisted according fascism the label "revolutionary" because the ideology was not "taken seriously." See, e.g., Michael Mann, *Fascists* (New York: Cambridge University Press, 2004). I discuss this in Chapter 5.

spread revolution escalated. In other words, Britain, France, Germany, and Italy were in Cell 2 and then Cell 4. The Italian fascist state aided fascist movements abroad in Britain and France, and possibly Germany. In Britain and France, these fascist movements were insignificant; thus, they were in Cell 1 and then Cell 3 when Mussolini began aiding these movements. Germany was in Cell 2 or Cell 4, depending on the ambiguous assessments of Italian aid to the Nazis.

The reaction to fascism and communism is for the most part a confirmation of the theory, though in different ways. In contrast to their reaction to the Soviet Union, Western statesmen sought to integrate Mussolini into the European order and downplayed radical fascist ideology, which is expected given that Britain and France had no significant fascist movement. This is in stark contrast to their reaction to the Soviet Union, which precluded what would have been an obvious balancing strategy against Germany. The Allied powers were consistently hostile toward the Bolsheviks, even when it made geopolitical sense to accommodate them in order to create a balancer against Germany. The German situation was more complicated. The Allied powers at times aligned with the Bolsheviks, even aiding the revolution, in contrast to what the domestic contagion effects theory would project. But there was also significant apprehension of the Soviets, and so the Allied powers refrained from joining with the Soviets in a partition of Poland, a key foreign policy goal, precisely because of their contagion concerns. The attempts by Italy to spread fascism abroad drew little concern. There was much more apprehension about the actions of the Bolsheviks in spreading revolution abroad, but great power hostility was not especially correlated with such activities: the great powers were hostile toward the Bolsheviks before the latter acted as much of a platform, and their hostility declined somewhat as the Soviets ramped up Comintern activities.

Finally, in Chapter 6 I examine the response to the Iranian Revolution by the principal powers in the Middle East: Iraq, Syria, Egypt, and Saudi Arabia. Significant Islamist revolutionary opposition movements existed in these states prior to the Iranian Revolution, with the exception of Saudi Arabia initially. The Iranian Revolution acted as a platform to spread revolution abroad in Iraq and Saudi Arabia, ramping up in 1980. Thus, Syria and Egypt populated Cell 2, Saudi Arabia was in Cell 1, then briefly in Cell 2, then Cell 4. Iraq was in Cell 2 and then Cell 4 as Iran ramped up attempts to spread revolution abroad.

I argue that it was the Iraqi fear of contagion from the Iranian Revolution that was the critical cause of the Iran-Iraq War and that restructured the alignment pattern of the Middle East more generally. It explains the anomaly, from a balance-of-power perspective, of states now balancing against a weakened Iran. The Syrian-Iranian relationship, however, is an exception, where foreign policy goals trumped the concern of contagion effects, in contrast to what the domestic contagion effects theory would predict. The actual outbreak of the Iran-Iraq War was due to Iran's acting as a platform in spreading revolution—an ideal case for the influence of a platform. But the power of the model in the region is evidenced in several ways—the fear of the revolution spreading predated substantial Iranian involvement with revolutionary Islamists, and, more strongly, there were contagion concerns about Sunni Islamist opposition groups, which never developed any significant tie with Iran.

In Chapter 3, I begin with an analysis of the proverbial "dog that did not bark"—the ancien régime's response to democratic revolutions.

3

Democratic Revolutions and the Ancien Régime

The two most prominent instances of democratic revolutions prior to the French Revolution were the American Revolution and the Dutch Patriot Revolt. These would be the first steps in what was later termed the "age of democratic revolutions," where the basic struggle was over whether sovereignty was vested in kings or in people.[1] They present a puzzle: in both these cases, the oldest monarchy in Europe (France) supported the self-styled patriots—those fighting for the rights of people over kings, just prior to when the French monarchy was overthrown. One German source proclaimed at the beginning of the American Revolution, "Since the interest of every sovereign is to suppress rather than to support a rebellion, the Americans cannot hope for foreign aid."[2] Why would a monarch support a popular uprising against a king? What explains French policy? Was French policy an anomaly among the great powers?

French policy was no anomaly. While not all of the European powers supported these revolutions, whether they did was driven by how these revolutions played into their existing geopolitical alliances rather than the concerns of revolutionary contagion. French policy is a puzzle for the ideological theory of international relations, where states with different ideologies conflict. But its policy and the policy of the other great powers are consistent with my theory. The domestic contagion effects theory asserts that leaders will fear the contagion of revolutions when there are significant opposition movements of a similar type within their own country. Because there were no significant revolutionary movements among the great powers, including France, there was no significant fear of the demonstration effects of these revolutions. As the theory also predicts, without this fear of contagion, ideological factors had little salience in international politics, which allowed a realpolitik policy to be pursued. Although there is some acknowledgment of how these revolutions could serve as dangerous models, the powers' reactions to these revolts are explained in traditional geopolitical terms. Spain is a partial exception. There were concerns in

---

[1] R. R. Palmer, *The Age of the Democratic Revolution* (Princeton: Princeton University Press, 1959).
[2] Horst Dippel, *Germany and the American Revolution, 1770–1800*, trans. Bernhard A. Uhlendorf (Wiesbaden: Franz Steiner Verlag GMBH, 1978), 196.

Revolutionary Contagion and International Politics. Chad E. Nelson, Oxford University Press. © Oxford University Press 2022. DOI: 10.1093/oso/9780197601921.003.0003

Madrid about the demonstration effect of the American Revolution as an anti-colonial revolt, although these apprehensions did not prevent Spain from aiding the Revolution.

This chapter analyzes the response to the American and Dutch uprisings by addressing the following questions: Did leaders have a fear of the spillover effects these revolutions could have on their own rule? Was this fear correlated with the presence of revolutionary movements within their polities? Did the fear of contagion prompt hostility to the revolution and cooperation among states with similar fears? I assess the independent variables: the extent to which these revolutions acted as platforms and models, and whether there was a significant revolutionary opposition movement in any of the major powers analyzed.[3] I then assess the international effects of the revolution/revolt by analyzing the policies of the great powers toward each other and the revolutionary state before and after the revolution.

The American Revolution

The American Revolution germinated in the tension that developed between king and colonies after the Seven Years' War. The war had drained the British state, and King George III attempted to increase his revenue from the empire. The colonists bitterly resented this. Britain attempted to consolidate its authority and stifle dissent, especially in restive Massachusetts, but instead it provoked widespread open rebellion. Royal authority dissolved and local communities organized popular governments. Military hostilities broke out in 1775, and the Second Continental Congress issued the Declaration of Independence in 1776.

Model

The United States served as a model for what it opposed and for what it was for. The American Revolution was an anti-colonial revolt. It was Europe's first overseas colony to successfully revolt and could be considered a dangerous example for other colonies, especially Europe's New World possessions. It was also clear from the beginning what kind of government the rebellious colonists wished to

---

[3] The great powers are the same throughout the period covered in this and the next chapter: Britain, France, Prussia, Austria, and Russia. In the response to the American Revolution, however, I exclude an analysis of British policy, since they had an obvious motive to suppress the revolt. An analysis of Spanish policy, however, is included. Spain was no longer considered a European great power in the late eighteenth century, but its navy and colonial possessions ensured that it was a major maritime power; indeed, France's policy toward the Americans is intertwined with Spanish policy.

form: a republic. The basic distinction between this regime type and the great powers was that sovereignty would lie with the people rather than with a king. Moreover, the rebelling colonists spoke in universal terms. The Declaration of Independence stated that men have certain rights, governments are instituted to uphold those rights, and when a government does not uphold those rights, the people have the right to overthrow it.

Platform

The universalistic language of the Declaration of Independence was not intended, however, to announce a foreign policy platform of world revolution. The Americans did not expect—and were not expected—to act as a platform in the strongest sense of the word: carrying on military expeditions to spread republics abroad. Even after they secured independence, they were weak, internally divided, and on the other side of the ocean from Europe. They did harbor ambitions to expand their holdings in North America. Part of the colonists' umbrage at British control before the Revolution was the fact that the British had attempted to restrict them from colonizing beyond the Appalachians. Their shrewd negotiations concluding the War of Independence secured them a huge swath of land up to the Mississippi, but their ambition did not stop there. Many envisioned an American continent without colonies or monarchies. Beyond the British, this aspiration most obviously affected Spain. But American expansion into Spanish lands either by the spread of their confederation or by the emergence of other republican empires was a future possibility that they were obviously not emphasizing to the Spanish.[4]

Even though the Americans were not capable of acting as a military platform to spread republics abroad, did they engage in less direct steps to encourage republican movements or sentiments in other lands, such as disseminating propaganda or organizing opposition movements? Almost without exception, the extent to which they acted as a platform was the dissemination of propaganda concerning their own cause rather than advocating the overthrow or even the reform of other regimes.

---

[4] The instructions for the American commissioners going to France in 1776 illustrates this sensitivity: "Should Spain be disinclined to our Cause, from an Apprehension of Danger to his Dominions in South America, you are empowered to give the strongest Assurances, that that Crown will receive no Molestation from the United States, in the Possession of those Territories." *Journals of the Continental Congress, 1774–1789*, vol. 5 (Washington, DC: Government Printing Office, 1906), 816. The American attempts to assure Spain "continued through to the peace negotiations." Thomas E. Chávez, *Spain and the Independence of the United States: An Intrinsic Gift* (Albuquerque: University of New Mexico Press, 2002), 233n7.

The most important American diplomat, Benjamin Franklin, spread propaganda for the American cause, but he studiously refrained from suggesting that the ideals that motivated the Americans should be applied in Europe.[5] One possible exception, his behind-the-scenes effort to derail the Society of the Cincinnati, a veterans' organization founded in the United States in 1783, exhibits his caution and restraint. He considered the hereditary and quasi-aristocratic nature of the group a dangerous precedent for the American republic. Although limited by his official position, he helped Honoré Mirabeau, the French writer and future revolutionary, write an attack on the society and had it translated into English and printed. Franklin had his own essay translated and circulated it among his French friends, but he did not dare publish what was in essence an attack on the existing social order in France.[6] The only reason he took action was because of its implications for the United States. He remained silent, for example, during the democratic revolution in Geneva that was crushed by the French. Franklin's fraternizing with the elite "reassured the French privileged classes that the American Revolution posed no threat to them."[7]

The closest the Americans came to fomenting unrest abroad was John Adams's mission to the Netherlands. Adams came into a situation much different from that in France. The stadtholder, William V, was the hereditary head of state of the Dutch Republic, and was closely aligned with the British. The opposing Patriot movement used the diplomatic recognition of Adams and thus the American cause as a weapon against the stadtholder. There to solicit loans and recognition from the Dutch during the American Revolution, Adams took a different tack than Franklin, attempting through his writings and associations to win popular support for the American cause and thus force William's hand. He even on

[5] Franklin wrote several articles and provided material for the French government-backed journal, *Affaires de l'Angleterre et de l'Amérique*, whose purpose was to provide news of the War of Independence and support the American cause. His famous printing press at his residence in Passy "produced little more than government documents, legal forms, and pieces for amusement." Jonathan R. Dull, "Franklin the Diplomat: The French Mission," *Transactions of the American Philosophical Society* 72, no. 1 (1982): 26. See Luther S. Livingston, *Franklin and His Press at Passy* (New York: The Grolier Club, 1914). The one letter attributed to Franklin that hinted at subversion, "To the Good People of Ireland," which alludes to the future possibility of an Irish revolt, turns out not to have been written by him. Claude A. Lopez, ed., *The Papers of Benjamin Franklin, Volume 27: July 1 Through October 31, 1778* (New Haven: Yale University Press, 1988), 504. For an overview of American propaganda in France, see Peter Ascoli, "American Propaganda in the French Language Press During the American Revolution," in *La Révolution Américaine et l'Europe* (Paris: Centre National de la Recherche Scientifique, 1979).

[6] William Doyle, *Aristocracy and Its Enemies in the Age of Revolution* (New York: Oxford University Press, 2009), 122–23. It was later published in France in 1790 as a justification for the abolition of the nobility. Durand Echeverria, *Mirage in the West: A History of the French Image of American Society to 1815* (Princeton: Princeton University Press, 1968), 56–57.

[7] Jonathan R. Dull, "Benjamin Franklin and the Nature of American Diplomacy," *The International History Review* 5, no. 3 (1983): 353. Dull describes Franklin as picturesque and unfrightening—the soothing face of revolution, like Zhou Enlai or Maxim Litvinov. Jonathan R. Dull, *Benjamin Franklin and the American Revolution* (Lincoln: University of Nebraska Press, 2010), 67.

one occasion uttered explicitly subversive statements against the stadtholder.[8] But his subversiveness was not so much a particular statement as the cause he represented and the language of representative democracy that he introduced. Adams claimed he "was not an enthusiast who wishes to overturn empires and monarchies for the sake of introducing republican forms of government," and his actions were motivated by a zeal for the American cause more than by an attempt to spread revolution in Holland.[9]

Overall, there was not any significant attempt by the Americans to spread their doctrines abroad. They promoted their own cause, which they thought would be an implicit cause for reform in Europe. There was a notion among Americans that their cause was "the cause of all mankind," but they were not expecting a significant amount of change in Europe in the near term, let alone revolution.[10] They left the regimes of Europe undisturbed.[11]

If their diplomacy was conventional, their aims were not. The Declaration of Independence has been portrayed as "decidedly *un*revolutionary" because it was signaling that the United States would abide by the norms of European interstate conduct so that it would be granted independence.[12] But the document was not just about signaling future diplomatic conduct. It was arguing that the colonies were now rightfully "*free* and independent states," and using quite radical language to do so. The United States was not acting as a platform, but it was certainly a revolutionary model. Its independence was in itself a potential challenge to imperial rule, and the form of government that it was establishing was a potential challenge to monarchies.

---

[8] Edward Handler, *America and Europe in the Political Thought of John Adams* (Cambridge, MA: Harvard University Press, 1964), 110. For more on Adams in the Netherlands, see James H. Hutson, *John Adams and the Diplomacy of the American Revolution* (Lexington: University Press of Kentucky, 1980), 75–116; Page Smith, *John Adams, Volume I: 1735–1784* (Garden City: Doubleday & Company, 1962), 481–535.

[9] Handler, *America and Europe in the Political Thought of John Adams*, 102.

[10] John C. Rainbolt, "Americans' Initial View of Their Revolution's Significance for Other Peoples, 1776–1788," *The Historian* 35, no. 3 (1973): 418–433. Beyond the assumption that Europe was not ripe for revolution, there was a consensus among American revolutionaries that, although they would exploit European rivalries to secure their independence, they wanted to keep out of the cockpit of Europe as much as possible for the sake of their democracy.

[11] Even Jefferson, until June 1789, would do little to spur on the French Revolution: "The existence of the independent United States, simply as a fact, was a subversive influence on the old order in Europe, but Jefferson did nothing to make it more so." R. R. Palmer, "The Dubious Democrat: Thomas Jefferson in Bourbon France," *Political Science Quarterly* 72, no. 3 (1957): 402.

[12] David Armitage, *The Declaration of Independence: A Global History* (Cambridge, MA: Harvard University Press, 2007), 65. Armitage and others stress that the Declaration's primary audience was an international one, but the Declaration's content (the document begins with establishing a right to revolution when one's universal rights of equality are violated) and the careless way it was transmitted to France, what one would expect to be the primary overseas audience, brings this claim into doubt. Maier argues that the Declaration was "first and foremost for domestic consumption." Pauline Maier, *American Scripture: Making the Declaration of Independence* (New York: Alfred A. Knopf, 1997), 131. At least a fundamental purpose of the Declaration was to justify what they were doing to an internal audience.

Revolutionary Opposition in the Ancien Régime

There was no significant democratic revolutionary opposition movement in the great powers in the Ancien Régime. European conservatives in the nineteenth century, reacting to the French Revolution, perpetuated the idea that the Enlightenment had propagated anti-monarchical ideas that had hastened the French Revolution and revolutionary movements throughout Europe. In fact, if the Enlightenment had a political impact in this period, it worked largely in the service of enhancing the consolidation of monarchical rule. A principal struggle of the eighteenth century was the battle between the constituted bodies of the feudal order, particularly representing the aristocracy, and the power of the absolute monarchies. Enlightenment thinkers were strong allies of the monarchy in this regard. Many of the philosophes were less concerned with the form of government than with the reforms they advocated. Men such as Voltaire or the physiocrats held the (well-grounded) opinion that enlightened policies such as religious toleration or free trade were best brought about by absolutist monarchs. Many of the monarchs of the age—Catherine the Great, Maria Theresa, Joseph II, and Frederick the Great—were attracted to some of these ideas, as well as to the general mantle of "enlightened monarch," because they legitimized the consolidation of their states against the aristocratic reaction.

There was, however, a "Radical Enlightenment," a set of works that advocated more far-reaching change, among them more democratic principles.[13] Writings of this ilk were marginal but began to develop in the 1770s and 1780s. Philosophes such as Diderot and Raynal, who once endorsed enlightened absolutism, rejected it.[14] But it would be a mistake to regard the Radical Enlightenment as constituting a significant revolutionary movement in Europe. There was a marked variation in the extent to which such ideas had spread in Europe. But even in France, the epicenter of the Enlightenment, those seeking more radical reform were a small minority; nor were they an organized political resistance. The extent of organization and mobilization was the reading groups and freemasonry clubs where ideas were exchanged. Neither of these associations in this period had overtly revolutionary goals, or were perceived as having such.[15]

---

[13] Jonathan Israel, *A Revolution of the Mind: Radical Enlightenment and the Intellectual Origins of Modern Democracy* (Princeton: Princeton University Press, 2010).

[14] Leonard Krieger, *An Essay on the Theory of Enlightened Despotism* (Chicago: University of Chicago Press, 1975), 20–21.

[15] For an exposition on freemasonry in this context, see Margaret C. Jacob, *Living the Enlightenment: Freemasonry and Politics in Eighteenth-Century Europe* (New York: Oxford University Press, 1991). Freemasons "in the first instance identified with power." (160) Following the French Revolution, however, masonic lodges were condemned by conservatives as revolutionary cabals.

Opposition in France

The most developed movement for political reform on the Continent was in France. Although there were grievances against the monarchy, there was no revolutionary movement dedicated to overthrowing it. As one scholar notes, it was the French Revolution that made revolutionaries in France, rather than revolutionaries making the Revolution.[16] In the 1770s and 1780s there was increasing disgruntlement over the international and domestic problems the country faced. There were three sources that served as the basis of reforms. First was the Enlightenment. As discussed, one strand of the Enlightenment was in favor of increasing the power of the king, which would give him the ability to enact the reforms needed. The radical strain, however, advocated the constriction of the king's power in favor of a more limited monarchy or, rarely, even the abolition of monarchy. Another source of inspiration was French constitutional history. This was especially popular among conservative members of the aristocracy who wished to restore their power vis-à-vis the king. The final source of reforms was the example of other nations. Most often, this was Great Britain. There were "liberal" reformers who yearned for the political rights enjoyed in Britain as well as those aristocrats who envied the power of the aristocrats there. One of the effects of the American Revolution was to displace England as the nation worth emulating among the small set of radicals. But even these, in terms of both ends and means, were not revolutionaries. Even Condorcet, a great admirer of America and republicanism, declared at the time, "France will remain a monarchy, because it is the only system of government suitable to her wealth, to her population, to her extent, and to the existing political system in Europe."[17] Almost no one was calling for the overthrow of the monarchy by violent means or otherwise to establish a republic, and no one was organizing to bring about that end.[18] The few critics do not meet the threshold as a significant revolutionary movement, and there is no evidence that the king or his advisors thought that there was a significant revolutionary movement in France.

---

[16] William Doyle, *Origins of the French Revolution* (New York: Oxford University Press, 1988), 213.

[17] J. Salwyn Schapiro, *Condorcet and the Rise of Liberalism* (New York: Harcourt, Brace and Company, 1934), 79.

[18] There were a few exceptions. Some of the most incendiary words were written by Diderot in his section on the American Revolution for Raynal's famous *Histoire des deux Indes*, where he explicitly approved insurrection against tyrannical monarchs by oppressed people. Brissot as well was one of the very few genuine revolutionaries. Even Jonathan Israel, a strong proponent of the impact of the radical philosophes on the French Revolution, argues they were "deliberate, conscious revolutionaries albeit not in the sense of being planners of revolutionary action but rather as ideologues preparing the ground for revolution." Jonathan I. Israel, *Democratic Enlightenment: Philosophy, Revolution, and Human Rights, 1750–1790* (New York: Oxford University Press, 2011), 437, 809; Palmer, *The Age of the Democratic Revolution*, 260–61.

Opposition in Austria and Prussia

In German lands, including Prussia and Austria, there was extremely wide support for monarchy. This characterized not just those who were content with the existing order, but also the reformers, who thought absolute monarchy was the best system to bring Enlightened reforms about.[19] Enlightenment reforms were particularly embraced by Joseph II of Austria, who faced stiff opposition in the 1780s as he pressed forward far-reaching changes, including an attempt to abolish the special rights enjoyed by the estates. Most notably, the Austrian Netherlands teetered toward open revolt in 1787. The aristocracy did not reject monarchy; they rejected Joseph's radical reinterpretation of monarchy. Neither Maria Theresa, who preceded Joseph, nor Frederick of Prussia attempted such radical reforms of the social structure.

Opposition in Russia

In Russia, Catherine II had her share of opponents. She had just finished repressing the Pugachev revolt when the American Revolution broke out. This revolt, though, was about local grievances and lacked ideological content.[20] There is no evidence that Catherine perceived it as a wider ideological challenge to her rule.[21] There is little evidence of opposition of a more revolutionary nature in Russia. The Enlightenment had begun to penetrate the top stratum of Russian society. In fact, a leading thinker of the Russian Enlightenment was Catherine herself, who wanted to use the ideas to consolidate her rule. A few Russian thinkers could be considered part of the Radical Enlightenment because they began to consider revolutionary ideals, but they did not remotely constitute a significant movement organizing for revolution.

[19] Eberhard Weis, "Enlightenment and Absolutism in the Holy Roman Empire: Thoughts on Enlightened Absolutism in Germany," *The Journal of Modern History* 58 (1986): S181–S197. Krieger notes that even the increasing "preoccupation with the rights and liberties of the subject" in German political literature "did not inspire theoretical alternatives to enlightened absolutism." Leonard Krieger, *The German Idea of Freedom: History of a Political Tradition* (Boston: Beacon Press, 1957), 71. See also Diethelm Klippel, "The True Concept of Liberty: Political Theory in Germany in the Second Half of the Eighteenth Century," in *The Transformation of Political Culture: England and Germany in the Late Eighteenth Century*, ed. Eckhart Hellmuth (New York: Oxford University Press, 1990), 447–66.

[20] Isabel de Madariaga, *Russia in the Age of Catherine the Great* (London: Weidenfeld and Nicolson, 1981), 270.

[21] Although the Pugachev revolt could be considered an anti-colonial revolt against the Russian Empire, just like the American Revolution, Catherine II and her advisors did not consider her Empire and the overseas British Empire in the same class. David M. Griffiths, "Nikita Panin, Russian Diplomacy, and the American Revolution," *Slavic Review* 28, no. 1 (1969): 4.

Opposition in Spain

In Spain, Charles III presided over a period of cultural and economic revival; his steady leadership was widely popular. There was no political group that advocated a departure from absolute monarchy.[22] To the extent that Enlightenment ideals penetrated Spain, they circulated among the very top stratum, particularly the king and his advisors. Charles III implemented extensive reforms advocated by Enlightenment thinkers to make the state bureaucracy more efficient and centralized, which brought about resistance in Spain's American Empire. The weakness of the Spanish state had left the Spanish American elites largely autonomous; the centralizing tendencies of the Bourbon reforms prompted resistance among the creoles. The resistance for the most part stopped well short of outright independence movements. Rebellion was certainly not unknown in the Spanish Empire, especially among the lower classes. These disturbances were localized, however, and aimed at the redress of specific grievances, such as high taxes; moreover, they generally operated within the political culture, as a form of bargaining, much the same way urban riots operated in early modern Europe. They were usually confined to particular classes and had no wider revolutionary dimension.[23]

However, there were several large-scale rebellions, culminating in the 1780s with the Comunero Rebellion in New Granada and the Túpac Amaru II and associated insurrections in Peru, the latter of which was the largest rebellion ever against Spanish rule. These rebellions combined the lower-class and creole resentment of Bourbon fiscal and administrative reform. Several Spanish officials asserted a connection between the revolts and the American Revolution.[24] The revolts may have had in common a reaction against reforming imperial bureaucrats, but the ideology that imbued the American Revolution had not really affected the Spanish Empire, and it does not seem to have played a role in the revolts at all. Only a few thinkers absorbed the republican ideas of the Americans. Although there is a tendency to view the colonial revolts in hindsight, as precursors to the independence movements that would sweep the

---

[22] Richard Herr, *Eighteenth-Century Revolution in Spain* (Princeton: Princeton University Press, 1958), 231.

[23] Anthony McFarlane, "Civil Disorders and Popular Protests in Late Colonial New Granada," *The Hispanic American Historical Review* 64, no. 1 (1984): 18; Brian R. Hamnett, "Process and Pattern: A Re-examination of the Ibero-American Independence Movements, 1808–1826," *Journal of Latin American Studies* 29, no. 2 (1977): 288.

[24] Anthony McFarlane, "The American Revolution and the Spanish Monarchy," in *Europe's American Revolution*, ed. Simon P. Newman (New York: Palgrave Macmillan, 2006), 41; Peggy K. Liss, *Atlantic Empires: The Network of Trade and Revolution, 1713–1826* (Baltimore: Johns Hopkins University Press, 1983), 128, 130.

empire a few decades later, they are better thought of as the aristocratic resistance to enlightened reform going on in Europe.[25] In sum, Spain had no significant revolutionary opposition movement at home, and there was no significant republican movement in the colonies. Whether there was an anti-colonial revolutionary movement is somewhat more ambiguous, but it seems there was not, particularly before Spain's involvement in the American Revolution.

Opposition in Britain

The British obviously had a revolutionary opposition in America, although they underestimated its extent at first. But was there such an opposition in the mother country? The nature of the British regime was different from that of the great powers on the Continent. There was no absolute monarchy and the aristocracy held much more power. But as in Europe, there was fear among the opposition that the king was centralizing power. This was the case in both wings of the opposition—the conservatives and the radicals. The conservatives, much more prominent than the radicals, looked to a past where the aristocracy was more in balance with the king. Radicals wanted to expand the political space. Radicalism in Britain got a boost from the American Revolution—there was an increased call for greater representation.[26] The movement, though, in terms of both ends and means, was not revolutionary. The radicals' goal was to enact reforms, most notably strengthening the House of Commons against the king and insisting on greater representation. The limited political mobilization that occurred generally tried to work within the system and eschewed violence.[27]

Section Summary

Although Europeans of the 1770s and 1780s lived in an era when there was a sense of change in the air, hardly anyone anticipated that those changes could

[25] Anthony McFarlane, "Rebellions in Late Colonial Spanish America: A Comparative Perspective," *Bulletin of Latin American Research* 14, no. 3 (1995): 334.
[26] Edward Royle and James Walvin, *English Radicals and Reformers, 1760–1848* (Lexington: University Press of Kentucky, 1982), 27–28; John Brewer, *Party Ideology and Popular Politics at the Accession of George III* (New York: Cambridge University Press, 1976), 201–16.
[27] H. T. Dickenson notes that the radicals of this period "did their best to use the existing political process." Even in the demonstrations of the followers of the radical John Wilkes, "violence [was] not usually seen as a means of applying pressure to the ruling elite. There was certainly nothing revolutionary about these disturbances. . . . Wilkes himself and nearly all the radicals of the period had a horror of mob violence." H. T. Dickinson, "Radicals and Reformers in the Age of Wilkes and Wyvill," in *British Politics and Society from Walpole to Pitt, 1742–1789*, ed. Jeremy Black (London: Macmillan, 1990), 139, 144.

include the replacement of the leading monarchies of Europe with republics, let alone organized to bring about that possibility. Reform was the order of the day, but most who sought reform wanted the king to implement it, and the biggest reaction to monarchical authority was the aristocratic resistance to the centralizing reform of monarchies. More radical ideas were aired, particularly in France, but they were still in the realm of ideas rather than organized political action. In the New World, there were revolts in the Spanish Empire; whether these were full-blown independence movements is somewhat ambiguous, but it seems doubtful.

International Relations Prior to the American Revolution

To assess whether the American Revolution affected patterns of international politics, I first examine relations among the great powers prior to the Revolution. The system was characterized by two poles of antagonism, France-Britain and Austria-Prussia, and by a weakening France that wanted to regain its former standing. Both Austria and Spain were allied with France, though Spain was enemies with Britain and Austria was not. Russia was allied with Prussia, and both had an ambivalent posture toward Britain.

Relations between the great powers in this period were shaped by the aftermath of the Seven Years' War. Britain had emerged from that conflict dominant over France, having entirely eradicated the French from North America. Britain was, however, relatively isolated from the Continent. Britain's focus was on internal and overseas matters. Although it tepidly searched for allies in Europe, it was no longer able to exploit the threat of France because of France's weakened position. Not only had France lost much of its overseas empire, but it was saddled with debt. France had also previously repaired its relations with Spain—it had renewed its "Family Compact" during the Seven Years' War. The Spanish navy nicely complemented the French army, and they shared the common enemy of Britain. The British were the biggest threat to the Spanish Empire, having taken over Florida in 1763, which put them in a prime position to control the Gulf of Mexico, and having infiltrated the Central American coast. British contraband trade to the colonies was also a major threat to the closed Spanish imperial trading system. In Europe, they controlled former Spanish territories such as Gibraltar and Minorca. Most importantly, Portugal, Spain's enemy next door and across the ocean, was supported by Britain. More recently, though, Spain had felt abandoned by France in its conflict with Britain over the Falklands.

Both Britain and France had little influence on the Eastern powers, and sat back as Prussia, Austria, and Russia engaged in the first partition of Poland in 1772. Relations on the Continent were still shaped by the Diplomatic Revolution during the War of Austrian Succession, which had brought about an alliance between Austria and France. Austria had partnered with France as the best means to wrest back the province of Silesia from Prussia, and broke with Russia. Austria and Prussia were antagonistic, and with Austria in the French camp, Prussia had gravitated to the British camp. Prussia had been abandoned by Britain in the Seven Years' War, but it did not want to distance itself from Britain for fear that the British would side with rival Austria. Austria was in an alliance with France, which prohibited an alliance with Britain, but it too did not want to antagonize Britain for fear of drawing Prussia closer to Britain. A Russian-Prussian alliance was the core of what was called the Northern System. Britain was affiliated with these states, but not in an alliance. Britain and Russia were regarded as having similar interests and enemies, and there were attempts by both sides in the early 1770s to draw up a formal alliance, but relations had cooled notably after Britain rebuffed Russia's efforts to form an alliance in 1773. Among other reasons, Russia required as the price of the alliance British support of Russian conquests of the Ottoman Empire, which the British refused.

Regarding great-power relations with Britain, then, France was looking to get back at Britain, its habitual enemy, from its losses in the Seven Years' War. Spain also was no friend of Britain. The other powers had ambiguous relations with Britain.

Predictions

Because of the lack of significant revolutionary opposition movements in the great powers, the domestic contagion effects theory predicts that there will be no significant fears of contagion, and thus this fear will not affect their reaction to the American Revolution.

This is in contrast to the expectations of a theory that emphasizes ideological differences. According to that theory, the European monarchs should be uniformly hostile towards the American democrats. As seen in Table 3.1, I show instead that the great powers' support or lack of support of the American Revolution was based on their previous stance toward Britain, as my theory predicts. One minor exception was Spain, which evinced fears of anti-colonial demonstration effects, though this was due more to their structural vulnerability than to existing anti-colonial movements, and it ultimately did not determine Spanish policy.

Table 3.1 Response to the American Revolution

Great Power	Stance Toward Britain Prior to American Revolution	Significant Liberal Revolutionary Movement?	Prediction of Stance Toward American Revolution Given Revolutionary Movement	Outcome
France	Hostile	No	Unaffected by fears of contagion	Allies with Americans
Spain	Hostile	No (but debatable anti-colonial movement)	Unaffected by fears of contagion	Allies (indirectly) with Americans
Prussia	Ambivalent	No	Unaffected by fears of contagion	Neutral
Austria	Ambivalent	No	Unaffected by fears of contagion	Neutral
Russia	Ambivalent	No	Unaffected by fears of contagion	Neutral

International Relations of the American Revolution, 1775–1783

The Bourbon Powers and the American Revolution

The French and Spanish would eventually provide critical aid to the American revolutionaries to secure their independence. This may seem like the inevitable byproduct of their rivalry with Britain. In fact, there were many hesitations as they moved to secretly aid the rebels and then intervene militarily. These hesitations, though, had to do not with the fear of contagion, but with a variety of other factors. The lack of significant revolutionary movements meant that there was no fear of contagion in France. There were some such concerns in Spain, but not enough to significantly influence its foreign policy.

Even before the American Revolution began, French statesmen anticipated the possibility of a rebellion in the American colonies and war with Britain. They sent spies to America to assess the military and political situation.[28] In 1774, the comte de Vergennes became the minister of foreign affairs under the new king, Louis XVI. Vergennes drafted a memorandum on foreign affairs for the young

[28] C. H. Van Tyne, "French Aid before the Alliance of 1778," *The American Historical Review* 31, no. 1 (1925): 23–29.

king that stressed France's current position of weakness in Europe as a whole and the need to rectify the situation. Although relations with Britain were currently peaceful, that was merely because of Britain's American troubles. A war with Britain was only a matter of time.[29] The French began building up their naval strength, and acted with restraint toward Britain because they were not ready for war. When relations between Spain, France's ally, and Portugal, Britain's ally, deteriorated over border disputes in South America, Spain proposed to attack Portugal directly, while Britain was distracted. Louis XVI wrote to Charles III, tactfully refusing to support Spain.

Upon the outbreak of open rebellion among the American colonists, Vergennes acted with caution, not knowing how serious the Americans were about becoming independent, or their ability to maintain a military. However, after receiving a favorable report from an envoy, Vergennes forwarded to the king a justification for aiding the Americans and wrote one of his own, which was debated in the king's council. He argued that it was desirable that the war last at least another year, which could be furthered by aiding the Americans in secret, so that Spain and France could rearm. His only warning of the danger of American independence in the document was that it would provoke in Britain a desire for compensation by seizing French colonies.

The king asked his chief minister and advisors for position papers. Vergennes's second memoir was explicit about the opportunity France faced: cutting America free could weaken Britain and alter the balance of power in favor of France. Using common mercantilist assumptions, Vergennes argued that Britain's monopoly of American trade was a great source of its strength and that denying that trade would harm the British economy and thus the country's ability to finance war and provide subsidies. The memoir dismissed the fear that the independent colonies would behave aggressively in the New World, because the war would wear them out for quite a while, and it was presumed that they would establish a republic, or many small republics, and republics did not have the spirit of conquest.[30] The only resistance to Vergennes's plan among the ministers was from Turgot, the controller-general of finances. He did so not because he thought that supporting democrats overthrowing a monarchy would set a dangerous precedent, but because the policy would not achieve the objectives it sought. It would not significantly weaken Britain, but it could derail the economic reforms he was attempting to implement.

---

[29] Orville T. Murphy, *Charles Gravier, Comte de Vergennes: French Diplomacy in the Age of Revolution, 1719–1787* (Albany: State University of New York Press, 1982), 213–19.

[30] Samuel Flagg Bemis, *The Diplomacy of the American Revolution* (Bloomington: Indiana University Press, 1967), 26–27; Jonathan R. Dull, *The French Navy and American Independence: A Study of Arms and Diplomacy, 1774–1787* (Princeton: Princeton University Press, 1975), 36–44.

In the discussion of France's policy toward the American Revolution, there was no expression of concern that the revolution could have a demonstration effect on France's internal politics. Some have detected resistance from Louis to aiding the rebels, and supposed the king was not fond of the implications of supporting rebel subjects. There is some evidence that he was not as enthusiastic as Vergennes.[31] But there appears to be no evidence that the king thought there would be negative repercussions to aiding the rebels and bringing about a republic. To the extent that he had hesitations, they seem to be based on his ethical qualms about secretly helping the Americans while France and Britain were at peace and on his concern about French finances.

The king got over his scruples. In May 1776, Louis XVI approved one million livres' worth of munitions to be covertly shipped to the Americans. Vergennes had previously asked Jerónimo Grimaldi, the Spanish minister of state, whether Spain would join France in providing secret assistance to the Americans. Grimaldi responded, "It is certainly desirable to us that the revolt of these people keep up, and we ought to want the English, and them, to exhaust themselves reciprocally."[32] Spain was involved in a conflict with Portugal, and it had a clear interest in keeping Britain occupied so that it did not openly aid its ally. Spain's policy toward America was derivative of its conflict with Portugal. Charles III matched the French funds. The Americans and French worked out a scheme for the Americans to buy "on credit" supplies, often directly from the French arsenals, that were worth many times the initial funds provided. The French also allowed American merchant ships to port at French possessions, which greatly assisted contraband trade. Meanwhile, the Spanish governor of Louisiana, Bernardo de Gálvez, provided munitions to the Americans.[33]

In August 1776, Vergennes proposed to Spain a war against Britain. The Americans were proving the strength of their resistance (the British had withdrawn from Boston), the French military was in a better state of readiness, and he was now convinced that Britain was behind the Portuguese aggressions against the Spanish. Spain countered that the plan had to include its designs on Portugal. Because this could, in Vergennes's perception, risk a general European war, he dropped the matter. In addition, the news of Washington's rout on Long Island brought momentary doubts that the Americans could keep the revolt going. In the meantime, France continued to build up their arms and approved another

[31] This should not be overemphasized. Hardman and Price note: "There are no signs whatsoever of friction or testiness on the king's part towards Vergennes over the policy towards England's American colonies. The most we can find are traces of procrastination on the part of the king." John Hardman and Munro Price, eds., *Louis XVI and the Comte de Vergennes: Correspondence 1774–1787*, Studies on Voltaire and the Eighteenth Century, vol. 364 (Oxford: Voltaire Foundation, 1998), 53.

[32] Bemis, *The Diplomacy of the American Revolution*, 24.

[33] John Walton Caughey, *Bernardo de Gálvez in Louisiana, 1776–1783* (Berkeley: University of California Press, 1934), 85–101.

clandestine loan for the Americans. Both France and Spain allowed American privateers to enter their harbors, and increasing pressure from Britain over the issue had Vergennes worried about a British ultimatum. When he again felt out the Spanish position in the summer of 1777, he found the Spanish were much less receptive. They had reconciled with Portugal, so conflict with Britain was less urgent. The British, long aware of French and Spanish aid to the colonists, were willing to overlook it rather than precipitate open warfare.

In January 1778, however, France openly allied with the Americans. The American victory at Saratoga was thought to have convinced the French of the Americans' competence, but recent losses had also shown they could not get the job done without overt assistance, especially from the French navy, which was now ready to enter into battle.[34] The French did this despite not having the Spanish onboard.[35] They engaged in a calculated risk—attempting to knock the British out of the war with one campaign. When this did not work, they desperately needed Spain and its ships of the line to join the fight.

The Spanish still thought it was better to let both the British and the Americans bleed. Since its dispute with Portugal was settled, Spain's primary rationale for conflict with Britain had disappeared and its interest in intervening in the American revolt was much less clear. Spain considered the benefits of an independent America weakening Britain, but it had doubts. America would possibly be just as aggressive as the British in North America, although the French tried to convince the Spanish that America would be a weak confederation of republics, consumed with their own divisions.[36] The Spanish minister in Paris, Pedro Aranda, had from the beginning advocated an open alliance with America to cut down the English.[37] But an independent United States would also set a dangerous precedent for Spain's own colonial empire. This concern was expressed, from the initial rejection of Aranda's proposal to ally with the United States to the end of the conflict, by all the major figures in Spanish statecraft.[38] After it

[34] Dull, *The French Navy and American Independence*, 89–91.

[35] It is somewhat puzzling that the French decided to strike out on their own when the king had long been insistent that action in regard to the Americans be only taken in concert with Spain. Hardman and Price speculate that in addition to the timing, the final factor that convinced the king to make an alliance was the king's desire to support their ally Austria in the conflict over Bavarian succession. Hardman and Price, *Louis XVI and the Comte de Vergennes*, 65, 72.

[36] Edward S. Corwin, *French Policy and the American Alliance of 1778* (Princeton: Princeton University Press, 1916), 110–11.

[37] Aranda would later supposedly pen a memoir in 1783 warning about the dangers of the United States, proposing far-reaching colonial reform, and claiming to have opposed aid by France and Spain to the United States. There are doubts about the authenticity of the memoir, but if it is authentic, Aranda is misrepresenting his previous position. See Arthur P. Whitaker, "The Pseudo-Aranda Memoir of 1783," *The Hispanic American Historical Review* 17, no. 3 (1937): 295; Almon R. Wright, "The Aranda Memorial: Genuine or Forged?," *The Hispanic American Historical Review* 18, no. 4 (1938): 445–60.

[38] Grimaldi, Minister of State Floridablanca, Charles III, and Aranda voiced these concerns. See, e.g., Chávez, *Spain and the Independence of the United States*, 58–59; McFarlane, "The American

made peace with Portugal in 1777, Spain decided that the negatives of interven-tion in the American war outweighed the positives; it refused to join the French in their alliance with the United States and even discontinued its secret aid to the Americans.[39] Spain was not about to do any favors for France, having felt it had again been left to fend for itself in the recent war with Portugal. Minister of State Floridablanca told Vergennes, "We do not wish to commit Spain to entering the war merely in order to frighten England into making a peace from which nothing but the independence of the United States would be obtained."[40] Given the ambiguous benefits of American independence, they were not willing to go to war to bring it about.

The French, however, were desperate to get Spain into the fight. Spain eventu-ally figured they could get more out of the deal to make involvement in the war worth it. The Spanish proceeded to skillfully bargain, under the guise of media-tion, with the British and French for the price of their neutrality. Britain was not willing to pay the price of Gibraltar for Spanish neutrality, so Spain turned to France. Spain added a host of territories beyond Gibraltar to its demands. Because of France's need of Spanish resources, Vergennes capitulated on all demands. He also gave up his request that the Spanish acknowledge American independence prior to the termination of the war. The king, Floridablanca relayed, fearful of the "example he would give to his own possessions," would "not recognize the independence of the United States until the English themselves would be forced to do so by a treaty of peace."[41] Thus, Spain entered the war on the side of France, although not formally allied with the United States.

Spain attempted to ensure the containment of the United States. It reconquered Florida and sent expeditions up the Mississippi to lay claims as far as the Ohio Valley. If it could control the Mississippi, it could limit Americans mostly to the Atlantic seaboard—any settlement across the mountains would be limited to a small population of subsistence farmers if they could not get their goods to market. Floridablanca at one point even proposed to Vergennes that America be a feudal dependency of England—they could be reduced to a "sort of anarchy which would render them absolutely nothing."[42] The Americans, at one point desperate to obtain an alliance with Spain, sent John Jay with instructions

Revolution and the Spanish Monarchy," 33; Corwin, *French Policy and the American Alliance of 1778*, 193; Liss, *Atlantic Empires*, 71.

[39] Jonathan R. Dull, *A Diplomatic History of the American Revolution* (New Haven: Yale University Press, 1985), 91.

[40] A. Temple Patterson, *The Other Armada: The Franco-Spanish Attempt to Invade Britain in 1779* (Manchester: Manchester University Press, 1960), 45.

[41] Corwin, *French Policy and the American Alliance of 1778*, 193.

[42] Richard B. Morris, *The Peacemakers: The Great Powers and American Independence* (New York: Harper & Row, 1965), 45.

to part with the Mississippi if necessary. The Spanish rejected the proposal be-cause they thought they could hold on to the Mississippi anyway. Their fortunes changed when Cornwallis surrendered in Yorktown. France, financially de-pleted, wanted the war to end, and hoped it could get Spain to abandon Gibraltar if France supported Spain's claims to the Mississippi and Ohio valleys, which the Americans had little claim over. The Americans, getting suspicious of a deal between France and Britain, made their own deal with Britain, and France and Spain eventually conceded.

To what extent, then, was there among French statesmen a fear of revolu-tionary contagion, and did this have any impact on French policy toward the American Revolution? Did it seem odd to contemporaries that the oldest mon-archy in Europe was playing a pivotal role in bringing about the republic's ex-istence? This sentiment was not unknown at the time. When Vergennes asked diplomat Jean Louis Favier to write a legal justification of the alliance the king had just made with the Americans, Favier instead questioned the wisdom of the alliance: "Would it be proper to put into the mouth of a King of France or his minister paradoxical assertions concerning *natural liberty, inalienable and in-admissible rights of the people and its inherent sovereignty*, which have not ceased to be repeated, commented, ransacked, and compiled for two centuries, from François Hottoman's *Vindiciæ contra tyrannos* to J. J. Rousseau's *Contrat social*? Would it be prudent even? . . . If the King, if the government, appeared to pro-fess such maxims, would we ourselves be exactly safe from their application and from their being turned against us?"[43] Some of the radical philosophes and their opponents expressed similar reasoning.[44]

But to the extent the government exhibited these concerns, it did so in an ef-fort to tone down the anti-monarchical rhetoric. The king himself noted in the margin of a memorandum by Vergennes justifying the French government's involvement in the American Revolution, in which he had asserted that France had only recognized a people already free, "This observation could au-thorize . . . England to openly help the malcontents so often agitated in Brittany, our Protestants, and all the French opposing royal authority."[45] This concern,

[43] Bernard Fäy, *The Revolutionary Spirit in France and America* (New York: Harcourt, Brace and Company, 1927), 483–84.

[44] Even before the Revolution began, Diderot expressed surprise that a translation of John Dickenson's *Letters from a Farmer in Pennsylvania* would appear in France: "Because Dickenson was writing for Americans they did not conceive that his Letters were addressed to all men. . . . They allow us to read things like this, and they are amazed to find us ten years later different men. Do they not realize how easily noble souls must drink of these principles and become intoxicated by them?" Echeverria, *Mirage in the West*, 35. Simo-Nicholas Henri Linguet expressed the same sentiment out of alarm: "In calling the English Crown to account, it is the abuses of all monarchies that they are attacking. . . . The blind hope of being able perhaps to imitate them some day and even of being aided by them in breaking our own chains, this is what wins the insurgents so many friends among us." Fäy, *The Revolutionary Spirit in France and America*, 94.

[45] Corwin, *French Policy and the American Alliance of 1778*, 8n11a.

however, did not have an effect on French foreign policy, and French censorship of democratic ideas was notably lax.

The French government engaged in a propaganda effort to provide domestic support for its policies toward the American Revolution. It covertly backed a journal, the *Affaires de l'Angleterre et de l'Amérique*, which published narrations of the conflict, translations of the state constitutions, and critiques of England. The journal exercised some prudence concerning political matters that could apply to France, but it even published long extracts from Thomas Paine's *Common Sense*, albeit with an editorial critique of Paine's diatribe against monarchies.[46] The Spanish also did not heavily censor news about the American Revolution in its colonies.[47]

The American Revolution has been described as opening up a Pandora's box in France, out of which poured revolutionary ideas that were subversive of the political and social order.[48] The revolution in America certainly got many French men and women thinking about ideas that would eventually have sub- versive implications, and it provided a safe means by which they could at least indirectly consider ideas such as liberty, equality, constitutionalism, and popular sovereignty. But the revolution's effects in encouraging radicalism should not be exaggerated. First of all, the bulk of public support for the American Revolution and the policies of France was for something like nationalistic reasons—getting back at the hated English.[49] Even those who were inspired by the liberal ideals of the American Revolution stopped well short of being revolutionary. The comte de Ségur, who fought in the American war and would go on to participate in the French Revolution, in 1782 expressed a sentiment common among progres- sives: "The liberty for which I am going to fight inspires in me great enthusiasm, and I would like my own country to possess as much of it as is compatible with our monarchy, our status, and our customs."[50]

An older generation of historians even maintained that the Franco-American alliance was at least in part the result of a movement in France in favor of li- berty and the king's desire to court public opinion, but this has been thoroughly

---

[46] Francis Acomb, *Anglophobia in France, 1763–1789* (Durham: Duke University Press, 1950), 83– 85; Fäy, *The Revolutionary Spirit in France and America*, 89–90. On another occasion, Vergennes even paid to have Paine's tract, which argued for the universality of the American Revolution, published in France. Janet L. Polasky, *Revolutions Without Borders: The Call to Liberty in the Atlantic World* (New Haven: Yale University Press, 2015), 46. Censer notes that the government "systematically played a dangerous game by allowing news that, though favorable at the level of foreign policy, promulgated democratic ideas." Jack R. Censer, *The French Press in the Age of Enlightenment* (New York: Routledge, 1994), 16.

[47] Mario Rodríguez, "The Presence of the American Revolution in the Contemporaneous Spanish World," *Proceedings of the Pacific Coast Council on Latin American Studies* 6 (1977–1979): 15–24.

[48] Echeverria, *Mirage in the West*, 42.

[49] Acomb, *Anglophobia in France*, 69–88.

[50] Claude Fohlen, "The Impact of the American Revolution on France," in *The Impact of the American Revolution Abroad* (Washington, DC: Library of Congress, 1976), 225.

discredited.[51] The popularity of the American cause in France was not primarily due to the Americans' political philosophy, and at any rate, the idea to intervene came "not from the *salon* but the Foreign Office."[52] In fact, the only evidence that Vergennes feared a contagion effect from supporting American independence was the possibility of it serving as a model for anti-colonial revolt in French colonies in the New World.[53] If this was a genuine concern of Vergennes, it was not serious enough to prevent him from securing American independence. A consensus has emerged that the French intervened in the American Revolution to recover, at the expense of Britain, their international position—in other words, to restore the balance of power.[54] Any other negative consequences were brushed aside.

Spain did not care that the Americans were establishing a republic, which is to be expected given its lack of a significant republican revolutionary movement. However, America's example as an anti-colonial revolt was a cause of concern. What is curious is the degree to which Spanish leaders felt that the problem of American independence would be mitigated by the strategy of not openly backing the rebels. Grimaldi had told Aranda that "the rights of all sovereigns to their respective territories ought to be regarded as sacred, and the example of a rebellion is too dangerous to allow of His Majesty's wishing to assist it *openly*."[55] The king was insistent that Spain not recognize the United States, at least not before England had. If the United States became independent, it would not acknowledge the Spanish role in bringing that about, which would to some extent delegitimize the king's rule.[56]

[51] See George Bancroft, *History of the United States of America, from the Discovery of the Continent*, vol. V (New York: D. Appleton and Company, 1888), 256; Fäy, *The Revolutionary Spirit in France and America*, 44; Ben C. McCary, *The Causes of the French Intervention in the American Revolution* (Toulouse: Édouard Privat, 1928), 118–19, 210–11.

[52] Acomb, *Anglophobia in France*, 72–74; Corwin, *French Policy and the American Alliance of 1778*, 2.

[53] In 1775, Vergennes had written to the French ambassador in London, "Far from seeking to profit by the embarrassment in which England finds herself on account of affairs in America, we should rather desire to extricate her. The spirit of revolt, in whatever spot it breaks out, is always of dangerous precedent; it is with moral as with physical diseases, both may become contagious. This consideration should induce us to take care that the spirit of independence, which is causing so terrible an explosion in North America, have no power to communicate itself to points interesting to us in [that] hemisphere." M. Guizot and Madame Guizot de Witt, *The History of France from the Earliest of Times to 1848*, trans. Robert Black, vol. 5 (Boston: Aldine Book Publishing Co., n.d.), 450; Claude Manceron, *The French Revolution*, trans. Nancy Amphoux, vol. 2, *The Wind from America* (New York: Alfred A. Knopf, 1978), 153. It is not clear how seriously this statement should be taken, given that his policy was to profit from the embarrassment of England.

[54] This is the position of the leading scholars on the issue: Corwin, *French Policy and the American Alliance of 1778*; Bemis, *The Diplomacy of the American Revolution*; Dull, *The French Navy and American Independence*; Dull, *A Diplomatic History of the American Revolution*; Murphy, *Charles Gravier*; Larrie D. Ferreiro, *Brothers at Arms: American Independence and the Men of France and Spain Who Saved It* (New York: Alfred A. Knopf, 2016).

[55] Corwin, *French Policy and the American Alliance of 1778*, 108, emphasis added.

[56] Hull notes that a formal alliance "would have mocked Charles's own imperial position," but covert aid had the effect of "preserving the dignity of a monarch while at the same time delivering

Contagion concerns prevented the Spanish from acknowledging what they were obviously doing, but that did not fundamentally change Spain's foreign policy of securing American independence. The Spanish gave secret aid to the Americans. They used their vital navy to prosecute a war with Britain. If contagion concerns were paramount, they could have sat the war out. But American independence could weaken the British, and they had significant carrots, especially Gibraltar, dangled before them, as well as the opportunity to constrain a future American state. They took a calculated risk, and although they achieved some success, such as capturing Florida and Minorca, they did not get Gibraltar; nor did they contain the United States, owing to the generous British terms. In sum, there *were* concerns about anti-colonial contagion, perhaps driven more by the empire's structural vulnerabilities than by the somewhat ambiguous anti-colonial movement in its colonies. But this concern was not strong enough to alter Spain's policy of aiding America.

The Eastern Powers and the American Revolution

Russia, Prussia, and Austria had only a peripheral concern with the American Revolution. Fears of contagion did not affect their foreign policy. Their policy toward the Revolution was a product of their ambiguous policy toward Britain.

In the fall of 1775, Russia rebuffed a British request for Russian troops to help suppress the rebellion. Catherine and her foreign minister, Nikita Panin, did not necessarily see the humbling of Britain as a bad thing.[57] They had no desire to get bogged down in the American revolt, or go to war with the Bourbon powers once they got involved. Russia rejected a British proposal for an alliance in 1778. Catherine and Panin were irritated at the British policy of detaining neutral ships. Catherine wanted to free Russian foreign trade from its dependence on the British merchant navy and make use of the heightened demand for Russian goods, primarily naval stores, during a maritime war. She needed other nations to have access to Russian ports. In 1780, Catherine issued a declaration of "armed neutrality," which outlined principles to govern neutral trade, and was joined by Prussia and Austria, among others.

---

heavy blows against the common enemy." Anthony H. Hull, *Charles III and the Revival of Spain* (Washington, DC: University Press of America, 1980), 252.

[57] Nikolai Bolkhovitinov, *The Beginnings of Russian-American Relations, 1775–1815*, trans. Elena Levin (Cambridge, MA: Harvard University Press, 1975), 5–6; Bolkhovitinov, *Russia and the American Revolution*, trans. C. Jay Smith (Tallahassee: The Diplomatic Press, 1976), 6–12; H. M. Scott, *British Foreign Policy in the Age of the American Revolution* (Oxford: Clarendon Press, 1990), 217–20.

The League of Armed Neutrality favored the Americans.[58] The Continental Congress thought they spied an opening and sent a representative to Russia to negotiate recognition and a treaty of commerce. Instead, he sat in his hotel room, ignored for two years. Russia looked after its own interest, which only incidentally benefited the Americans. Catherine at one point offered to mediate between the two sides, who rejected the proposal, but by 1780 she had no interest in a settlement. Her "Greek Project," expelling the Turks from Europe, meant she did not want the war to end. She wanted the other powers occupied.

Soviet historians argued Catherine was against the American Revolution because of the political ideals it represented, but the evidence does not bear this out.[59] A historian writing before the Russian Revolution outlined well her position: "Catherine neither liked nor disliked the Americans. She probably knew none of them personally, and cared little about their theories of government. She took an interest in the American Revolution because it affected English and European politics."[60] Her lack of contagion concerns is expected by the domestic contagion effects theory given the lack of a significant revolutionary opposition movement in Russia. There was a radical, Alexander Radischev, who penned an ode to the American Revolution in the 1780s, and published, in Russian, extracts of some of the American state constitutions.[61] But those such as Radischev were in a distinct minority. One scholar notes that it is possible to count on one's fingers the number of progressive Russian thinkers who looked with favor upon the American Revolution.[62]

Catherine compared the American war for independence to that of the Dutch against the Spanish and that of the Corsicans against the French. She had intervened in the latter to thwart French expansion into the Mediterranean. She did not have similar interests in opposing the British.[63] Panin did think that revolting colonists set a dangerous precedent for those who had colonies in the New World, but he did not consider Russia to be in this category.[64] At one point, he told the British representative that Catherine could be trusted as a mediator to

---

[58] Madariaga argues that it played a bigger role in the diplomacy of the era than supposed—frustrating British efforts to find allies on the Continent. Isabel de Madariaga, *Britain, Russia, and the Armed Neutrality of 1780* (New Haven: Yale University Press, 1962), 466.

[59] David M. Griffiths, "Soviet Views of Early Russian-American Relations," *Proceedings of the American Philosophical Society* 116, no. 2 (1972): 148–56.

[60] Frank A. Golder, "Catherine II and the American Revolution," *The American Historical Review* 21, no. 1 (1915): 92.

[61] David Marshall Lang, *The First Russian Radical: Alexander Radischev, 1749–1802* (London: George Allen and Unwin, 1959), 171–75.

[62] David M. Griffiths, "American Commercial Diplomacy in Russia, 1780 to 1783," *The William and Mary Quarterly* 27, no. 3 (1970): 410.

[63] David M. Griffiths, "Catherine the Great, the British Opposition, and the American Revolution," in *The American Revolution and "a Candid World,"* ed. Lawrence S. Kaplan (Kent: Kent State University Press, 1977), 86–89.

[64] Russia did have a few trading posts in Alaska at the time, but this was not an object of concern.

watch over Britain's interests because "she disapproved of French recognition of the Americans as a blow to monarchical solidarity."[65] But the British rightly did not think she was moved by this sentiment.[66]

As with Russia, neither of the German powers had fears of contagion, and geopolitical factors dominated their policy—or lack thereof—toward the Americans. Prussia and Austria had similar approaches. Because of their mutual antipathy, each had a strong incentive to remain cordial with Britain (and thus maintain a strict neutrality vis-à-vis the American situation) so that Britain did not side with its rival.

Frederick the Great, ruler of Prussia, has sometimes been regarded as having a relatively pro-American policy, either out of sympathy for the Americans or because of anger against Britain for its abandonment of Prussia during the Seven Years' War. Frederick, like Catherine, criticized British policies toward the Americans as counterproductive. However, he also did not mind that Britain was being humbled and occupied outside Europe. Frederick confided to his minister in France at the outset of the Revolution, "The more the affairs of the colonies keep the British court busy and embarrassed, the less it can meddle in the affairs of the other powers, and that is always a great point gained."[67]

Prussia's policy was one of cautious neutrality. American representatives came to Prussia with the hope of recognition and/or an opening up of commercial relations. They got neither. Frederick remained friendly with the American representatives so that, if the conditions arose, he could negotiate a commercial treaty with them. But the time was not ripe. As Frederick's foreign minister told the American representative, "The king is very much disposed to please your constituents; but, on the other hand, his majesty in the present circumstances, as you well know, cannot embroil himself with the court of London."[68] Prussia at this point was only days away from war with Austria over its attempt to control Bavaria. But even in times when there was not an acute crisis, Frederick could not afford to antagonize the British out of fear that they would court the Austrians, and because of the substantial trade connections between Prussia and Britain.[69]

Like Russia, Prussia's neutrality was not unfavorable for the Americans. Frederick sent clear signals to the French that he would not side with Britain in

---

[65] Madariaga, *Britain, Russia, and the Armed Neutrality of 1780*, 99.

[66] They emphasized to the Russians how America would be an economic competitor and that it was in Russia's interest that Britain remained strong. Regarding Panin, Griffiths notes, "Never in his talks with various diplomatic representatives did Panin evince any sort of legitimist sentiment." Griffiths, "Nikita Panin, Russian Diplomacy, and the American Revolution," 4.

[67] Henry M. Adams, *Prussian-American Relations, 1775–1871* (Cleveland: The Press of Western Reserve University, 1960), 5n5.

[68] Francis Wharton, *The Revolutionary Diplomatic Correspondence of the United States*, vol. 2 (Washington, DC: Government Printing Office, 1889), 350.

[69] Horst Dippel, "Prussia's English Policy after the Seven Year's War," *Central European History* 4, no. 3 (1971): 205.

order to encourage France's pro-American policy.[70] But Frederick's policy was not driven by sympathy for the American colonists, or by what he thought of the American form of government. Though he closely followed the American crisis, he took "no note whatsoever of the domestic development of America."[71] He was interested in the revolt insofar as how it affected international politics and how Prussia could profit.

This is expected by the domestic contagion effects theory given the lack of significant democratic revolutionary opposition resembling the Americans. In German lands, there was widespread coverage of American affairs, though political and constitutional issues were usually neglected. Even so, the way that the vocabulary of the American Revolution was translated into feudal terms—"state assemblies," for example, was translated as "estates"—illustrates the degree to which the Germans did not comprehend many of the ideals that motivated the Americans.[72] Some Germans expressed approval of the American Revolution, and considered that Americans were now exercising rights that Germans already enjoyed. In 1784, a minister in Frederick's government wrote an essay for the occasion of the king's birthday: "On the Forms of Government, and Which One Is the Best?" The birth of the new American republic, he said, "has given us a new phenomenon." But he considered republics as passé: "We have to wait at least a half century in order to see whether this new Republic or confederated body will consolidate its form of government. At the moment, its existence is not yet evidence in favor of the republican form."[73] The lecture indicates the tone of philosophical speculation that existed at the time rather than alarm over political agitation.

Of all great powers, Austria was least involved in the diplomacy of the American Revolution. That revolution was on the periphery of the foreign policy concerns of Maria Theresa, her son, Joseph II (the co-regent until Maria's death in 1780), and Kaunitz, the long-standing state chancellor. The Austrian court kept relatively well abreast of the events in America.[74] But Austrian policy was not warm to the American cause. An American attempting in 1777 to gain recognition for the rebels while in Vienna could not even get an audience with the court. "There is a cold tranquility here that bodes us no good," he reported.[75]

---

[70] Paul Leland Haworth, "Frederick the Great and the American Revolution," *The American Historical Review* 9, no. 3 (1904): 474.

[71] Dippel, *Germany and the American Revolution*, 61.

[72] Ibid., 69–70.

[73] Willi Paul Adams, "German Translations of the American Declaration of Independence," *The Journal of American History* 85, no. 4 (1999): 1326.

[74] The court physician, Jan Ingenhousz, was a personal friend of Benjamin Franklin's and was reporting on the situation for the court. Franklin, aware that Joseph took an interest in his correspondence with Ingenhousz, did his best to put England in a bad light. Timothy K. Conley and Melissa Brewer-Anderson, "Franklin and Ingenhousz: A Correspondence of Interests," *Proceedings of the American Philosophical Society* 141, no. 3 (1997): 290.

[75] Wharton, *The Revolutionary Diplomatic Correspondence of the United States*, vol. 2, 327.

Austria never recognized the Americans and forbade the Austrian Netherlands from trading with the rebels. Their most significant foray into the conflict was their mediation proposals, which were rebuffed and then bypassed when the belligerents chose direct negotiations.[76]

Why were the Austrians unsympathetic to the Americans? One explanation is that the Austrians feared the Americans could be a dangerous model. While traveling in France in 1777, Joseph II was supposedly asked his opinion of the American revolt and responded, "My trade is to be a royalist."[77] One scholar doubts the authenticity of this statement, noting that "this kind of interpretation of the American Revolution was much more characteristic of the period of the French Revolution," and not surprisingly the remark is handed down from the 1790s. He concludes that Joseph II "was not cognizant of the revolutionary character of American ideas and of their antimonarchical trend."[78] However, this was not the only such statement. The British ambassador in Vienna reported that Joseph told him he was "extremely concerned for the difficulties which embarrass the King's government. The cause in which England is engaged, is the cause of all sovereigns, who have a joint interest in the maintenance of due subordination and obedience to law, in all the surrounding monarchies."[79] He was possibly telling the British what they wanted to hear, but perhaps these remarks indicate that he did have an ideological antipathy toward the Americans.

Nevertheless, there is no evidence that this sentiment was the decisive factor affecting Austrian policy toward the Americans. What was shaping Austrian policy was its relationship with England in the context of its grand strategy. Ever since the "Diplomatic Revolution" orchestrated by Kaunitz in 1756, Austria was allied with its former enemy, France, to aid it against the Prussians, who had become the Austrians' primary enemy. This prohibited an outright alliance with England, but the Austrians and English remained on good relations. There were two reasons behind Kaunitz's cultivation of English friendship: prevention of a British-Prussian rapprochement, and an insurance policy to retain the possibility of a British alliance should the French alliance collapse.[80] These geopolitical factors dominated decision-making regarding the Americans.

[76] Morris, The Peacemakers, 153–58, 173–90.

[77] See Derek Beales, Joseph II: In the Shadow of Maria Theresa, 1741–1780, vol. 1 (New York: Cambridge University Press, 1987), 385.

[78] Dippel, Germany and the American Revolution, 62–63.

[79] William Coxe, History of the House of Austria from the Foundation of the Monarchy by Rhodolph of Hapsburgh to the Death of Leopold the Second, vol. 2 (London: Luke Hansard and Sons, 1807), 548.

[80] Scott, British Foreign Policy in the Age of the American Revolution, 86.

The American Revolution and the Ancien Régime

In 1854, Leopold von Ranke claimed that the American Revolution was more important than all earlier revolutions because it was a complete turnover in principles.[81] But did contemporaries recognize this? More specifically, did they see the revolution as a potential threat because of spillover effects, and did that affect their foreign policy? Some have said that it did. The historian Lawrence Kaplan, for example, claims that the French alliance with the United States was a dangerous departure from typical eighteenth-century statecraft. Prussia, Russia, and Spain "appreciated the dangers to all monarchies in the success of the American experiment."[82] He is wrong on both counts.

Concerning the claim that the American Revolution was regarded as a danger to monarchies, my theory asserts that the presence of a revolutionary movement triggers fears of spillover effects, which prompt patterns of hostility toward revolutions and cooperation among those states that have similar movements. There was no significant revolutionary opposition movement, and likewise there was little or no fear of the spillover effect. That fear was expressed in France, the country that had the strongest anti-monarchical sentiment, but this fear was still peripheral among policymakers. Consequently, the American Revolution did not affect any change in patterns of cooperation and conflict; the international reaction to it, rather, is explained by preexisting patterns of conflict and cooperation. Thus, the reactions of France, Russia, Prussia, Austria, and Spain (mostly) are a negative confirmation of the theory.

The domestic contagion effects theory, however, only imperfectly captures the matter of America having a negative demonstration effect on other colonies in the Americas. As we have seen, concern was voiced in France but especially in Spain on this matter. I assessed that there was no significant revolutionary movement in Spain itself, and there was no concern among Spanish policymakers regarding the fact that America's republican principles would prove contagious in either Spain or the empire. Whether there was a significant revolutionary anti-colonial movement in the Spanish Empire is somewhat ambiguous. The literature on the subject indicates that there was not, but this point can be contested. However, the noted fear by Spanish officials of a contagion effect from the American Revolution on the Spanish Empire seems more driven by the structural weakness of the empire—how overextended Spain was—rather than by whether significant revolutionary groups already existed. Officials thought more preemptively, wanting to prevent these groups from developing in the first place,

---

[81] Dippel, *Germany and the American Revolution*, x.
[82] Lawrence S. Kaplan, *Colonies into Nation: American Diplomacy, 1763–1801* (New York: The Macmillan Company, 1972), 108.

given the weakness of the empire. The intendant of Venezuela, who was witness to one of the biggest rebellions in Spanish America, said in 1781 that if Britain could not subdue its relatively close colonies, "what prudent human would not fear greatly an equal tragedy in the astonishingly extended dominions of Spain in these Indies?"[83] These contagion concerns, however, were still too abstract to have a decisive effect on Spanish foreign policy. Spain's rivalry with Portugal, and then its desire for a variety of prizes once its ally was committed to the American cause, dominated its concerns. In the end, Spain helped ensure American independence. Its concession was that they would not openly recognize America.

Regarding Kaplan's claim that the French response to the American Revolution was a departure from eighteenth-century diplomacy, this also is not the case. The other powers' policies were not driven by such ideological concerns. The great powers' response to the Dutch Patriot Revolt provides further data points to show that France's intervention was not a departure from eighteenth-century statecraft; rather, it exemplified the statecraft of the ancien régime.

The Dutch Democratic Revolution of the 1780s

Outbreak of Revolution

In the Dutch Republic, there was a long-standing antagonism between the stadtholder and the regent class. The stadtholder was the chief officer in charge of public order and upholding the law. After 1747, the position was pseudo-monarchical: it was hereditary, passed down through the House of Orange, and the stadtholder served simultaneously as chief of all seven provinces that made up the United Provinces. The regents were urban oligarchs, an unusual aristocracy that earned their income in large part through finance and trade. They exercised influence in their respective provinces and through the States General, an assembly of delegates from each of the seven provinces.

The American Revolution brought renewed criticism of the stadtholder, William V. The British were the traditional protectors of the stadtholder, and William V wanted to comply with British requests for assistance against the Americans. The regents, however, wanted to end their dependency on Britain and profit from trade with the Americans. The American Revolution also inspired a democratic movement—especially among the upper middle class, who had been excluded from the political system and called for a broader system of participation. A Dutch periodical declared that the Americans had reminded the Dutch

---

[83] Liss, *Atlantic Empires*, 128.

that "all nations have a right to seek liberty and to rise up against tyranny."[84] The 1781 pamphlet that became the Dutch equivalent of Thomas Paine's *Common Sense* exhorted, "Arm yourselves, elect those who must command you ... and in all things proceed like the people of America."[85] Those advocating popular sovereignty and the anti-stadtholder regents together made up what became known as the Patriot party, united in their opposition toward the stadtholder.

Anti-Orangist sentiment was fueled by what was considered the incompetent performance of William V in the Anglo-Dutch War of 1780–84. The stadtholder was blamed for the Netherlands' lackluster showing, and his tepid leadership was explained as loyalty to England over the Dutch Republic. The reaction against the defeat grew to a broader set of demands. Measures to curtail the stadtholder's power in the various assemblies multiplied, and the burghers began organizing "free corps" militias. In 1783, the Patriots scored a major victory by forcing the stadtholder's main advisor/executive from office. However, the decentralized nature of political power in the Dutch Republic that enabled the Patriots to initially flourish by seizing one municipal council at a time also prevented them from decisively consolidating power. There was no Bastille to storm, although the Patriots had done the closest equivalent in September 1785 by forcing William V and the princess from The Hague, which was the headquarters of the stadtholder and housed the assemblies of Holland and the States General.

Also beginning in 1785 the coalition between the regents and the burghers began to fall apart—many of the oligarchs began to fear the stadtholder less and the "democrats" more. The more radical Patriot movement spread nevertheless, taking on a much broader geographic and demographic character than traditional disputes with the stadtholder. In other words, the revolt was going beyond regaining traditional Dutch rights; it was a democratic revolution. By the summer of 1787, there was a low-level civil war. The Patriots had garnered control of three provinces, the stadtholder had two, and the two others were disputed. There seemed to be a stalemate, though many assumed that the Patriots would ultimately prevail, including at times the stadtholder himself, who was widely regarded as a weak and vacillating figure. Most assumed that the victor would be determined by the policies of the great powers, which is exactly what happened. Prussia intervened, with British diplomatic support, and crushed what would have been a Dutch democracy.

---

[84] Franco Venturi, *The End of the Old Regime in Europe, 1776–1789*, trans. R. Burr Litchfield, vol. 2 (Princeton: Princeton University Press, 1991), 529.

[85] Palmer, *The Age of the Democratic Revolution*, 330. For the effect of the American Revolution on the Patriot Revolt, see Simon Schama, *Patriots and Liberators: Revolution in the Netherlands, 1780–1813* (New York: Alfred A Knopf, 1977), 58–63; J. W. Schulte Nordholt, "The Impact of the American Revolution on the Dutch Republic," in *The Impact of the American Revolution Abroad* (Washington, DC: Library of Congress, 1976), 41–63; Jan Willem Schulte Nordholt, *The Dutch Republic and American Independence*, trans. Herbert H. Rowen (Chapel Hill: University of North Carolina Press, 1982).

Model

The revolt against the stadtholder could be considered, like all revolts, as a negative model in the general sense of encouraging rebellions against traditional authority, specifically encouraging the aristocracies to resist the centralizing demands of the monarchies. But the Patriots were also pushing a novel product—a republic based on popular sovereignty. Patriot ideology has been described as "a mélange of old and new attitudes towards the Dutch constitution."[86] The regent class pined for the Dutch Republic of old, where the oligarchs exercised the decisive power, as in the other old republics of Europe ruled by aristocracies, such as Venice and Geneva. This stood in marked contrast with the monarchies of the great powers. But the radicals who came to dominate the Patriot movement and who had significantly expanded the idea of popular sovereignty stood at an even greater contrast. They more often spoke in universal terms to justify their republic based on the rights of people over kings.

Platform

The Patriot Revolt did not act as a significant platform in spreading revolution. The Dutch Republic had weakened considerably since its golden age in the seventeenth century. It remained an important trading and financial center, but it was clearly a second-rate power. Although the Dutch Republic was not much of a military threat, it was well suited to act as a platform in more indirect ways. The Dutch had been disseminators of potentially subversive materials. Because of their looser restrictions on the press, some of the books by the philosophes that were banned in France were available via the Republic. However, by the time of the Patriot Revolution, Dutch publishers were no longer significantly involved in exporting books and pamphlets to other countries.[87] The revolt did not reverse this trend. There does not seem to be any evidence that the Patriots spent their energy specifically targeting other states with revolutionary propaganda, although their political tracts would eventually make their way especially to France and have an impact on the French Revolution. In summary, the Patriot Revolt was not acting as a platform toward any of the powers, but it did serve as a potential model.

---

[86] Schama, *Patriots and Liberators*, 68.

[87] Jeremy D. Popkin, "Print Culture in the Netherlands on the Eve of the Revolution," in *The Dutch Republic in the Eighteenth Century: Decline, Enlightenment, and Revolution*, eds. Margaret C. Jacob and Wijnand Mijnhardt (Ithaca: Cornell University Press, 1992), 282.

International Relations Prior to the Dutch Patriot Revolt

To assess how the Patriot Revolt affected patterns of international politics, I examine the relations of the great powers among each other and toward the Dutch Republic prior to the revolt. Most importantly, the Dutch traditionally had been either neutral or in the British sphere of influence. Britain had gone to war with the Republic in 1780 to ensure that a pro-British stadtholder held sway.

As discussed, the American Revolution did not change the patterns of conflict and cooperation among the great powers, although the French were now vindicated and the British seemed more isolated from the Continent than ever, and also in a state of decline. A big change on the Continent was that with Maria Theresa's death in 1780, Joseph II emerged as sole ruler of Austria. Prussia, as well as France, worried about the consequences, as it was widely assumed that he would engage in a more aggressive policy. Relations between France and Austria were strained because Joseph rightly believed the French were trying to use the alliance to restrain him, but they remained allies for the simple reason that Joseph could not afford a rupture, which would bring about an alliance between Prussia and France. Joseph had allied with Catherine in order to get Russian support for Austrian policies in Germany and perhaps the Balkans, and to slowly wean Russia from Prussia. Russia, on the other hand, wanted Austrian support against the Ottomans. The British, set back by the American loss, were trying to gain allies, sounding out Russia and Austria.

Regarding the relations between the great powers and the United Provinces, the latter's general policy in the eighteenth century, especially after the threat of France receded, was to steer clear of the rival European power blocs, although with a tilt toward Britain. Britain traditionally regarded the United Provinces as its sphere of influence—the British had a commercial, security, and imperial interest in preventing the Republic from coming under the sway of other powers, particularly France. Dutch neutrality in the Seven Years' War had angered Britain when Dutch trade aided France, but they avoided conflict. Both the British and the Prussians supported the stadtholder. The stadtholder's wife was Frederick the Great's niece. The French preferred that the United Provinces be neutral rather than in the British sphere of influence, but the revolt would provide an opportunity to put them in their camp.

The Dutch involvement in the War for American Independence was both a cause and consequence of the increasing division internally, as the pro-British stadtholder and the merchant oligarchs diverged on matters of internal and foreign policy. The war that Britain launched on the Dutch during the conflict was traditionally thought to have been a British attempt to keep the Dutch from providing the French with supplies and thus aiding the American cause. Perhaps even more important than that, war was a means to shore up support for the

Table 3.2 Response to the Dutch Patriot Revolt

Great Power	Stance Toward Dutch Republic Prior to Revolt	Significant Liberal Revolutionary Movement?	Prediction of Stance Toward Patriot Revolt Given Revolutionary Movement	Outcome
Britain	Aligned with stadtholder	No	Unaffected by fears of contagion	Allies with stadtholder
Prussia	Aligned with stadtholder	No	Unaffected by fears of contagion	Allies with stadtholder
France	Ambivalent	No	Unaffected by fears of contagion	Allies with Dutch patriots
Austria	Ambivalent	No	Unaffected by fears of contagion	Neutral
Russia	Ambivalent	No	Unaffected by fears of contagion	Neutral

stadtholder against the regents and keep the United Provinces in the British orbit.[88] This was a miscalculation, as the war only expanded opposition toward the stadtholder.

Predictions

Like with the American Revolution, the domestic contagion effects theory expects that, given the lack of significant revolutionary opposition movements in the great powers, as previously established, there would be no significant fears of contagion. And, correspondingly, this factor would not affect international politics.

Like the case of the American Revolution, a theory that emphasized ideological differences would expect uniform hostility among the monarchs to a democratic movement. This did not happen, as seen in Table 3.2. Instead, I show that the great powers' support or lack of support of the Dutch Patriots would be based on other motivations for their statecraft. For France, it was an opportunity to wrest the Dutch Republic from the British sphere of influence, and thus it supported revolutionaries. Britain wanted to preserve its sphere of influence, and

---

[88] H. M. Scott, "Sir Joseph Yorke, Dutch Politics and the Origins of the Fourth Anglo-Dutch War," *The Historical Journal* 31, no. 3 (1988): 571–89. The issue of neutral rights and the position of the stadtholder were related. The stadtholder's lack of standing meant he was unable to prevent the Dutch accession to the League of Neutrality.

thus was against the revolutionaries. Geopolitical calculations drove statecraft. The Prussians had their prestige on the line when threats were made against their family (the stadtholder wife), and they ultimately decided to crush the revolutionaries for this reason. The Russians and Austrians had little at stake in the matter.

International Relations of the Patriot Revolt, 1783–87

The Revolt and the French Alliance

The French had welcomed the growth of opposition toward the pro-British stadtholder as well as Dutch neutrality in the war between the British and French, though they let Dutch events develop on their own. The Patriots had reached out to them, but the French did not want the responsibility of more allies to defend while they were involved in the American conflict. The Dutch were more valuable to them as trading neutrals. They urged the Republic to join the League of Armed Neutrality. Even in 1783, when the Patriots scored major victories against the stadtholder and the American conflict was over, the French remained aloof. The Patriots again the following year reached out to the French for an alliance.

The potential alliance held out several advantages for France. It would wrest the state from the British sphere of influence, which would increase France's sway over the English Channel. Dutch overseas colonies, especially the Cape of Good Hope, could allow action against British India. The Dutch also had a sizable navy, although the French had not been impressed with their military contribution in the American Revolution. And a commercial alliance would perhaps help the struggling French economy. Vergennes at one point wrote the king, "Of all the alliances, that with the [Dutch] Republic is the most advantageous and the least subject to drawbacks."[89]

However, Vergennes was initially hesitant to a commitment beyond a commercial alliance. This was not due to concerns that the Patriots might set a negative example for France. The reason for pause was the potential reaction of other great powers. Frederick of Prussia might oppose the Patriots, given that the stadtholder's wife was his niece. More importantly, he feared that the alliance was too much of an affront to Britain. There was an ambiguity in Vergennes's policy toward the British. On the one hand, Vergennes desired stability and the status quo. His policy toward the American conflict can be defended on these grounds as an attempt to restore the balance between France and Britain. On the other hand, there was an opportunistic temptation to take advantage of

---

[89] John Hardman, *Louis XVI* (New Haven: Yale University Press, 1993), 95.

Britain while they were weak.[90] Vergennes at first moved cautiously on the Dutch matter, fearing that kicking the British while they were down might provoke further recriminations when he desired stability. Nevertheless, many in the French council were actively pressing a general alliance. Vergennes went along, and even acted as though he was in favor of aiding the Patriots all along, probably because he did not want to put up a fight given his weakened position in the court.[91]

Before the alliance could be signed, though, France had the complication of their Austrian allies to deal with. The Dutch Republic was a neighbor of the Austrian-controlled Netherlands (roughly modern Belgium). Joseph II saw an opportunity to push a variety of demands on the Republic now that the Dutch were not allied with Britain. He was encouraged by the British, who sought out the Austrians for an alliance, while the Prussians were encouraging the Dutch to remain firm. The French were not pleased that war was about to break out between an ally and a potential ally. They regarded the crisis as primarily the result of Joseph's "torrent of ambition."[92] Facing French resistance, Joseph raised—not for the first time—the possibility of trading the Austrian Netherlands for Bavaria, which was probably his primary goal all along.[93] Louis XVI resisted this too. In addition to French opposition, Frederick organized a league of German princes to oppose the exchange.[94] Given the difficulties, Joseph backed down and France brokered a settlement that granted Joseph a few secondary demands. Louis XVI had essentially abandoned Austria. Joseph recognized that his alliance with France was more of a means by which France contained him, but he dared not break with the French, even though Britain was courting him. As many other contemporaries did, he overestimated French strength and British weakness. A peace treaty between Austria and the United Provinces was signed in France in November 1785. The following day, an alliance was struck between France and the States General of the United Provinces.

---

[90] Dull makes the strongest case for the defensive inclination of Vergennes' policies, and notes that after the balance of power was corrected following American independence, Vergennes told Louis that "the power of France should be used to not to gain extra territory, but rather to maintain the public order of Europe and to prevent the destruction of the different powers with form the equilibrium of Europe." Dull, *The French Navy and American Independence*, 340. Vergennes pursued a trade treaty with Britain in large part as a means to Anglo-French reconciliation. However, Vergennes's aggressive policies in the Netherlands and in India worked against this aim.

[91] Murphy, *Charles Gravier*, 464–65; Alfred Cobban, *Ambassadors and Secret Agents: The Diplomacy of the First Earl of Malmesbury at the Hague* (London: Jonathan Cape, 1954), 26; Hardman and Price, *Louis XVI and the Comte de Vergennes*, 389.

[92] Murphy, *Charles Gravier*, 408.

[93] Munro Price, *Preserving the Monarchy: The Comte de Vergennes, 1774–1787* (New York: Cambridge University Press, 1995), 190; Derek Beales, *Joseph II: Against the World, 1780–1790*, vol. 2 (New York: Cambridge University Press, 2009), 390.

[94] The British king George III, as possessor of Hanover, joined this league, the Fürstenbund, which complicated potential rapprochement between Britain and Austria. Jeremy Black, *British Foreign Policy in an Age of Revolutions, 1783–1793* (New York: Cambridge University Press, 1994), 93–98.

The British and Prussian Reaction

With the Austrian problem out of the way and the alliance with the Dutch Republic and France concluded, British policy was at a low point. This was not because the British had contagion concerns because of Patriots coming to power, but because they were losing an ally. The seasoned, enterprising British ambassador to The Hague, Sir James Harris, had been requesting funds to organize a pro-English, pro-stadtholder party. Prime Minister William Pitt's cabinet's initial response was that nothing could be done to reverse the loss,[95] but they began to provide Harris with funds in the hope that events would eventually work to their favor. The funds through 1786, however, were still modest—they were considerably outspent by the French funding of the Patriots.[96] The British faced other obstacles. The stadtholder, William V, was well known as a weak figure, and Prussia was not willing to intervene with England on his behalf.

What drove Prussian's policy toward the United Provinces was not Frederick's familial relation with the princess, nor fears of contagion, but Prussia's foreign policy agenda. He had told his niece, the stadtholder's wife, that they would have to concede to the Patriots' demands. He was relatively unconcerned with the position of the stadtholder, as long as he was allowed to hold some honorific title.[97] There were two factions in the Prussian court, one pro-French and the other pro-British. Frederick, who firmly controlled policy, was in the French camp. He viewed the British as a sinking ship and not really a Continental power. In the spring of 1785, the British had sounded out Frederick on a proposal that they would back him in the Bavarian matter if he would help them with the Dutch Republic, but he demurred. An Anglo-Prussian alliance would be no match against the alliance of France, Spain, Austria, and Russia, he said, and the Republic was under France's firm control.[98] Frederick's most important foreign policy aim was resisting Austria, and this was better accomplished via an alignment with France.

The British recognized that Frederick had his eye on a French alliance. In 1786, Britain was still courting Joseph for an alliance. It was taken as a given that if the British had their pick of alliances, they would choose Austria.[99] This tempered Britain's approach to Prussia, which was reciprocated. Even if the British could court Prussia, it was not necessarily enough to entice them to intervene in the

---

[95] John Ehrman, *The Younger Pitt: The Years of Acclaim* (London: Constable, 1969), 522; James Harris Malmesbury, *Diaries and Correspondence of the Earl of Malmesbury*, vol. 2 (London: Richard Bentley, 1844), 80.

[96] Cobban, *Ambassadors and Secret Agents*, 110–20.

[97] Ibid., 56–57.

[98] Black, *British Foreign Policy in an Age of Revolutions*, 94.

[99] As Harris observed, they could not warm to Prussia until the Austrian door was shut, and they only wanted to do this when "Austria is irrevocably cemented to France." Malmesbury, *Diaries and Correspondence of the Earl of Malmesbury*, vol. 2, 219; Richard Lodge, *Great Britain and Prussia in the Eighteenth Century* (Oxford: Clarendon Press, 1923), 163–64.

Republic, which could spark a war with France and possibly Austria.[100] British prime minister Pitt emphasized peace and economic reconstruction and signed a trade treaty with France in September 1786. Prussia was willing to let France have free rein in the United Provinces; the British were not as complacent, but their policy largely consisted of biding their time.

The Revolt Radicalizes and the Powers Watch

While Britain waited, the revolution progressed to the brink of civil war. The regents had been splitting from Patriot ranks as the movement radicalized. In July 1786, William V was removed from command of the garrison at The Hague. It became clear that France did not have control of the Patriots. The French expressed their surprise but did not want to apologize for the Patriots, and suggested that Berlin advise the stadtholder to accept the situation. In August and September, the Patriots were able to take control over a large part of the armed forces, which were traditionally under the control of the stadtholder; surprisingly, he held firm against Patriot demands. The French risked alienating Prussia by supporting the Patriots' agenda. Both Prussia and Britain assumed that the French would moderate the Patriots' aims. But the French had largely bought into those aims. The French ambassador in Berlin was told by Vergennes, "It is more important for us to preserve the alliance of Holland than to show compliance to the King of Prussia by favoring a Prince who is by his sentiments, and even by his instinct, an enemy of France."[101]

The French assumption that they could take Prussia for granted was initially correct. Frederick the Great had died in August 1786, and some British officials thought that his successor, Frederick William II, the brother of the stadtholder's wife, would be more sympathetic to the stadtholder's cause. But there was no appreciable change in Prussian policy. Frederick William wrote to the princess that the provinces that supported the stadtholder should appeal to Britain, as it was more of a concern to them. Whatever obligation he may have felt to his sister, he had the traditional Prussian concern, which was Austria; he did not want to alienate France given rumors of Austrian and Russian plans to revive the Bavarian exchange, or even attack Prussia.[102]

There was some disagreement among French officials about relying on the Patriots, but this was not over concerns over their ideology. Vergennes was

---

[100] Ehrman, *The Younger Pitt*, 524.
[101] Cobban, *Ambassadors and Secret Agents*, 77.
[102] Black, *British Foreign Policy in an Age of Revolutions*, 135; Lodge, *Great Britain and Prussia*, 169.

concerned about limiting French policy to one faction. He wanted a combination of the aristocratic and democratic factions for stability's sake. While he thought the elimination of the stadtholder would be the best means of getting rid of British and Prussian influence, he did not think the Patriot party was strong enough to impose that solution.[103] The French envoy to the Dutch Republic, Joseph Mathias Gérard de Rayneval, instead took the view that the French should operate through the leaders of the Patriots, who were dependent on France, and he proposed a solution that essentially left the Patriots in charge and the stadtholder stripped of his power.[104] Frederick William accepted the plan, but the Princess of Orange did not and called for negotiations to end. Rayneval accepted this—the Patriots would now impose their will, and that would relieve France of its obligations to Prussia. Frederick William's response was that "if the stadtholder chose to ruin himself he could not prevent him."[105]

The situation was bad for Britain, whose policy depended on the cooperation of Prussia, but it could at least console itself that France was increasingly weakened and distracted by domestic problems. Louis XVI announced in December 1786 his decision to call the Assembly of Notables to deal with the state's fiscal problems. Although there was disagreement, some British officials thought that France's economic problems would mean a hesitancy to get involved in Dutch issues.[106] Pitt supported Harris but warned him not to overcommit. He wanted maneuverability, which would allow him to take advantage of opportunities that arose but also permit him to extricate himself if need be.

Harris's attempt to rally pro-stadtholder forces in the first half of 1787 made progress. The Patriots were driving more regents into the stadtholder camp. The French were having difficulty controlling the Patriots, partly because of the lack of clear direction coming from the many French agents. There was a policy drift even before Vergennes died in February. Pitt made clear that he was not willing to go to war over the issue. King George was even more reluctant: he was concerned about costs and felt that Britain had best steer clear of Continental affairs. However, Pitt convinced the king to go along and he approved of more funding, although he would not commit himself further. Harris hoped that a well-timed insurrection might spur British policy forward.[107] He soon got his catalyst.

---

[103] Cobban, *Ambassadors and Secret Agents*, 98.

[104] They had, said Rayneval, "no other existence but that which France gave them" and thus would do their bidding. Murphy, *Charles Gravier*, 471.

[105] Cobban, *Ambassadors and Secret Agents*, 104.

[106] Black, *British Foreign Policy in an Age of Revolutions*, 131–32.

[107] Ibid., 262.

The Arrest of a Princess and Foreign Intervention

In the summer of 1787, the Princess of Orange attempted to break the stalemate by going to The Hague to rally Orangist forces and propose a moderate settlement to force the Patriots' hand. This launched a series of unanticipated events. The princess was captured and temporarily detained by the Patriot Free Corps forces until she retreated. The supposed indignity of her treatment prompted outrage in Prussia, which she and Harris used to their advantage to press for Prussian intervention. The Patriots appealed to France to mediate, while the princess appealed to Prussia and Britain for protection. Frederick William demanded an apology from the States General and assembled a force of twenty thousand men, but he was still hesitant to get involved for the same reasons he had earlier cited. The French, meanwhile, spread rumors that they were amassing troops on the border of the Austrian Netherlands, while in private they tried to get their Patriot allies to apologize and accept mediation. The Patriots, convinced of their strength and the backing of France, refused.

A game of brinkmanship was going on between Prussia, Britain, and France over the Republic, and France was gradually losing. No power wanted war, but France least of all, given its economic difficulties. Britain and Prussia became increasingly convinced that French threats of intervention were a bluff. The position of Britain was hardening as a result. This encouraged the Prussians, who had not wanted to be left in the lurch by a wavering Britain. The two began coordinating their policies. But the decisive factor that prompted the Prussians to intervene was the Ottoman declaration of war against Russia.[108] A necessary condition for Prussian intervention was that they not go to war with the French, but even with that satisfied, Prussia did not want to intervene, because of the risk of leaving itself open to an Austrian attack. The Russo-Turkish War, however, ensured that the Austrians would be tied up elsewhere. In September 1787, Prussian forces invaded the United Provinces, handily defeating the Patriot Free Corps, and reinstalled the stadtholder.

France, Prussia, Britain, and the Question of Contagion

Did the fear of revolutionary contagion to any extent influence policymakers in their approach to the Dutch Revolt, either the Prussians in their decision to crush the Patriots, the British in their decision to support the Prussians, or the French in their decision to abandon the Patriots? For France, two prominent scholars of French policy of the period have claimed that this factor did play a role. Orville

---

[108] Cobban, *Ambassadors and Secret Agents*, 177.

Murphy states, "Louis XVI soon began to doubt the wisdom of supporting the Patriots when he learned more about their liberal political ideals. It was one thing to support Republicans in faraway America; it was another thing to encourage them so close to home."[109] Munro Price makes a similar claim about Vergennes.[110]

There is not much evidence to back those claims up. The king did tell his foreign minister that he would rather renounce the Dutch alliance "than see the country given over to a pure democracy."[111] Part of the king's concern may have been the negative example the democratic revolution was setting. Just as he did during the American Revolution, Louis criticized the tone of a report for French officials favoring the Patriot cause—he disliked any language that was "revolutionary."[112]

The more salient concern among French officials seems to have been whether a democratic ally would be reliable. Rayneval reported in March 1787 that "the king has no interest, nor any reason to promote democracy; I could even say that such a government would lose the Republic or at least render the ally useless, because it is impossible to devise and undertake anything with the democrats."[113] Vergennes had expressed the same concern to Rayneval in his last letter before he died.[114] In 1786, the French ambassador to The Hague had written to Vergennes, attempting "to show that the ideas of the Patriots were not as alarming as they might seem at first sight." While they appealed to the rights of the people, "by this word *people* is not meant the most wretched part of the nation, men deprived of the means of living in a condition of comfort. Only the class of bourgeois possessing a certain capital and contributing in a certain proportion to the expenses of the Republic is included in this term."[115] This would not have assuaged the king if he had been worried about a demonstration effect from the Dutch. The French constituent assembly established a few years later during the French Revolution had similar restrictions. The alarm the ambassador was

---

[109] Orville T. Murphy, *The Diplomatic Retreat of France and Public Opinion on the Eve of the French Revolution, 1783–1789* (Washington, DC: The Catholic University of America, 1998), 83.

[110] "Having set aside his principles and supported the American insurgents in 1778, he was clearly not prepared to extend the same favor a second time to the Dutch Patriots." Munro Price, "The Dutch Affair and the Fall of the Ancien Régime, 1784–1787," *The Historical Journal* 38, no. 4 (1995): 904. Likewise, Simon Schama says, "the French government knew full well that it was one thing to applaud the advent of liberty thousands of miles away across the Atlantic, quite another to foment sedition on the doorstep of their own kingdom." Schama, *Patriots and Liberators*, 126.

[111] Cobban, *Ambassadors and Secret Agents*, 139.

[112] Piere de Witt, *Une invasion prussienne en Hollande en 1787* (Paris: E. Plon, Nourrit et Cie, 1886), 186. Interestingly, Vergennes himself sometimes lapsed into the language of the Patriot cause. For example, he praised one agent of France as playing a great role as a defender of liberty. Cobban, *Ambassadors and Secret Agents*, 108.

[113] H. T. Colenbrander, *De patriottentijd*, vol. 3 (The Hague: Martinus Nijhoff, 1897–99), 116.

[114] Cobban, *Ambassadors and Secret Agents*, 102.

[115] Ibid., 71–72.

attempting to quell had to do not with whether Patriot ideology would be replicated in France, but with whether the allies that France was committing themselves to were reliable. This was at the same time the French were expressing alarm at the disorder in their ally, the United States, which the French thought was due to the "phantom of democracy."[116]

The reliability of the Patriots ended up being a major problem for the French, but Versailles did not give up on the Patriots until the economic crisis forced its hand. In the summer of 1787 there was a divide in the French cabinet concerning Dutch policy, and the debate was dominated by the question of what policy would help resolve France's domestic crisis. The secretary of state for war, the marquis de Ségur, and the secretary of state for the navy, the marquis de Castries, advocated military intervention. Castries told Louis, "Present the idea of *la gloire* to Frenchmen and you will effect the most useful . . . diversion from the present turmoil."[117] Others opposed intervention. Vergennes's replacement, Montmorin, occupied a middle position—he wished to avoid committing France to war, but he thought that it could get away with bluffing and Britain and Prussia would back down.[118] But Louis took the opinion of the finance minister, Loménie de Brienne: "France was not in a position to interfere in the quarrels of her neighbors."[119] It is not credible, wrote the Austrian diplomat in Paris, "that the Versailles ministry, in such straits, would risk getting involved in a war that would make bankruptcy inevitable."[120]

Missing from the debate over intervention was the notion that the French should abandon the Patriots because they were setting a dangerous example. There does not appear to be much evidence that French officials viewed the domestic developments in the Dutch Republic beyond the lens of French foreign policy interests.[121] Price notes that Vergennes was the minister most attached to absolute monarchy in France, and most sympathetic to the stadtholder, while other ministers who supported the Patriots also tacitly condoned the nobles' revolt against the king during the French pre-revolution.[122] However, Vergennes was not particularly sympathetic to the stadtholder—he specifically said that he was indifferent to his fate.[123] France gave up on the Patriot cause not because it

---

[116] Murphy, *The Diplomatic Retreat of France*, 102–3.

[117] Hardman, *Louis XVI*, 128–29.

[118] Jeremy J. Whiteman, *Reform, Revolution and French Global Policy, 1787–1791* (Burlington: Ashgate, 2003), 56–61.

[119] Jean Egret, *The French Prerevolution*, trans. Wesley D. Camp (Chicago: The University of Chicago Press, 1977), 42.

[120] Ibid., 41.

[121] Murphy notes, "Neither Rayneval nor Vergennes saw that the Patriots were not simply the creatures, or pawns, of international politics." Murphy, *Charles Gravier*, 470.

[122] Price, "The Dutch Affair and the Fall of the Ancien Régime, 1784–1787," 904–5.

[123] Colenbrander, *De patriottentijd*, vol. 3, 91.

thought Patriot ideology was a threat to France's internal stability, but when it determined it did not have the resources to continue.

There is also little evidence that the British government supported the suppression of the revolution because of its domestic consequences. For the British, like the French, domestic developments in the Dutch Republic had relevance only insofar as they affected British foreign policy. Foreign Secretary Carmarthen had even on several occasions been willing to abandon the stadtholder and support the Patriots if it would serve British interests.[124] A contemporary history of the Patriot Revolt written by a British radical accused King George of wanting to crush the Patriots: "The sovereign . . . is doubtless much attached to the cause of a prince, whose prerogatives so nearly resemble his own, and whose house has so long been connected with the royal family of Britain."[125] In fact, as noted, it was the king that was pushing against involvement in the Patriot Revolt. Harris, the British official most familiar with the Patriots, did tell the foreign minister that "this leveling spirit which has gone forth will if left to itself produce a total subversion of good order and good government."[126] But he did not use this as any kind of lobbying point for British intervention. The British had a problem with the Patriots not because of their ideological agenda for the United Provinces, but because they were pro-French, while the stadtholder was pro-British.

There is no evidence that Fredrick William suppressed the revolution out of fear of the domestic consequences for Prussia. In the aftermath of the arrest and detention of the Princess of Orange and the lack of an apology from the Patriots, John Adams expressed disdain that Prussia would intervene in "a Romantick quarrel to revenge an Irreverence to a Princess, as Silly a Tale as the Trojan Wars on Account of Helen."[127] The arrest of the princess was not the only factor in the king's decision to intervene, as we have seen; he had to be reasonably sure that France and Austria would stand aside and Britain would support him, which accounted for the significant delay between the princess's arrest and his decision to invade. But the arrest was the motive that he expressed when the opportunity arose.[128] Frederick William does not seem to have feared that he could face a

---

[124] Cobban, *Ambassadors and Secret Agents*, 64, 86.

[125] *History of the Internal Affairs of the United Provinces, from the Year 1780 to the Commencement of Hostilities in June 1787* (London: G. G. J. and J. Robinson, 1787), 349. This anonymous work was written by William Godwin. Peter H. Marshall, *William Godwin* (New Haven: Yale University Press, 1984), 70.

[126] Cobban, *Ambassadors and Secret Agents*, 212.

[127] Peter Nicolaisen, "John Adams, Thomas Jefferson, and the Dutch Patriots," in *Old World, New World: America and Europe in the Age of Jefferson*, ed. Leonard J. Sandosky et al. (Charlottesville: University of Virginia Press, 2010), 113.

[128] Another possible motive of intervention was to increase British-Prussian cooperation. T. C. W. Blanning, *The Origins of the French Revolutionary Wars* (New York: Longman, 1986), 52.

similar treatment; it was, rather, that the treatment of his sister was an insult to his honor.[129]

Russia and Austria, the Onlookers

The Russians did not play any direct role in the Dutch Revolt, nor did they appear to have much interest in it. Catherine had had dealings with the Dutch Republic in the past when it touched on her larger foreign policy interests: she sought Dutch entry into her League of Armed Neutrality (though she was not willing to intervene when the Republic got tangled up with Britain), and she had supported her ally Joseph in his schemes concerning the Bavarian exchange.[130] The fate of the United Provinces, though, was peripheral to her interests. She was not particularly close with either the British or the French. Her conflict with the Turks was her major concern, which nevertheless had a critical indirect effect on the Dutch Revolt. Her war with the Ottomans brought in Austria, which gave Prussia the freedom to crush the Dutch Revolt without having to worry about Austria. But this was a byproduct of Russian policies, not a deliberate plan.

Austria had a greater interest in the fate of the Dutch Republic, but Joseph was also not directly involved. From a foreign policy perspective, one might expect that he would be supportive of the French against the Prussians. On the other hand, one might expect him to want to see the revolution crushed, given that a revolt was brewing in his neighboring province. In fact, a report from Brussels to Kaunitz in May 1787 claimed that the disturbances in the United Provinces were exciting discontented elements in Belgium.[131] Joseph was indifferent, as exhibited in a revealing interview he had with the British minister to Austria, Robert Murray Keith, in July 1787. Joseph explicitly stated that the fate of the stadtholder was of no concern to him, and when Keith pressed Joseph with the assertion that the revolt was emboldening his rebellious subjects in the Austrian Netherlands, Joseph downplayed its effects.[132] He even encouraged the Patriots

[129] The arrest and detention of Princess Wilhelmina was widely regarded as an indignity and insult to Frederick William that he would have to respond to. The concept of honor, prestige, and face in international politics is explored by Barry O'Neill, *Honor, Symbols, and War* (Ann Arbor: The University of Michigan Press, 1999).

[130] Madariaga, *Britain, Russia, and the Armed Neutrality of 1780*, 310; Madariaga, *Russia in the Age of Catherine the Great*, 390–92.

[131] Thomas K. Gorman, *America and Belgium: A Study of the Influence of the United States Upon the Belgian Revolution of 1789–1790* (London: T. Fisher Unwin Ltd., 1925), 11.

[132] After Keith relayed King George's sympathy for Joseph's problems in the Austrian Netherlands, Joseph responded that the king knew from experience "that it is the unhappy lot of monarchs to see their upright intentions" misunderstood. The Americans had abandoned their duty and allegiance from "false notions of liberty" and only gained anarchy and confusion as a result. He noted his own problems in the Netherlands with "new-fangled dabblers in what *they* call patriotism." But when Keith asserted that the "independence of [the Dutch] Republic and the maintenance of its *ancient* constitution . . . were matters of very essential importance to the House of Austria," Joseph pushed

fleeing the Republic after the Prussian invasion to settle in Belgium for economic reasons.[133]

Joseph did not think the Patriot Revolt was a big factor encouraging rebellion among his subjects, and he believed (mistakenly) he had the situation under control. He also did not have strong foreign policy preferences on the matter. His hostility toward the Prussians had subsided. He now considered Austro-Prussian reconciliation a priority. And especially given that France had abandoned him in his dispute with the Dutch in 1785, he was not about to go out of his way to further their aims where he had no immediate interest. At any rate, his attention was directed elsewhere, to the Balkans, in light of the Russo-Turkish War.[134]

The Patriot Revolution and the Ancien Régime

Some thinkers in the late 1780s viewed the Patriot Revolt in a larger framework, as part of a movement toward democracy. A British radical was confident that even if the revolt was crushed, the cause would go on: "The Northern Hercules may cut off the heads of the Lernaean Hydra, but they will infallibly sprout again more fierce and numerous than ever. Thus a new republic of the purest kind is about to spring up in Europe; and the flame of liberty, which was first excited in America, and has since communicated itself in a manner more or less perfect to so many other countries, buds fair for the production of consequences not less extensive than salutary."[135] This view was prescient, but rare, and not shared by leaders of states. Even though the Patriot Revolt culminated at the same time as what would later be regarded as the preliminary events of the

back: "Whatever concern foreign powers may have in keeping the Dutch Republic from falling to pieces, it can be of little, very little, importance indeed, to any other crowned heads save those who are related by blood or affinity to the Prince of Orange, whether there is, or is not, a stadtholder in Holland" or "whether his powers are enlarged or curtailed." Keith responded that the lawless Patriots would seek to "spread the same infectious spirit of licentious democracy and wild innovation among their neighbors the Flemings" if they "remained masters at home." Joseph granted that the Patriots have been "extremely desirous to make proselytes . . . But it is not from them alone that my subjects in the Netherlands have borrowed the spirit of turbulent and mistaken patriotism." He listed instances of aristocratic resistance to monarchs, most notably condemning Louis's calling the Assembly of Notables. Gillespie Smyth, ed., *Memoirs and Correspondence (Official and Familiar) of Sir Robert Murray Keith*, vol. 2 (London: Henry Colburn, 1849), 208–18. Beales notes that Keith's interview is probably the fullest account of Joseph talking, yet this "remarkable" document is relatively ignored by diplomatic historians. Beales, *Joseph II*, vol. 2, 522.

[133] R. T. Turner, "Europe and the Belgian Revolution, 1789–90," PhD thesis, University of California, Los Angeles, 1944, 152.

[134] Joseph even turned around troops sent to deal with the troubles in the Austrian Netherlands and marched them toward the Balkans to grab the spoils of the Ottoman Empire. Jeremy Black, "Sir Robert Ainslie: His Majesty's Agent-Provocateur? British Foreign Policy and the International Crisis of 1787," *European History Quarterly* 14, no. 3 (1984): 263.

[135] *History of the Internal Affairs of the United Provinces*, 345.

French Revolution, the great powers saw the revolt through the prism of tradi-tional ancien régime diplomacy.[136]

There is little evidence that there were fears of the revolution as a source of contagion among leaders. The ideological distances between the monarchs and the democrats did not affect policy because the domestic ideological trigger of opposition groups at the heart of the domestic contagion effects theory was not present. The reaction to the revolt reflected international politics rather than altered it. The most striking policy is that of France, which effectively com-mitted to the Patriots and their radical agenda even though they were right on France's doorstep. Given the lack of significant revolutionary movements, my theory does not expect that leaders would be fearful of contagion, and thus these fears would not dictate policy. The cases are largely a negative confirmation of the theory. The one possible exception is Austria. The brewing rebellion in the Austrian Netherlands was of a very different character than the revolt in the Dutch Republic. Put simply, the disturbance in the Austrian Netherlands was a revolt of the right—a conservative reaction—whereas the Patriot movement was a revolt of the left.[137] But Joseph did not seem to perceive the differences. He saw both disturbances as part of a broader trend of subjects unjustly resisting the will of their monarchs. Nevertheless, this did not affect his foreign policy toward the Republic or the other powers. The Austrian uprising he could crush on his own.

Conclusion

The beginning of this chapter posed a puzzle: Why did the oldest monarchy in Europe support the patriots in America and the Dutch Republic? Was there any fear that these revolts would embolden its own opposition? What about the other powers? It may seem foolhardy, especially of France, to encourage a movement that would engulf France and then much of the rest of Europe in only a handful of years. As has been discussed, the American Revolution served to bolster the view of the Radical Enlightenment and the general feeling among Frenchmen that they were in a new age and that French political institutions needed radical

---

[136] Marc H. Lerner, "Radical Elements and Attempted Revolutions in Late 18th-Century Republics," in *The Republican Alternative: The Netherlands and Switzerland Compared*, eds. André Holenstein, Thomas Maissen, and Maarten Prak (Amsterdam: Amsterdam University Press, 2008), 311; Wayne Ph. te Brake, "Provincial Histories and National Revolution in the Dutch Republic," in *The Dutch Republic in the Eighteenth Century*, eds. Margaret C. Jacob and Wijnand Mijnhardt (Ithaca: Cornell University Press, 1992), 61.

[137] In contrast to the Dutch Republic, there were almost no democrats in the Austrian Netherlands. Israel, *Democratic Enlightenment*, 881. For an overview of the uprising, see Janet L. Polasky, *Revolution in Brussels* (Hanover: University Press of New England, 1987), 35–83; J. Craeybeckx, "The Brabant Revolution: A Conservative Revolt in a Backward Country?," in *Revolutions in the Western World, 1775–1825*, ed. Jeremy Black (New York: Routledge, 2016), 389–423.

reform. The model of America was used to further the radical agenda in 1789.[138] There is also evidence that the Dutch Patriot movement emboldened French reformers. For example, the *Leidse Ontwerp*, an important Dutch Patriot manifesto of political rights, was originally written in French, published in France in 1788, and possibly influenced the drafting of the Declaration of the Rights of Man in 1789.[139]

From a realist perspective, the policies of the powers seem inevitable. France sided with the Americans and the Dutch Patriots to weaken the British; the British tried to wrest the United Provinces back from the French. In fact, there was a good deal of contingency in these policies: it was not inevitable that France would side with the United States, especially ahead of Spain, or that the British or Prussians would not abandon the stadtholder.[140] But in the end the policies of the great powers look quite like the realist playbook that seems to fit the diplomacy of the ancien régime well: states exploiting revolutions for geopolitical gain, taking sides with the opposing side of one's rival, regardless of ideological differences between states.

However, the idea that these revolutions could serve as models was by no means absent. Reformers cheered on the revolutions. The American Revolution, for example, was considered to be "a new lesson for despots."[141] Condorcet claimed, "It is not enough that the rights of man be written in the books of philosophers and the hearts of virtuous men; the weak and ignorant must be able to read them in the example of a great people. America has given us this example."[142] Turgot wrote that the Americans "are the hope of the human race; they may well become its model."[143] This is exactly what conservatives feared. A German thinker declared, "God help all monarchs if their subjects should agree with the Americans' principles, which arise from a perverted and fanatical

[138] See Joyce Appleby, "America as a Model for the Radical French Reformers of 1789," *The William and Mary Quarterly* 28, no. 2 (1971): 267–86. Beyond the ideological link, the American Revolution's role in weakening the French state by draining the finances was a concern at the time, and has been commonly cited as a reason for the financial collapse that preceded the French Revolution, but this seems to be overblown. The amount France spent on the American war is often exaggerated, and it has been argued that it was the monarchy's fiscal policy of abandoning reforms in the 1780s, rather than the debt acquired by the American war and before, that brought on the crisis. See Robert D. Harris, "French Finances and the American War, 1777–1783," *The Journal of Modern History* 48, no. 2 (1976): 233–58; Eugene White, "Was There a Solution to the Ancien Régime's Financial Dilemma?," *The Journal of Economic History* 49, no. 3 (1989): 545–68. By 1792, though, Louis XVI would say that he never thought about the "American adventure" without regret. John Hardman, *The Life of Louis XVI* (New Haven: Yale University Press, 2016), 108.

[139] Jeremy D. Popkin, "Dutch Patriots, French Journalists, and the Declarations of Rights: The *Leidse Ontwerp* of 1785 and Its Diffusion in France," *The Historical Journal* 38, no. 3 (1995): 553–65.

[140] Scott, *British Foreign Policy in the Age of the American Revolution*, 208; Cobban, *Ambassadors and Secret Agents*, 210–11.

[141] Dippel, *Germany and the American Revolution*, 196–97.

[142] Durand Echeverria, "Condorcet's *The Influence of the American Revolution on Europe*," *The William and Mary Quarterly* 25, no. 1 (1968): 91.

[143] Echeverria, *Mirage in the West*, 69.

interpretation of liberty."[144] A Frenchman expressed that, despite his wish to humiliate England, "I cannot desire that rebels should exist or be successful."[145] Although the American Revolution did not yet "ignite the world," the lines between reformers and conservatives were being drawn even before the French Revolution.[146]

Of all the monarchs, Gustav III of Sweden had the most antipathy toward the American Revolution over concerns of contagion. When France openly allied with the United States, he wrote to his ambassador in Paris that "the action of the French ministry, it seems to me, has deviated from the principles of justice and practical interests, and from state principles of nations that have been in force for centuries. I cannot admit that it is right to support rebels against their king. The example will find only too many imitators in an age when it is the fashion to overthrow every bulwark of authority."[147] Gustav's hostility toward the American cause was due to his own experience as a monarch struggling to establish an absolutist system.[148] But these concerns were not enough to trump geopolitical interests. He also did not have a revolutionary democratic movement to contend with. He set aside his apprehensions to help his French ally.[149]

French foreign minister Vergennes had stated why he crushed a revolutionary uprising in Geneva in 1782 while he aided the Americans: "The insurgents whom I am driving from Geneva are agents of England, while the American insurgents are our friends for years to come. I have dealt with both of them, not by reason of their political systems, but by reason of their attitudes towards France. Such are my reasons of state."[150] His statement exemplifies the foreign policy priorities of the ancien régime and the realist perspective. On the other hand, Vergennes also commented, "I study the Genevese disputes as a politician; for it is to be feared that, after their writings have sown discord at home, they may spread

---

[144] Dippel, *Germany and the American Revolution*, 196.

[145] Acomb, *Anglophobia in France*, 74; Echeverria, *Mirage in the West*, 62–63.

[146] Regarding the American Revolution igniting the world, see Jonathan Israel, *The Expanding Blaze: How the American Revolution Ignited the World, 1775–1848* (Princeton: Princeton University Press, 2017).

[147] H. A. Barton, "Sweden and the War of American Independence," *The William and Mary Quarterly* 23, no. 3 (1966): 420.

[148] Gustav's father had been more of a figurehead presiding over the Diet, but, fearing that Sweden would end up like Poland, which had recently undergone its first partition, Gustav and Vergennes orchestrated a coup and dissolved the Diet. For this he had many critics, though not democratic revolutionaries.

[149] However, the king's hostility remained. He forbade the Swedish colonels in French forces to accept membership into the American Society of the Cincinnati, because he considered it unwise to allow them to be honored by subjects who had revolted against their legitimate sovereign: "Too recently having ourselves escaped from our troubles that there should not still exist, no doubt, some germs of our former divisions, it is my duty to avert anything which could reawaken such ideas." Barton, "Sweden and the War of American Independence," 426–27.

[150] Murphy, *Charles Gravier*, 400. The contradiction in French policy was "much commented on and highlighted by radical publicists like Mirabeau and . . . Brissot." Israel, *Democratic Enlightenment*, 869.

fanaticism which characterizes them abroad, and their neighbors may pass from curiosity to imitation."[151] Albert Sorel noted, "This was unusual language for a statesman of the old régime," a penetrating political insight into an upheaval that was to be the French Revolution in miniature.[152] The king had expressed similar concern: "While the political differences at Geneva were confined to matters of mere dispute, it was to be doubted whether France had any right to take notice of them. But now, when principles, destructive of all society, have established there one set of people, who tyrannise over and imprison the other; now that this usurpation has seized on an authority disputed by all classes; I owe it to Genevese government, who I am protective, to give them relief."[153] The bad example of Geneva may have been a motive for the French crushing the uprising there, but it also happened to coincide with their geopolitical goals, because the revolutionaries were also viewed as agents of England.[154] The situation was the reverse in the Dutch and American cases, where the revolutionaries were the enemies of England. Geopolitical motives trumped other factors.

Although there may be more fear of contagion among leaders than is expressed in the evidentiary record, ultimately geopolitical concerns prevailed in France and elsewhere. There was some concern about contagion, but it proved too abstract, too much of a distant probability that was overwhelmed by immediate, concrete geopolitical interests. In sum, these cases are largely a negative confirmation of the theory. With the possible exception of the Spanish New World and the Austrian Netherlands, there was no significant revolutionary movement in these powers, and thus the fear of contagion was not an important factor in international politics. The following chapter tells a very different story.

---

[151] John Lewis Soulavie, *Historical and Political Memoirs of the Reign of Lewis XVI*, vol. V (London: G. and J. Robinson, 1802), 209.

[152] Albert Sorel, *Europe and the French Revolution: The Political Traditions of the Old Regime*, trans. Alfred Cobban and J. W. Hunt (London: Collins, 1969 [1885]), 171.

[153] Soulavie, *Historical and Political Memoirs of the Reign of Lewis XVI*, vol. V, 228.

[154] For the French policy toward Geneva, see Richard Whatmore, *Against War and Empire: Geneva, Britain, and France in the Eighteenth Century* (New Haven: Yale University Press, 2012), 139–76.

4

Liberal Revolutions and the Concert of Europe

In 1820–21, revolution gripped Spain, Portugal, Italy, and Greece. The revolutions stood for sovereignty of the people against the sovereignty of kings, if in a milder form than the American Revolution and Dutch Patriot Revolt. As in Chapter 3, the revolutions were in weak states not attempting to spread revolution abroad. The great powers were also the same: Austria, Britain, France, Prussia, and Russia. What is puzzling about the great powers' behavior is the striking contrast in their reaction to these revolutions compared to their earlier treatment of the American and Dutch revolts. In particular, these revolutions were not seen as opportunities to advance these states' geopolitical advantage. Why not? Great powers are generally assumed to focus on their position relative to other great powers. Thus, their interest would be to shift power away from their rivals. These revolutions provided an opportunity to do so. France and Russia could have used the Italian revolutions to undermine Austrian hegemony in Italy. Russia could have used the Greek revolt to undermine the Ottomans. France could have used the revolt in Portugal to sideline Britain. The other powers could have used the Spanish Revolution to exclude French influence.

The domestic contagion effects theory accounts for these puzzles. In this period, unlike the period in which the revolutions of the preceding chapter took place, there was a change in the nature of the domestic political opposition within the great-power states. The governments of each state believed that their own population harbored revolutionary movements with ideological similarities to the revolutions. This caused a fear of contagion, which prompted great-power hostility toward the revolutionary state and cooperation with other great powers. There were disagreements about the correct solution to the revolutions and a fear that other states would exploit these revolts for geopolitical gain, but the great powers did not take advantage of these revolutions to undermine a rival, as they had with the American Revolution and the Dutch Patriot Revolt. Some leading scholars, such as historian Paul Schroeder, have dismissed the importance of the fear of revolutionary contagion as a cause of restraint, as emphasized by my theory, but they are wrong, as I demonstrate in what follows.

In examining the great-power reactions to these revolutions, I first assess the theory's two independent variables: (1) how the revolutions were models and

Revolutionary Contagion and International Politics. Chad E. Nelson, Oxford University Press. © Oxford University Press 2022. DOI: 10.1093/oso/9780197601921.003.0004

the extent to which they acted as platforms, and (2) whether there was a significant revolutionary opposition movement in any of the great powers. I then assess the international effects of the revolutions by analyzing the policies of the great powers toward each other and the revolutionary state before and after the revolutions.

Revolutions of 1820–21

In January 1820, military detachments in Spain preparing to embark for the New World to suppress the rebels in Spanish America rose up against the absolutist king, Ferdinand VII. At first, the revolt seemed to fizzle, but what might have been mere military sedition became much broader. Uprisings occurred throughout Spain. Forces sent to put them down joined their ranks instead. The revolutionaries called for a reinstatement of the Spanish Constitution of 1812. This constitution, established while Napoleon's forces occupied Spain and the king was held in captivity, had created a constitutional monarchy subject to a parliament elected with universal male suffrage, as well as other freedoms. When Ferdinand VII was restored to power he had declared the constitution null and void. But in the face of uprisings and a disloyal army, the king was forced to accept the constitution in March 1820.

In neighboring Portugal, there was a similar military revolt in the north in August 1820. They demanded the return of King John VI from Brazil, where he had been residing since the Napoleonic invasion, and the adoption of a constitution. The regency ruling in his place rejected those demands, but was soon ousted by an uprising in Lisbon that joined with the rebellion in the north. A constitution was drawn up based on relatively broad suffrage. King John was compelled to sign an oath to the constitution when he returned.

Shortly after word of the Spanish events reached the Kingdom of the Two Sicilies, the army rose in Naples and joined with the Carbonari, a clandestine revolutionary organization. They forced King Ferdinand of the Two Sicilies to adopt a constitution modeled on the 1812 Spanish version. In March 1821 a revolt broke out in Piedmont. King Victor Emmanuel abdicated in favor of his brother, Charles Felix. Charles Albert, ruling in Charles Felix's absence, adopted the Spanish Constitution, subject to Charles Felix's approval.

Also in March 1821, an officer of Greek descent in the Russian army, Alexander Ypsilantis, entered the Danubian Principalities with a contingent of soldiers and called on all Christians to overthrow the Ottoman Empire. He was the leader of a secret organization whose purpose was to overthrow Ottoman rule of Greece. While his own efforts fared poorly, the rebellion spread to the Greek islands, and Ottoman rule of Greek lands was cast in doubt. These were the first revolutions of post-Napoleonic Europe, and the fact that they followed one after the other—and had clear links to the Spanish Constitution—was ominous to many great-power statesmen.

Model

The revolutions in 1820–21 served as a model for overthrowing the existing order. But they also stood for something else: the principle of popular sovereignty over the rights of kings. The goal of the revolts in the Iberian Peninsula and in Italy was to change institutions and the legitimizing principles of government by constitutionally limiting the king's power. There was an array of opinions among the revolutionaries, from the moderate liberals to the radicals, regarding the extent to which they wished to further curtail the powers of kings and expand political rights. Few were advocating the abolition of monarchy altogether, and thus the movement was not as radical as the American Revolution, the Dutch Patriot Revolt, or France in 1792. If anything, these revolutions should have been seen as less threatening and safer to endorse, except for the rise of domestic oppositions with this ideology. The 1812 Spanish Constitution that inspired the revolts of 1820–21, though, provided a system of universal male suffrage and a unicameral parliament. This was a radical contrast to the absolute monarchies of the Eastern powers and, to a lesser extent, the conservative constitutional monarchies of Britain and France.

The conflict in Greece was not directly about the existing form of government. It was a separatist revolt motivated especially by religion (Greek Orthodox against Muslim), which was conjoined with nationalism (Greek against Turk). Even this revolt, however, had a liberal dimension. Liberals within the independence movement proclaimed a republican constitution in January 1822, although it only existed on paper.[1] The Greek national cause also had a liberal hue. Greece's position in the historical consciousness of Europeans as the birthplace of democracy rallied liberals to the cause.[2]

---

[1] Douglas Dakin, "The Formation of the Greek State, 1821–33," in *The Struggle for Greek Independence*, ed. Richard Clogg (New York: Macmillan, 1973), esp. 165–66.

[2] This movement was not limited to liberals and radicals, though its most famous devotee, Lord Byron, was one. For an exposition, see C. M. Woodhouse, *The Philhellenes* (London: Oxford University Press, 1973); William St. Clair, *That Greece Might Still Be Free: The Philhellenes in the War of Independence* (London: Oxford University Press, 1972); Theophilus C. Prousis, *Russian Society and the Greek Revolution* (DeKalb: Northern Illinois University Press, 1994).

Platform

The revolts of 1820–21 occurred in the periphery in weak states that mostly did not attempt to act as a platform. Certainly, there was no attempt to spread revolution to the great powers, and only marginal attempts in neighboring states.

Indeed, the only notable "platform" actions were the Neapolitans against the Papal States, and even this case exhibits the caution of the revolutionary states. Some Neapolitan Carbonari volunteers helped the Carbonari revolting in two small Papal States that were enclaves in Neapolitan territory in July 1820 and in February 1821, and irregular bands marched into some other towns.[3] The Neapolitan government, though, was at pains to earn the goodwill of its neighbors. Its minister of foreign affairs even tried to portray the revolution as a mere reorganization of government to convince the great powers of its unquestionable legitimacy, which warranted their continued recognition.[4] It disavowed the actions of the irregulars and refused to recognize the rebels of the Papal State enclaves as fellow citizens. The government strained to convey that it was not in the business of exporting revolution, even shutting down a newspaper critical of Austria. A senior military commander of Naples did invade the neighboring Papal States to meet Austrian forces there.[5] But this occurred only when facing imminent Austrian intervention, and even then, his actions were unauthorized by the Naples government. It was a *response* to great-power intervention rather than what *provoked* it. In another instance, Portugal faced propaganda from Spain, although British foreign minister Lord Castlereagh thought the activities of Spanish agents were exaggerated by Portugal in an appeal for British help.[6] Castlereagh's warnings to Spain not to interfere helped keep them quiet.

Even if the revolutionaries desired the spread of liberal institutions, these states were too concerned with their own survival to offer much in the way of proselytizing directed at their neighbors or the great powers themselves. Even more, they knew that acting as a platform would only give the great powers more excuse to crush them. These revolts acted as models, but not as significant platforms in spreading revolution abroad.

[3] Joseph H. Brady, *Rome and the Neapolitan Revolution of 1820–1821: A Study of Papal Neutrality* (New York: Columbia University Press, 1937), 20–26, 123–39.
[4] George T. Romani, *The Neapolitan Revolution of 1820–1821* (Evanston: Northwestern University Press, 1950), 105.
[5] Ibid., 163–66; John A. Davis, *Naples and Napoleon: Southern Italy and the European Revolutions (1760–1860)* (New York: Oxford University Press, 2006), 314.
[6] C. K. Webster, *The Foreign Policy of Castlereagh, 1815–1822* (London: G. Bell and Sons, 1947), 251, 253.

Liberal Opposition Among the Great Powers

Was there a significant revolutionary opposition movement in the great powers of a similar character as these revolts? The French Revolution and subsequent upheavals had transformed the domestic politics of the great powers in the decades since the American Revolution and Dutch Patriot Revolt. All great powers now had a significant revolutionary opposition. The principal source of contention during the late ancien régime had been aristocratic resistance to the centralizing monarchs. After the Napoleonic Wars, this struggle was transformed. Monarchy and aristocracy were now united in their rejection of the principles of the French Revolution. Differences remained, including the old debate over the society of orders versus the centralizing state, and whether the goal should be conservation (preserving what remained of the old order) or reaction (returning to the old regime). But these differences paled in comparison to their opposition to revolutionary forces. There was a renewed emphasis on using religion to bolster the political and social order—the marriage of throne and altar. In many quarters there was an anti-Enlightenment attitude, as Enlightenment thought was now seen as undermining the thrones rather than supporting them. Instead, the forces of order pushed a Romanticism that glorified the past.

The principal instigators of change were groups variously dubbed "liberals" or "radicals." Their basic aim was to make the state more accountable to the people, but how that goal of popular sovereignty was interpreted varied widely, as did the means to achieve it. A common objective of liberals was to limit monarchies to constitutions that would institute parliamentary systems with a limited franchise and other constraints on the monarchy. Meanwhile, the radicals advocated for democracy—full equality under the law and universal male suffrage. They tended to be even more anti-clerical than the liberals, and many were explicitly anti-monarchical. Liberals and radicals, with their emphasis on popular sovereignty, were also in this period associated with another political ideal: nationalism. In post-Napoleonic Europe, radicals were more explicitly revolutionary, in both ends and means. Whether the groups advocating liberalism were revolutionary depended partly upon what regime they operated under, which helped determine whether they would be working within the system for reform or provoking revolution to institute such changes. But all of the great powers had a significant domestic revolutionary opposition movement.

Opposition in Russia

All the Eastern powers—Austria, Prussia, and Russia—were absolute monarchies, but Russia was the absolute monarchy par excellence, where the tsar's will carried considerable weight. Ironically, the man who occupied that position had liberal, even republican sympathies. Alexander had ascended to the throne in 1801 with plans for reform, including the notion that the autocracy should be based on law rather than whim. His liberal advisor, Michael Speransky, even pressed for a constitution with a national legislative assembly. However, Alexander rejected Speransky's plans as undermining the autocracy.[7] When Alexander granted a constitution to Poland in 1815, he also suggested that he was about to introduce one for Russia.[8] But though he requested a draft of a Russian constitution largely based on the Polish model, nothing came of it.[9] Alexander was in favor of constitutionalism, by which he meant an orderly system of government based on the rule of law.[10] By the time the constitution was ready in 1820 Alexander had cooled on reform, largely because of the revolutionaries he perceived to be in his midst.

Alexander's concern about revolutionaries was not unfounded. Poland was where revolutionary agitation was first manifested. The Polish parliament increasingly angered the tsar when it bucked his will. He authorized the Polish king to take extraconstitutional measures to tame the opposition in parliament.[11] This caused some of the Polish opposition to turn revolutionary.[12] In addition, revolutionary secret societies operated in Russia. As it became clear that Alexander would not enact liberal reforms, opposition hardened among secret societies in the Russian army. Some army officers, affected by their time abroad during the French Revolutionary and Napoleonic Wars, hoped to see liberal reforms at home. The Union of Salvation, founded in February 1816, was home to lively disagreements over whether a constitutional monarchy or even a republic should be sought, and whether to pursue it through legal or extralegal means (including

[7] Gooding convincingly argues that Speransky was a closet revolutionary who wished to transform the system from within to a constitutional monarchy on the pattern of Britain. Alexander became convinced of this and he was deposed. John Gooding, "The Liberalism of Michael Speransky," *The Slavonic and East European Review* 64, no. 3 (1986): 401–24.

[8] Janet M. Hartley, "The 'Constitutions' of Finland and Poland in the Reign of Alexander I: Blueprints for Reform in Russia?," in *Finland and Poland in the Russian Empire: A Comparative Study*, eds. Michael Branch, Janet Hartley, and Antoni Mączark (London: University of London, 1995), 56.

[9] This was not made public until Polish rebels found a copy in Warsaw in 1830 and published it. Not only did Czar Nicholas suppress the Polish revolt, but he gathered all but two of the 1,580 not yet distributed copies of the constitution and burned them. George Vernadsky, "Reforms Under Czar Alexander I: French and American Influences," *The Review of Politics* 9, no. 1 (1947): 60–64. The proposal is reproduced in Marc Raeff, *Plans for Political Reform in Imperial Russia, 1730–1905* (Englewood Cliffs: Prentice Hall, 1966), 110–20.

[10] Hartley, "The 'Constitutions' of Finland and Poland," 41–45.

[11] Frank W. Thackeray, *Antecedents of Revolution: Alexander I and the Polish Kingdom, 1815–1825* (New York: Columbia University Press, 1980), 54–78.

[12] When reminded by Alexander's "delegate" to Poland, Nikolai Novosil'stov, that the constitution had been granted to them, and that it was possible to take it away, a leader of the liberal opposition responded, "Then we will become revolutionaries." Ibid., 76.

regicide).[13] In 1820, when the government caught wind of its activities through defectors, the organization officially disbanded.[14] However, the group continued under two secret organizations, a northern branch and a southern one. The northern branch, despite the adoption of a republican platform in 1820, became a stronghold of more conservative liberals, whereas the radical republican Pavel Pestel dominated the southern society.[15]

The year 1820 was a watershed both for the revolutionary movements in Russia and for Tsar Alexander's perception of them. The inspiration from the revolutions abroad, in combination with the tsar's failure to reform and his suppression of revolutions abroad (especially in Spain), spurred on the revolutionaries.[16] These groups, known as the Decembrists, later launched an aborted revolution when Alexander died in 1825. In 1820, however, there was a mutiny among the Semenovsky Regiment, the tsar's favored regiment. Although the mutiny was driven by poor treatment at the hands of their new commanding officer, investigators also found two seditious notes condemning the regime. Alexander was convinced the Semenovsky Revolt had revolutionary intentions and was linked to the broader revolutionary movement, which had to be crushed before it threatened the Russian government.[17] Alexander always rejected revolution at home or abroad. His interpretation of "liberalism" did not include limiting his own authority. When liberal reforms became associated with bottom-up pressure—revolutionary demands from the army, no less—he became decidedly reactionary. By 1820, reform ambitions were over.

Opposition in Prussia and Austria

Prussia had gone further in the direction of reform than Russia. After defeat at the hand of Napoleon, Prussian statesmen enacted reforms, including creating a draft army and dismantling feudal obligations, in an attempt to mobilize the population behind the state. King Frederick William III promised a constitution with representative institutions several times, the last time in May 1815,

---

[13] Anatole G. Mazour, *The First Russian Revolution, 1825* (Stanford: Stanford University Press, 1962), 66–68.

[14] Ibid., 83.

[15] For more on Pestel, see Patrick O'Meara, *The Decembrist Pavel Pestel: Russia's First Republican* (New York: Palgrave Macmillan, 2003).

[16] John Gooding, "Speransky and Baten'kov," *The Slavonic and East European Review* 66, no. 3 (1988): 408; Isabel de Madariaga, "Spain and the Decembrists," *European History Quarterly* 3, no. 2 (1973): 146; Richard Stites, "Decembrists with a Spanish Accent," *Kritika: Explorations in Russian and Eurasian History* 12, no. 1 (2011): 5–23.

[17] Joseph L. Wieczynski, "The Mutiny of the Semenovsky Regiment in 1820," *Russian Review* 29, no. 2 (1970): 176.

as the Allied armies were preparing for their last battle with Napoleon.[18] When the war was over, the king's (always tepid) enthusiasm for reform cooled markedly. Reformers petitioned the king, and various organizations promoted liberal reform, such as those that organized around the gymnasiums (schools). Most significant were the German university students and faculty, many of them veterans, who advocated liberal rights and democratic constitutions. These groups grew rapidly, and in October 1817 they organized a festival in Jena and burned symbols of conservative oppression. Even one reformer was taken aback by the rhetoric: "The demand for a constitution is getting dangerously out of hand, and some Jacobin yeast is mixed in with it."[19] Prince Karl von Hardenberg, prime minister and orchestrator of Prussian reforms, wrote Klemens von Metternich, the foreign minister of Austria, expressing the need to "suppress the revolutionary tendency . . . and Jacobinism, which is almost everywhere raising its head."[20]

The emperor of Austria, Francis II, had never contemplated the far-reaching reform the Prussians had considered. Francis II had endured the execution of his aunt, Marie Antoinette, by revolutionaries in Paris and faced what he considered a Jacobin conspiracy at home. His modus operandi was repression. When several South German states wrote limited constitutions in 1818, it increased pressure for reform. For Francis II, Prussia was the key to stemming the liberal tide. Metternich put strong pressure on Prussia to suppress the agitating groups, and connected those groups with the larger movement for constitutional reform. "A national assembly composed of representatives of the people would mean the dissolution of the Prussian state," he said, "because such an innovation cannot be introduced in a great state without revolution or preparing for revolution."[21] A democratic constitution in Prussia, Metternich wrote Francis, would result "in the complete overthrow of all existing institutions."[22]

The threat both Prussia and Austria perceived from revolutionary activity brought them together. In 1819, a radical theology student assassinated a conservative playwright and publicist. This was interpreted as part of a larger conspiracy of university radicals. Metternich won Prussia's support to pass the Carlsbad Decrees in the German Confederation—a series of acts that coordinated and

---

[18] Whether this representative system would work in a corporate manner or a parliamentary form was left unclear. For elaborations on the reform movement, see Matthew Levinger, "Hardenberg, Wittgenstein, and the Constitutional Question in Prussia, 1815–22," *German History* 8, no. 3 (1990): 257–77; Walter M. Simon, *The Failure of the Prussian Reform Movement, 1807–1819* (Ithaca: Cornell University Press, 1955).

[19] Simon, *The Failure of the Prussian Reform Movement*, 134.

[20] Matthew Levinger, *Enlightened Nationalism: The Transformation of Prussian Political Culture, 1806–1848* (New York: Oxford University Press, 2000), 139.

[21] Simon, *The Failure of the Prussian Reform Movement*, 139.

[22] Robert D. Billinger Jr., *Metternich and the German Question: States' Rights and the Federal Duties, 1820–1834* (Newark: University of Delaware Press, 1991), 21.

enforced strict press censorship and created a central investigating committee to repress revolutionary agitation. The Confederation was strengthened to allow the Federal Diet to provide troops to ensure state governments kept the lid on revolutionary activity. While most of the movement for democratic constitutions was not explicitly advocating the overthrow of the state, there was a perception among Austrian and Prussian leaders that a revolutionary movement was at hand. Both states feared that even mild reforms could get out of hand, as had happened in France in 1789.[23] "I tell you," Metternich told his wife in 1819, "the world was in full health in 1789 in comparison with its state today."[24] His biographer reports that Metternich "lived under the constant fear that he would become the target of an attack."[25]

Austria also had to worry about revolutionary movements elsewhere in the empire, especially in Italy. While Metternich had perhaps overestimated the revolutionary movement in Germany, in Italy it was underestimated. Metternich had been quite concerned about the revolutionary secret fraternities. In 1816 he said, "The troubled temper of Italy in general necessitates a ceaseless watch on the efforts of agitators in all parts of the peninsula."[26] By the time he and Emperor Francis traveled through Italy in 1819, he reported "some revolutionary dispositions which are common to a great mass of the population," but he did not consider the situation ripe for revolution. Among other matters, he saw no leadership yet plenty of divisions among the sects.[27] He would shortly be proven wrong.

Opposition in France

France in this period is described as having a "protoparliamentary" system with a "pseudoconstitution."[28] After the Allies twice deposed Napoleon, they

---

[23] Levinger, *Enlightened Nationalism*, 144.

[24] Paul R. Sweet, *Friedrich von Gentz: Defender of the Old Order* (Madison: University of Wisconsin Press, 1941), 221.

[25] Wolfram Siemann, *Metternich: Strategist and Visionary*, trans. Daniel Steuer (Cambridge, MA: Harvard University Press, 2019), 616.

[26] Donald E. Emerson, *Metternich and the Political Police: Security and Subversion in the Hapsburg Monarchy (1815–1830)* (The Hague: Martinus Nijhoff, 1968), 60. See also his letter to Emperor Francis, November 3, 1817, in Richard Metternich, ed., *Memoirs of Prince Metternich, 1815–1829*, vol. III (London: Richard Bentley & Son, 1881), 98–99. One report in 1817 estimated that there were 700,000 in Italy who sought a republic or a highly limited constitutional government. Emerson, *Metternich and the Political Police*, 67; see in general 57–86. A detailed examination of the secret societies in Lombardy-Venetia, and Austrian attempts to curb their influence, is in R. John Rath, *The Provisional Austrian Regime in Lombardy-Venetia* (Austin: University of Texas Press, 1969).

[27] Paul W. Schroeder, *Metternich's Diplomacy at Its Zenith, 1820–1823* (Austin: University of Texas Press, 1962), 23. In fact, revolutionaries planned to seize the emperor and Metternich during their visit, but the plot was foiled when they changed their route. Mark Jarrett, *The Congress of Vienna and Its Legacy: War and Great Power Diplomacy After Napoleon* (New York: I. B. Tauris, 2013), 233.

[28] Gordon Wright, *France in Modern Times* (New York: W. W. Norton & Company, 1995), 89, 92.

reinstated the Bourbons to the throne. King Louis XVIII issued the Charter of 1814, which proclaimed the divine right of kings. Under the charter, the king embodied executive power and initiated legislation, though the Chamber of Peers and Chamber of Deputies, the latter an elected body with an electorate limited to the very wealthy, could vote on taxes and laws.[29] Louis XVIII recognized that reinstituting the ancien régime was not feasible, despite the demands of the ultra-royalists, who wanted to turn back the clock. But his concessions were hardly satisfying to those on the left, a range of actors from the (more dominant) liberals who advocated constitutional monarchy (like Britain's) to republicans. Another opposition group was the Bonapartists, who were joined by many of the liberals and republicans during Napoleon's hundred-day rule, which was something like a revolution modeled on 1789. All of these groups were persecuted during the "White Terror" that followed the uprising.[30]

There was no shortage of groups unhappy with the regime, but in the immediate aftermath of the second Bourbon restoration, stability was mostly welcomed. The king's ministers took a relatively moderate course, which convinced many liberals to work within the system. The Indépendants, as the collection of Bonapartists, liberals, and republicans were known, increased their power in the elections held in the fall of 1819. The government also reached out to Bonapartist officers who had been banished from the army, in an attempt to mold a more monarchist, elitist army.[31] There were nevertheless rumblings: secret societies were established, such as L'Union, founded by Joseph Rey, who in 1816 attempted a republican coup. There were minor army uprisings and unrest at the universities.[32]

In 1820, the level of revolutionary agitation increased significantly. In February, a Bonapartist assassinated the Duc de Berri, the only Bourbon considered likely to produce an heir to the throne. The ultra-royalists seized the moment. They blamed the center and left for creating the climate for the assassination. They forced the resignation of the centrist head of the government, strict censorship was reinstated, and the government was given the authority to arrest and detain individuals without trial. Moreover, after violent debate, electoral reform was passed, which ensured that the conservatives would retain a hold on

---

[29] Only about 0.3 percent of the population, the largest taxpayers, were enfranchised. The state actually granted tax rebates to reduce the number of those eligible to vote.

[30] See Daniel Phillip Resnick, *The White Terror and the Political Reaction After Waterloo* (Cambridge, MA: Harvard University Press, 1966).

[31] Richard Holroyd, "The Bourbon Army, 1815–1830," *The Historical Journal* 14, no. 3 (1971): 540.

[32] Pamela M. Pilbeam, *Republicanism in Nineteenth-Century France, 1814–1871* (London: Macmillan, 1995), 71–80; E. Guillon, *Les complots militaires sous la restauration, d'après les documents des archives* (Paris: E. Plon, Nourrit et Cie, 1895); R. S. Alexander, *Bonapartism and Revolutionary Tradition in France: The Fédérés of 1815* (New York: Cambridge University Press, 1991), 248–79.

power.[33] This convinced many on the left that they could no longer work with the regime. Lafayette, for example, at this stage began actively plotting against the monarchy.[34]

The Charbonnerie—a collection of revolutionary secret societies, several formed before 1820—was inspired by the Italian Carbonari, and was founded by revolutionaries who had fled to Naples following prosecution after an earlier uprising. It boasted perhaps fifty thousand members. The aim was to infiltrate the army and use it against the regime. Several conspiracies were launched from 1821 to 1823, but all were successfully repressed.[35]

Opposition in Great Britain

The political system that some of the more moderate liberals in France aspired to was one like Great Britain's. Britain stood out among the great powers for having confirmed the ascendancy of the parliament vis-à-vis the monarchy in 1688. After about 1810, the parliament and the cabinet had grown more autonomous from the monarchy, as George III became incapacitated and his son George IV had character deficits that undermined the monarchy. Compared to the standards of parliamentary democracy, though, Britain was actually fairly similar to its Continental peers. Only 2.5 percent of the population was enfranchised to vote for the lower house of Parliament; the landed aristocracy still overwhelmingly dominated the government.[36]

Yet some wanted this to change. After 1815, associations agitating for reform, called Union societies or Hampton clubs, sprang up, but they were soon declared illegal. Reformers such as William Cobbet advocated universal suffrage and annual parliaments, but he explicitly advised against "secret Cabals" and suggested instead that supporters of reform "trust to individual exertion and

---

[33] The number of deputies' seats was expanded from 258 to 430, with the new 172 members selected by the richest quarter of the electorate in each district of France. Because this group also voted on the original 258 seats, it was dubbed the "law of the double vote." Consequently, the left lost heavily in the elections of November 1820. The assassination and political consequences for the Bourbon Restoration are elaborated in David Skuy, *Assassination, Politics and Miracles: France and the Royalist Reaction of 1820* (Montreal: McGill-Queen's University Press, 2003).

[34] Sylvia Neely, *Lafayette and the Liberal Ideal, 1814–1824: Politics and Conspiracy in an Age of Reaction* (Carbondale: Southern Illinois University Press, 1991), esp. 146.

[35] A chronicle of the movement and its context is Alan B. Spitzer, *Old Hatreds and Young Hopes: The French Carbonari Against the Bourbon Restoration* (Cambridge, MA: Harvard University Press, 1971). See also P. Savigear, "Carbonarism and the French Army, 1815–1824," *History* 54, no. 181 (1969): 198–211.

[36] Robert Justin Goldstein, *Political Repression in 19th Century Europe* (Totowa: Barnes & Noble Books, 1983), 4–5. For an evocative portrait of the conservative nature of the political system, see Élie Halévy, *England in 1815* (London: Ernest Benn Limited, 1964), 108–200.

open meetings."[37] The most popular radical orator of the day, Henry Hunt, used mass rallies of dubious legality to pressure the government. He would reiterate his peaceful intent, but warn the government to adopt the demands of the movement or it would face revolutionary consequences.[38] The Spenceans, named after revolutionary Thomas Spence, had even more radical aims that included land redistribution. A minority in that group aimed to create a spark that would ignite revolution across the country.[39]

Revolutionary agitation seemed to build up steam in the second half of the decade. A mass rally in December 1816 outside London led to a Spencean armed march and attack on the Tower of London. Three months later, the "Blanketeers," thousands of blanket-carrying weavers from Manchester, gathered to march to London to petition the regent before they were dispersed. Several months later, there was an armed uprising by textile workers in Pentrich, in Derbyshire.[40] The wave of unrest continued in 1819, when a crowd of over sixty thousand, the largest mass meeting in British history, gathered to hear Henry Hunt speak outside of Manchester. The Yeomanry Cavalry dispersed the gathering, killing eighteen people and injuring about seven hundred in what was dubbed the Peterloo Massacre.[41] A radical later wrote that he made up his mind on that day "that the time for Reform was past and the hour of Revolution had come."[42]

In the aftermath of Peterloo, there was revolutionary activity in the manufacturing areas of the north and London. In February 1820, a group of Spenceans in London plotted to murder the entire cabinet, but government spies foiled their plans. The leaders of what became known as the Cato Street Conspiracy were hung and then decapitated. In the Glasgow area at the same time, authorities arrested members of the Committee for Organizing a Provisional Government, who had been causing unrest.[43]

---

[37] Malcom I. Thomis and Peter Holt, *Threats of Revolution in Britain, 1789-1848* (London: The Macmillan Press, 1977), 42.

[38] John Belchem, *"Orator" Hunt: Henry Hunt and English Working-Class Radicalism* (New York: Oxford University Press, 1985).

[39] An overview of the radicals and their activities for this period is in Thomis and Holt, *Threats of Revolution in Britain*, 29–84; Edward Royle, *Revolutionary Britannia? Reflections on the Threat of Revolution in Britain* (Manchester: Manchester University Press, 2000), 42–60; David Worrall, *Radical Culture: Discourse, Resistance and Surveillance, 1790–1820* (Detroit: Wayne State University Press, 1992), 77–200; T. M. Parssinen, "The Revolutionary Party in London, 1816–20," *Bulletin of the Institute of Historical Research* 45, no. 111 (1972): 266–82; Iain McCalman, *Radical Underworld: Prophets, Revolutionaries and Pornographers in London, 1795-1840* (New York: Cambridge University Press, 1988), 97–177; J. Ann. Hone, *For the Cause of Truth: Radicalism in London, 1796-1821* (New York: Oxford University Press, 1982), 270–354. Also see the citations in the following notes.

[40] John Stevens, *England's Last Revolution: Pentrich, 1817* (Buxton: Moorland Publishing Company, 1977).

[41] Robert Poole, *Peterloo: The English Uprising* (New York: Oxford University Press, 2019).

[42] Royle, *Revolutionary Britannia?*, 53.

[43] P. Berresford Ellis and Seumas Mac A'Ghobhainn, *The Scottish Insurrection of 1820* (London: Pluto Press, 1989).

Historians have debated the extent to which these revolutionary groups threatened Britain. An older position viewed the disturbances in postwar Britain as apolitical protests against economic conditions. Some still consider those who had revolutionary aims to be an insignificant minority. Recent historical work, however, has challenged this view partly by taking seriously governmental reports of seditious activity.[44] What has never been questioned is that the government regarded the revolutionary threat as significant, as indicated by its actions. After the Spa Field riots, habeas corpus was suspended, followed shortly by the Seditious Meeting Act, which made it illegal to hold a meeting of more than fifty people. Following Peterloo, the government passed the reviled Six Acts, which, among other things, further restricted public meetings, imposed heavy fines on seditious literature, increased the tax on newspapers and pamphlets to decrease their circulation, prohibited unauthorized military drilling, and empowered local magistrates to search private property for arms. The government also heavily infiltrated radical organizations with spies.

No doubt the government exaggerated the extent of revolutionary activity by blurring the sometimes thin line between advocating radical reform and supporting revolution. As Lord Sidmouth, home secretary and former prime minister, stated, "An organized system has been established in every quarter, under the semblance of demanding parliamentary reform, but many of them, I am convinced, have that specious pretext in their mouths only, but revolution and rebellion in their hearts."[45] The assumption of both the authorities and the revolutionaries was that some revolutionary spark could tip much of the populace.[46] Castlereagh, whose job it was to shepherd bills such as the one suspending habeas corpus through the House of Commons, made a provision in his will so that his wife could sell her diamonds if necessary in the event of a revolution. After the Cato Street conspiracy, he carried two loaded pistols in the pockets of his breeches.[47]

---

[44] Royle makes the assumption that "those responsible for policy at the Home Office were not stupid and that the evidence presented to them was neither wholly fabricated nor distorted beyond credibility." Royle, *Revolutionary Britannia?*, 6. Some have played down certain uprisings as the product of spies and agents provocateurs, but Royle and others point out that these agents merely brought to light and in some cases led what was already a genuine movement. See his review of the historiography in ibid., 1–10.

[45] Philip Ziegler, *Addington: A Life of Henry Addington, First Viscount Sidmouth* (London: Collins, 1965), 349.

[46] Prime Minister Liverpool despaired that the economic difficulties they were facing would not have accounted for the political disturbances had it not been for the French Revolution, which had "shaken all respect for established authority and ancient institutions . . . I am sanguine enough to believe that the great body of the population is still sound, but it is impossible to say how long it will remain so." Charles Duke Yonge, ed., *Life and Administration of Robert Banks, Second Earl of Liverpool, K.G., Late First Lord of the Treasury: Compiled from Original Documents*, vol. II (London: Macmillan and Co., 1868), 431.

[47] C. J. Bartlett, *Castlereagh* (London: Macmillan, 1966), 183; Peter Quennell, ed., *The Private Letters of Princess Lieven to Prince Metternich, 1820–1826* (New York: E. P. Dutton, 1938), 17.

Section Summary

In Chapter 3, we saw that a growing number of thinkers, especially in France and Britain, questioned the foundations of the ancien régime. But this was still in the realm of philosophical speculation. Political contestation accepted the basic premises of the existing order. After the French Revolution, this changed markedly; the nature of the system was called into question in all the great powers. Leaders were aware in 1820–21 that their legitimacy was rejected by some and tenuous among others. To be sure, revolutionaries explicitly organizing and agitating for change were a small minority, like revolutionaries always are, but they were considered a dangerous threat in all the great powers. The possibility that they could tip the scales against the regime could not be ruled out. The concerns of the ruling classes were exhibited in the system of repression they established. Measures such as employing secret police and censorship to control the public atmosphere had not been unknown during the period of the ancien régime, but those activities were now greatly expanded.[48] But domestic repression alone was not seen as adequate; instead, the great powers' concerns about revolutionary potential also shaped their priorities in the international system.

International Relations Prior to the Revolutions

To assess whether the revolutions of 1820–21 affected patterns of international politics, I first examine relations among the great powers and toward the soon-to-be revolutionary states prior to these revolts. I will show that all the great powers were in an alliance with each other. The alliance was, however, somewhat uneasy and uncertain. While the status quo was largely congenial to Britain, Austria, and Prussia, there were fears that Russia and France could emerge as revisionist powers who would attempt to undermine the post-Napoleonic order settled so laboriously at Vienna in 1815.

The great powers that emerged from the Napoleonic Wars were the same as twenty-five years prior: France, Great Britain, Russia, Austria, and Prussia. Britain emerged from the conflict as the leading naval and commercial power. On the Continent, Russia was the predominant military power, as exhibited by its occupation of Paris in 1814. Austria led the newly established German

---

[48] See Beatrice de Graaf, *Fighting Terror After Napoleon: How Europe Became Secure After 1815* (New York: Cambridge University Press, 2020), chaps. 5–6; and the works authored or edited by Robert Goldstein: *Political Repression; The Frightful Stage: Political Censorship of the Theatre in Nineteenth-Century Europe* (New York: Berghahn Books, 2009); *Political Censorship of the Arts and the Press in Nineteenth-Century Europe* (New York: St. Martin's Press, 1989); *The War for the Public Mind: Political Censorship in Nineteenth-Century Europe* (Westport: Praeger, 2000).

Confederation, although in practice it conceded that northern Germany was in Prussia's sphere. Notably, there was no post-settlement renewal of the Prussian-Austrian rivalry. Prussia cooperated with Austria and even followed its lead. Prussia, still the weakest of the great powers, had gained territory in the Vienna Settlement to serve as a barrier against French expansion. Lombardy was returned to Austria, and Venetia was added to it. The Italian states not under direct Austrian control were under Austrian protection.

The French situation was in flux. The four other powers had twice defeated Napoleon. According to the Second Treaty of Paris, France was limited to the borders of 1790, had to pay an indemnity, and had to undergo a military occupation by the Allied powers. The Quadruple Alliance maintained those terms and provided to "renew their Meetings at fixed periods . . . for the purpose of consulting upon their common interests . . . and for the maintenance of the Peace of Europe."[49] The Allies had been relatively generous with France, but there was resentment within France and fear among the Allies that discontent could lead to further upheaval in France. The Bourbons feared the Allied occupation might completely discredit their monarchy, and the Allies agreed to withdraw their troops and fix the final sum of reparations. They also invited France into the alliance system.

Yet despite the expanded alliance, the other powers feared France from both a geopolitical and ideological perspective. They feared the domestic instability in France, which could lead to yet another revolution and an expansionist France spreading its ideals across Europe. France had been reduced in size and spheres of external influence. Whether it would try to regain territory or spheres of influence was thus an open question.

The Italian peninsula, formerly under French domination but now in the Austrian sphere, was seen as "a likely point of collision for Habsburg and French interests."[50] Piedmont's ambassador to Russia had written a memorandum for Alexander in 1818, detailing the long history of rivalry there. He stated, "Neither France nor Austria will ever consent to yield to each other," and he predicted the rivalry would upend European peace.[51] The Kingdom of Sardinia (which also included Piedmont, Nice, and Savoy) had traditionally danced between France and Austria. The kingdom moved into the French camp after it feared Britain would not protect it from becoming a victim of Austrian expansion under Joseph II. During the French Revolutionary Wars, France annexed most of Sardinia's territory. The Congress of Vienna reestablished the kingdom and added the territory once ruled by the Republic of Genoa to strengthen it as a barrier against French

---

[49] Jarrett, *The Congress of Vienna and Its Legacy*, 168.
[50] David Laven, "Austria's Italian Policy Reconsidered: Revolution and Reform in Restoration Italy," *Modern Italy* 2 (1997): 10.
[51] Ibid.

expansion. Vulnerable to France without the help of Austria, Sardinia was also wary of Austrian domination.

A similar dance between the Bourbons and the Habsburgs occurred in the Kingdom of the Two Sicilies. During the Revolutionary Wars, it was conquered by France, with the exception of Sicily, which was under British protection. The Allies eventually deposed Joachim Murat, Napoleon's former general who was ruling over the kingdom. They restored the old king, Ferdinand, as King of the Two Sicilies. Like other Italian states, the Two Sicilies was in the Austrian sphere of influence.

There was a subtler shift in the spheres of influence in the Iberian Peninsula. Spain had traditionally been an ally of France, and Portugal an ally of Britain. The upheavals of the French Revolution led to Napoleon occupying Spain and the Portuguese monarchy fleeing to Brazil. The British ultimately beat back the French presence in Portugal and then Spain. Both Iberian countries emerged from the wars weakened and consumed with maintaining order at home and in their empires. Portugal remained an ally of Britain, while Spain attempted to move closer to the Continental powers, particularly Russia, because of its dissatisfaction with British mediation between Spain and its former colonies.

Though an ally, Russia was also a potential threat, especially to Austria and Britain, from a geopolitical and ideological perspective. It had the largest army, and there were fears Russia could, for example, ally with France to gain Polish territories denied it at Vienna. Metternich proposed to Castlereagh in 1817 an Austro-British alliance to check the Russians. One long-standing Russian target was the Ottoman Empire. The eighteenth century saw Ottoman losses to the Habsburg and Russian Empires, and Russia emerged as its predominant threat toward the end of the century. The Ottomans showed little ability to resist Russian advances. Russia had even sponsored a revolt in Greece during the Russo-Turkish War of 1768–74. Catherine's "Greek Project" was to partition the Ottoman dominions in the Balkans between Austria and Russia, establish an independent Romania, and restore the Byzantine Empire under Catherine's grandson.

Russia's Balkan dreams had to be deferred when Joseph II died and Austria became consumed with the effects of the French Revolution. France had been the traditional protector of the Ottoman Empire against Habsburg and then Russian aggression. In the course of the Napoleonic Wars, the Ottomans allied with all the major protagonists at some point, and their strategy of picking the winning side was successful—they avoided partition and emerged with only a minimal loss of territory. However, the Ottomans were still weak, and dependent on the restraint or balancing of great-power rivalries to continue to prevent partition. Britain and France had no designs on the Balkans, and Austria, reversing its old position, did not want to extend its territory south. Whether Russia would resume its aggression toward the Ottoman Empire was an open question.

Alexander's ideological predispositions were as worrisome as his geopolitics. At times, Alexander seemed to favor liberal ideals, as evident in his establishment of an autonomous constitutional monarchy in Poland. Before 1820, he claimed that every nation should have the type of government that best suited it (e.g., not necessarily an absolute monarchy). He even suggested that the Bourbon collapse upon Napoleon's return meant the old charter was not liberal enough to reconcile throne and people.[52] Austria feared that Russian aims were to block Austrian influence in Germany and Italy, and that Alexander's agents there were promoting liberalism. Russia's diplomacy did not soothe their fears. The tsar helped block an effort by Metternich to make an Italian confederation modeled on the German one, and his agents did have extensive contact with the Carbonari in Italy.[53] Under the influence of his liberal foreign minister, Count Ioannis Capodistria, he did not endorse the Carlsbad Decrees. Instead, he sounded out Castlereagh on a joint demarche against them, infuriating Prussia and Austria.[54]

Alexander's ideological dalliances prevented any broader uptake of his proposals for an alliance that would regulate the internal affairs of states. While the powers were negotiating the Second Treaty of Paris in 1815, Alexander had proposed an alliance among the four Allied powers whereby they would commit to shun the selfish diplomacy of the ancien régime. Instead, sovereigns and peoples would unite to defend the sacred principles of the Christian gospel. Metternich revised the final version, eliminating the condemnation of the past as well as the future vision of merging states, attempting to shape it into a conservative alliance of sovereigns committed to Christian principles.[55] Similarly, the tsar's proposal that the Allied powers should guarantee the whole Vienna Settlement, as well as meeting occasionally to survey the internal affairs of European states, was rebuffed by Britain and Austria. Castlereagh argued that no British government would accept such a commitment on the Continent, particularly in support of absolutist governments. Metternich, on the other hand, feared the possibility of a tsar with liberal proclivities meddling in Germany and Italy.

In 1818, Alexander again proposed a general alliance, guaranteeing not only the existing territorial settlement between states, but also the political order

---

[52] Pawl W. Schroeder, *The Transformation of European Politics, 1763–1848* (New York: Oxford University Press, 1994), 523.

[53] Alan J. Reinerman, "Metternich, Alexander I, and the Russian Challenge in Italy, 1815–20," *The Journal of Modern History* 46, no. 2 (1974): 262–76.

[54] C. M. Woodhouse, *Capodistria: The Founder of Greek Independence* (London: Oxford University Press, 1973), 211–12.

[55] Although the Holy Alliance would become known as an enforcer of conservatism, to the tsar at this stage, it was pact of rulers to peoples. It did not uphold one regime type—the tsar even invited the United States to join, though it declined.

within states, backed up by an international army with the Russian army at its core. The Prussians, who were most fearful of French ambitions toward the Rhineland, were keen on this idea, but Austria and especially Britain were not. Castlereagh again could not sell that kind of involvement on the Continent. Metternich was attracted to the idea of an alliance that preserved the political order. Neither Britain nor Austria was comfortable with giving Russia an excuse to meddle across the Continent.

Before the revolutions in 1820, then, all the powers were allied with each other. The alliance was not without tensions. Austria and Britain were most content with the status quo, with Prussia following Austria's lead. They cast a wary eye, however, on Russia and France. There was an unease about whether Allied unity would break down and the politics of cutthroat competition would return.

Predictions

We have already seen that there was a significant liberal revolutionary movement in all the great powers, so the domestic contagion effects theory predicts that these regimes would fear contagion, cooperate with each other, and be hostile toward the revolutions that broke out in 1820–21. As Table 4.1 shows, this is precisely what we see. Moreover, in no case did a great power use one of the revolutions as a pretext for advancing its geopolitical position against one of the other great powers. This stands in contrast to the response to the American and Dutch revolutions, where domestic opposition was not present and geopolitical ambitions dominated the great powers' policy toward revolution.

Other theories have different expectations. The ideological perspective coincides with the domestic contagion effects theory, unless one regards as insufficient the ideological distance between the revolutionaries espousing a radical form of constitutional monarchy and the conservative constitutional and pseudo-constitutional monarchies of Britain and France. If that is the case, then perhaps there would be a divergence of strategies, with absolutist monarchies hostile toward the revolutionaries, and Britain and France not.

The practice of exploiting revolutions for geopolitical gain, regardless of ideological differences, is in line both with realist expectations and with the behavior of the great powers discussed in Chapter 3. From this perspective, one would expect that states would try to use revolutions to undermine others' sphere of influence. France would be looking to use the liberal revolts in the Italian peninsula to undermine the Austrian sphere of influence, just as Metternich feared. Russia might join with France. Russia would back a Greek revolt, as it had done before, to undermine the Ottoman Empire. The former Quadruple Alliance, especially

Table 4.1 Responses to the Revolutions of 1820–21

Great Power	Significant Liberal Revolutionary Movement?	Prediction of Stance Toward Revolutions Given Revolutionary Movement	Potential Revolutions to Support for Geopolitical Advantage	Outcome
France	Yes	Hostile	Support revolutions in Italy to undermine Austrian sphere of influence; support revolution in Portugal to undermine British sphere of influence	Hostile toward revolutions
Britain	Yes	Hostile	Support Spanish Revolution to prevent an extension of French influence; take Sicily back	Hostile toward revolutions
Prussia	Yes	Hostile	Support revolutions in Italy to undermine Austrian sphere of influence	Hostile toward revolutions
Austria	Yes	Hostile	Support Spanish Revolution to prevent an extension of French influence	Hostile toward revolutions
Russia	Yes	Hostile	Support Greek Revolt to break up the Ottoman Empire; support revolutions in Italy to undermine Austrian sphere of influence	Hostile toward revolutions

Britain and Austria, would aim to keep the French influence out of Spain. Other powers, especially France, would try to limit British influence in Portugal.

None of this happened. The outbreak of revolutions in Spain, Portugal, Naples, Piedmont, and Greece inspired fears of contagion among great-power leaders that affected their foreign policies in a manner that was hostile to the revolutionary state and cooperative with other states. There were big disagreements about how to proceed, but basic agreement about the desired end: to crush revolutions. I turn first to Spain, where revolution first broke out.

International Relations of the Liberal Revolutions of the 1820s

Initial Response to the Spanish Revolution

The great powers were unified in their hostility to the revolution in Spain—a hostility that would characterize their reaction to all the revolutions in this period. They were not angling to align with the revolutionaries for geopolitical advantage. Their main disagreements were about whether the Alliance should suppress the Spanish Revolution.

The great powers treated the news of the revolt with varying degrees of alarm. In Britain, France, and Austria, the initial military insurrection did not actually garner much attention. All three expected the Spanish government would suppress the uprising, and all also were consumed with domestic matters. But when the king was forced to restore the radical constitution of 1812, the anxiety of the great powers spiked. Metternich feared a chain reaction; Wellington told French prime minister Richelieu that the revolution was a catastrophe greater than Napoleon's return from Elba. Meanwhile, the tsar was less concerned with the 1812 constitution than with the military insurrection.[56] Spanish revolutionaries wrote to the tsar, asking him to approve of the 1812 constitution. It is one indication that revolutionaries placed their hopes in the tsar, which was a source of alarm for other powers. Instead, their approach to him provoked Alexander to issue a circular to the other powers calling for a congress. Even before the triumph of the revolution, the tsar sent a dispatch to the Allies supporting intervention should the king not suppress the revolt. Prussia seconded the tsar's concern, and Hardenberg wrote to Castlereagh about the dangerous example set by Spain.[57]

Castlereagh, however, in his state paper of May 5, objected to the Alliance meeting, both because he thought it would be ineffective and because he did not want the Alliance to have a general policy of regulating the internal affairs of other states.[58] This was not because Britain did not fear revolutionary contagion and

---

[56] Had the principles of the 1812 constitution emanated from the throne, the tsar said, they would be "conservative" and thus legitimate. Arising from an insurrection, they were "subversive." Russell H. Bartley, *Imperial Russia and the Struggle for Latin American Independence, 1808–1828* (Austin: University of Texas Press, 1978), 135.

[57] Lawrence J. Baack, *Christian Bernstorff and Prussia: Diplomacy and Reform Conservatism, 1818–1832* (New Brunswick: Rutgers University Press, 1980), 80; Charles William Vane, ed., *Correspondence, Despatches, and Other Papers, of Viscount Castlereagh, Second Marquess of Londonderry*, vol. 12 (London: John Murray, 1853), 223–24; Webster, *The Foreign Policy of Castlereagh*, 227–33; Schroeder, *Metternich's Diplomacy at Its Zenith*, 26.

[58] Castlereagh provided a litany of reasons why he thought intervention would be ineffective: There was as yet no one to negotiate with. A statement from the Allies would inflame rather than mollify the revolutionaries. A faction of Spanish moderates was already trying to reform the 1812 constitution, and an Allied declaration would make their job harder. Force was not an option. The Spanish

was not hostile toward the revolution. As the domestic contagion effects theory predicts, there was no distinction between Britain and the Continental powers on that score. But that did not mean they had the same strategy to suppress revolution. We may all agree that the Spanish revolt is a "dangerous example" and inconsistent with monarchical Government," Castlereagh said, and "may also agree, with shades of difference, that the consequence of this state of things in Spain may eventually bring danger home to all our own doors, but it does not follow, that We have therefore equal means of acting upon this opinion."[59] King Ferdinand VII's cause was not popular with the British public, and Britain had to temper its public support of counterrevolutionary measures in ways the "purely monarchical" states such as Russia did not. "In this country at all times, but especially at the present conjuncture, when the whole Energy of the State is required to unite reasonable men in defence of our existing Institutions"—here he is referring to the recent revolutionary activity—"public sentiment should not be distracted or divided, by any unnecessary interference of the Government in events, passing abroad, over which they can have none, or at best but very imperfect means of control."[60]

Castlereagh thought the Alliance should limit itself to what its members could agree on, and the states would not be able to agree to a general principle upon which to intervene in the internal affairs of other states. This was not a new argument from him; he had rejected the Russian proposal in 1818 to expand the scope of the alliance for the same reasons.[61] He favored states stamping out revolution on their own as much as possible, without involving Britain. On the same day as the state paper was issued, he wrote to his ambassador in Austria, his brother, to convey to Austria his pleasure at the work of the Carlsbad Decrees in stamping out revolutionary activity in Germany, much as he passed the Six Acts to suppress similar revolutionary activity at home.[62] "Although we have made an immense progress against Radicalism," he wrote Metternich, "the monster still lives."[63] Britain's commitment to counterrevolution in private but its obligation

would never accept Allied occupation. (He used Wellington as his authority, and the context was the ferocious Spanish resistance to Napoleon's occupation a decade earlier.) And troops would not be available to suppress internal dissidents, while the armies would get contaminated by revolutionary ideals. Finally, military intervention would weaken indebted states, making them more vulnerable to revolt. The state paper is reprinted in A. W. Ward and G. P. Gooch, eds., *The Cambridge History of British Foreign Policy, 1783–1919*, vol. II, *1815–1866* (New York: Macmillan, 1923), 623–33.

[59]   Ibid., 627–28.
[60]   Ibid., 628–29.
[61]   Castlereagh's memorandum on the Russian proposal is reproduced in C. K. Webster, *The Congress of Vienna, 1814–1815* (London: G. Bell & Sons, 1934), 166–71.
[62]   Webster, *The Foreign Policy of Castlereagh*, 197–98.
[63]   Vane, *Correspondence, Despatches, and Other Papers, of Viscount Castlereagh*, vol. 12, 259.

to work within the constraints of public opinion would characterize its reaction to these revolutions.

Metternich followed Castlereagh's lead. He rejected Allied intervention using many of the same arguments. He thought that the Spanish revolution could be reversed without direct military intervention, and he objected to Russian and French intervention in Spain. He was still apprehensive of the tsar's liberal sensibilities, he did not want Russian troops marching through Germany on their way to Spain, and he did not want to encourage a Franco-Russian alignment. He did not trust the French army—if it was loyal, it should remain within France to protect Louis XVIII. If not, a Spanish expedition could be an excuse to overthrow the French king. He also did not favor the other states' suggested solutions to the Spanish problem. Both France and Russia had proposed not merely that the revolution should be suppressed, but also that a moderate constitution, like the French charter, could be granted by royal will rather than through insurrection, thereby reconciling king and subjects. Metternich welcomed what he regarded as the tsar's newfound zeal against revolution, and sought to steer him in a more conservative direction. But at this stage he was content to let the Spanish Revolution burn itself out, and only assist Spanish royals with money and arms at the royals' initiative.[64] The great powers were not considering how to take advantage of the Spanish Revolution for geopolitical gain; they were united in their opposition towards it, given the fear of revolutionary contagion, even if they preferred different means by which to contain it.

Revolution in Naples

The Spanish revolt spread to Naples in July. The Italian revolutions provided a prime opportunity for Russia and especially France to undermine the Austrian sphere of influence by siding with the revolutionaries, but these opportunities were not taken, given the fear of revolutionary contagion. Austria was immediately alarmed by the Italian situation—Metternich "varied his metaphors between conflagrations, torrents, and earthquakes."[65] The outbreak at Naples was a surprise; the kingdom was regarded as relatively well governed, in contrast to Spain. Metternich saw it as the most stable of all the Italian states he had visited on his tour the previous year. One option was to let the Neapolitans stew in their own juice and hope for a counterrevolutionary coup d'état, but that possibility was considered too dangerous given the fear of contagion. Metternich decided

---

[64] Schroeder, *Metternich's Diplomacy at Its Zenith*, 28–29; Harold Temperley, *The Foreign Policy of Canning, 1822–1827* (London: Archon Books, 1966), 17.

[65] Webster, *The Foreign Policy of Castlereagh*, 264.

that the revolution must be crushed. On the military front, he began reinforcing his army in Lombardy-Venetia. But the diplomatic front was just as important. He wanted the moral support of the other powers. The Italian and German states (including Prussia) supported Metternich. Whatever fear they had of Austrian hegemony was superseded by a fear of revolutionary contagion. Their concern was rather that Austria might not send enough troops to fully crush the revolution.[66]

Britain was on Austria's side against the revolution. The British representative in Naples expressed alarm at the effect the revolution would have on Italy and sympathized with Austria's concerns about the security of its possessions. In private, Wellington told Austrian and Russian representatives that "it is time to make an example" and the Austrians "must march."[67] Castlereagh urged Metternich to crush the revolution. He also reassured Metternich that he would have nothing to do with revolutionaries in Sicily, as there was some suggestion that they would appeal to Britain for help. Officially, however, he was clear that Austria could not expect direct British assistance or even moral support. Certainly, the Alliance should not be summoned for the cause. Still, Metternich was pleased at Britain's private endorsement.

Metternich's bigger concern was the tsar. He had been complaining about Alexander's previous support of liberals, particularly in Italy. This encouragement from Russia convinced some revolutionaries they would be protected from Austrian repression. Metternich worried that with the tsar's support, emboldened revolutionaries would rise throughout Germany and Italy.[68]

Russia and France had a similar reaction—both condemned the revolution, but both were hesitant to simply let Austria have its way. France feared Austria would strengthen its influence in Italy and the British would create a protectorate

---

[66] Schroeder, *Metternich's Diplomacy at Its Zenith*, 44. There is a parallel with the Gulf states accepting Saudi hegemony through the formation of the GCC in the face of threats from the Iranian Revolution, discussed in Chapter 6. One partial exception was the Papal States, which Austria would have to march through to invade Naples. Cardinal Consalvi, the secretary of state for the Papal States, desired to see the revolution crushed but did not want to openly support Austrian policy in order to uphold his position of neutrality in disputes between Christian princes, and so as to not provoke a Neapolitan invasion. He was also wary of Austrian domination, but did not want to be an obstacle to counterrevolution. Rather than formally grant Austrian troops passage, he requested that Austria not ask so that he could accept a fait accompli and preserve his neutrality. Alan J. Reinerman, *Austria and the Papacy in the Age of Metternich: Between Conflict and Cooperation, 1809–1830*, vol. I (Washington, DC: The Catholic University Press of America, 1979), 78–81; Brady, *Rome and the Neapolitan Revolution of 1820–1821*, 57–63.

[67] Webster, *The Foreign Policy of Castlereagh*, 263; Quennell, *The Private Letters of Princess Lieven to Prince Metternich*, 53.

[68] For Italy, see Reinerman, "Metternich, Alexander I, and the Russian Challenge in Italy"; Romani, *The Neapolitan Revolution of 1820–1821*, 111; Webster, *The Foreign Policy of Castlereagh*, 95, 182; Metternich, *Memoirs of Prince Metternich*, 261. For Metternich's fear that Russia would use liberal movements to undermine Austria's domination of the German Confederation, see Enno E. Kraehe, "Austria, Russia and the German Confederation, 1813–1820," in *Deutscher Bund und deutsche Frage 1815–1866*, ed. Helmut Rumpler (Munich: Verlag, 1990), 274–75.

over Sicily, increasing the British presence in the Mediterranean. Richelieu, though, promised Metternich that he could "count on us that we will do all in our power to prevent the evils that no one more than us has to fear."[69] He indicated he would happily see Metternich crush the revolution on his own, but also suggested an Allied forum to show a united front against revolution. Russia too pushed for an Allied forum to deal with the problem, which would give it a say in what the outcome would be for the Neapolitan government. Metternich had no desire for such input, principally because elements in both France and Russia wanted to modify the constitution in Naples to resemble the French charter. Metternich was opposed; he wanted an absolute monarchy. Since working through the Alliance would alienate Britain, Metternich proposed an informal Allied conference, committed in advance to the moral support of Austria. Castlereagh let it be known that he could not even publicly announce Britain's policy of refusing recognition to the revolutionary regime for fear of the public reaction.

Metternich could ignore France and Britain, but not Russia. He needed Russia's blessing to act unilaterally in Naples. Russia insisted on an Allied conference, and Metternich tried in vain to bring Castlereagh around to the idea, arguing that without the Alliance the revolution would triumph and Alexander would be unrestrained. But Castlereagh, worried that Metternich's plans would embarrass him and his government, said that Britain was now forced to take a position of neutrality on the Naples question. This in turn had ripple effects on France. The French foreign minister admitted, "We find ourselves in a certain way forced by the conduct of England to modify our original intentions."[70] Neither constitutional power could be seen consorting with the Holy Alliance against a revolution. Thus, Austria, Prussia, and Russia arranged a conference to be held at Troppau, Austria, in October 1820, with Britain and France sending only observers.

With Prussia backing Austria, could Metternich win Russia to his position? His worry was the possible sway the tsar's liberal foreign minister had over him. Capodistria was no revolutionary, but he thought the antidote to revolution was liberal constitutionalism.[71] He opposed Austria's proposals to reinstall

---

[69] Guillaume de. Bertier de Sauvigny, *France and the European Alliance, 1816–1821: The Private Correspondence of Metternich and Richelieu* (Notre Dame: University of Notre Dame Press, 1958), 94–95.

[70] Schroeder, *Metternich's Diplomacy at Its Zenith*, 57.

[71] Capodistria told his diplomats, "The infection which menaces all the states of Europe is formidable only to the extent that governments open an access to it by unpardonable improvidence." Governments had to choose between the "wise and reasonable establishment of liberal ideas or the reversion of old institutions." Metternich's advisor Friedrich von Gentz assessed that Capodistria "mistakenly believes that the maintenance of order is compatible with the ascendancy of liberal ideas." Woodhouse, *Capodistria*, 243; Patricia Kennedy Grimsted, *The Foreign Ministers of Alexander I: Political Attitudes and the Conduct of Russian Diplomacy, 1801–1825* (Berkeley: University of California Press, 1969), 235.

Ferdinand in Naples as absolute ruler. Metternich played his hand well. He jus-tified intervention based on the secret agreement Naples had made with Austria not to change its form of government without Austria's consent and on the ge-neral danger the revolution posed to Europe. Metternich sidestepped a debate on the merits of different forms of government by insisting it was up to the le-gitimate sovereign to decide—in an uncoerced manner—what he preferred. He added a provision that the government established must not be "in opposition to the internal tranquility of neighboring states."[72] This, of course, meant the re-instatement of the king on absolutist terms. Metternich reminded the tsar that neither Russia nor Austria was a constitutional state.

At this point, the tsar did not need much convincing. He was already souring on liberal causes after his frustrations in Poland and the internal developments in France. He came to Troppau via Warsaw, where he had refused to lift the recent censorship decree and secretly authorized his brother to override the Polish con-stitution if need be.[73] His alarm at the military revolts in Spain and Naples was magnified by the Semenovsky Revolt, which occurred while he was at Troppau. As previously discussed, Alexander believed that military revolt was part of a wider international revolutionary conspiracy. He backed unilateral Austrian action to crush the revolution in Italy; Capodistria was sidelined. The prelimi-nary Protocol of Troppau stated the matter in more general terms: "States which have undergone a change of government, due to revolution, the results of which threaten other States, ipso facto cease to be members of the European Alliance, and remain excluded from it until their situation gives guarantees of legal order and stability. If, owing to such alterations, immediate danger threatens other States, the Powers bind themselves, by peaceful means, or if need be by arms, to bring back the guilty State into the bosom of the Great Alliance."[74]

Metternich risked upsetting Britain, his natural geopolitical ally, in favor of Russian support against revolution. He hoped that at least the British would hold their tongue. Castlereagh made public his arguments in the state paper, omit-ting reference to concerns about revolution at home, to distance his govern-ment from the actions of the Eastern powers as parliamentary members and the public railed against the government for associating with the Holy Alliance. But the Austrian ambassador to London accurately described him as "like a great lover of music who is at Church; he wishes to applaud but he dare not."[75] Indeed, Castlereagh agreed with the counterrevolutionary aims of Austrian policy. The reaction in France was much the same. Some on the left eyed a chance to re-store French influence in the Italian peninsula, as well as support a more radical

[72] Schroeder, *Metternich's Diplomacy at Its Zenith*, 77.
[73] Jarrett, *The Congress of Vienna and Its Legacy*, 247.
[74] Ward and Gooch, *The Cambridge History of British Foreign Policy*, 37–38.
[75] Webster, *The Foreign Policy of Castlereagh*, 326.

regime. Conservatives backed Austrian actions for the opposite reason. French policy in the face of these forces was to do nothing and hope the Austrians completed their work quickly, while France, like Britain, publicly distanced itself from Austria's actions.[76]

Revolution in Piedmont

While the great powers reconvened their Troppau conference in Laibach in 1821, the revolution in Piedmont broke out. The king of Piedmont appealed to Austria for support. Russia's local representative pushed for mediation to prevent Austrian intervention, but Alexander supported crushing the revolution and proposed to march a hundred thousand men to do so. In part, this was to discourage French meddling. Some, including Metternich, thought that France was behind this revolution, and not without reason. The French representative in Turin urged his government to support the uprising, and his predecessor had been removed in 1820 because of his ties with the liberals.[77] The French government, though, refused to support revolutionaries. It proposed to mediate, but the British did not support this. Castlereagh preferred that the revolt be suppressed by the Russians rather than the French or Austrians, if it could not be put down internally.[78] All the powers, France and Britain more discreetly, approved of the quick work made of the revolution. Loyal Piedmontese troops, assisted by Austrian troops, crushed the revolution in April. Liberals in Italy who had counted on the support of the French, the British, and Alexander were sorely mistaken.

This was a remarkable concession for France in particular. Piedmont had previously been in the French sphere of influence, but the Vienna Settlement had placed it in Austria's camp. Some French thought France should have a policy of

---

[76] Guillaume de Bertier de Sauvigny, *The Bourbon Restoration*, trans. Lynn M. Case (Philadelphia: The University of Pennsylvania Press, 1966), 175–76. The divide in French foreign policy was not entirely left-right. Ultra-royalist Count Pierre Blacas wanted to check Austria and draw closer to Russia, though he did not want a radical regime in Naples. Schroeder, *The Transformation of European Politics*, 609.

[77] Ambassador Dalberg was in trouble with the French government for being "too liberal." He was against Austrian domination of Italy, and his residence was a gathering place for the "club of plotters." His successor, Count La Tour du Pin, urged his government to get behind the revolution. Federico Cuarto, ed., *Le relazioni diplomatiche fra la Gran Bretagna e il Regno di Sardegna, I serie: 1814–1830*, vol. I (Rome: Istituto Storico Italiano, 1972), 234; Cesare Spellanzon, *Storia del risorgimento e dell'unità d'Italia*, vol. 1 (Milan: Rizzoli, 1933), 843; Piotr Kozlovski, *Diorama social de Paris* (Paris: Honoré Champion, 1997), 99; Guillaume de. Bertier de Sauvigny, *Metternich et la France après le Congrès de Vienne*, vol. 2 (Paris: Hachette, 1970), 481; Narciso Nada, *Le relazioni diplomatiche fra l'Austria e il Regno di Sardegna, I serie: 1814–1830*, vol. 2 (Rome: Istituto Storico Italiano, 1970), 36–37, 48. The British diplomat in Tuscany also attempted to push back against Austrian actions, but Castlereagh shut him down. John Bew, *Castlereagh: A Life* (New York: Oxford University Press, 2012), 498–99.

[78] Webster, *The Foreign Policy of Castlereagh*, 329–31.

returning Piedmont to its sphere by supporting revolutionaries. Politicians on the left in the Chamber of Deputies had been excoriating the government for the loss of French influence in Italy. "Those who have some knowledge of the politics that preceded the period of our Revolution know that France hastened to stop the enlargement of Austria in Italy," liberal opposition leader Horace Sébastiani declared. "So! Today Austria advances towards Naples."[79]

There was a concern among the French leadership about Austrian domination of the Italian peninsula, as well as an unease about how French acquiescence to Austrian hegemony would look at home, but this was secondary to their greater interest in crushing revolutions. France would accept Austrian hegemony if it served that aim. The French foreign minister himself outlined a possible French strategy in response to the revolutions in Italy: "There is no doubt that if she [France] wanted to take 30,000 men beyond the Alps, throughout Italy people would throw themselves in their arms . . . and, supposing that the other Powers want to oppose this union, they would have much to do in regards to attitudes in Europe. France, moreover, by thus placing herself at the head of ideas and constitutional undertakings, would be able to exercise among them an advantageous influence."[80] But it became clear that this option was no longer possible, and it was clear why: "In other circumstances," he later said, "France could have conceived the idea of acting alone in this role that suits her better than the other Powers; but today she would expose herself to the danger, immense for herself and for Europe, of encouraging, against her will, the spirit of revolution."[81] Again, the great powers were united in the goal of preventing revolutionary contagion, even at the expense of geopolitical gain, as the domestic contagion theory expects.

Revolution in Greece

Word of the Greek revolt reached the great powers as they were conferring at Laibach. At stake was not just the nature of a regime, but the fate of the Ottoman Empire and the expansion of Russian power. The officer in the Russian army who initiated the revolt intended to incite a war between Russia and Turkey, which would enable the liberation of Greeks from Ottoman rule. It was feared that such a war could lead to the collapse of Ottoman rule, which was in fact the aim of Alexander's grandmother Catherine.

Alexander's initial response provided some comfort to the other powers. He disavowed any involvement and gave the Turks a green light to repress the

---

[79] *Archives parlementaires de 1787 à 1860*, vol. 30, deuxième série (Paris: Librairie Administrative de Paul Dupont, 1875), 448.

[80] Bertier de Sauvigny, *Metternich et la France après le Congrès de Vienne*, vol. 2, 332.

[81] Ibid., 365.

uprising. He thought the same forces in Greece were behind revolutionary movements elsewhere in Europe, including the mutiny of one of his own regiments, and pledged not to aid the rebels.[82] The revolt in the Danubian Principalities, ruled by Greeks, was relatively easily repressed, but the revolt in Greece was genuinely popular. The Turks' brutal suppression tactics, including massacres and the hanging of the Patriarch of Constantinople, increasingly raised the ire of the Russians, who claimed the right to protect Orthodox subjects. Other violations against Russian treaty rights included direct Turkish occupation of the Danubian Principalities, interference with Russian trade through the straits, and the destruction of Russian property in Constantinople. Russia broke ties with the Turks in July 1821, but the Turks were uncompromising.

None of the other great powers wanted to see the Greek revolt succeed. Austria hoped the Turks would crush the revolution as quickly as possible. Metternich feared a war could stimulate revolutionary activity across Europe, and he supported Turkish rule because "the interest of Europe pronounces against any major political change."[83] He considered it a "firebrand thrown by the radicals between the great powers and especially between Austria and Russia."[84] He funneled to the tsar reports that the revolutionaries were only waiting for the outbreak of war between Russia and Turkey to make their move.[85] Metternich pressed the Pope to condemn the Greek revolt, not wanting Alexander or other Catholic states to have an excuse to favor Greek independence.[86]

Metternich also conferred with Castlereagh to restrain Alexander. Britain had no interest in the collapse of the Ottoman Empire and an expansion of Russian influence, and Castlereagh was not sympathetic to the Greek revolt. Alexander did not appreciate what he regarded as Austro-British collusion against him, and at one point reached out to the French for an alliance against the Ottomans. There was some support on both the left and right in the Chamber of Deputies to exploit the Greek situation,[87] but the cabinet under Richelieu declined, and the new ultra-royalist cabinet under Villèle continued that policy. "While desiring

---

[82] Webster, *The Foreign Policy of Castlereagh*, 358–59.

[83] Schroeder, *Metternich's Diplomacy at Its Zenith*, 173.

[84] M. S. Anderson, *The Eastern Question, 1774–1923* (New York: St. Martin's Press, 1966), 59.

[85] Whether it was due to Metternich's reports or not, the tsar accepted this view: "If we reply to the Turks with war the Paris directing committee will triumph and no government will be left standing. I do not intent to leave a free field to the enemies of order. At all costs means must be found of avoiding war with Turkey." Ibid., 72.

[86] Metternich's strong efforts to get the Pope to condemn the Greek revolt and also the Carbonari shows how he viewed the Pope as playing a critical role in supporting the established order, the so-called union of throne and altar, and the importance Metternich placed on preserving a larger moral climate that would insulate the powers against revolution. Alan J. Reinerman, "Metternich, the Papacy, and the Greek Revolution," *East European Quarterly* 12, no. 2 (1978): 177–88; Alan Reinerman, "Metternich and the Papal Condemnation of the 'Carbonari,' 1821," *The Catholic Historical Review* 54, no. 1 (1968): 55–69.

[87] Webster, *The Foreign Policy of Castlereagh*, 380.

a rapprochement with Russia, which places us in a position more like those of England and Austria," Richelieu stated, "it is necessary to try to avoid anything that could harm the union between the five powers, even in the case where the Turkish war could break out. This union is the most powerful of the paths against the invasion of revolutionary principles."[88] Prussia was the most outwardly sympathetic to Russian aims, though it too urged restraint.

The Alliance thus clearly pushed Russian restraint, but they had nothing more than moral leverage to use against Russia. The British took the strongest stance, but merely threatened neutrality in any possible Russo-Turkish war. Russian leadership knew there would not be any significant resistance by the great powers to their action against the Ottomans, and moreover expected that a war with Turkey would be relatively easily won. Plus the tsar had a compelling list of reasons to fight: geopolitical advantage, economic interests, and the situation of the Orthodox Christians. It is not surprising that many Russian officials advised Alexander to take action, not the least of which was one of his foreign ministers, Capodistria.[89]

Alexander, however, refused to intervene, leading to the resignation of Capodistria. Why did Alexander not take action? However much he despised the sultan, Alexander saw him as the legitimate ruler and the Greeks as Jacobin usurpers. "I could have permitted myself to be swept along by the enthusiasm for the Greeks," he told the Prussian envoy, "but I have never forgotten the impure origin of the rebellion or the danger of my intervention for my allies."[90] And any conflict with Turkey would only aid the revolutionary cause. To the British ambassador he said, "I am sensible of the danger which surrounds us all. When I look to the state of France and the new Ministry—when I see the state of Spain and Portugal, when I see, as I do see, the state of the whole world, I am well aware that the smallest spark which falls upon such combustible materials may kindle a flame which all our efforts may perhaps hereafter be insufficient to extinguish."[91]

Paul Schroeder pointedly claims that Alexander's policy was driven by the desire to preserve the Alliance rather than by an anti-revolutionary strategy.[92] But Matthew Rendall rightly critiques this as a false dichotomy.[93] In the tsar's

[88]   Bertier de Sauvigny, *Metternich et la France après le Congrès de Vienne*, vol. 2, 519.
[89]   This is well documented in Matthew Rendall, "Russia, the Concert of Europe, and Greece, 1821–29: A Test of Hypotheses About the Vienna System," *Security Studies* 9, no. 4 (2000): 59–71. He decisively refutes the claims of Korina Kagan that Russia was restrained by the balance of power. Korina Kagan, "The Myth of the European Concert: The Realist-Institutionalist Debate and Great Power Behavior in the Eastern Question, 1821–1841," *Security Studies* 7, no. 2 (1997/98). For Capodistria's efforts to persuade the tsar, see Grimsted, *The Foreign Ministers of Alexander I*, 256–74; Woodhouse, *Capodistria*, 260–78.
[90]   Cited in Henry A. Kissinger, *A World Restored: Metternich, Castlereagh and the Problems of Peace*, 1812–1822 (Boston: Houghton Mifflin, 1957), 308.
[91]   Webster, *The Foreign Policy of Castlereagh*, 388.
[92]   Schroeder, *The Transformation of European Politics*, 621.
[93]   Rendall, "Russia, the Concert of Europe, and Greece," 71.

view, the major purpose of the Alliance was to ward off revolution. He told the French ambassador in 1822, "The only aim of the Alliance is that for which it was formed: to combat revolution."[94]

Dealing with the Revolution in Spain

With the Italian revolts crushed and the Greek situation put to the side, the polarization and anarchy in Spain commanded the attention of the great powers. After the failure of a royalist coup in 1822, Ferdinand VII repeatedly appealed to the tsar and the French to come to his rescue. Frenchmen, conservative and liberal, had been crossing the border to aid their respective sides. The French government had already sent troops in 1821 to the Pyrenees as a cordon sanitaire to contain an outbreak of yellow fever in Spain. In June 1822, they reinforced the troops and renamed them a "corps d'observation." The French government was also covertly aiding the royalists.[95]

There were three camps in the French government on the Spanish matter: one wished to crush the revolution in concert with the Allied powers, another desired France to crush the revolution on its own, and a third wanted to stay out.[96] Most had largely been in the third camp, for the same reasons that Allied powers had misgivings about French action against Spain. Some in the French government were dissatisfied with the Spanish king and were concerned that, once restored, he would continue his misrule, which would foment radicalism. The more important concern in the French government and among the Allies was that French intervention might not only be unsuccessful at stamping out revolution in Spain, but also could lead to revolution in France.

French intervention could be costly and dangerous, given the unreliability of the army and the potential for French forces to get bogged down in Spain. Government officials worried that a military intervention in Spain would provide an opportunity for liberal elements in the French army to turn on the monarchy. The French had ample evidence that the reliability of the troops intervening in Spain was a real problem, including propaganda being circulated, conspiracies that had been uncovered, and defections to Spain. At a review of troops in 1820, for example, an officer had stepped out of line and told the Duc de Berri, heir to the throne and soon to be assassinated, that if he wanted to send them to Spain, they would refuse to obey.[97] The French Charbonnerie instigated

---

[94] Irby C. Nichols, *The European Pentarchy and the Congress of Verona* (The Hague: Martinus Nijhoff, 1971), 91.

[95] Ibid., 33.

[96] Bertier de Sauvigny, *The Bourbon Restoration*, 186–89.

[97] Savigear, "Carbonarism and the French Army," 204.

several uprisings that were repressed, but these events reminded everyone of the danger.[98] All the Allied powers were worried that a French intervention in Spain might precipitate the military turning on the Bourbons.[99]

Alexander advocated creating a European army to put an end to the revolution. He first suggested that the suppression could be done directly, but when Austria objected, he proposed that the army could stand by to protect France from revolution in the event that the French intervened in Spain. Metternich tried to gently point out the difficulties in this position. Alexander demanded that the possibility of intervening in Spain be a major part of the upcoming great-power conference in Verona.

Metternich, with Prussia at his side, was hostile to the Spanish Revolution, but he had few good options. For both geopolitical and ideological reasons he disliked the idea of either Russia or France marching into Spain. Uncomfortable with encouraging either Russian or French ambitions, he also feared that they would encourage Ferdinand to grant a constitution as a compromise. "A king must never make the sacrifice of any part of his authority whatsoever," Metternich claimed. "The only sense of the word Constitution that is admissible in the monarchical system is that of an organization of public powers under the supreme, indivisible, and inalienable authority of the monarch. . . . In every other sense, Constitution is the equivalent of anarchy and the supposed division of powers is the death of monarchical government."[100]

As Metternich counted on Castlereagh to help restrain Russia and France, he considered Castlereagh's suicide just before the Verona conference (largely dedicated to the Spanish problem) as a personal blow. Castlereagh's replacement was George Canning, whom Metternich despised as a shameless opportunist who would undermine the principles of European peace for the sake of popularity at home. In fact, the differences between Castlereagh and Canning were more of style. Their position on intervention in Spain was essentially the same: they hoped the revolution would burn itself out and a moderate government would emerge. Both were irritated at French meddling that polarized the Spanish situation. Canning consistently opposed French intervention in Spain and was particularly worried France would get bogged down in Spain, which might incite revolution in France itself.[101] Canning sent Wellington to Verona as an observer to help prevent French intervention.

---

[98] Nichols, *The European Pentarchy and the Congress of Verona*, 30.

[99] That their concern was warranted would be illustrated in 1830, when a French expedition to Algeria prompted a revolution.

[100] Schroeder, *Metternich's Diplomacy at Its Zenith*, 201n22.

[101] Temperley's influential work argues that Canning actually favored French intervention in Spain as a means to separate France from the Continental powers and break the great-power concert system, which was disliked by British public opinion and thought to restrain British freedom of action. But Yamada decisively refutes this argument. Temperley, *The Foreign Policy of Canning*;

At Verona, France did seek—but did not get—Allied approval for intervention in Spain.[102] Metternich had proposed instead a plan of joint "moral" action to get all five powers to break their relations with Spain. But Montmorency, the French foreign minister, broached the issue of Allied approval for an invasion (exceeding his instructions in doing so). Alexander, shifting away from the idea of a European army, now supported a French intervention. He was still worried about the intervention causing the fall of the monarchy in France, but he wanted the Spanish Revolution crushed. Knowing the objections to Russian forces doing it, he decided to support the French and be ready to march to Paris if the Bourbons were overturned there.[103] Austria and Prussia waffled. Metternich tried to tie the French to an Allied policy of breaking relations with Spain and supporting French aid to the royalist rebels.[104] French prime minister Villèle, however, did not want to break relations with Spain until France was ready to march, and that time was getting close. As the counterrevolution in Spain was collapsing, government support grew for a more belligerent French policy.

By January 1823, King Louis XVIII had decided on war. Metternich dropped his opposition when he realized his fear of France imposing a moderate constitution was misplaced.[105] Canning still opposed French intervention. He attempted to get the Spaniards to modify their constitution, but when they refused, he gave up. The French army crossed into Spain in the spring of 1823, quickly crushed the revolution, and reinstalled Ferdinand on the throne. Metternich wrote Foreign Minister Chateaubriand a congratulatory note: "I regard it as one of the happiest chances, as much for the consolidation of matters in France, as for the weal of the entire social body, that it has been part of the destiny of a country, which has been the asylum of so many insurrections, to be called upon to strike a blow at revolution, from which, if struck with vigour, it can never revive."[106] Canning, pleased his fears had not been realized, remarked, "Never had an army done so little harm and prevented so much of it."[107] French prime minister Villèle had feared the British would openly back a constitutional regime, which could be a means to exclude French influence, but this did not happen.

Norihito Yamada, "George Canning and the Spanish Question, September 1822 to March 1823," *The Historical Journal* 52, no. 2 (2009): 343–62.

[102] Nichols, *The European Pentarchy and the Congress of Verona, 1822*, 135.

[103] Jarrett, *The Congress of Vienna and Its Legacy*, 327.

[104] The British, though, thought the strategy would only embolden the radicals and marginalize the moderates.

[105] Metternich still made a secret agreement between Ferdinand and the eastern powers that he would not promise any changes while in captivity. Schroeder notes that Ferdinand kept the spirit if not the letter of the agreement by making many promises to the revolutionaries and repudiating them all once French forces liberated him. Schroeder, *Metternich's Diplomacy at Its Zenith*, 235.

[106] M. de. Chateaubriand, *The Congress of Verona: Comprising a Portion of Memoirs of His Own Times*, vol. II (London: Richard Bentley, 1838), 35.

[107] Bertier de Sauvigny, *The Bourbon Restoration*, 193.

There was thus considerable friction among the great powers over how they should handle the Spanish Revolution, but this was a debate about tactics rather than goals. They shared hostility toward a radical regime in Madrid. There was resistance to France marching into Spain, but that resistance was not grounded in an apprehension over the expansion of French influence to Spain. This in itself is remarkable given the efforts the great powers had exerted to get France out of Spain only a few years prior. Instead, it was out of a concern that French intervention could lead to more revolution. When this did not happen, the great powers were satisfied.

Great-Power Response to Portugal

When revolution spread to Portugal in September 1820 after the Spanish Revolution, the great powers reacted negatively, though not identically so. Britain, and George Canning in particular, has been portrayed as advocating liberalism in Portugal. In fact, the British were not fond of the radicalism of the revolution, and were willing to live with either a moderate constitutional monarchy like their own or something more conservative. The Continental powers preferred something more conservative and were alarmed at how the Portuguese could influence Spain. The Continental powers might have backed whatever faction was anti-British in an attempt to remove Portugal from the British sphere of interest—whether radicals who were hemmed in by the British, or elements in the military that wanted to end British influence—but that kind of policy was never considered, and so the Continental powers would have to live with a moderate constitutional monarchy.

Castlereagh pressured King John to come back from Brazil, but warned the king that he should not rely on the Holy Alliance to "reconquer" Portugal by force, nor would Britain support reestablishing absolute authority. The king returned in July 1821 and accepted the new constitutional regime, but the domestic crisis remained. The counterrevolutionaries in the Court and liberals in the Cortes pulled in opposite directions. Castlereagh hewed to a middle line—he would not support an absolutist reaction by King John, but he would not be tied to the radical agenda of the liberals, even when they pressed for a British guarantee against the Holy Alliance and threatened to bind themselves to revolutionary Spain.[108]

The British waited for the conservative reaction within Portugal to strengthen. Emboldened by the French invasion of Spain in 1823, the son of King John, Dom Miguel, and a portion of the army rose up in May 1823. They compelled the king

[108] Webster, *The Foreign Policy of Castlereagh*, 250–55.

to dismiss the Cortes and withdraw the radical constitution based on the Spanish Constitution of 1812. The king immediately promised to grant another constitution (though he did not). He did appoint moderates to his cabinet, among them a pro-British foreign minister, who called on the British to help repress the reactionaries. Canning refused. Often portrayed as a defender of liberalism, Canning wrote in private that the counterrevolution "is just what one could wish." "Those revolutionists," he said, were "the scum of the earth" and "fierce, rascally, thieving, ignorant ragamuffins, hating England and labouring with all their might to entrap us into war."[109]

The Continental powers pressured King John to revoke his promise to issue a constitution. In the spring of 1824 he did issue a decree to reassemble the Cortes in the form of the ancien régime estate system, far from a democratic parliamentary system. Nevertheless, Dom Miguel used this as a trigger for a coup against his father. He assembled troops and surrounded the king's palace. The diplomatic corps forced their way in and insisted on the safety of the king. Eventually the standoff broke. Dom Miguel backed down and was sent into exile.

With the reactionaries now gone, there were two main factions in the Court: the pro-French and the pro-British. France's ambassador aggressively courted the king and promised French military aid. The French foreign minister let Britain know that the French ambassador in Portugal was taking unauthorized steps, and stated the French had no designs on Portugal. The French ambassador further got himself into trouble by approving of King John's summoning of the Cortes, which infuriated Spain and the Holy Alliance. He was sent on a leave of absence. Britain eventually sidelined the pro-French faction through diplomatic means. King John's "moderate" absolutism reigned, with British support.

The king never issued another constitution. When he died in 1826, his eldest son, Dom Pedro, ascended the throne. But Dom Pedro, king of Brazil and a genuine liberal, renounced the crown for himself (to keep the crown in Brazil) and gave it to his eight-year-old daughter. He also granted Portugal a moderately liberal constitution.[110] The monarchs on the Continent were infuriated. Metternich said, "It threatens with death and destruction the social order, for it would be difficult not to regard the revolution sanctioned in Portugal as a true unchaining [of forces]." He predicted a chain reaction with effects on Spain and from there on

[109] Joceline Bagot, ed., *George Canning and His Friends: Containing Hitherto Unpublished Letters, Jeux d'Esprit, Etc.*, vol. II (London: John Murray, 1909), 183.

[110] The liberalism of Dom Pedro is elaborated in Neill Macaulay, *Dom Pedro: The Struggle for Liberty in Brazil and Portugal, 1798–1834* (Durham: Duke University Press, 1986). The constitution was a modified version of Brazil's 1824 constitution. Knowing he had to give up Portugal to keep Brazil, he decided to strike a blow for liberty, though he deliberately devised the Portuguese constitution as less liberal, granting a house of lords for the hereditary nobility and absolute veto power for the king. Ibid., 191–92; Gabriel Paquette, "The Brazilian Origins of the 1826 Portuguese Constitution," *European History Quarterly* 41, no. 3 (2011): 444–71.

France, Italy, and all of the rest of Europe.[111] The Holy Alliance was in a bind. They had previously skirted debates over the merits of the liberal constitutions put forth by the revolutions in Spain and Italy by simply arguing that the compacts were not granted by the legitimate monarch and were therefore unacceptable. But in this case, it was the legitimate monarch who had granted the constitution.

Canning also was bothered by the upheaval. He thought the constitution was too liberal, even though it was less so than Britain's. He also had to reassure the other powers that Britain was not responsible for Dom Pedro's actions. But Canning desired to keep a policy of nonintervention in internal affairs, and besides, Britain was hardly in a position to reject the right of a king to issue a constitution.

The Continental powers warned Portugal not to engage in propaganda, particularly toward Spain. Metternich committed Austria to defending Spain if its internal security was menaced from Portugal. The Russian ambassador in France and the French prime minister thought Portuguese isolation would prompt civil upheaval, which could do away with the constitution and resolve the matter internally.[112] Just as Britain had made clear it would not tolerate attacks on Spain, it also stressed that Portuguese actions should not provide excuses for outside powers to intervene there. Nevertheless, Spain began to arm Portuguese dissidents and place them at the border. Portugal demanded that Spain disperse the dissidents, but to no avail. It appealed to Great Britain for help, and multiple incursions into Portugal finally compelled Canning to act. He decided to dispatch troops to Portugal to shore up the Portuguese regime. He made noise about protecting liberty, which was popular at home and alarmed the Continental powers, but the real motive for his intervention was to protect an ally.[113]

On the whole, then, the Continental powers supported absolutism in Portugal. Britain was content with a moderate absolutism. As long as Portuguese institutions were not too radical, Britain's concern was the perseverance of a Portugal that was allied with it. In the end, this required British support for a moderate constitutional monarchy, which Canning sold to great effect at home. Portugal was an important British ally, and if the past was prologue, one might expect the French to support whatever party, even radicals, that would undermine British influence there. But that did not happen because such geopolitical

---

[111] Temperley, *The Foreign Policy of Canning*, 367.

[112] Ibid., 370.

[113] His claim in his famous address to Parliament that if war came, Britain "could not . . . avoid seeing ranked under her banners all the restless and dissatisfied of any nation with which she might come into conflict" was seen by Continental powers as dangerously seditious. However, even in this address he specifically stated his intention was not to defend the domestic institutions of Portugal. R. Therry, ed., *The Speeches of the Right Honourable George Canning*, vol. 6 (London: James Ridgway & Sons, 1836), 90–91.

temptations were outweighed by the imperative to suppress revolutionary impulses.

Conclusion

The European domestic and international politics of the period analyzed in this chapter were fundamentally different from that described in Chapter 3. It is taken as given among historians that the nature of political contestation *within* regimes had changed; whether this was true *among* regimes is more controversial. But even those who accept that international politics had changed do not necessarily attribute this to the change that occurred within states. This, however, is the basic premise of my theory.

The domestic contagion effects theory asserts that leaders fear the spread of revolutionary contagion when there are significant revolutionary movements within their own borders. This is indeed what occurred. In all the great powers, in contrast to what we saw in Chapter 3 regarding the ancien régime, there was a significant revolutionary movement of the same character as revolutions abroad, and this was directly tied to their fear of contagion. Unlike in the previous era, the fear of contagion was no longer distant and hypothetical. The Semenovsky Revolt in Russia, the Cato Street Conspiracy in Britain, the assassination of the Duc de Berri in France—these events convinced rulers they had revolutionaries in their midst, and so had a direct bearing on their fear of contagion from the revolutions sweeping Europe.

To be sure, there were different perceptions of what was revolutionary. Britain and France did not regard regimes that instituted a conservative constitutional monarchy as inherently threatening, because from the British and French perspectives, that type of regime was not very revolutionary: both already had a monarchy limited by a constitution and a parliamentary body, although representation was extremely restricted. They were, however, alarmed by more radical revolutions—those that greatly expanded the "democratic" nature of the state— because this is what some of their domestic opposition was pressing for.

The domestic contagion effects theory also asserts that leaders' fear of contagion will be driven more by the characteristics of the host (the presence of preexisting revolutionary movements affiliated with the revolution) than by characteristics of the infecting agent (whether revolutionary states acted as platforms or as mere models). This chapter and the last provide solid evidence for this claim. The extent to which revolutionary states acted as platforms is held constant—the American Revolution, the Dutch Patriot Revolt, and the revolutions in Spain, Portugal, Naples, Piedmont, and Greece all acted as models and not platforms. And yet there is a striking difference in the fear of contagion that corresponds to the change in the opposition facing these powers. Even revolutions in peripheral places were a problem.

Great-power leadership worried the mere example of these revolutions could erode the order in their states and the legitimacy of their existing institutions and could inspire revolutionaries, regardless of any actions taken by the revolutionary state. The revolutionary wave spread, after all, without any revolutionary state spreading it.[114] Chateaubriand, arguing for French intervention in Spain, declared, "People say that [the Spanish] revolution is isolated, confined to the Peninsula whence it cannot spread. As if, in the state of civilization that the world has reached, there were any states in Europe that were strangers to each other!"[115] That these revolutionary states did not act as platforms made it more difficult for some leaders to justify intervention against them. Metternich hoped Naples would have a more belligerent foreign policy so that he would have a better excuse to crush its revolution.[116] Thus, the perceived problem with the revolutions of 1820–21 was not what they were *doing*, but their mere *existence*.

My theory also asserts that great-power fears of contagion would mean that a policy of domestic suppression alone would seem insufficient. Instead, states also would be hostile to a revolutionary state itself and would cooperate with states that had similar opposition movements. This is what occurred. Despite increased capacity to surveil and suppress their domestic opponents, leaders felt these domestic measures did not provide adequate regime security. States were uniformly hostile toward the revolutions of 1820–21.

The relatively more liberal Britain was no exception. It did not mind conservative constitutional regimes—those with a very restrictive franchise like its own—but it loathed the radical regimes. Even Canning, the supposed apostle of liberalism, expressed in private a preference for Continental authoritarianism. Rather than having "free" states established there, it was "much better and more convenient for us to have neighbors, whose Institutions cannot be compared with ours in point of freedom."[117] Canning, who opposed any parliamentary reform at home, found it useful to draw out how distinctly free Britain already was compared to the Continent.[118]

---

[114] For a work that chronicles these revolutions as a whole, see Richard Stites, *The Four Horsemen: Riding to Liberty in Post-Napoleonic Europe* (New York: Oxford University Press, 2014).

[115] Irene Collins, *Government and Society in France, 1814–1848* (New York: St. Martin's Press, 1970), 34.

[116] Schroeder, *Metternich's Diplomacy at Its Zenith*, 98–99.

[117] Harold Temperley and Lillian M. Penson, *Foundations of British Foreign Policy from Pitt to Salisbury: Documents Old and New* (London: Cambridge University Press, 1938), 87.

[118] On the other hand, conservative constitutional monarchies were preferred as an antidote to Jacobinism that could develop in the face of a strict absolutism. See Günther Heydemann, "The Vienna System Between 1815 and 1848 and the Disputed Anti-Revolutionary Strategy: Repression, Reforms, or Constitutions?," in *"The Transformation of European Politics, 1763–1848": Episode or Model in Modern History?*, eds. Peter Krüger and Paul W. Schroeder (New York: Palgrave Macmillan, 2002), 188–91.

Shared hostility toward revolutions did not prescribe the same strategy among all the great powers. They initially hoped that the revolution in Spain would burn itself out and the matter would be taken care of internally. France and Russia initially in Italy and Britain on the Iberian Peninsula pressed for reforms, a way of subverting the revolution that would take the more revolutionary aspects out of it. The more common strategy was to crush the revolution, or let it be crushed by another power.

We also see support for the claim that states with similar revolutionary movements and thus analogous fears of contagion will cooperate with each other, often overriding geopolitical temptations. There were undoubted moments of disagreement during this period, but they are often overstressed. Even if the great powers could agree on the undesirability of revolution, leaders could not always agree on a common solution, and this division led to the demise of regular conferences between the powers. There was rivalry and mistrust, despite similar aims. But to focus on this discord is to miss the forest for the trees, to focus on the conflict that did happen versus the (much greater) potential conflict that did not.

The contrast to how even more liberal revolutions were treated during the ancien régime is notable. In that period, revolutions were a means to exploit other powers, irrespective of ideological considerations. Competition between great powers did not vanish after the Napoleonic Wars, of course, but the level of cooperation is much more striking than any remaining conflict. These great powers could have attempted to exploit these revolutions for their geopolitical gain. France—a frustrated power and potential revisionist state—could have exploited liberal sympathy in Germany and Italy to weaken Austrian hegemony there. Russia faced similar temptations and could have cooperated with France in this regard. However, a Franco-Russian alliance, Metternich's worst nightmare, never materialized. Similarly, Britain could have used the revolution in the Two Sicilies to establish a British protectorate there.

Another remarkable change in international politics was that only a few years after the Napoleonic Wars, the great powers, particularly Britain, put aside their fears of French expansion and accepted France's occupation of Spain and the restoration of Ferdinand VII. The powers' initial resistance to the French invasion was not about resisting French expansion, but rather about concern that the French would get bogged down, perhaps provoking a revolution within France. France also could have exploited the revolutionary situation in Portugal to push Britain out, yet it did not do so.

Sometimes anti-revolutionary strategy and geopolitical aims conflicted fairly directly. The Prussian, lesser German, and Italian states' acceptance of Austrian hegemony out of concern for the general social order was a remarkable turn in international affairs. The Russian response to the Greek revolt was the most spectacular case of the divergence of anti-revolutionary strategy and geopolitical aims. Alexander had every incentive but the anti-revolutionary one to support the revolt, and his unparalleled position of power made it easy to act. Yet he acted to leave the despised Ottoman sultan in power.

The issue of great-power restraint stressed here rhymes with what Paul Schroeder has described as a "transformation" of European politics.[119] Unrestrained self-aggrandizement was replaced with a relatively cooperative international order. The question is why this happened. Schroeder is surely right that the simple distribution of power does little to explain the great powers' post-Napoleonic restraint, particularly in contrast to the previous period. The domestic contagion effects theory goes further and stresses that the fears of the great powers regarding revolutionary potential in their own societies and in Europe more generally helps undergird that transformation.

Schroeder's purely systemic argument plays down the notion that statesmen moderated their behavior to avoid internal revolution.[120] According to Schroeder, leaders did not fear revolution; they feared war. He goes so far as to say that the great powers were lax about stamping out revolutions, and "one of the distinguishing features of the Vienna era, compared to the earlier and later ones, was that it was relatively easy and safe to promote revolution."[121] He does not support his claim, and he cannot. Certainly, the weight of evidence provided here is to the contrary. As one leading scholar notes, nineteenth-century revolutionaries rotting in jail would surely be surprised to learn that it was "easy and safe" to promote revolution.[122]

The problem is Schroeder's overcommitment to separating issues of international conflict and domestic order. He claims that "when someone like Metternich said, as he did at every turn at every crisis, that the existence of the social order was at stake, he meant first and foremost [the] international order."[123] But Schroeder's own earlier work on Metternich shows clearly that Metternich saw war and revolution as two sides of the same coin, and he feared both.[124] For him, as for the other great powers, the domestic order was dependent on a stable

---

[119] Schroeder, *The Transformation of European Politics*. Schroeder's thesis has generated a significant debate. See the exchanges in *The American Historical Review* 97, no. 3 (1992); *The International History Review* 16, no. 4 (1994); *Orbis* 40, nos. 1–2 (1996); Peter Krüger and Paul W. Schroder, eds., *"The Transformation of European Politics, 1763–1848": Episode or Model in Modern History?* (New York: Palgrave Macmillan, 2002). Schroeder elaborates the restraint of Russia in Paul W. Schroeder, "Containment Nineteenth Century Style: How Russia Was Restrained," *The South Atlantic Quarterly* 82, no. 1 (1983).

[120] Paul W. Schroeder, "Did the Vienna Settlement Rest on a Balance of Power?," *The American Historical Review* 97, no. 3 (1992): 700; *The Transformation of European Politics*, 802.

[121] Schroeder, *The Transformation of European Politics*, 673.

[122] T. C. W. Blanning, "Paul W. Schroeder's Concert of Europe," *The International History Review* 16, no. 4 (1994): 711. For an overview of the repressive measures of European states, see Goldstein, *Political Repression*.

[123] Schroeder, *The Transformation of European Politics*, 802.

[124] Schroeder, *Metternich's Diplomacy at Its Zenith*, esp. 243.

international order.[125] Lose the latter, great-power leaders were convinced, and the former was likely to fall as well. As Richelieu stated to Metternich, "There is only one interest in European politics, that of maintaining social order. It is a question of preventing widespread conflict, and all the particular, undermining motives that so greatly occupied our diplomatic predecessors seem insignificant if they do not completely disappear before such a great interest."[126] Even when the possibility of war between great powers was not on the table, one could not flirt with the old policy of exploiting revolutions for geopolitical gain.

[125] Another theoretical perspective uses the same events as an example of how concert diplomacy is what established the restraint between the powers. Mitzen argues that public diplomacy was the means of restraint. Having to justify their foreign policies meant they "were able to cooperate publicly when they could not privately." The opposite was the case—they could cooperate privately, because they had the same counterrevolutionary goals, but the constitutional monarchies had a hard time cooperating publicly. The forum of the concert perhaps facilitated coordination, but it does not explain the underlying reason they wanted to cooperate. Jennifer Mitzen, *Power in Concert: The Nineteenth-Century Origins of Global Governance* (Chicago: The University of Chicago Press, 2013), 102–41; Jennifer Mitzen, "Reading Habermas in Anarchy: Multilateral Diplomacy and Global Public Spheres," *American Political Science Review* 99, no. 3 (2005): 412.

[126] Bertier de Sauvigny, *France and the European Alliance*, 100.

5

Communist and Fascist Revolutions in Europe

Revolutions in Russia and Italy toward the end of World War I and in its aftermath brought communists and fascists to power. There are several puzzles regarding the international reaction to these two revolutionary movements. First, there are large disparities in how these movements and the states that headed them were treated. While revolutionary communism generated huge anxiety abroad, revolutionary fascism did not. Likewise, a broadly status quo Soviet power sparked hostility among and was ostracized by Europe's status quo powers, whereas revisionist Italy was embraced by the same countries. This is puzzling from a balance-of-power perspective. Despite the need to balance against Germany, the Allies refused to align with the Soviets. Instead, they relied on Poland and lesser states, which exacerbated the problem of containing Germany rather than solving it.

What explains these puzzles? Other great powers feared revolutionary communism more than revolutionary fascism. But why was this the case? I argue that they made clearer analogies to their own domestic challengers, who looked far more like communists than like fascists. This is consistent with my theory that leaders will fear the contagion of revolutions when they have opposition movements of a similar type and that this fear of contagion will be independent of the policies of the revolutionary state attempting to promote revolution abroad. Communist/socialist movements were widespread, and there were corresponding widespread fears of contagion, which was not the case with fascism. The domestic contagion effects theory predicts that fear of contagion prompts hostility toward the revolutionary state and cooperation among states with similar movements. This did occur and explains these puzzles.

I examine the response to these revolutions by the principal powers of the region: Britain, France, Germany, Italy (in the case of the Russian Revolution), and the Soviet Union (in the case of the Italian fascist revolution). With each revolution, I assess the independent variables: how the revolutionary state served as a model and acted as a platform in spreading revolution abroad and whether there were significant revolutionary socialist or fascist movements in the great powers. I then assess the international effects of the revolution by analyzing the policies of these powers toward the revolutionary state and toward each other before and after the revolution. I find my theory is validated in many but by no

Revolutionary Contagion and International Politics. Chad E. Nelson, Oxford University Press. © Oxford University Press 2022. DOI: 10.1093/oso/9780197601921.003.0005

means all aspects. This chapter is a hard case for the domestic contagion effects theory in the sense that it covers a period of intense geopolitical competition that pushed states to act in ways that are counter to what my theory predicts, and this is indeed what happened to some extent with German policy in particular—Germany's aid to the Bolsheviks during the war, and its collaboration with them after.

The Russian Revolution

In 1917, Russia went from being ruled by the most autocratic regime in Europe to being ruled by one of the most radical socialist sects. The first stage of the 1917 revolution, the February Revolution, forced the tsar to abdicate, and two sources of power emerged. A committee from the Russian parliament, the Duma, created the Provisional Government, which was dominated by liberals. But the government had to contend with the soviets, or councils of workers and soldiers that had arisen in the revolt. In these soviets, socialist parties predominated. V. I. Lenin, the leader of the Bolsheviks, which was one faction in the split of the Marxist Russian Social Democratic Labor Party, called for the proletariat to overthrow the Provisional Government to create a socialist society. The Bolsheviks were increasingly influential in the soviets, and in the October Revolution their Red Guards marched on the Winter Palace and removed the Provisional Government. This began the Bolshevik struggle to stay in power. In a bitter civil war, they faced an array of enemies across the political spectrum, among ethnic groups in the former Russian Empire, and from outside, including the great powers. They had more or less prevailed by 1921.

Model

The Russian Revolution served as a model in several ways. It served as a model for overthrowing existing regimes, although its target, the tsarist regime, was uniquely autocratic. More striking was what the revolution was for. The February Revolution had established what seemed to be a democratic regime dominated by liberals. The October Revolution moved the regime to the far left. In a narrower historical context, the October Revolution served as a model of people rising up to take their country out of war, which was the demand of the Bolsheviks and central to their appeal at the time: peace, land, and bread. The most important way that the October Revolution served as a model was in the broad sense of bolstering common socialist aims. Those aims stretched from a radical redistribution of wealth and expansion of labor rights, at a minimum, to the abolition of capitalism and private property. The socialist movement across Europe, which had been pushing for these goals and gaining momentum, now had its example.

Whether the revolution was a direct model for other Marxists was a contentious theoretical debate. The revolution deviated from orthodox Marxism by having a socialist revolution in a backward agrarian economy. More importantly, Lenin's emphasis on the vanguard party that would shape the working class was controversial in socialist circles. Some thought that socialism could not emerge under a "dictatorship of the proletariat." Lenin would face resistance to his insistence that the Bolshevik Revolution served as a model for the tactics that should be used by other socialist movements.[1]

Platform

The Bolsheviks used their state to spread revolution, although this did not really pick up until around 1920, and that aim coexisted uneasily with other foreign policy goals. When the October Revolution succeeded, there was a notion among the Bolsheviks that the revolution had to spread, otherwise it would be crushed. Leon Trotsky, the first foreign minister, echoed a common sentiment when he declared at the outset of the revolution, "Either the Russian Revolution will create a revolutionary movement in Europe, or the European powers will destroy the Russian Revolution!"[2] But the new regime's first year was consumed with barely hanging on to power in Russia; it mostly relied on the revolution to spread organically. The People's Commissariat of Foreign Affairs (Narkomindel) in the new state established a department of international propaganda aimed primarily at the soldiers of the Central Powers, including prisoners of war and troops on the Eastern Front. They also helped set up communist parties in the former territories of the Russian Empire. The fall of the German and Austro-Hungarian Empires in November 1918, the subsequent communist insurrections, and the need to preempt a revival of the Second International prompted the Bolsheviks to more systematically organize their efforts at spreading revolution. In March 1919, the Bolshevik party began the first congress of the Comintern—a forum of Marxist parties from around the world, dominated by the Bolsheviks. Their aims were not modest: "We will facilitate and hasten the victory of the communist revolution in the entire world."[3] Although it was disorganized and a "negligible

[1] For a discussion of this debate, see Fernando Claudin, *The Communist Movement*, vol. 1 (New York: Monthly Review Press, 1975), 56–62.

[2] John Reed, *Ten Days That Shook the World* (New York: Boni and Liveright, 1919), 143.

[3] John Riddell, *Founding the Communist International: Proceedings and Documents of the First Congress, March 1919* (New York: Pathfinder Book, 1987), 222. Studies on the Comintern include Kevin McDermott and Jeremy Agnew, *The Comintern: A History of International Communism from Lenin to Stalin* (London: Macmillan, 1996); Silvio Pons, *The Global Revolution: A History of International*

force" in its first year of existence, the Comintern increasingly attempted to help organize and finance revolutionary parties abroad.[4] The Comintern gradually evolved from a forum of Marxist parties to essentially an arm of the Soviet state, although what became the Soviet Union always maintained the fiction that the Comintern was independent of the state.

The Bolsheviks' foreign policy has been characterized as a dual policy represented by the Comintern, which emphasized spreading world revolution, and the Narkomindel, which emphasized diplomacy.[5] There has been debate over the relative emphasis of these two policies in early Soviet foreign policy, but following the early Cold War, scholars have increasingly placed emphasis on the willingness of the Bolsheviks, and Lenin in particular, to cut deals with capitalist states to ensure the survival of the Soviet state and thus the revolution.[6] Lenin certainly had the goal of the socialist revolution spreading abroad.[7] But he was a pragmatist willing to bend the theory to new circumstances, to alter tactics and perhaps strategy to achieve an end goal in light of new realities. Given that the Bolsheviks considered the Soviet state to be surrounded by stronger imperialist countries bent on destroying them, Lenin said that "of course" they had to consider a possible alliance with one capitalist state against another.[8] But, as Lenin said, even if they did not have the coercive means to spread revolution abroad, "socialism has the force of example."[9]

Communism, 1917-1991 (New York: Oxford University Press, 2014), 7–75; Tim Rees and Andrew Thorpe, *International Communism and the Communist International* (Manchester: Manchester University Press, 1998); Claudin, *The Communist Movement*, vol. 1; Branko Lazitch and Milorad M. Drachkovitch, *Lenin and the Comintern*, vol. 1 (Stanford: Hoover Institution Press, 1972).

[4] Edward Hallett Carr, *The Bolshevik Revolution 1917-1923*, vol. 3 (Baltimore: Penguin Books, 1953), 170.
[5] Jon Jacobson, "On the Historiography of Soviet Foreign Relations in the 1920s," *The International History Review* 18, no. 2 (1996): 352.
[6] This is characteristic of the predominant works on early Soviet foreign policy: Richard K. Debo, *Revolution and Survival: The Foreign Policy of Soviet Russia 1917-1918* (Toronto: University of Toronto Press, 1979); Richard K. Debo, *Survival and Consolidation: The Foreign Policy of Soviet Russia 1918-1921* (Montreal: McGill-Queen's University Press, 1992); Teddy J. Uldricks, *Diplomacy and Ideology* (London: Sage Publications Ltd., 1979); Jon Jacobson, *When the Soviet Union Entered World Politics* (Berkeley: University of California Press, 1994); Michael Jabara Carley, *Silent Conflict: A Hidden History of Early Soviet-Western Relations* (Lanham: Rowman & Littlefield, 2014).
[7] Melograni argues that Lenin never wanted world revolution because he thought revolution elsewhere would marginalize the Bolsheviks and possibly prompt a counterrevolutionary invasion against the Soviet state, but this is a decidedly minority position, and contradicts Lenin's lifetime commitment to world revolution. Piero Melograni, *Lenin and the Myth of World Revolution* (Atlantic Highlands: Humanities Press International, Inc., 1989).
[8] Debo, *Survival and Consolidation*, 314.
[9] V. I. Lenin, *Collected Works*, vol. 31 (Moscow: Progress Publishers, 1965), 457.

Socialist Opposition Among the Great Powers

There were significant numbers of socialists, broadly construed, in each great power. Whether there was a significant revolutionary movement depends on whether we speak of these groups' ultimate goals or their short- and long-term tactics. All Marxists, for example, ultimately had revolutionary goals. Many thought they could only achieve these goals via a violent overthrow of the state but that the time for this was not yet ripe.[10] Others thought that the time for revolution, or at least mass strikes and other extralegal behavior, was now. The distribution of these groups varied by country. Britain had few Marxists and fewer ready for direct revolutionary action against the state. Italy probably had the most bellicose leftist movement, seemingly on the verge of revolution in 1914. Germany and France were closer to Italy on that spectrum.

This socialist movement was a long time coming. The late nineteenth and early twentieth centuries witnessed increasing industrialization, growing urbanization, and the emergence of a mass society, including mass production and mass media. Conventions were challenged in the arts and sciences, and also in politics. On the left, the socialist movement was characterized by its rejection of the individualism of liberalism, including its democratic/radical wing. Socialism was not a new political ideology, but in the late nineteenth century it became a major force, buoyed by rapid industrialization and the economic instability of the period. The socialist movement included anarchists and other strains, but Marxism in particular spread widely beginning in the 1880s. Marxism was in theory a revolutionary ideology, calling for the overthrow of existing regimes. However, many advocated working for change within existing political institutions, at least for the time being. The Second International, a loose coalition of socialist parties formed in 1889 and dominated by the German Social Democrats (SPD) and the French Section of the Worker's International (SFIO), promoted an extended period of accommodation and increasingly forced out of the organization those who called for revolutionary action. The expellees, in turn, denounced these organizations' moderation.[11]

---

[10] A prominent example is Karl Kautsky, one of the leaders of German Marxism. See John H. Kautsky, *Karl Kautsky: Marxism, Revolution and Democracy* (New Brunswick: Transaction Publishers, 1994), esp. 71.

[11] A minority of socialists abandoned even the aim of revolution in favor of reform, most notably Edward Bernstein in his work *Evolutionary Socialism*. Peter Gay, *The Dilemma of Democratic Socialism: Edward Bernstein's Challenge to Marx* (New York: Columbia University Press, 1952); Julius Braunthal, *History of the International*, vol. 1 (New York: Frederick A. Praeger, 1967), 255–84. Reformists were a minority, but the majority who rejected reformism in theory actually practiced it. Although the term "communism" is sometimes used to distinguish revolutionaries from the moderate/reformist "socialists," this was in development in the period discussed in this chapter. Lenin had revived the use of the term "communism" during World War I to distinguish his hard-line brand of socialism from others. By the late 1920s, what it meant to be a communist was someone who toed the Moscow line. In the period covered here, leaders would refer to their radical socialists, and

In Germany, the SPD was not only the largest socialist party in Europe, but the largest political party in Germany by far, capturing about 35 percent of the vote in the landmark 1912 election.[12] The SPD prior to World War I exemplified socialists attempting to work within the system. The party had been repressed under Bismarck, but the anti-socialist laws were not renewed in 1890, and the SPD emerged as a legitimate political party. The party platform rejected direct revolutionary action, not wanting a reinstatement of the anti-socialist laws. The 1905 revolution in Russia inspired the left within the SPD to push for a more revolutionary direction, to "act in the Russian manner," but most socialist leaders thought that those who urged revolutionary tactics, such as Rosa Luxemburg, were inappropriately applying the Russian situation to Germany, where they could work through existing parliamentary institutions. There was an increasing number of SPD leaders, though, who were considering extraparliamentary actions such as mass strikes to democratize the voting system.[13]

France also had a significant socialist movement. The SFIO grew in the prewar years, capturing about 17 percent of the vote in the 1914 election.[14] Like the SPD, it worked within existing political institutions. Marxists in France faced greater competition from other socialists, and socialists had more competition from the democratic radicals. There were also revolutionaries in other left-wing groups. The General Confederation of Labor (CGT) in France was the opposite of most leftist organizations—the leadership was much more radical than its members.

In Italy, socialists were a significant force. The Italian Socialist Party (PSI) received 17.6 percent of the vote in the 1913 elections.[15] Rather than drifting in a more conservative direction in the prewar years, it was radicalizing. The "Red Week" of June 1914, where there were widespread riots and strikes, was one

---

Bolsheviks, as socialists, as would the Bolsheviks themselves. I assess the broad socialist ideological "family." For these movements in this period, see Albert S. Lindemann, *A History of European Socialism* (New Haven: Yale University Press, 1983), 133–219; Donald Sassoon, *One Hundred Years of Socialism: The West European Left in the Twentieth Century* (New York: I. B. Tauris, 1996), 5–31. For the Second International, see James Joll, *The Second International 1889–1914* (London: Weidenfeld and Nicolson, 1955); Julius Braunthal, *History of the International*, vol. 1, 195–384.

[12] Chris Cook and John Paxton, *European Political Facts, 1900–1996* (New York: St. Martin's Press, 1998), 206. For reviews of the socialist movement in Germany, see Gary P. Steenson, *"Not One Man! Not One Penny!": German Social Democracy, 1863–1914* (Pittsburgh: University of Pittsburgh Press, 1981); Heinrich Potthoff and Susanne Miller, *The Social Democratic Party of Germany*, trans. Martin Kane (Bonn: Dietz, 2006), 50–77.

[13] Jens-Uwe Guettel, "Reform, Revolution, and the 'Original Catastrophe': Political Change in Prussia and Germany on the Eve of the First World War," *The Journal of Modern History* 91, no. 2 (2019).

[14] Cook and Paxton, *European Political Facts*, 203. For an overview, see Robert Wohl, *French Communism in the Making, 1914–1924* (Stanford: Stanford University Press, 1966), 1–82.

[15] Cook and Paxton, *European Political Facts*, 222. For an overview, see Alexander De Grand, *The Italian Left in the Twentieth Century: A History of the Socialist and Communist Parties* (Bloomington: Indiana University Press, 1989), 15–30.

indication of that radicalism. There were also revolutionary syndicalists and anarchists.[16]

In Britain, the attraction to Marxist socialism was markedly smaller.[17] The Labor Party was a distant third among the three major political parties, although this was in good measure due to voting restrictions on the working class.[18] Although Britain is somewhat of an outlier regarding revolutionary socialists, it was not an exception to the increasing labor strife that afflicted all the great powers. Hundreds of thousands of workers took part in strikes that were violently suppressed. One historian notes, "England was not perhaps on the brink of a revolution as understood on the Continent. British labor did not revolt against patriotism in the name of class loyalty nor did it seek to abolish the state or even capitalism. But in the pursuit of more restricted objectives—recognition of the unions, increase of wages, reduction of hours it was making preparations by the employment of a new strategy to involve England in a class war on a scale in excess of anything previously witnessed."[19]

Large socialist movements existed in all the great powers, although their commitment to the violent overthrow of existing regimes varied. The Second International determined in 1907 that in the event of war, it should take advantage of "the economic and political crisis created by the war to arouse the population and hasten the overthrow of capitalist rule."[20] However, when World War I came, the socialists shirked from the task. The divides between left, right, and center factions within the socialists widened. Radicals supported a mass strike, the right were unabashed patriots, and many of the parties' leadership supported the generally pro-war membership.[21] As the war continued, more gravitated toward the anti-war position.

While many of the socialists had determined they would work within the system, they had not dropped their revolutionary goals. Prudent leaders should assume that the tactics of radical groups can change rapidly depending on the situation, and probably they should care at least as much about challengers' goals as about their tactics. Thus, I assume that leaders' fears of contagion are driven

---

[16] Carl Levy, "Italian Anarchism, 1870–1926," in *For Anarchism: History, Theory, and Practice*, ed. David Goodway (New York: Routledge, 1989): 25–78; Charles Lloyd Bertrand, "Revolutionary Syndicalism in Italy, 1912–1922," PhD thesis, University of Wisconsin, 1969.

[17] For an overview of the radical left in Britain, see Walter Kendall, *The Revolutionary Movement in Britain, 1900–21: The Origins of British Communism* (London: Weidenfeld & Nicolson, 1969); Stanley Pierson, *Marxism and the Origins of British Socialism* (Ithaca: Cornell University Press, 1973); Keith Laybourn and Dylan Murphy, *Under the Red Flag* (Thrupp: Sutton Publishing, 1999), 21–39.

[18] Michael Mann, *The Sources of Social Power*, vol. 2 (New York: Cambridge University Press, 1993), 634.

[19] Élie Halévy, *A History of the English People in the Nineteenth Century*, vol. 6, book II (New York: Peter Smith, 1952), 482.

[20] Carl E. Schorske, *German Social Democracy, 1905–1917: The Development of the Great Schism* (Cambridge, MA: Harvard University Press, 1955), 83.

[21] Italy was an exception in this regard.

not just by those who are already employing revolutionary tactics, but also by those who have revolutionary aims. By this measure, Germany, Italy, and France clearly meet the threshold of "significant revolutionary movement" that the domestic contagion effects theory argues will trigger fears of revolutionary contagion. The British case is more ambiguous. A significant number of people wanted to dismantle the aristocratic class that was still very much running the country, and the amount of labor unrest, especially before and after the war, was unprecedented. But in their means and in their aims they were generally more moderate than parallel groups on the Continent. For this reason I categorize Britain as "ambiguous."

International Relations Prior to the Russian Revolution

To assess whether the Russian Revolution disrupted the patterns of conflict and cooperation that existed before the Revolution, I briefly review those patterns. In short, Russia, prior to the Revolution, was no longer in an alliance with the other autocratic powers, Germany and Austria. It was fighting a war against those powers in alliance with France, Britain, and Italy.

After its unification in 1871, Germany had, under Bismarck, pursued a strategy of isolating France and preventing the formation of a coalition against Germany. Bismarck resuscitated the old conservative grouping of monarchs, the Three Emperors League of Austria-Hungary, Germany, and Russia, though there were strains between Austria-Hungary and Russia, particularly concerning the Balkans. Germany signed a formal alliance with Austria, the Dual Alliance, in 1879, and Italy joined in 1882 to make it the Triple Alliance. Germany also had signed the Reinsurance Treaty in 1887 with Russia, which pledged neutrality if the other party went to war. France was thus isolated. However, Kaiser Wilhelm dismissed Bismarck and shortly thereafter did not renew the Reinsurance Treaty in 1890. A direct consequence of this was the alliance between republican France and autocratic Russia by a series of agreements signed in 1892–94.

Britain stood at a distance from these blocs, enjoying its "splendid isolation," though it made up with its principal adversaries of the nineteenth century at the turn of the new century. After almost going to war in 1898, it resolved its major differences with France in the Entente Cordial in 1904. In 1907, the Anglo-Russian Convention resolved many of their imperial disputes. This was specifically motivated by the increasing friction between Britain and Germany.

At the outbreak of World War I, Britain was not obligated to side with France and Russia, but did so. The Triple Alliance that bound Germany, Austria-Hungary, and Italy was a defensive alliance, and on the grounds that Italy's allies had not provided it with prior consultation, Italy took a position of neutrality, and then assessed which side would offer greater territorial spoils. The Allies convinced Italy to join them in the Treaty of London in 1915 by promising it territorial concessions in Austria and the Balkans. Thus, on the eve of the Russian Revolution, Russia, Britain, Italy, and France were in an alliance at war with Germany and Austria-Hungary.

Predictions

Given the assessment of the socialist movements in the great powers, the theory predicts there would be relatively uniform hostility toward the Russian Revolution. Whether Britain had a significant revolutionary socialist movement was ambiguous, though I assumed rulers would in that case err on the side of caution and believe they had a significant movement. From that perspective, one would expect leaders to be hostile toward the revolution. Hostility toward Russia would constitute a departure from alignments prior to the Revolution, as seen in Table 5.1.

Alternative theories have different expectations. Some geopolitical pressures in this case push in the opposite direction of the domestic contagion effects theory's prediction. In the immediate context of the war, one might expect that the attitude toward the communists would be dictated by war demands: Germans would be favorable to the Bolsheviks as long as they kept Russia out of the war. Likewise, the Allies would be hostile toward the Bolsheviks if they kept Russia out of the war or were generally pro-German. In the longer term, though, one might expect a reversion to the pattern that existed before the Revolution, simply because of the need to contain German power. In other words, balance-of-power

Table 5.1 Response to the Russian Revolution

Great Power	Stance Toward Russia Prior to Revolution	Significant Revolutionary Socialist Movement?	Prediction of Stance Toward Revolutionary Russia Given Revolutionary Movement	Outcome
Britain	Aligned with	Ambiguous	Hostile	Hostile
France	Aligned with	Yes	Hostile	Hostile
Germany	Hostile	Yes	Hostile	Sometimes supportive, sometimes hostile
Italy	Aligned with	Yes	Hostile	Hostile

pressures would cause a reconstitution of the Franco-British-Russian alignment against Germany.

We will see that the alternative theories have some merit. But the expectations of my theory are also validated, even in the face of significant geopolitical pressure. The Germans initially aided the Bolsheviks during the war, though there were considerable disagreements among themselves about this policy. The Allied powers were hostile toward the Bolsheviks, even when the Bolsheviks were reaching out to them because of their conflict with Germany. Allied intervention and hostility persisted after the war. An even bigger consequence for international politics than intervention in the Russian Revolution was the creation of a postwar system that had lost Russia as a balancer against Germany, in large part because of the hostility of the Allied powers due to contagion concerns. In what follows, I will illustrate that these outcomes were motivated in part by the theory of this book.

International Relations of the Russian Revolution, 1917–25

British, French, and Italian hostility toward the Russian Revolution was relatively constant, whereas Germany's hostility ebbed and flowed. I track the policies toward the Russian Revolution in several stages: the initial response toward the upheavals in Russia prior to the October Revolution; the chance for the Allies to reach out to the Bolsheviks while they faced a German invasion; Allied military intervention, both during and after World War I; the Polish situation; and policies after Allied military intervention had ended.

German and Allied Response to the Upheaval in Russia Prior to the October Revolution

Although the unfolding of the Russian Revolution was largely a result of state collapse under the strain of war and subsequent domestic developments, the foreign policy of Germany played a role. This was a part of a broader German strategy to incite chaos in the Allied powers, weaken their war effort, and take one of the powers out of the conflict. In what has been described as "by far the most elaborate strategy of sabotage on an international level ever conceived to that point in history," Germany aided insurrectionists from India to Ireland in the British, French, and Russian Empires.[22]

---

[22] Stanley G. Payne, *Civil War in Europe, 1905–1949* (New York: Cambridge University Press, 2011), 19. For a brief overview, see Fritz Fischer, *Germany's Aims in the First World War* (New York: W. W. Norton and Company, 1967), 120–54.

In the Russian Empire, Germany encouraged nationalist separatists, such as Finnish and Ukrainian movements, as well as social revolutionaries. Their goal in encouraging the social revolutionaries was, at least initially, to sow instability to convince the tsar to sue for peace. But the tsar was not amenable, and the policy became one of either causing havoc or replacing the existing government with one willing to sue for peace. This was a policy shrouded in secrecy for understandable reasons. A key intermediary was Alexander Helphand, a German Social Democrat of Russian origin, who had contact with revolutionaries in Russia. German diplomats were taking a calculated risk in encouraging the leftists in Russia. The potential advantages of ending the war on their terms, though, overwhelmed their apprehensions. After Helphand's failure to ignite a general strike and revolution in January 1916, State Secretary for Foreign Affairs Gottlieb von Jagow, an aristocrat who was opposed to the policy of revolutionary provocation, reasserted himself. The Foreign Ministry significantly reduced its support for fomenting revolution, although it continued to back separatist movements.[23]

The Russian Revolution proceeded despite the Germans' partial abandonment of this policy. The Germans were apprehensive, however, that the Provisional Government might renew Russia's war effort. One German diplomat put forth the options: if Germany thought it could not sustain the war effort, it could try to negotiate with the Provisional Government, but if it continued the war, the right step was to "create the greatest possible degree of chaos in Russia" by supporting the extremists.[24] This is what the Germans did. The German General Staff, using their connections with Helphand, assisted in returning Lenin to Russia, putting him on a train and transporting him from his exile in Switzerland across Germany, after which he could continue on to Petrograd to take part in the October Revolution; they also provided money to the Bolsheviks.[25] Lenin was an outspoken opponent of the war. He soon was in Russia demanding that the Provisional Government immediately sue for peace. The Germans thought that Lenin would be unable to hold power without their support, and that given the narrow base of Bolshevik support, the

---

[23] Z. A. B. Zeman, *Germany and the Revolution in Russia, 1915–1918* (London: Oxford University Press, 1958), 23; Z. A. B. Zeman and W. B. Scharlau, *The Merchant of Revolution* (London: Oxford University Press, 1965), 190.

[24] Zeman, *Germany and the Revolution in Russia*, 31.

[25] There is still controversy over the extent of German money provided to Russian revolutionaries. The materials the Provisional Government released to prove the Bolsheviks were foreign agents contain no evidence themselves of funds being transferred from Germany to the Bolsheviks, but there is other evidence of extensive financial support. See Sean McMeekin, *The Russian Revolution: A New History* (New York: Basic Books, 2017), 129–36, Semion Lyandres, *The Bolsheviks' "German Gold" Revisited: An Inquiry into the 1917 Accusations* (Pittsburg: University of Pittsburg Press, 1995).

Bolsheviks would never be able to control the chaos and thereby present a threat to Germany.[26]

The Allied response to the tsar's abdication and the Provisional Government (initially dominated by liberals) depended on the new government's position toward the war. World War I was a stalemate at the time, but it would not be if Russia took itself out of the war, or was taken out of the war due to domestic chaos. Just as the Germans were apprehensive about the new government in Russia reinvigorating the war effort, there were hopes on the Allied side. But those hopes turned to doubts given the domestic developments in Russia. Foreign Minister Pavel Milyukov was forced to resign in May after protests against his vow to continue the Allies' war aims. The Mensheviks and social revolutionaries who dominated the Petrograd soviet demanded that the Provisional Government end the war. The Allies pressed Russia to continue. The Provisional Government split the difference: they vowed to continue a defensive war where the goal was peace without annexations and indemnities.

The increasing radicalization of the revolution was tied to the question of whether Russia would stay in the war, since leftists wanted to get out of the war. The events in Russia were largely emboldening those abroad who simply wanted out of the war rather than a new political system, though there were hints of the latter as well. Anti-war socialists in Britain, Italy, Germany, and France all rejoiced at the progress.[27] In Germany, the Independent Social Democratic Party, the USPD, split from the SPD in April 1917 over the SPD's continued support for the war. Most of the prewar radicals moved to this party. With the exception of Russia and Italy, though, the anti-war stance was still a minority position in the socialist parties.

The Provisional Government attempted to organize a conference of European socialist parties to outline the end of the war, and leaders' reaction to the conference showed their concerns about the demonstration effects of the Russian Revolution.[28] France initially wanted to send pro-war socialists to convince the Russian socialists to stay in the war. President Raymond Poincaré met with General Pétain and asked him whether he could keep the army in control if the French delegates went to the socialist conference. Pétain replied that he could not. When Poincaré pointed out that if the Russian front collapsed, the Germans would be able to move seventy-five divisions to the Western Front, Pétain responded. "Yes,

---

[26] Wayne C. Thompson, "Voyage on Uncharted Seas: Kurt Riezler and German Policy Towards Russia, 1914–1918," *East European Quarterly* 12, no. 2 (1980): 180.

[27] Stephen White, "Soviets in Britain: The Leeds Convention of 1917," *International Review of Social History* 19, no. 2 (1974): 165–93; Carr, *The Bolshevik Revolution*, vol. 3, 19; Philippe Bernard and Henri Dubeif, *The Decline of the Third Republic, 1914–1938*, trans. Anthony Forster (New York: Cambridge University Press, 1985), 55; Wohl, *French Communism in the Making*, 86.

[28] See Rex A. Wade, *The Russian Search for Peace* (Stanford: Stanford University Press, 1969).

but the danger of an attack by 75 German divisions is distinctly less serious than the demoralization of our army."[29] France refused to allow its socialists to attend the conference. At the time, there were strikes in the munitions industries and an outburst of mutinies in the army, some even forming soldiers' councils to march on the capital. They seemed to spread "like fire in dry prairie grass."[30] Poincaré noted in his diary that soldiers cried: "Down with the war. Long live the Russian Revolution."[31] Italy had the same concerns that the Russian Revolution would embolden their anti-war socialists.[32]

Germany and the Allies' Hostility Toward the October Revolution

The October Revolution was met with immediate hostility among the Allies. They agreed not to recognize the new regime, and the British and French went about attempting to unite and aid the anti-Bolshevik forces. The embargo that had been placed on the Central Powers was extended to include Russia. The expectation that the Bolsheviks would not last long started to give way when they realized the fragmented state of the opposition, something that would constantly plague Allied intervention in Russia.

For the Germans, it was a realization of their foreign policy aims toward Russia. They negotiated a ceasefire with the new regime in December 1917. This peace, though, was not permanent. They demanded extensive territorial concessions from the Bolsheviks, and resumed their invasion to get their terms.

The Bolsheviks had a vigorous debate about what their policy toward the outside world should be. Immediately upon gaining power, they had issued decrees calling not only for peace but also for the working classes of the world to liberate those who labor. When negotiations with Germany began, some, such as Lenin, wanted peace even at the very heavy price of losing key parts of the former Russian Empire. Others, such as Bukharin, wanted to engage in a revolutionary war of liberation. They instead picked Trotsky's middle way of "no war, no peace," an attempt to drag out negotiations to give time for a revolution to occur in Germany. This strategy was not working, however. The Germans continued to march east, and there was a faction in the German government pushing for the overthrow of the Bolsheviks.[33] Lenin used all his powers of persuasion and the threat of stepping down to convince his fellow Bolsheviks to

---

[29] Wohl, *French Communism in the Making*, 92.

[30] Ibid., 88.

[31] Ibid.

[32] Giorgio Pettrachi, *La Russia Rivoluzionaria nella politica italiana: Le relazioni Italo-Sovietiche, 1917–1925* (Rome: Guis. Laterza & Figli, 1982), 10–11.

[33] Fischer, *Germany's Aims*, 502.

come to a deal with Germany, known as the Treaty of Brest-Litovsk.[34] It was a severe peace deal—Soviet Russia agreed to relinquish Finland, the Baltic states, Belarus, and Ukraine in return for staying alive. The Germans (or their proxies) crushed socialist forces in these places. For example, they decisively intervened in the Finnish Civil War against the Reds and in favor of the Whites, and they supported a right-wing coup against the socialist republic in Ukraine.

What was the Allied response to the standoff between the Bolsheviks and the Germans? The Bolsheviks had done plenty to earn the animus of the Allied powers. They were an ideological rival, and they preached revolution. They encouraged soldiers to turn the war into civil war by turning their weapons against their true enemy, the capitalist order. In early 1918, the Bolsheviks nationalized banks and industries and announced they would not be paying off the tsar's debts. This particularly hit the French, who had extensive investments in Russia. They also published the Allies' secret treaties that contained their war aims. This was particularly damaging in Italy, where the government's cynical motives for entering the war were revealed.

But there is one reason the Allies might have nevertheless reached out to the Bolsheviks: they could be an ally against Germany. The Bolsheviks' most proximate threat was the invading German armies. For this reason, the Bolsheviks were reaching out to the Allies.[35] This was true even after the Treaty of Brest-Litovsk and up until mid-May 1918 because the peace between Russia and Germany was uncertain.[36]

There were figures in both the British and French governments that wanted to reach an accommodation with the Bolsheviks rather than throw them to the Germans by remaining indifferent. In the words of an American who had Prime Minister David Lloyd George's ear, "Let's make them our Bolsheviks."[37] In a remarkable two-day discussion in the British War Cabinet over whether to grant a British emissary the authority to come to an understanding with the Bolsheviks, Lloyd George, a member of the Liberal Party, had said, "My view is that Russia is our most powerful ally now in Germany." This flabbergasted Robert Cecil, British undersecretary of state for foreign affairs, who responded that it was a "dangerous thing to suppose revolution was 'catching' only in Germany."[38] The

---

[34] For details of the negotiations between the parties and the debate among the Bolsheviks about how to respond, see Borislav Chernev, *Twilight of Empire: The Brest-Litovsk Conference and the Remaking of East-Central Europe, 1917–1918* (Toronto: University of Toronto Press, 2017); John W. Wheeler-Bennett, *Brest-Litovsk, the Forgotten Peace, March 1918* (London: Macmillan & Co, 1963); Debo, *Revolution and Survival*, 45–169.

[35] Trotsky told the British unofficial representative that the German danger was uppermost in his mind, and "now is the big opportunity for the allied governments." Lenin was even willing to accept military support. R. H. Bruce Lockhart, *Memoirs of a British Agent* (London: Putnam, 1934), 228; Carr, *The Bolshevik Revolution*, vol. 3, 58.

[36] Jonathan D. Smele, *The "Russian" Civil Wars, 1916–1926* (London: Hurst & Company, 2015), 46.

[37] Lloyd C. Gardner, *Safe for Democracy* (Oxford: Oxford University Press, 1984), 158.

[38] Ibid., 166.

Conservative members of Lloyd George's coalition cabinet resisted, and nothing was pursued.

Discussions of rapprochement got further in France. The Ministry of War advocated a limited rapprochement with the Bolsheviks since they were the only unifying force in Russia that could attempt to resist Germany and provide a balance of power in Europe. The French Foreign Ministry, however, successfully resisted this approach. They argued that anti-Bolshevik factions in Russia would be lost to the Germans or wiped out if there was a policy of rapprochement with the Bolsheviks, and France needed to look beyond the narrow military advantage to the threat the Bolsheviks posed to France's political and economic interests.[39]

The Italians were more straightforwardly counterrevolutionary, never considering a rapprochement with the Bolsheviks, afraid as they were about the demonstration effects the Bolsheviks were having in Italy.[40] The architect of Italian foreign policy, the foreign minister, could get along with different regime types, but he "saw in the Soviet Union not a national government, but an ideological statement; not a potential friend, or even a rival, but a mortal enemy."[41]

In sum, the Allies never seriously pursued a policy of rapprochement with the Bolsheviks, and for a brief period both the Germans and the Allies were on the same side against them.

Allied Military Intervention in the Civil War and the German Response

The Allied policy would be one of basic hostility toward the Bolshevik government through the duration of the war, using both covert and overt means to destroy the regime. They poured money into anti-Bolshevik groups such as the Volunteer Army and the Union for Defense of Motherland and Liberty. Their diplomats participated in a variety of covert activities designed to bring down the regime.[42] And they began to militarily intervene in the Russian Civil War. British, French, and Italian forces, along with the Americans and the Japanese,

---

[39] Michael Jabara Carley, "The Origins of the French Intervention in the Russian Civil War, January–May 1918: A Reappraisal," *The Journal of Modern History* 48, no. 3 (1976): 438.

[40] Pettrachi, *La Russia Rivoluzionaria nella politica italiana*, 33, 44.

[41] H. James Burgwyn, *The Legend of the Mutilated Victory* (Westport: Greenwood Press, 1993), 319.

[42] For some of the discussion on the covert means, see Robert Service, *Spies and Commissars* (New York: Public Affairs, 2012); John W. Long, "Searching for Sidney Reilly: The Lockhart Plot in Revolutionary Russia, 1918," *Europe-Asia Studies* 47, no. 7 (1995); Gordon Brook-Shepherd, *Iron Maze: The Western Secret Service and the Bolsheviks* (London: Macmillan, 1998); Jonathan Schneer, *The Lockhart Plot: Love, Betrayal, Assassination and Counterrevolution in Lenin's Russia* (New York: Oxford University Press, 2020)

sent troops to northern Russia, Siberia, Vladivostok, the Caucasus, Ukraine, and the Baltics.[43]

What were the motives of this military intervention? The Allies themselves and an older generation of scholarship emphasized the need, at least during the war, to reconstitute the Eastern Front against the Germans. This was a better way to sell what was going on to a domestic audience, and indeed this was a factor, but there was more to it than that. An Allied military intervention in northern Russia, for example, was ostensibly to safeguard military stockpiles there, but it also provided a secure base from which anti-Bolshevik forces could operate. France used intervention as a means to secure some of its tsarist investments. Their goal, though, was not just to secure investments, but to overthrow the Russian regime. This goal was due in good part to ideological hostility, not in any abstract sense, but in the sense that Bolshevism broadly represented a dangerous ideology that could spread to subvert the social and political order within France.[44] Allied overt operations were an extension of those covert ones. There were multiple reasons for intervention, but the fact that their activities continued after they thought they could reconstitute the Eastern Front, and even after the war ended, is evidence of their counterrevolutionary aims.

One would think that the Germans, having succeeded in taking the Russians out of the war and having cut off a good chunk of the territory of the former Russian Empire, and facing the fight of their lives on the Western Front, would be satisfied with the east and turn their attention west. This was indeed the tactic of Foreign Secretary Richard von Kühlmann, who had stated, despite the strangeness of conservative Germany supporting a socialist government in another country: "Bolshevik rule means the weakness of Russia, and we still have a great interest in that."[45] However, there was considerable pressure within the German government—from German diplomats in Moscow, from the military, and from "the entire German Right"—to abandon Germany's policy of supporting the Bolsheviks and to reach out to counterrevolutionary groups.[46]

These tensions would coexist in German policy. General Erich Ludendorff promoted a conservative Russia with Ukraine intact and allied with Germany— an authoritarian "world state structure."[47] He and others in the German government wanted to outbid the West in their courting of counterrevolutionaries

---

[43] For an overview, see Ian C. D. Moffat, *The Allied Intervention in Russia, 1918–1920* (New York: Palgrave Macmillan, 2015).

[44] This is emphasized by Michael Jabara Carley, *Revolution and Intervention: The French Government and the Russian Civil War* (Kingston: McGill-Queen's University Press, 1983).

[45] Konrad H. Jarausch, "Cooperation or Intervention? Kurt Riezler and the Failure of German Ostpolitik 1918," *Slavic Review* 31, no. 2 (1972): 385.

[46] Ibid., 386.

[47] Quoted in Adam Tooze, *The Deluge: The Great War, America and the Remaking of the Global Order, 1916–1931* (New York: Penguin Books, 2014), 161.

rather than side with the Bolsheviks. This was not the fragmentation of the Russian Empire and the turn to the Western Front envisioned by Kühlmann. The kaiser agreed with Ludendorff's aims, although he wanted to uphold Brest-Litovsk temporarily. German diplomats in Russia toed the official line of supporting the Bolsheviks, but they were authorized to make covert contact with and fund counterrevolutionary groups—the very groups the Allies were also in contact with.[48] They promised these groups that the Brest-Litovsk treaty applied only to the Bolsheviks, and could be revised or revoked if there was a new regime. Ludendorff prepared troops to march against the Allied position in Murmansk, Russia, via Petrograd. He planned on crushing the Bolsheviks, but he was temporarily dissuaded by opposition to the plan in the German government and the Reichstag majority, who wanted to keep Russia weak and focus on events in the West. The failure of the German offensive on the Western Front in the spring and summer of 1918 suddenly put an end to the German regime and their ostpolitik plans.[49] As Trotsky said, "It is absolutely certain that at the time of the October Revolution, if we had had to contend with a victorious Germany, with peace concluded in Europe, Germany would not have failed to crush us."[50] Ironically, the Allied actions on the Western Front and the promise of a larger American involvement caused the Germans to sue for peace, which saved the Russian Revolution by preventing the Germans from crushing it.[51] Just before the Germans signed the November armistice, they severed ties with the Soviets and expelled the Soviet diplomats, who had been attempting to foment revolution in Germany.

Given the pressures of fighting the biggest war the world had ever seen, one might expect that all policy would be directed toward winning the war and that the domestic contagion effects theory's emphasis on contagion concerns causing hostility toward the Bolsheviks would count for little. We do see evidence of that—Germany aiding revolution is not what my theory would predict. But even in the German case, we see hesitation and attempts at counterrevolutionary policies. And the Allied intervention in Russia was clearly not only about reconstituting a front against Germany. The Allies did not seriously attempt a rapprochement with the Bolsheviks when the Germans were invading Russia, even though the Bolsheviks were reaching out to the Allies, and continued to fight them even after they gave up on reconstituting the Eastern Front. This tells us their policy was motivated by more than defeating the Germans.

---

[48] Thompson, "Voyage on Uncharted Seas," 184.

[49] Ludendorff was still considering military action in Russia—"Operation Schlusstein"—until September 1918. Martin Kitchen, *The Silent Dictatorship: The Politics of the German High Command Under Hindenburg and Ludendorff, 1916–1918* (New York: Holmes & Meier Publishers, 1976), 225–26.

[50] Leon Trotsky, *Problems of Civil War* (New York: Pathfinder Press, 1970), 18.

[51] Brian Pearce, *How Haig Saved Lenin* (London: Macmillan, 1987).

As the war ended, there was a wave of upheaval that spurred revolutions throughout Europe. The Austro-Hungarian Empire disintegrated and the Weimar Republic replaced the German Empire. There was the Spartacus uprising in Berlin, and the Bavarian Soviet Republic was briefly established. In Hungary, the communist Béla Kun briefly established the Hungarian Soviet Republic before the Czechs and Romanians crushed it with the aid of France. In Vienna, there was a workers uprising.[52] All European countries faced severe economic problems and an influx of demobilized troops, which led to a corresponding upsurge of radicalism among labor groups and political parties. Although counterrevolutionaries repressed leftist revolutions, Europe seemed to be a boiling cauldron. In a memorandum to the Paris Peace Conference, Lloyd George said, "The whole of Europe is filled with the spirit of revolution."[53]

In the aftermath of the war, continued Allied intervention in Russia was more blatantly counterrevolutionary. The Soviets, fearing what the Allies could do with a free hand, proposed peace negotiations with a wide array of concessions, including the payment of Russian debts, territorial concessions, and a promise to cease the export of revolutionary propaganda. "The only real question," Soviet diplomat Maxim Litvinov said, was whether the Allies "would allow the Soviet Government to exist. If they would, an agreement would not be difficult to reach."[54] Bolshevik sincerity was not put to the test, as the Allies spurned these offers. In other words, there was not a bargain to be had about the revolutionary state acting as a platform to spread revolution or any other negotiable issue because the problem was the existence of the revolutionary state. Robert Cecil wrote, "Now that our enemies are defeated, the chief danger to this country is Bolshevism."[55] The French foreign minister concurred: "The Bolshevik problem is no longer a purely Russian affair; it is now an international question. . . . [A]ll the civilized countries should unite to oppose this anarchic contagion which should be fought in the same way as an epidemic."[56]

There were debates, however, about how to proceed. Some, such as Winston Churchill in Britain and French marshal Ferdinand Foch, wanted a much greater Allied commitment to defeat the Soviets. These calls were spurned, and Allied intervention muddled along in a relatively limited manner. There were several obstacles toward successful Allied intervention in the Russian Civil War. On

---

[52] For these upheavals, see, for example, F. L. Carsten, *Revolution in Central Europe 1918–1919* (Berkeley: University of California Press, 1972); Oszkár Jászi, *Revolution and Counterrevolution in Hungary* (New York: H. Fertig, 1969); David W. Morgan, *The Socialist Left and the German Revolution* (Ithaca: Cornell University Press, 1975); Pierre Broué, *The German Revolution, 1917–1923*, trans. John Archer (Leiden: Brill, 2005).

[53] Francesco S. Nitti, *Peaceless Europe* (London: Cassel and Company, 1922), 94.

[54] Debo, *Survival and Consolidation*, 29, 11–33.

[55] Debo, *Revolution and Survival*, 388.

[56] Carley, *Silent Conflict*, 17.

the Allied side, there was intense domestic pressure against a larger-scale inter-vention in Russia, particularly from the left; another factor was that resources were already stretched thin. The Allies' limited efforts probably would have been sufficient, however, if the enemies of the Bolsheviks had been more united. The so-called White forces encompassed groups of varying political perspectives, from monarchists committed to the old regime to socialists, and were riven with personal rivalries. There were large-scale mutinies among French soldiers in the Ukraine and French sailors in the Black Sea. The Bolshevik propaganda made a simple point: *The war is over—why are you still fighting?*[57]

These difficulties led to the end of direct Allied intervention. The French withdrew their military forces in 1919, and began drawing down their financial support of anti-Bolshevik forces in 1920. They shifted their limited resources to shoring up and preventing Soviet infiltration of the cordon sanitaire—the eastern European states that would serve as a buffer against Bolshevism.[58] In June 1919, Italy had cancelled its military expedition to the Caucasus because of economic difficulties at home. Meanwhile, a British cabinet meeting in January 1920 con-cluded, "There can be no question of making active war on the Bolsheviks, for the reason that we have neither the men, the money, nor the credit, and public opinion is altogether opposed to such a course."[59]

In sum, with the war ended and no need to reconstitute the Eastern Front, one might expect a reversion to pre-revolution alliances to check German power. But the Allies were still dedicated to the overthrow of the Bolshevik regime. Evidence suggests that this was at least partially for reasons consistent with the domestic contagion effects theory. And although they had to give up their military inter-vention, this did not change their basic hostility toward the regime.

Contagion Concerns, Poland, and the Alliance System of Interwar Europe

The domestic contagion effects theory predicts hostility toward the Bolsheviks, and we see this in Allied and German policies toward Poland and the Polish-Soviet War. While much attention has focused on the Allied intervention in Russia, the situation in Poland is of more lasting importance for international rela-tions in Europe. Poland exhibits how the fear of Bolshevism shaped the alliance

---

[57] Carley, *Revolution and Intervention*, 144. The mutiny was more motivated by soldiers wanting to come home than their pro-Soviet position, but it was not seen that way by both pro- and anti-com-munist partisans. Andrew Orr, "The Myth of the Black Sea Mutiny: Communist Propaganda, Soviet Influence and the Re-Remembering of the Mutiny," *French History* 32, no. 1 (2018): 86–105.

[58] Carley, *Revolution and Intervention*, 182–86.

[59] G. H. Bennett, *British Foreign Policy During the Curzon Period, 1919–1924* (London: St. Martin's Press, 1995), 65.

system that would characterize interwar Europe. Prior to the Russian Revolution, France and Russia were allies, and they were allies for a simple balance-of-power reason: to contain a rising Germany. This was an alliance between the least ideologically compatible states in Europe—an autocracy and a republic. Why was there not a similar move in the aftermath of the war?

That question is particularly salient during the war between the Soviets and the Poles. After all, France knew even by 1920, when the war occurred, a few salient facts about its international situation. First, the Germans bitterly resented the constraints put on it by the Versailles Treaty. Second, the Americans, and increasingly the British, were not willing to sufficiently back France in its attempts to restrain Germany. Third, it was increasingly clear that the Bolsheviks would emerge as the victor from the civil war. This situation cried out for an alliance with the Bolsheviks to constrain Germany. Indeed, a French intelligence report in March 1920 noted that the reconstitution of a great Russian state was "necessary for a balance of power in Europe. By an unexpected turn of events, this Russia of the future might develop from the present efforts of Lenin and Trotsky."[60] A strategy to rely on Poland and other eastern European states to balance against Germany was grossly inferior to one that included Russians, as Poland had a tenth of the population of Russia.

In fact, even though it might involve Germany retaking territory taken away from it at Versailles, one could make the case it would be better for the Allied powers if Poland did not exist. This buffer state created a situation where Russia and Germany did not have to worry about the other as much as when they were at each other's throats. An invasion of a Western-allied Poland by either Germany or Russia would prompt the West to come to Poland's aid. Thus, rather than having a situation where Germany and Russia were neighbors, which would prompt fear of the other and a reason for both to court the West, those concerns were reduced considerably. Instead, Germany could threaten cooperation with the Soviets and have the West come to it. Mutual hostility toward Poland could also be a source of collaboration between Germany and the Bolsheviks. What then explains not only French policy but also the policy of the other great powers toward Poland?

Poland in fact was critical to understanding not only the postwar settlement, or lack thereof, but also why there was not a peace settlement in 1917 when it had long been obvious that the war had reached a stalemate. The Germans had committed themselves to an independent Poland that would essentially be a satellite of the Central

[60] Michael Jabara Carley, "The Politics of Anti-Bolshevism: The French Government and the Russo-Polish War, December 1919 to May 1920," *The Historical Journal* 19, no. 1 (1976): 173. Litvinov reminded the French of their interest in a strong Russia. Michael Jabara Carley, "Prelude to Defeat: Franco-Soviet Relations, 1919–39," *Historical Reflections* 22, no. 1 (1996): 162.

Powers.[61] On the other hand, one of the tsar's key war aims, along with annexing Constantinople, was to incorporate the Central Powers' Polish provinces into a semiautonomous Polish province.[62] The French had long been sympathetic toward the Poles, but the French government would not get involved in Polish matters as long as the Russian Empire was France's ally in the war. Sympathy toward the Poles' plight was particularly strong in the United States, and Wilson made the establishment of an independent Poland a cornerstone of his version of a just peace.[63] The Russian Provisional Government announced in March 1917 the creation of an independent Polish state, and the French began aiding the Polish army in June.

French, British, and Italian policymakers, though, had decidedly mixed feelings about a possible independent Polish state. After the Provisional Government's announcement, the British foreign minister, Lord Balfour, voiced skepticism of the use of Poland as a buffer state, noting that "the existence of Poland would mean that there was no longer a German-Russian frontier, and this would prevent Russia from coming to the assistance of France in the event of German attack."[64] The French position toward Poland was ambiguous and dependent on what was going to happen in Russia. If a conservative regime could be established in Russia, then the alliance with that regime could be resumed, and thus an independent Polish state would not be advantageous.[65] In Italy too, as long as it was thought that the Bolshevik regime would not rule Russia, the leadership was not in favor of the breakup of the Russian Empire precisely because it would remove a balancer against Germany.[66]

There were two main Polish movements prior to the creation of the state: a leftist regime based in Poland, supported by the Polish Socialist Party and a radical peasant party led by Joseph Pilsudski, and a right-leaning regime based in Paris, the KNP, led by Roman Dmowski. The French worried about connections between the leftists in France and the Polish left, and that Pilsudski was not sufficiently anti-Bolshevik, and perhaps pro-German. In fact, Pilsudski was more nationalist than socialist, and he was stridently anti-Bolshevik. He viewed the

---

[61] See David Stevenson, "The Failure of Peace by Negotiation in 1917," *The Historical Journal* 34, no. 1 (1991): 74.

[62] Alexander Dallin et al., *Russian Diplomacy and Eastern Europe 1914–1917* (New York: King's Crown Press, 1963), 1–77.

[63] Christopher G. Salisbury, "For Your Freedom and Ours: The Polish Question in Wilson's Peace Initiatives, 1916–1917," *Australian Journal of Politics and History* 49, no. 4 (2003): 481–500; Louis L. Gerson, *Woodrow Wilson and the Rebirth of Poland, 1914–1920* (New Haven: Yale University Press, 1953).

[64] Kay Lundgreen-Nielsen, *The Polish Problem at the Paris Peace Conference*, trans. Alison Borch-Johansen (Odense: Odense University Press, 1979), 60.

[65] Ibid., 71.

[66] Pettrachi, *La Russia Rivoluzionaria nella politica italiana*, 53.

leftist government as a "Pasteur injection against Bolshevism."[67] There were ties between Pilsudski and French leftist figures, but the rest of the apprehensions were misguided. On the other hand, the British, especially Lloyd George, worried that the KNP was too reactionary and that its policies could lead to a revolution favoring the extreme left.[68] They saw the Pilsudski regime as the regime saw itself—as an antidote to Bolshevism. Thus, although there were disagreements between the British and French over Polish politics, these were tactical disagreements with the same anti-revolutionary goal in mind. The separate factions on the left agreed to merge, and Pilsudski outmaneuvered Dmowski to become the chief of state.

Poland emerged from the Versailles Conference as an independent state, considered the "linchpin of the *cordon sanitaire*."[69] This was not the only motive for the creation of Poland. The thirteenth of Wilson's Fourteen Points called for an independent Polish state, exhibiting the principle of self-determination that was to legitimize the peace settlement. Self-determination figured somewhat into British calculations, but it counted for very little to the French. For them, Poland was about balancing against Germany and, as a foreign ministry memorandum said, it "was a necessary barrier between Russian Bolshevism and a German revolution."[70] Both of these motives had to do with the threat of Bolshevism spreading—the latter more directly, but the former because the only reason France was considering Poland as a balancer is because the French did not want Soviet Russia to play that role. Stephen Walt argues that although French hostility toward Bolshevism was significant, its overriding goal was the future containment of Germany.[71] But in fact it was the opposite. If containing the Germans was the primary goal of French policy, then there would be a simple solution: support Russia rather than Poland.

The Poles began a strategy of expanding their borders to the east by the use of force. In this, they were for the most part encouraged by the French. The French became Poland's military supplier. Poland's incursions to the east culminated in the Polish-Soviet War. There is controversy over when the Polish-Soviet War began, some dating it to the beginning of skirmishes in February 1919, when the Poles combatted Soviet forces advancing as the German army withdrew. But the most notable escalation was Pilsudski's invasion of Ukraine in April 1920. The Poles had put out feelers to the French, and the French had tacitly encouraged

[67] Kay Lundgreen-Nielsen, "The Mayer Thesis Reconsidered: The Poles and the Paris Peace Conference, 1919," *The International History Review* 7, no. 1 (1985): 77.

[68] Ibid., 81.

[69] Arno Mayer, *Politics and Diplomacy of Peacemaking: Containment and Counterrevolution at Versailles, 1918–1919* (New York: Alfred A. Knopf, 1967), 603.

[70] Piotr S. Wandycz, *France and Her Eastern Allies, 1919–1925* (Minneapolis: University of Minnesota Press, 1962), 22.

[71] Stephen M. Walt, *Revolution and War* (Ithaca: Cornell University Press, 1996), 153.

their invasion, seeing it as a means to topple the Bolshevik regime.[72] The British, however, thought the Polish invasion foolhardy because they figured it would likely rally the Russians around the Bolshevik regime and possibly lead to the disintegration of Poland.[73] As was the case in the divide between the constitutional and absolutist monarchies in the 1820s, both Britain and France had counterrevolutionary objectives but differences over tactics and strategy.

The Bolsheviks then made the fateful decision to push on toward Warsaw. The British had at this point proposed a border that came to be called the Curzon Line, named after the British foreign minister, who also issued a threat that Britain would intervene on Poland's side if the Red Army crossed that line. In a reversal of the Soviet deliberations over the Brest-Litovsk treaty, Lenin proposed marching the Red Army into Poland, but the bulk of the Bolshevik leadership, including Trotsky, was opposed.[74] What were the aims of the Soviet advance? There is no document containing the Soviet war aims, but it appears that Lenin supposed he could communize Warsaw, a "revolution from without."[75] After they controlled the lands of the former Russian Empire, the Bolsheviks would then attempt to negotiate a peace with the Germans and Allies.[76] And of course there was the hope that the revolution would spread organically to Germany. The Soviets interpreted the recent Kapp Putsch as "Germany's Kornilov Affair," which had precipitated a leftist uprising in the Ruhr, and thought revolution was not far off.[77]

One might suppose, from a geopolitical perspective, that this was the Allies' chance to set things straight—let the Soviets carve up Poland and pit a more powerful united Soviet Russia against Germany. But this was not the case. The Allies, and the French in particular, provided critical aid to the Poles, including a French loan and military mission, which allowed them to stave off the Bolsheviks' advance.[78] Lloyd George was more ambiguous. While he threatened the possibility of war with the Soviets, the British labor movement threatened a general strike if he proceeded.[79]

[72] Carley, "The Politics of Anti-Bolshevism."
[73] Lundgreen-Nielsen, The Polish Problem, 82.
[74] Robert Service, Lenin: A Political Life, vol. 3 (Bloomington: Indiana University Press, 1995), 118–20.
[75] Marc H. Lerner, "Attempting a Revolution from Without: Poland in 1920," in The Anatomy of Communist Takeovers, ed. Thomas T. Hammond (New Haven: Yale University Press, 1975).
[76] Debo, Survival and Consolidation, 408–11; Thomas C. Fiddick, Russia's Retreat from Poland, 1920 (London: Macmillan, 1990).
[77] Smele, The "Russian" Civil Wars, 156.
[78] Michael Jabara Carley, "Anti-Bolshevism in French Foreign Policy," The International History Review 2, no. 3 (1980): 410–31.
[79] Richard H. Ullman, The Anglo-Soviet Accord (Princeton: Princeton University Press, 1972), 184–232; L. J. Macfarlane, "Hands Off Russia: British Labour and the Russo-Polish War, 1920," Past and Present 38 (1967): 126–52.

The Soviet failure to defeat Poland implicates both Allied and German policies. The "Miracle of the Vistula"—the turning point of the Soviet advance, where they failed to capture Warsaw and were eventually routed—was a close call. One of the reasons for the Soviet failure was the tactic of sending their forces northwest of Warsaw rather than concentrating them there. There were several reasons for this move. One was to prevent Allied supplies from reaching Warsaw, but there was also a political reason—to occupy the Polish Corridor so that it could be turned over to the Germans in a negotiation.[80]

Why had the Germans not responded to the Soviets' overtures? The head of the German desk in the Polish Foreign Ministry "correctly concluded" that Germany " 'found it impossible to reconcile its foreign policy, which demanded the annihilation of Poland, with its domestic policy, which was very largely directed by the fear of a Spartacist uprising."[81] A Reichswehr colonel wrote a memorandum that claimed "it can only be agreeable to us if Poland should cease to exist. On the other hand, we must also take the measures necessary to prevent Bolshevism from flooding Germany after the destruction of Poland."[82] His idea was to strengthen domestic repression on leftist groups while pursuing German foreign policy aims. But for the German government, that was too risky. Ruling-class strategies extended to foreign affairs. While they welcomed the destruction of Poland and with it the Versailles system, the "concern of the government at the time seemed to be less with the foreign political or strategic consequences of a Soviet victory than with its domestic impact on the latent revolutionary situation in Germany."[83] German labor was sympathetic to the Bolshevik cause and refused to transport any war matériel to Poland. The government was forced into a position of neutrality.

Poland revealed the contagion concerns of the powers. There were differences in tactics between Britain and France, but they had the same counterrevolutionary aims. The policies they pursued would have a big effect on the structure of international relations in the interwar period. Rather than resorting to Soviet Russia balancing Germany, France attempted to use Poland—a most inferior substitute—for that job. If the Allies had felt constrained by the doctrine of self-determination, they could have used the Polish-Soviet War as an excuse to see Poland extinguished. But they did not take that opportunity. Even Germany did not take up the chance to destroy the Versailles system by linking hands with

[80] Jerzy Borzecki, *The Soviet-Polish Peace of 1921 and the Creation of Interwar Europe* (New Haven: Yale University Press, 2008), 86. For details of the attempted negotiations, see Robert Himmer, "Soviet Policy Toward Germany During the Russo-Polish War, 1920," *Slavic Review* 35, no. 4 (1976).

[81] Harald Von Riekhoff, *German-Polish Relations, 1918–1933* (Baltimore: Johns Hopkins University Press, 1971), 30.

[82] F. L. Carsten, *Reichswehr and Politics: 1918 to 1933* (Oxford: Oxford University Press, 1966), 69.

[83] Von Riekhoff, *German-Polish Relations*, 29.

the Soviets and dividing Poland. Destroying the Versailles Treaty may have been their primary foreign policy goal, but they could not bring it about when they were in the throes of revolutionary agitation. Poland, then, illustrates the hostility of all the powers toward the Bolshevik regime, as the domestic contagion theory expects.

From Crushing to Containing the Bolsheviks

The end of military intervention by the great powers in the Russian Revolution meant new measures had to be taken to contain or transform the menace. The last attempt to snuff out the Bolsheviks by military means involved British and French attempts to aid the Kronstadt revolt, an anti-Bolshevik insurgency. By 1921, it was clear the Bolsheviks were going to remain in power. The Allies eventually restored diplomatic relations with the Soviet Union in 1924, but their relations have been described as a "cold peace" or "silent conflict." The embargo against the Soviets was lifted in 1920, and in both Britain and Germany some in the government thought that economically engaging the Soviets was the best way to undermine the revolution. It would also have the additional benefit of improving their economies, which had faced a serious postwar depression that exacerbated domestic instability. In Britain, this plan was quite controversial.[84]

In the German government, there was wider acceptance of increasing economic ties. As the leader of German policy toward Russia at the time, Ago Maltzan, said in December 1920, "Bolshevism cannot be destroyed from without by means of radical military measures, but can only be undermined from within. One must . . . bring about the evolution of Bolshevism."[85] Germany had another motive to court the Soviets: to achieve its primary foreign policy goal of breaking the constraints of Versailles. Allied sanctions against Germany and the terms of Versailles had pushed Germany toward the Soviets, but diplomatic relations severed in 1918 had not been restored. Talks in June 1919 and April 1920 were broken off by the Germans. The Bolsheviks, "for all their talk of wanting to develop far-reaching cooperation, still hoped for revolution in Germany," and that is precisely what Germans feared.[86] Germans did not appreciate Soviet attempts to encourage revolution at the same time as there were communist insurrections in Germany. Merely courting the Soviet Union, though, could prompt the

[84] Stephen White, *Britain and the Bolshevik Revolution: A Study in the Politics of Diplomacy, 1920–1924* (New York: Holmes & Meier, 1979), esp. 235.

[85] J. David. Cameron, "To Transform the Revolution into an Evolution: Underlying Assumptions of German Foreign Policy Toward Soviet Russia 1919–1927," *Journal of Contemporary History* 40, no. 1 (2005): 11. See also J. David. Cameron, "Carl Graap and the Formation of Weimar Foreign Policy Toward Soviet Russia from 1919 until Rapallo," *Diplomacy and Statecraft* 13, no. 4 (2002): 75–95.

[86] Debo, *Survival and Consolidation*, 343.

western powers to appease Germany so that it would not be further drawn to an alliance with the Soviets. And there were tangible benefits to be had. Versailles put limitations on the size of the German military and its ability to develop military technology. At the Treaty of Rapallo in 1922 Germany overcame its apprehensions. It normalized relations with the Soviets, and secretly agreed that the German military would train Soviet soldiers and construct military equipment on Soviet territory.[87]

Despite the German incentives, cooperation with the Soviets remained limited. Although much has been made about the contacts between Weimar Germany and Soviet Russia, it is striking how restricted their interactions were. Gustav Stresemann, the architect of Weimar foreign policy from 1923 until 1929, regretted that an agreement had been signed with the Bolshevik government, but he found it useful to balance between the West and the Soviets. He warned those advocating a closer relationship with the Soviets that the latter were intent on a German revolution. He supported economic engagement for the benefits to Germany as well as a means to "so bind up the Russian economy with the capitalist system of the Western European powers that we thereby pave the way for an evolution in Russia which in my opinion presents the only possibility of creating a state and an economy out of Soviet Russia with which we can live."[88] The Soviets did not take the bait. German policymakers by the mid-1920s had concluded that this policy was a failure. There were hesitations from the Soviet side, seeing as they correctly viewed it as a means to undermine their system of government. There were hesitations from the German side regarding political cooperation, both because the Germans did not want to excessively antagonize the Allies and because of the conservative German government's own ideological antipathy toward the Soviets.[89] As Stresemann confided to his diary, "To enter into a marriage with communist Russia is like going to bed with the killer of one's own people."[90] On the other hand, Stresemann had an interest in the Bolsheviks remaining in power because he thought, no doubt correctly, that if the bourgeois were to take over in Russia, there would inevitably be an alliance with France.[91]

There was then a degree of accommodation with the Soviet regime, although part of the reason to cooperate with the regime in terms of trade ties was so

---

[87] For some of the main works on this relationship, see Aleksandr M. Nekrich, *Pariahs, Partners, Predators: German-Soviet Relations 1922–1941* (New York: Columbia University Press, 1997); Kurt Rosenbaum, *Community of Fate: German-Soviet Diplomatic Relations 1922–1928* (Syracuse: Syracuse University Press, 1965); Gerald Freund, *Unholy Alliance* (London: Chatto and Windus, 1957).

[88] Cameron, "To Transform the Revolution," 18.

[89] As Gatzke says, "The main obstacle to real friendship was communism." Hans W. Gatzke, *European Diplomacy Between Two Wars, 1919–1939* (Chicago: Quadrangle Books, 1972), 40.

[90] Hans W. Gatzke, "Von Rapallo nach Berlin Stresemann und die Deutsche Rußlandpolitik," *Vierteljahrshefte für Zeitgeschichte* 4, no. 1 (1956): 12.

[91] Jonathan Wright, *Gustav Stresemann: Weimar's Greatest Statesman* (Oxford: Oxford University Press, 2002), 403–04.

that they could undermine the revolutionary regime. And tensions remained. German-Soviet cooperation was more extensive, but still limited. German ambiguity toward the Soviet Union is not a confirmation of my theory, but neither is it a refutation. Ideological factors interacted in complex ways with geopolitical pressures. One development of note is that the relations between the revolutionary regime and Europe somewhat improved at a time when the Soviets were more active as a platform in spreading revolution abroad by using the Comintern to finance and coordinate communist parties in European states that answered to Moscow.

Cooperation Among Counterrevolutionaries

International rivalries did not stop in the face of the Russian Revolution. This was a time of intense competition between the great powers, obviously among the belligerents during the Great War, but also in its aftermath, and even among the Allies. Even in the response to the Russian Revolution, one of the factors that hampered Allied intervention was distrust between the Allies as they angled for opportunities in post-revolutionary Russia, as well as divisions over how to best prevent the spread of revolution. Of course, that conflict of interest paled in comparison to that between the Allies and Germany. The Russian Revolution did not prompt states to drop their weapons and stop the war. But such an expectation would be unrealistic. What is surprising is the extent to which the fear of contagion led to cooperation. Most stunning was the period in 1918 when the Germans on one side and the British, French, and Italians on the other were slaughtering each other on the battlefield, yet indirectly cooperating in Russia—both trying to crush the Bolsheviks.

More significant for international politics is how the fear of contagion from the Russian Revolution encouraged cooperation among the victors and the vanquished in the postwar world. Arno Mayer may have overstated matters when he claimed "the Paris Peace Conference made a host of decisions, all of which, in varying degrees, were designed to check Bolshevism."[92] But there is no question that the Paris Peace Conference happened under the shadow of the threat of Bolshevism, and this significantly affected how the Allies responded to Germany. Fritz Klein notes that "the problem of Germany's possible radicalization and its importance for the peace negotiations were constant themes" during the Versailles period.[93] The Versailles peace is still denounced in textbooks as excessively harsh

---

[92] Mayer, *Politics and Diplomacy of Peacemaking*, 9.
[93] Fritz Klein, "Between Compiègne and Versailles: The Germans on the Way from a Misunderstood Defeat to an Unwanted Peace," in *The Treaty of Versailles: A Reassessment After 75 Years*, eds. Manfred F. Boemeke, Gerald D. Feldman, and Elisabeth Glaser (Cambridge: Cambridge University Press, 1998), 210.

on Germany, but the historiography on this question has disagreed fundamentally.[94] As Zara Steiner argues, the Versailles Treaty was the most moderate of the postwar settlements.[95] Most obviously, Germany lost very little of its territory, unlike with the settlement in 1945. It was also moderate in comparison to the Brest-Litovsk treaty the Germans forced on the Bolsheviks. But even the reparations issue, which was famously denounced by John Maynard Keynes as a Carthaginian peace—and which was supposedly pushed by the French, who demanded revenge—turns out not to be as it has been portrayed.[96] The French especially were willing to take a softer line with Germany, and the reparations were not beyond Germany's ability to pay, especially when the sum was consistently revised downward. One reason for the relatively soft approach, though not the only one, was the fear of the spread of Bolshevism in Weimar Germany and from there to the rest of Europe. The simple prediction of the theory that there would be cooperation among states that had similar movements did not hold across the board, but again we see the mechanism at work, and it did prompt an increase in cooperation.

The Communist Revolution and the European Powers

In line with the domestic contagion effects theory, there were serious fears of revolutionary contagion from the Russian Revolution in all the great powers, stemming from their significant domestic socialist/communist movements. The one ambiguous case is Britain. Not coincidentally, that was where the leader the least concerned about revolutionary contagion was found: Lloyd George.[97] And not coincidentally, he was the most accommodating toward the Soviets. Although I consider it ambiguous whether Britain had a significant revolutionary socialist movement, British leaders' fear of contagion was, for the most part, not ambiguous.

[94] For reviews, see Sally Marks, "Mistakes and Myths: The Allies, Germany, and the Versailles Treaty 1918–1921," *The Journal of Modern History* 85, no. 3 (2013): 632–59; Marc Trachtenberg, "Versailles Revisited," *Security Studies* 9, no. 3 (2007): 191–205.

[95] Zara Steiner, *The Lights That Failed: European International History 1919–1933* (New York: Oxford University Press, 2005), 608.

[96] See Marc Trachtenberg, *Reparations in World Politics: France and European Economic Diplomacy, 1916–1923* (New York: Columbia University Press, 1980); Sally Marks, "The Myth of Reparations," *Central European History* 11, no. 3 (1978): 231–55.

[97] In February 1918, he had even said that he "had no fear that Bolshevism was a formidable menace to the internal peace of this country." Michael Kettle, *The Allies and the Russian Collapse: March 1917–March 1918* (Minneapolis: University of Minnesota Press, 1981), 224. This was not the case with his conservative colleagues in the war cabinet, none of whom had his past as a radical liberal. Ullman, *The Anglo-Soviet Accord*, 469. George thought that a Bolshevik Russia would be a weakened one, with the borderlands achieving self-determination, which would be a good outcome for the British Empire.

Regarding the platform versus model issue, the Soviet state was not going to spread revolution by force of arms to the great powers, as was the case with the French Revolution. The Soviet state lay prostrate even after it emerged victorious from the civil war. That is, the Soviets had developed a powerful state apparatus vis-à-vis internal enemies, but they were still quite weak vis-à-vis external ones. It is clear that Soviet attempts to spread revolution abroad through less direct means—spreading propaganda, organizing and financing revolutionary groups, and the like—were a major irritant. For example, Britain made its diplomatic recognition conditional on the Soviets not carrying on revolutionary activities in Britain, as did Germany in the Brest-Litovsk treaty.[98] But the fear of contagion was not dependent on the revolutionary state acting as a platform. In fact, Western leaders were most fearful of contagion in the period from 1917 to about 1921, and in Germany to 1923, when, with the partial exception of the Bolsheviks' activities in Germany, the Soviets were doing little to promote revolution abroad. What amplified the contagion effect was more the major dislocations in the host countries combined with the fact that similar revolutionary movements existed in their polities. As Adam Ulam stated, "There was little fear as yet of Soviet or Communist *power* . . . when Western statesmen expressed fear of Bolshevism or anarchism (and those terms were used almost interchangeably), they were afraid of the *example* of Russian Communism stirring up social trouble in their own countries and, under the precarious economic conditions of the post-war world, making impossible the return of the pre-1914 pattern of political stability."[99] When the Comintern began more directly coordinating the activities of communist parties that had formed, contagion fears had already peaked. In fact, the host countries could have thanked the Soviets for interfering in their countries, which contributed to a fracturing of the leftist movement in this period, as the Soviets insisted on communist parties that would do their bidding and purged and vilified other leftists.[100] The Soviet activities were certainly not welcomed, and generated a considerable amount of diplomatic friction, but they do not explain the fear of contagion and consequent hostility toward the Soviet state.

[98] For how the Comintern's activities affected relations with Britain, see Gyoohyoung Kahng, "Intervention and Coexistence: The Comintern's Revolutionary Propaganda in Great Britain and Anglo-Soviet Relations, 1920–1927," PhD thesis, Ohio University, 1998; Roger Schinness, "The Conservative Party and Anglo-Soviet Relations," *European Studies Review* 7, no. 4 (1977): 393–407.

[99] Adam B. Ulam, *Expansion and Coexistence* (New York: Praeger Publishers, 1968), 98, emphasis in the original.

[100] There is widespread agreement that these policies had a negative effect on the political left, although Lindemann places much of the blame for the fracturing on indigenous debates. Albert S. Lindemann, *The "Red Years": European Socialism Versus Bolshevism 1919–1921* (Berkeley: University of California Press, 1974).

Regarding the more important issue of the international effect of the fears of contagion, the theory makes a strong claim that this factor will shape patterns of cooperation and conflict in international politics, and it does so to get a sense of just how powerful that factor is. In the context of a world war and its aftermath, it may be surprising that the fear of contagion was still manifested in foreign policy. For Germany, the results are mixed. Their aid to the Bolsheviks and their cooperation with them once in power is the opposite of what the theory would expect. On the other hand, we do see fear of contagion manifested. Some in the German government wanted to break from the Bolsheviks even while fighting a war for their survival on the Western Front. Even more significant is that after the war the Germans, whose number one foreign policy priority was to break the shackles of Versailles, did not take the opportunity to come to an agreement with the Soviets to partition Poland.

The Allies were more consistent in their hostility toward the Bolsheviks. The Russian Revolution turned the alliances of World War I on their head. The fear of the Russian Revolution emboldening leftist movements in their own countries was at the heart of this hostility from the beginning of the revolution, as is evidenced in the Allies spurring a reconciliation with the Bolsheviks against the Germans in 1918 and then continuing after the war.

Though Allied intervention in Russia garners most of the attention, the bigger effect of contagion fears on international politics is how those fears structured interwar Europe. The entire Versailles settlement was directed at western Europe. What was not settled was eastern Europe, which had been and would be the primary source of conflict in both world wars. And what is most notable is the lack of a balancing coalition against Germany, as there had been prior to the Russian Revolution. This would provide Germany with the opportunity to defy the constraints of the Versailles system. The international system in Europe was fundamentally unstable even in the 1920s. It was clear after 1923 (after French occupation of the Ruhr and the Dawes Plan) that the Versailles settlement would not be backed by force. Despite the "Locarno spirit"—the reintegration of Germany with the West at the Locarno conference of 1925—France was planning the Maginot Line before the rise of Nazism and the onset of the Great Depression. The French did not have a balancer against Germany, so they gritted their teeth and hoped for the best. A neorealist perspective highlights the basic continuity between the 1920s and 1930s given the structural situation in Europe, in contrast to the conventional wisdom's emphasis on the rise of Nazism in Germany. This is an important point. There were larger structural problems than Hitler, who would exploit preexisting vulnerabilities. But it is also important to note that a factor very much outside the neorealist perspective—domestic ideological threats—is critical to explaining how that structure was created. Russia was anathema because of its revolutionary threat, and thus was unacceptable as a balancer.

Italian Fascist Revolution

At the same time as leaders were fearing a communist wave sweeping through Europe, there emerged a new ideological movement: fascism. In March 1919, Benito Mussolini founded the fascist movement in Italy, a collection of groups that espoused Italian nationalism and anti-socialism through radical social programs. The movement grew rapidly in the "Red years," 1919–20, when demobilized peasants occupied lands and workers occupied factories. Fascists organized paramilitary squads that intervened in the class conflict. They formed the National Fascist Party (PNF) in late 1921, though they retained their paramilitary squads. By the summer of 1922, they were informally militarily occupying large parts of central and northern Italy. In October 1922, the PNF threatened to stage a coup if Mussolini was not made head of government. The king complied and appointed him prime minister. Mussolini formed a government with both fascists and nonfascists. He exercised increasing control, and by 1925 he had dispensed with parliamentary institutions altogether. Despite their noise about totalitarianism, the fascist dictatorship had to coexist with other institutions, such as the monarchy and the church.

One main reason why fascist regimes—Mussolini's regime, as well as Hitler's—are sometimes not regarded as revolutionary is because of the way these movements came to power. Their road to power made use of extralegal threats and the use of violence, but they used the system in place to ascend to office. More important for our purposes is the fact that they had to, at least initially, cooperate with elements of the old regime to maintain their power. This is another reason fascist regimes, and even fascist movements, have sometimes not been accorded as revolutionary: their ideology was not taken seriously. Fascism was an ideological "latecomer."[101] This new force had no long-standing texts and was known more for what it was against—liberalism and communism—than what it was for. The traditional Marxist interpretation was that fascism was counterrevolutionary rather than revolutionary, not just because of the Marxists' teleology of themselves in the revolutionary vanguard, but because they saw fascism as little more than a stooge for capitalist interests. These issues are important in explaining the reaction to the Italian fascist revolution, as I will discuss in what follows.

Nevertheless, the consensus of fascist studies is that fascism was a revolutionary movement.[102] It was not only against liberalism and communism, but

[101] Juan J. Linz, "Some Notes Toward a Comparative Study of Fascism in Sociological Historical Perspective," in *Fascism: A Reader's Guide*, ed. Walter Laqueur (Berkeley: University of California Press, 1976), 4–8.
[102] Michael Mann, *Fascists* (New York: Cambridge University Press, 2004); Philip Morgan, *Fascism in Europe, 1919–1945* (London: Routledge, 2003); George L. Mosse, *The Fascist Revolution: Toward a General Theory of Fascism* (New York: H. Fertig, 1999); Stanley G. Payne, *A History of Fascism,*

against conservatism as well—despite the fascists' tactical cooperation with conservative forces. Fascism produced no systematic theory, but the basic outlines are clear enough: the movement aimed to overturn the old social and political order and replace it with a new order that emphasized the nation-state. Fascism rejected the individualism of liberalism and the communitarianism of socialism based on class and insisted on a communitarianism based on the nation-state. There was also a common emphasis on means—rejecting democracy in favor of strongmen who would implement the popular will, and favoring violence and militarism.[103] Their aim of overthrowing the old social and political order and creating something new is what made them revolutionary.

Model

Fascism was a model for other groups that had the same enemies: liberalism and communism. Indeed, there was a surge of movements and regimes in the aftermath of the fascist takeover in Italy that took inspiration from its undermining of parliamentary democracy and its violence against the left. The fascist revolution was not just about what it was against. It stood for a new movement, a new ideology that represented, as Mussolini claimed, the wave of the future—the ideology of the twentieth century. Groups across Europe were inspired by this ideology. Thus, despite claims to the contrary, transnational nationalism is not a paradox.[104] Perhaps it was less naturally transnational than Marxism, which did not regard the nation-state system as legitimate. But in one sense fascist transnationalism had an easier time crossing borders. Unlike the Bolsheviks, who insisted on the Moscow party line, the Italian fascists assumed that the model of fascism would not be adopted in its entirety; rather, the principles of fascism would be adapted to each national environment. And this is what happened.

As with any ideological movement, there were significant differences within that movement. The most notable is the difference between the Italian

1914–1945 (Madison: The University of Wisconsin Press, 1995); Roger Eatwell, Fascism: A History (New York: Penguin, 1995); Roger Griffin, The Nature of Fascism (New York: Routledge, 1991).

[103] Two complementary definitions of fascism are Mann's, "the pursuit of a transcendent and cleansing nation-statism through paramilitarism" and Payne's, "a form of revolutionary ultranationalism for national rebirth that is based on a primarily vitalist philosophy, is structured in extreme elitism, mass mobilization, and the Führerprinzip, positively values violence as end as well as means and tends to normalize war and/or the military virtues." Mann, Fascists, 13; Payne, A History of Fascism, 14. See these works (Mann, 10–13; Payne 3–19) for a discussion on the definition of fascism, as well as Roger Eatwell, "On Defining the 'Fascist Minimum': The Centrality of Ideology," Journal of Political Ideologies 1, no. 3 (1996): 303–19.

[104] Arnd Bauerkämper, "Transnational Fascism: Cross-Border Relations Between Regimes and Movements in Europe 1922–1939," East Central Europe 37, nos. 2–3 (2010): 214–46.

fascist movement that emphasized the state and the Nazi movement that emphasized the nation, or race. But these differences should not obscure the commonalities and the fact that they viewed each other and were viewed as part of the same family. Given the nationalist emphasis of their ideology, fascist groups in non-Italian countries did not want to be seen as a foreign import. But this did not prevent them from being inspired by the Italian model.[105]

Platform

Even before he ascended to power, Mussolini was suggesting to others outside Italy that fascism was not a movement that was confined to Italians. In the 1920s, though, he was not always explicit about this, and he would say to foreign journalists that fascism was not for export. Italian efforts to support fascist movements abroad were sporadic. There was a tension between fascist ideologues who wished to support fascists abroad and the career diplomats of the Italian state, who did not. The Fasci all'Estero, which was set up to organize the fascist cells that had appeared in Italian immigrant communities abroad, also wanted to disseminate fascist ideology more broadly. In 1925, the leader of the Fasci all'Estero, Giuseppe Bastianini, worked on founding a "Fascist International" that would "irradiate a new civilization from the eternal city."[106] Not just the career diplomats objected. Some in the Fascist Party did not want to cooperate with some of the supposed fascist movements abroad that they regarded as simply reactionary. The fascist international was not established. Mussolini went on record to foreigners claiming that fascism was not for export.[107] The Fasci all'Estero ended up being absorbed into the Ministry of Foreign Affairs, where it could be watched by the diplomats.

In the late 1920s, though, the talk of a fascist international picked up, culminating in the early 1930s with the creation of the Action Committees for Roman Universality (CAUR).[108] This organization existed relatively independently from

[105] Beyond the variation among fascist movements and regimes, there were authoritarian movements and regimes that selectively adopted aspects of fascism. António Costa Pinto and Aristotle Kallis, *Rethinking Fascism and Dictatorship in Europe* (New York: Palgrave Macmillan, 2014).

[106] Cited in Luca de Caprariis, "'Fascism for Export'? The Rise and Eclipse of the Fasci Italiani All'estero," *Journal of Contempory History* 35, no. 2 (2000): 167.

[107] For example, in 1925 Mussolini had his minister write in *Foreign Affairs* that fascism does not profess to be a "formula applicable to the needs of all nations." It "remains a thing Italian." And he told a Norwegian journalist that fascism was not for export. Ibid., 169, 175.

[108] Michael Ledeen, *Universal Fascism: The Theory and Practice of the Fascist International, 1928–1936* (New York: Howard Fertig, 1972).

the Italian regime until 1936.[109] They held a gathering in Montreux in the fall of 1934, and representatives from fascist groups across the continent attended, including the Iron Guard from Romania, the Francistes from France, and the Falange from Spain. The Nazis were notably absent.[110] There was a rivalry among these fascist regimes over who represented the fascist banner, and a specific dispute over the place of race in fascism. The creation of a fascist international faced several obstacles, among them that nationalist movements could not be seen as foreign imports. For example, British fascist Oswald Mosley told an Italian representative of the CAUR that he could not join such an organization because it would be viewed as foreign.[111] Nothing concrete came from the Montreux conference, and the CAUR gradually faded into obscurity.

The lack of a formal fascist international did not prevent Mussolini from covertly aiding fascist groups. He met with aspiring fascist leaders, such as José Antonio Primo de Rivera of Spain, Oswald Mosley of Britain, and Georges Valois of France. He also gave aid to fascist groups—more extensive in the 1930s than in the 1920s. In France, Le Faisceau possibly received some financial support from Mussolini, though if so it was likely modest.[112] The Francistes, on the other hand, received one million francs between 1933 and 1936.[113] In Britain, Italian subsidies were one of the main sources of funds for the British Union of Fascists (BUF), second only to Mosley himself. This is evidenced by the fact that when the Italian tap was reduced and finally cut off altogether in 1937, it severely curtailed BUF activities.[114] The fascist regime had contact with Nazis and other German nationalists, although it is unclear whether it directly aided the Nazis.[115]

[109] Mauro Marsella, "Assessing European Fascism: The View from Mussolini's Italy," PhD thesis, McMaster University, 2006, 75.

[110] Ledeen, *Universal Fascism*, 115.

[111] Claudia Baldoli, "Anglo-Italian Fascist Solidarity? The Shift from Italophilia to Naziphilia in the BUF," in *The Culture of Fascism: Visions of the Far Right in Britain*, eds. Julie V. Gottlieb and Thomas P. Linehan (London: I. B. Tauris, 2004), 156. The Nazis criticized the BUF on this score for incorporating the term "fascism." See Stephen Dorril, *Blackshirt: Sir Oswald Mosley and British Fascism* (New York: Penguin Books, 2006), 343, 374.

[112] Allen Douglas, *From Fascism to Libertarian Communism: Georges Valois Against the Third Republic* (Berkeley: University of California Press, 1992), 128; Robert Soucy, *French Fascism: The First Wave, 1924–1933* (New Haven: Yale University Press, 1986), 99–100; Joel Blatt, "Relatives and Rivals: The Responses of the Action Française to Italian Fascism, 1919–1926," *European Studies Review* 11, no. 3 (1981): 275.

[113] Alain Deniel, *Bucard et le Francisme* (Paris: Jean Picollec, 1979), 61. The PPF in the late 1930s also received a small amount of Italian funds. Robert Soucy, *French Fascism: The Second Wave, 1933–1939* (New Haven: Yale University Press, 1995), 226–27.

[114] Thomas Linehan, *British Fascism 1918–1939: Parties, Ideology, and Culture* (Manchester: Manchester University Press, 2000), 110; Richard Thurlow, *Fascism in Britain* (London: I. B. Tauris, 1998), 107–8.

[115] See Alan Cassels, "Mussolini and German Nationalism, 1922–1925," *The Journal of Modern History* 35, no. 2 (1963): 137–57.

Fascist Opposition in the Great Powers

Most or all of the intellectual roots of fascism can be traced back to prewar France.[116] But these ideas were not a synthesized whole. That had to wait for a political movement that created it.[117] Fascism as a political movement was a distinctly post–World War I phenomenon. In the 1920s among the great powers, there was a significant fascist movement in Germany and insignificant movements in Britain and the Soviet Union. Whether there was a significant fascist movement in France is debatable based on one's definition of fascism, but if fascism is considered a revolutionary movement, there were no significant fascist movements.

Fascist Movements in Germany

In Germany, the National Socialist German Workers' Party (NSDAP), or Nazi Party, rapidly emerged as the leading fascist party in Germany. The party developed in a milieu of far-right völkish, or nationalist, movements, some of which predated the war, but which were sprouting up everywhere in postwar Germany. For example, the German Nationalist Protection and Defiance Federation, organized by the Pan-German League, and the Thule Society were to be key conduits into the Nazi Party. Many of these groups were authoritarian and anti-Semitic. Also, there were the Freikorps, militias formed to suppress the revolutionary left. The Staglhelm, or Steel Helmets, was the largest right-wing nationalist organization, but it was a veterans organization and not a political party.[118]

The German Workers' Party, founded in January 1919, had a recognizably fascist platform. It was renamed the NSDAP in 1920, and in 1921 Adolf Hitler emerged as its undisputed leader. The party mostly took over potential rivals—the German Socialist Party and the German Völkisch Freedom Party (DVFP). Nazi Party membership quickly grew from 1,100 in June 1920 to 55,000 in the

---

[116] Zeev Sternhell, *The Birth of Fascist Ideology*, trans. David Maisel (Princeton: Princeton University Press, 1994).

[117] Levy notes that "Sternhell and associates' contention that fascism was already fully formed in pre-1914 France, and perhaps Italy, is not convincing. Their treatment is far too disembodied from real social movements, institutions and politicians." Carl Levy, "Fascism, National Socialism, and Conservatives in Europe, 1914–1945: Issues for Comparativists," *Contemporary European History* 8, no. 1 (1999): 99.

[118] For these groups, see, for example, Barry A. Jackisch, *The Pan-German League and Radical Nationalist Politics in Interwar Germany, 1918–1939* (Burlington: Ashgate, 2012); Robert G. L. Waite, *Vanguard of Nazism* (Cambridge, MA: Harvard University Press, 1952); James M. Diehl, *Paramilitary Politics in Weimar Germany* (Bloomington: Indiana University Press, 1977); Reginald H. Phelps, "'Before Hitler Came': Thule Society and Germanen Orden," *The Journal of Modern History* 35, no. 3 (1963): 245–62.

autumn of 1923.[119] Moreover, they could count on the support of other paramilitaries and prominent right-wing figures that aligned with the Nazis, most
notably Erich Ludendorff. A parade of paramilitaries in September 1923, for example, had as many as 100,000 uniformed men taking part.[120] Their support,
however, was concentrated in Bavaria. They attempted a coup there in November
1923. After the Beer Hall Putsch, they garnered 6.5 percent in the elections of
May 1924. By December 1924, though, they only garnered 3 percent of the vote,
and in 1928, just 2.6 percent. Although they arguably slid into insignificance,
they came roaring back at the end of the decade. The elections of September 1930
and July 1932 saw their share rise to 18.3 percent and 37.4 percent, respectively.
Weimar politics polarized into the far left and far right. The far-right nationalist
party, the DNVP, took a turn toward fascism and their support drained to the
NSDAP. Hitler assumed the chancellorship in January 1933.

Fascist Movements in Britain

In marked contrast to Germany, British fascist groups existed, but they never
escaped "total insignificance."[121] In 1923, Rotha Lintorn-Orman founded the
small British Fascisti. Inspired by Mussolini's repression of the socialists, it en-
thusiastically took part in strikebreaking activities.[122] This was not much more
than an organization of reactionaries, and for the very reason that the Fascisti
were not fascist enough, some members split in 1925 to form their own organization.[123] A variety of "shoestring operations with minimal popular impact"
emerged, such as the Imperial Fascist League.[124] The most significant by far was
the British Union of Fascists. The BUF was a genuinely fascist movement, and
had one of the clearest programs of all fascist parties. Oswald Mosley, a former
leader in the Labor Party and a charismatic orator, founded the BUF in 1932
after an inspiring visit with Mussolini in Rome. The BUF's influence peaked in
1934, when it was briefly backed by Lord Rothermere and his *Daily Mail* newspaper, at the encouragement of Mussolini. However, the BUF was never more

[119] Dietrich Orlow, *The History of the Nazi Party: 1919–1933* (Pittsburgh: The University of
Pittsburgh Press, 1969), 55.
[120] Richard J. Evans, *The Coming of the Third Reich* (New York: Penguin Books, 2005), 190.
[121] Payne, *A History of Fascism*, 305.
[122] For works on British fascism, see Thurlow, *Fascism in Britain*; Linehan, *British Fascism*.
For the British Union of Fascists in particular, see Dorril, *Blackshirt*; Gary Love, "'What's the Big
Idea?': Oswald Mosley, the British Union of Fascists and Generic Fascism," *Journal of Contempory
History* 42, no. 3 (2007): 447–68.
[123] For an argument against the predominant thesis that the Fascisti were just "conservatism with
knobs on," see Paul Stocker, "Importing Fascism: Reappraising the British Fascisti, 1923–1926,"
Contemporary British History 30, no. 3 (2016): 326–48.
[124] Thurlow, *Fascism in Britain*, 41.

than a curiosity. It rapidly declined in popularity, largely surviving on subsidies from Mussolini and Mosley himself.

Fascist Movements in the Soviet Union

Like Britain, the Soviet Union had no significant fascist movement. In Imperial Russia, the 1905 revolution had spawned the creation of the Union of the Russian People in response, a right-wing aspiring mass movement, but it did not have revolutionary goals like fascism.[125] A significant fascist movement did not emerge in the Soviet Union when recognizably fascist movements were developing in other places in post–World War I Europe. In the aftermath of the fascist revolution in Italy, there were movements among Russian émigrés in places such as Paris, Berlin, Connecticut, and Manchuria that took inspiration from Mussolini's ideology.[126] They were disgusted with the failures of the Whites of the Russian Civil War, and saw fascism as a means to solve the Bolshevik threat. Russian fascists in Harbin, Manchuria, created what became the largest fascist movement, the All-Russian Fascist Party. The party grew after the Japanese takeover of Manchuria in 1932, and there were several brief mergers between it and other Russian émigré fascist parties. Nevertheless, these were not significant movements. There were probably only "several thousand" Russian fascists scattered across the globe, and no significant presence in the Soviet Union.[127]

Fascist Movements in France

France developed unambiguously fascist movements in the interwar period, particularly Le Faisceau and the Francistes. However, there is widespread agreement that these two groups were relatively insignificant. Le Faisceau was founded in 1925 by Georges Valois. Obviously inspired by the Italian model, Valois was looking to be the French Mussolini. Le Faisceau's influence peaked

---

[125] Hans Rogger, "Was There a Russian Fascism? The Union of Russian People," *The Journal of Modern History* 36, no. 4 (1964): 414; George Gilbert, *The Radical Right in Late Imperial Russia: Dreams of a True Fatherland?* (New York: Routledge, 2016): 227.

[126] John J. Stephan, *The Russian Fascists: Tragedy and Farce in Exile, 1925–1945* (New York: Harper & Row, 1978); Susanne Hohler, *Fascism in Manchuria: The Soviet-China Encounter in the 1930s* (London: I. B. Tauris, 2017); Erwin Oberlander, "The All-Russian Fascist Party," *Journal of Contemporary History* 1, no. 1 (1966): 158–73.

[127] Susanne Hohler, "Russian Fascism in Exile: A Historical and Phenomenological Perspective on Transnational Fascism," *Fascism* 2, no. 2 (2013): 123. The significance of fascist and far-right Russian émigrés was their contributions to the development of National Socialism. See Michael Kellogg, *The Russian Roots of Nazism: White Émigrés and the Making of National Socialism, 1917–1945* (New York: Cambridge University Press, 2005).

with demonstrations in the summer of 1926 that drew a self-reported ten thousand supporters.[128] Its support declined as the conservative Poincaré ministry took over from the "Cartel of the Left," the coalition of leftist parties that ruled from 1924 to the summer of 1926 and prompted much fervor on the right. In 1933, Marcel Bucard, a veteran of Le Faisceau, founded Francistes. As mentioned, it was subsidized by the Italian government. It had even less of a following than Le Faisceau.[129]

While Le Faisceau and Francistes were relatively insignificant, they can be thought of as part of a much larger collection of militant right-wing groups that were willing to use extralegal means to undermine the republic. The debate over whether there were significant fascist movements in France therefore hinges on whether right-wing groups such as Action Française and especially the Croix de Feu were fascist. Action Française was, as one book title proclaims, a group of "die-hard reactionaries."[130] Founded in 1899, this neomonarchist elitist group was the only significant survivor of the prewar authoritarian nationalist groups. The Croix de Feu was founded as a veterans association in 1927, but it became more political in the 1930s as a moderately authoritarian nationalist party. It became the largest right-wing movement in France, and possibly the largest political party in France on the eve of World War II.[131]

Most scholars have argued that these groups were not fascists, but there is dissenting opinion.[132] Robert Soucy, for example, insists these organizations and other far-right groups were fascist. The dispute is not as much about the nature of these organizations as about the nature of fascism. He considers fascism as essentially anti-Marxism. For Soucy, the only thing distinguishing fascism from "nonfascist" conservatism was the latter's support for democracy, although he

[128] Jules Levey, "George Calois and the Faisceau: The Making and Breaking of a Fascist," *French Historical Studies* 8, no. 2 (1973): 297.

[129] Soucy, *French Fascism*, 39–40.

[130] Edward R. Tannenbaum, *The Action Française: Die-Hard Reactionaries in Twentieth Century France* (New York: John Wiley & Sons, 1962).

[131] The Popular Front government dissolved the Croix de Feu in 1936, and it was replaced by the Parti Social Français, a political party.

[132] Most of the general works on fascism as well as those on fascism in France argue these groups were not fascist, but for the dissenters, see Robert Soucy, "Problematising the Immunity Thesis," in *France in the Era of Fascism: Essays on the French Authoritarian Right*, ed. Brian Jenkins (New York: Berghahn Books, 2005), 93nn4, 5. For reviews of the historiographical debate about French fascism, see Jenkins, ed., *France in the Era of Fascism*, well as Robert D. Zaretsky, "Neither Left, nor Right, nor Straight Ahead: Recent Books on Fascism in France," *The Journal of Modern History* 73, no. 1 (2011): 118–32; Sean Kennedy, "The End of Immunity? Recent Work on the Far Right in Interwar France," *Historical Reflections* 34, no. 2 (2008): 25–45; John F. Sweets, "Hold That Pendulum! Redefining Fascism, Collaborationism and Resistance in France," *French Historical Studies* 15, no. 4 (1988): 731–58. One significant group that was not initially fascist but increasingly had fascist attributes was the Parti Populaire Français, founded in 1936. Payne describes it as transitioning to full fascism under German occupation. Payne, *A History of Fascism*, 400. The Rassemblement National Populaire (RNP) was another fascist party that was founded during the war.

admits this was also slippery.[133] This serves Soucy's arguments that French fascism was a movement of the right rather than neither left nor right,[134] and that there was a significant fascist movement in France. But this does not comport with how most scholars of fascism, observers of fascists, and fascists themselves use or used the term. Even though there was overlap, fascism was not synonymous with reactionary or conservative politics.[135] The leader of Le Faisceau expressly founded the organization because Action Française was not fascist. The leader of the Croix de Feu resisted the push from some members to turn it into a fascist organization, and so they left for more radical groups. Italian fascists also had the notion of what is now known as the fascist minimum, and they regarded these groups not as revolutionary fascists but instead simply as counterrevolutionary.[136] They could be useful allies in the fascists' fight against the left, but not truly one of them. There was thus an insignificant fascism movement in France, unless one includes radical right movements not usually considered fascist.

Section Summary

Fascism was a transnational movement. The first wave, around Mussolini's "March on Rome," sprouted groups across Europe. The magnitude, though, was markedly different across the continent. This wave generated major movements in Austria, Hungary, Romania, Spain, and Germany. Elsewhere, the movements were minor. The second fascist wave, in the context of the Great Depression, increased the strength of fascist movements across the board but did not change the distribution of states with significant fascist movements. Fascist groups interacted with far-right authoritarian movements, and France had significant followings of the latter. But among the great powers, only Germany had a significant fascist movement.

International Relations Prior to the Italian Revolution

The European international politics of this post–World War I period was characterized by the ostracization of the Soviet Union, as we have seen, and a fragile relationship between the two status quo powers, Britain and France, and the

---

[133] Soucy, *French Fascism*, xv–xvi, 17–18.

[134] This is in contrast to Zeev Sternhell, *Neither Right nor Left: Fascist Ideology in France*, trans. David Maisel (Berkeley: University of California Press, 1986).

[135] The one major scholar of comparative fascism who regards Action Française as fascist defines fascism as a type of anti-Marxism. Ernst Nolte, *Three Faces of Fascism* (New York: Mentor, 1969), 40.

[136] Marsella, "Assessing European Fascism," 94–141.

potential revisionists, Germany and Italy. Germany resented the Versailles settlement, and although there was a range of opinion within Germany about the tack to take, the predominant sentiment favored resisting those constraints. They would erode the Versailles settlement by attacking the weakest link: the reparations issue. During Mussolini's March on Rome, the French were preparing an occupation of the Ruhr because of Germany's refusal to pay reparations. This was straining British-French relations, because the former thought the latter was taking too hard a line.

Italy, the weakest of the great powers, had long harbored revisionist aims. The Italians viewed their Risorgimento as incomplete (there were Italian communities not in the Italian state) and they wanted to make up ground in the European colonizing game. Their aspirations were delineated in the Treaty of London, which was their list of demands to enter World War I. Their slogan after the war was the "Treaty of London plus Fiume," the largely Italian city on the Adriatic. When they did not achieve all those goals, they called their victory in World War I a "mutilated" one. The Americans took the lead in blocking Italian aspirations in the Balkans, and the British and French went along. The dissolution of the Austrian and Russian Empires created an opportunity for an expansion of Italian influence along the Danube and territorial expansion in the Balkans. Here Italy clashed with France. France wanted to shore up these states to prevent the reestablishment of the Austrian Empire and the expansion of German power, and also so that these states could act as a bulwark against communism. On the other hand, France and Britain, but especially France, had a reason to court Italy as a balancer against Germany, particularly because Russia was no longer playing that role.

Germany was ambivalent toward Italy. Italy was a potential revisionist bedfellow, but Italy benefited from some of the Versailles settlement directed against Germany. One of Italy's territorial rewards from the former Austrian Empire, the South Tyrol, put Italy at odds with German nationalists given the region's primarily German population.

Predictions

Given the lack of significant fascist movements in great powers other than Germany, my theory expects that it would be business as usual between these powers, as there would be a lack of contagion concerns. What this might mean is that there would be a basic continuity in policy and the Italian Revolution would not significantly affect interstate relations, unless there was some other reason to take a hostile or beneficent stance toward the new regime, independent of contagion concerns. Germany, however, would be hostile toward Italy, given its fascist

Table 5.2 Response to the Italian Fascist Revolution

Great Power	Stance Toward Italy Prior to Revolution	Significant Revolutionary Fascist Movement?	Prediction of Stance Toward Revolutionary Italy Given Revolutionary Movement	Outcome
Britain	Aligned with, but tensions	No	Unaffected by fears of contagion	Aligned with, but tensions
France	Aligned with, but tensions	No	Unaffected by fears of contagion	Aligned with, but tensions
Germany	Ambivalent	Yes	Hostile	Ambivalent
Soviet Union	Hostile (driven by Italian hostility)	No	Unaffected by fears of contagion	Improved relations

movement. I have coded France as not having a fascist movement, but if we include the radical right in France more broadly, then we would expect hostility toward Italian fascism. Because there are two revolutionary movements in the same period, some contrasting predictions arise regarding Italian-Soviet relations, which I address in what follows. The fear of communist contagion would predict cooperation between Italy and the non-Soviet states, as well as Italian hostility toward the Soviets, though the lack of a fear of fascist contagion by the Soviets would mean that the Soviets would not necessarily be hostile toward fascist Italy.

Other theories have different expectations. The ideological theory expects hostility toward the fascist regime by the other great powers, which were communist and liberal regimes. Fascism, after all, was against liberalism as well as communism.[137] Another potential source of hostility toward the Italian fascist state, independent of ideological distances between regimes or concern about revolutionary contagion, is the foreign policy content of the fascist ideology, specifically its emphasis on war and expansionism. As noted, Italy already was a state not content with the status quo, which caused friction between it and Britain and France in particular. Fascism, though, seemed to promise revisionism on another level. Mussolini in fact directly targeted these states, even threatening French territorial integrity by calling for Italy to take over Nice and Sardinia, and

---

[137] One might claim that fascism was a lesser ideological threat for liberals than communism, but the "ideological" theory does not provide a means to assess this ex ante.

challenging the British Empire, as reflected in the slogan "The Mediterranean for the Mediterraneans!"[138]

We will see that the reactions to the Italian fascist revolution in some ways validate the domestic contagion effects theory, although in some ways they do not. As expected by the theory, in Britain, France, and the Soviet Union there was no fear of contagion of fascism given the lack of significant fascist movements, and thus that factor did not affect their bilateral relations with Italy, in contrast to what the ideological theory would expect. This is despite the fact that Italy ended up directly supporting fascist movements in Britain and France. To the extent ideological factors had salience for Britain and France, fascism was seen in a positive light because it was against the revolutionary left. This outweighed concerns Britain and France had about an aggressive fascist foreign policy. On the other hand, Germany had no significant contagion concerns from the Italian fascist revolution despite its significant revolutionary movement essentially because it already had what it regarded as a more significant revolutionary movement to deal with—the revolutionary left. And although the lack of concern from the Soviets about fascist contagion is to be expected from the theory, the Italian outreach to the Soviets is inconsistent with the theory of the book, given their revolutionary socialist history.

International Relations of the Italian Fascist Revolution, 1920s

British and French Reaction to the Italian Fascist Revolution

Given the lack of significant revolutionary fascist movements in Britain and France, the domestic contagion effects theory does not expect large fears of contagion, and thus the patterns of conflict and cooperation based on that fear of contagion would not arise. That is indeed what we see. British and French policymakers were somewhat apprehensive concerning fascist Italy's expansionist aims, but they looked beyond that. As Zara Steiner says, "In sharp contrast with their attitude towards the Soviet Union, [Western statesmen] sought Mussolini's participation in the European reconstruction process and minimized the danger of his radical nationalist revolution."[139] They did not have much concern about the ideological program in Italy. If anything, British and French policymakers were supportive of what fascism was accomplishing in Italy—namely, repressing the revolutionary left.

---

[138] Alan Cassels, *Mussolini's Early Diplomacy* (Princeton: Princeton University Press, 1970), 11.
[139] Steiner, *The Lights That Failed*, 314.

As discussed, fascism in Italy emerged during the "Red years," when workers were occupying factories. That colored British and French attitudes toward fascism. The British ambassador in Rome, who had witnessed the Russian Revolution as ambassador to St. Petersburg, provided an interpretation typical of the British government: the fascists had "rendered Italy a service by reawakening a more healthy patriotic spirit and by counteracting the revolutionary activities of the Extremists."[140] French diplomats had the same reaction.[141]

This attitude continued when Mussolini came to power. Austen Chamberlain wrote to the British ambassador in Rome, "It is not part of my business as Foreign Secretary to appreciate [Mussolini's] action in the domestic policies of Italy, but if I ever had to choose in my own country between anarchy and dictatorship, I expect I should be on the side of the dictator."[142] He did not refrain from judging Soviet domestic policies, and in fact what endeared fascists to the right-wing governments in France and Britain was that the fascists were crushing the socialists. Churchill, in a visit to Italy, told a press conference, "If I had been an Italian I should have been wholeheartedly with you from start to finish in your triumphant struggle against the bestial appetites and passions of Leninism."[143] Recognition of the new regime was never an issue. Just after coming to office, Poincaré and Curzon welcomed Mussolini to the Lausanne Conference, involving a new peace treaty with Turkey. They resisted Mussolini's demands for a mandate in Iraq, among other things, but his mere presence legitimized the new regime.

There were concerns about Mussolini's foreign policy ambition and the violence of the fascist regime, but these were mostly excused. The main cause of concern was not so much fascism's anti-liberalism, but the possibility that the fascists' violent tactics could further provoke the left. Regarding foreign policy, the Corfu incident of 1923 was an early indicator that the fascist rhetoric of expansion was not just rhetoric. Mussolini was looking for a pretext to take over the island of Corfu, and he got it when Italian diplomats were assassinated there, possibly with his knowledge. He issued an ultimatum to the Greeks designed to be rejected, and when it was, he occupied the island of Corfu. Although some in the League of Nations demanded a condemnation of Italy, Britain, and France got the matter sidelined to the Conference of Ambassadors, where they could control the investigation. They eventually forced the Greeks to pay reparations to

[140] A. F. Manning, "Reports of the British Embassy in Rome on the Rise of Fascism," *Risorgimento* 1 (1980): 34.
[141] Joel Richard Blatt, "French Reaction to Italy, Italian Fascism and Mussolini, 1919–1925: The Views from Paris and the Palazzo Farnese," PhD thesis, University of Rochester, 1976, 488–563.
[142] P. G. Edwards, "The Austen Chamberlain–Mussolini Meetings," *The Historical Journal* 14, no. 1 (1971): 157.
[143] R. J. B. Bosworth, "The British Press, the Conservatives, and Mussolini, 1920–1934," *Journal of Contempory History* 5, no. 2 (1970): 173.

Italy, but also forced the Italians to evacuate Corfu. The French especially pushed the Italian agenda. It was not a good start for the League of Nations, and it was an auspicious beginning to Italian foreign expansion. As Alan Cassels notes, "Those, and they were numerous and influential, who chose to regard Mussolini as an anti-Bolshevik bulwark and accepted him as a respected participant in European diplomacy, dismissed the episode as a momentary Fascist aberration. Yet nothing was further from the truth."[144]

The British and French had a general policy of accommodation with Mussolini. They pushed back on some of Mussolini's demands, but what is more notable is how obliging they were. They integrated him into the Locarno summit to pose as a good European, despite his revisionist aims. Much of his ambition was curtailed by Italian weakness, but the Corfu incident and other actions such as Italy's inroads into Albania signaled that ambition. The Franco-Italian relationship through the 1920s would face strains from a variety of causes: the French attempt to naturalize the Italians in Tunisia, competition for influence along the Danube, and the activities of Italian anti-fascist emigrants in France. The Cartel of the Left, the leftist coalition that ruled France from 1924 to 1926, was less sympathetic to the Fascist regime. But relations remained relatively friendly.

There were a variety of reasons for the cordiality of Britain and France toward fascist Italy. Sometimes there were narrow political interests. During the Corfu incident, for example, France wanted Italy to take its side in the Ruhr crisis at the time. But a key reason for France's broad amicability was its lack of contagion concerns about fascism and its contagion concerns about communism. The conservative governments in Britain and France, and the conservative movements in these states, were particularly enthusiastic about Italian fascism because of its role in destroying leftist forces there, even if very few wished to adapt fascism to Britain or France.[145] The radical right wing in France was sometimes jealous of fascism. It was a potential ideological rival. However, the leader of Action Française, who saw Le Faisceau spring from his ranks under the inspiration of Mussolini, considered Italian fascism to be a bulwark against the great communist threat: "The assassination of Mussolini would be the assassination of order in Western Europe."[146] Among British and French policymakers, there was the fear that if Mussolini was removed from the scene, someone worse would take his place.[147]

---

[144] Cassels, *Mussolini's Early Diplomacy*, 125.

[145] For the conservative reaction in Britain, see Philip Williamson, "The Conservative Party, Fascism and Anti-Fascism 1918–1939," in *Varieties of Anti-Fascism: Britain in the Inter-War Period*, eds. Nigel Copsey and Andrzej Olechnowicz, 73–97 (New York: Palgrave Macmillan, 2010). For the conservative and right radical reaction in France, see Blatt, "French Reaction to Italy," 674–775.

[146] Blatt, "Relatives and Rivals," 278.

[147] Peter Edwards, "The Foreign Office and Fascism 1924–1929," *Journal of Contempory History* 5, no. 2 (1970): 158; Blatt, "French Reaction to Italy," 791, 845, 901, 907, 912.

There does not appear to be much in the way of contagion concerns regarding fascism in the French government or the public at large, even when Mussolini was financing fascist groups in France. One conservative writer explicitly asked, "Could the contagion of the example install itself in France?" He was "one of the few French conservatives to extend disease terminology from the Left to Fascism." His answer was that the Italian experience was not relevant to France, which was "infinitely more ordered. Our neighbors demand a surgical operation and a great practitioner. . . . We need only some tonic."[148] Some on both the left and the right considered the possibility of fascist contagion, but not to France—they worried that the Italian fascist success could serve as a model for extreme German nationalists.[149] For France, this would be alarming from a foreign policy perspective, given the German nationalists' rabid resistance to the Versailles settlement. But it could be good news from a domestic perspective, because they would fight the left. In fact, just after Mussolini came to power, Poincaré was given a French intelligence report noting that Mussolini had for a long time been connected with German nationalist organizations, and the report put that in a positive light (from the perspective of Poincaré): "The Fascists tend to constitute a 'White International,' which would oppose the 'Red International.'"[150] Leftist contagion was the real concern. One historian notes that the French government's documents regarding revolutionary leftist parties in Italy from 1918 to the fascist takeover are contained in four and two-thirds bound volumes, whereas the period from the fascist takeover until November 1926, when all other political parties were banned, was only seventy-two pages of documents.[151] Clearly the French were pleased with the developments in Italy.

The fact that there were no contagion fears among the British is what we would expect given the lack of a significant fascist movement. Fascism was a "minor irritant." Even the leadership of the British Communist Party was more interested in fighting fascism abroad.[152] British authorities treated the BUF's Owsley, leader of the largest British fascist party, as "a figure of ridicule rather than a threat to the ability to protest."[153] To the extent they were alarmed, it was because they feared that the disorder associated with the BUF's rallies would encourage the growth of the much bigger anti-fascist movement, which was perceived by the British security services as a Communist Party front. The Communist Party was

[148] Blatt, "French Reaction to Italy," 580.
[149] Ibid., 628.
[150] Ibid., 812.
[151] William I. Shorrock, *From Ally to Enemy: The Enigma of Fascist Italy in French Diplomacy* (Kent: Kent State University Press, 1988), 25.
[152] Thurlow, *Fascism in Britain*, 87, 79.
[153] Dorril, *Blackshirt*, 346.

the main focus of the security services' activities.[154] The authorities were monitoring the BUF and were aware it was receiving funding from Mussolini, although the exact extent of Italian aid was not known until World War II. That very fact is indicative of the lack of concern with which they regarded not just the BUF, but Italian aid to the BUF.[155] That aid never affected British-Italian relations. Despite warnings from Italian officials that he was "flushing money down the sewer," Mussolini continued aid to the BUF until 1937.[156]

In sum, France and Britain did not react with hostility toward the fascist state, as an ideological theory would suppose. As was the case before Mussolini came to power, the British and French had differences with the Italians over aspects of their revisionism. The fascist state took revisionism to another level, and Britain and France pushed back against it. But they were not particularly alarmed at Italy's revisionist foreign policy. The anti-Bolshevik policies of the fascist regime were not the only reason for their pro-fascist policy. Another was that they needed to court Italy as a balancer against Germany. But that also involved contagion concerns—their strategic predicament of not having Russia as a balancer.

Soviet Reaction to the Italian Fascist Revolution

There is no evidence that the Soviets had any concern about fascist contagion to their own country, which is expected given the lack of a significant fascist movement. The Soviets had China ban the anti-communist and pro-fascist propaganda emanating from the insignificant fascist movement in Harbin, Manchuria.[157] However, there is no evidence that fascist movements abroad were more than an irritant. Fascism was not a domestic political threat. Fears of fascist contagion thus did not affect Soviet relations with Italy in any way.

The Soviets had other obvious reasons to dislike the fascists: the fascists were crushing the socialists. They responded negatively to the March on Rome, with Lenin threatening to remove the Soviet delegation from Italy. The Soviets treated fascism initially as a counterrevolutionary movement used by the primitive south European bourgeoisie. Some, though, recognized that fascism was distinct from standard counterrevolutionaries, and even noticed some similarities with

---

[154] Richard Thurlow, "Passive and Active Anti-Fascism: The State and National Security, 1923–45," in *Varieties of Anti-Fascism: Britain in the Inter-War Period*, eds. Copsey and Nigel Olechnowicz (London: Palgrave Macmillan, 2010), 168.

[155] Ibid., 169.

[156] The Nazis were more circumspect. Goebbels said that "fascism is a plant that does not grow in the soil of Britain." Although the Nazis eventually gave small amounts of aid to the BUF, Hitler, as he told Oswald directly, subordinated his relations with the BUF to courting British appeasers. Dorril, *Blackshirt*, 362, 341, 393.

[157] Hohler, *Fascism in Manchuria*, 4.

Bolshevik tactics. As one Soviet writer expressed, "Undoubtedly many of the novelties introduced by the Russian Bolsheviks float in the air like bacteria and are breathed involuntarily by Russia's worst enemies."[158]

Mussolini, though, sent positive signals to the Soviets about reconciling. He thought Italy had commercial interests in expanding trade with the Soviets. The Soviets, for their part, had an interest in breaking out of their diplomatic isolation. Italian de jure recognition of the Soviets could help do that, and possibly lead to trade deals that would help the industrialization of Russia. What followed was a series of ups and downs. On both sides, their diplomats' confidential reports, which denounced the other's regime, were inadvertently revealed, which complicated attempts to reconcile. Eventually the Soviets got the de jure recognition they demanded, and a trade deal was hammered out in 1924. The Soviets even requested a formal alliance with Italy in 1925, although Italy declined, for a variety of reasons.[159]

The fact that the Soviet policy toward Italy was not in any way conditioned by concern of fascist contagion is expected by the domestic contagion effects theory given the lack of fascist movements in the Soviet Union. The countries' limited rapprochement is to some extent anomalous for the ideological theory of international relations given their ideological distance. While Soviet policy toward Italy is expected in my theory, the Italian willingness to come to terms with the Soviets is anomalous given the Soviet Union's recently significant revolutionary socialist/communist movement. Part of the process of easing relations between the two was an Italian demand that Soviet Comintern activities be curbed, and those activities did trail off.[160] The Italian regime was bargaining with a regime rather than ostracizing it.

German Reaction to the Italian Fascist Revolution

German leaders had sufficient cause to worry about the contagion effects of the Italian fascist revolution. They already had a fascist movement to deal with, and it was emboldened by events in Italy. Adolf Hitler would recall in 1941, "The brown shirt probably would not have existed without the black shirt. The march on Rome, in 1922, was one of the turning-points in history. The mere fact that anything of the sort could be attempted, and could succeed, gave us an impetus."[161]

---

[158]   Cited in Stanley G. Payne, "Soviet Anti-Fascism: Theory and Practice, 1921–1945," *Totalitarian Movements and Political Religions* 4, no. 2 (2003): 5.

[159]   Pettrachi, *La Russia Rivoluzionaria nella politica italiana*, 253–59.

[160]   Ibid., 238.

[161]   Adolf Hitler, *Hitler's Table Talk, 1941–1944*, trans. Norman Cameron and R. H. Stevens (New York: Enigma Books, 2000), 10. The Nazi Party archive is full of newspaper clippings and other publications

Things like the Nazi salute came directly from the inspiration of the Italian fascists. The connection between the fascist movements was obvious, and even colored perceptions of the Nazis. British diplomats called Hitler the "Bavarian Mussolini."[162] Nazis themselves made the comparison. At a rally a week after Mussolini's ascent to power, a leading Nazi declared, "Germany's Mussolini is called Adolf Hitler."[163] Hitler kept a bust of Mussolini on his desk at party headquarters. In addition, there was a direct connection between the Italian fascists and the Nazis and other far-right nationalists. Mussolini had met with German far-right nationalists on a visit there shortly before coming to power. He may have even aided Nazis in their putsch, although if he did, he covered his tracks well. The German embassy in Rome thought Mussolini was "too clever to compromise himself."[164]

Despite this potential cause for concern, there is not a lot of evidence of contagion fears, because the Nazis were not regarded as a particularly salient threat. The German government's reaction to the Beer Hall Putsch of November 1923, directly inspired by the March on Rome, is illustrative. The Putsch was a surprise, but it was quickly dealt with by the Bavarian army. The German states of Württemberg and Baden arrested Nazi leaders, but "with the threat of a right radical revolution banished, the Bavarian question became a recurrent and irritating ache rather than a dangerous disease of the body politic."[165] It seemed less like the beginning of Nazism than the end. There were many other things that focused the minds of policymakers, among them the fact that Germany seemed to be on the brink of a communist revolution—there was a communist uprising in Hamburg just two weeks before the Putsch, and plans for insurrections elsewhere.[166] The Nazis were largely acquitted of their crimes, and Hitler served only a nine-month sentence.

Because the Nazis were downplayed as a threat, the fear of contagion was minimal and likewise did not have an appreciable effect on German-Italian relations. In foreign policy, Germany mostly stood aloof from Italy, as it had before the fascists came to power. Foreign Minister Stresemann was a conservative who looked at the radical right in Germany and elsewhere with some unease. When he died, Mussolini told his Council of Ministers his death was "an advantage to

about the March on Rome. See Christian Goeschel, *Mussolini and Hitler: The Forging of the Fascist Alliance* (New Haven: Yale University Press, 2018), 27.

[162] Detlev Clemens, "The 'Bavarian Mussolini and His 'Beerhall Putsch': British Images of Adolf Hitler, 1920–24," *The English Historical Review* 114, no. 455 (1999): 69.

[163] Ian Kershaw, *Hitler: 1889–1936 Hubris* (New York: W. W. Norton & Company, 1998), 180.

[164] Cassels, *Mussolini's Early Diplomacy*, 169.

[165] Harold J. Gordon, *Hitler and the Beer Hall Putsch* (Princeton: Princeton University Press, 1972), 455.

[166] Werner T. Angress, *Stillborn Revolution: The Communist Bid for Power in Germany, 1921–1923* (Princeton: Princeton University Press, 1963), 426–74.

us. Stresemann hated Italy and hated Fascism."[167] Stresemann did not like fascism, but it did not cause him to be hostile toward Italy. Germany recognized the new regime, and generally did not resist but rather observed Italian policies, sometimes approvingly, such as their efforts to displace French influence in the Balkans. But Germany, and Stresemann in particular, was largely ambivalent toward Italy.

Why did the two revisionist states not make common cause? Perhaps one reason for their coolness was a domestic political one—the distaste for fascism among Stresemann and his ilk.[168] It seems though the primary reason for Stresemann's ambivalence toward Italy revolved around his main foreign policy objective, which was to break free from the shackles of Versailles. Stresemann shared this goal with the far right (part of his coalition), which was constantly criticizing him for his timidity.[169] But for Stresemann, open resistance was not the way to achieve the policy objective. Instead, he would appear as a good European while Germany laid the groundwork to cast off the Versailles constraints. Openly allying with the reckless and revisionist Italy was not a means to this aim. In an early encounter, Mussolini asked the German ambassador whether Germany would be able to immobilize the French army in the event of a war between Italy and Yugoslavia. The stunned Stresemann refused to be tied down to such a reckless policy.[170] Mussolini's proposals for a German-Italian alliance were rebuffed. Mussolini on several occasions in the 1920s reached out to Germany to ask for support for his policy on the Balkans or the Danube region, and Stresemann would politely decline, not wanting to be so closely associated with a wild card that could jeopardize the more important understanding with Brittan and France.

The nadir of Italo-German relations illustrates the pressures Stresemann was working under. One area where Italy decidedly supported the Versailles settlement was its granting of South Tyrol, a German-speaking area, to Italy. German nationalists were furious about this. Hitler was an exception. He drew considerable heat for openly renouncing the German claim on South Tyrol for the purposes of aligning Germany and Italy together. Mussolini's Italianization of South Tyrol set off an acrimonious dispute. Stresemann did not want to be seen by the British and French as an adherent of pan-Germanism, but he was under domestic pressure to do something. He tried to reign in the German irredentists, but he also asked Mussolini to provide a gesture of conciliation to complement

---

[167] Cassels, *Mussolini's Early Diplomacy*, 159.

[168] This is suggested by John Hiden, *Germany and Europe 1919–1939* (London: Longman, 1993), 169; Vera Torunsky, *Entente der Revisionisten? Mussolini und Stresemann 1922–1929* (Keulen-Wenen: Böhlau, 1986), 175.

[169] Robert P. Grathwol, *Stresemann and the DNVP: Reconciliation or Revenge in German Foreign Policy, 1924–1928* (Lawrence: The Regents Press of Kansas, 1980).

[170] Cassels, *Mussolini's Early Diplomacy*, 154.

his efforts to defuse the situation. Mussolini responded negatively and an acrimonious exchange ensued, although Mussolini eventually relaxed the Italianization program and the crisis dissipated.[171]

Why was there not greater alarm at the contagion effect and thus a policy of hostility toward Italy? One answer could have to do with the significance of the Nazi movement itself. I have considered it significant, but an argument could be made that they were only significant in Bavaria until around 1924, and then their support dropped off. My theory, though, supposes that even if revolutionary movements are successfully suppressed, leaders will still be alarmed at the possibility they might reconstitute themselves, as the Nazis did. Even if the geographical limitation of Nazism is granted, when Nazi support picked up in the late 1920s across Germany, there still was not considerable alarm, at least among the center and right, the ruling coalition in Germany from late 1923 on.

Another possible reason for the lack of concern is that they did not perceive the revolutionary nature of the Nazis, and fascists in general. This, after all, was a new movement whose aims were not as clear as those of the communist movement. It was clearer what fascism was against. Added to this were the compromises the fascist movement had to make with conservative forces—the Italian one in power, and the German one trying to gain power through elections. The Nazi Party, which was initially almost named the Social Revolutionary Party, was not emphasizing its revolutionary nature to voters in 1929. Even French diplomats in Italy, close observers of fascism, initially confused fascism with conservatism or reactionary politics. A French diplomat in Milan in September 1922, for example, wrote to the embassy claiming that the program of the "pure fascists" resembled "the conservative main lines of the French party of nationalism." The French ambassador a month later described Mussolini coming to power as a "counterrevolution" that had thrown down the gauntlet "to the Bolshevik contagion."[172] It would eventually become clear enough that Nazis, and other fascists, were not traditional conservatives or merely reactionary. But even if they could spot the difference, the radical right, conservatives, moderates, and even conservative leftists shared the animus the Nazis and fascists more generally had against the revolutionary left.

The fundamental reason fascism was not regarded with greater alarm is because there was a simultaneous revolutionary movement from the left that was deemed a bigger threat. The Nazis would benefit throughout their rise to power from the presence of the communist threat. The legal system favored the extreme right over the extreme left.[173] Hitler's nine months in jail for attempting to

[171] Ibid., 280–82.
[172] Blatt, "French Reaction to Italy," 531, 550.
[173] Evans, *The Coming of the Third Reich*, 135–38.

overthrow the government is but one example of that. The Nazis came to power via conservatives who thought the Nazis were a useful tool against the leftists. Even the infamous Article 48 of the Weimar Constitution, which granted emergency powers to the president and was used by Hitler to seize dictatorial control, was drafted in the spring of 1919, when it was conceived that the president would need emergency powers to crush potential revolutionary uprisings on the left, and in fact was used for that purpose.[174]

There was concern across the political spectrum (even all the way to some in the SPD) of social revolution on the left, and so there was a corresponding willingness to cooperate with, or tolerate, the far right. After all, it was German president Friedrich Ebert, who epitomized the socialist who had abandoned the aim of revolution, who called on the Freikorps to put down communist revolutions. He said that he hated social revolution "like sin."[175] Not everyone agreed with his accommodating position, and Ebert's willingness to act more softly against the right than the left caused the SPD to withdraw from the coalition government in November 1923, never to return.[176] For much of the political spectrum, though, their main animus was the far left. The Nazis pilloried those such as Konrad Adenauer in the Center Party. Nevertheless, as late as 1932 Adenauer regarded the Nazis as a relative nuisance and focused instead on the communist threat.[177]

The Fascist Revolution and the European Powers

In sum, the reaction to the fascist revolution in Italy was in some ways as expected by the domestic contagion effects theory. There were no significant fascist movements in three of the great powers: Britain, France, and the Soviet Union. Consequently, there were no significant fears of fascist contagion in those states, and the Italian Revolution did not significantly affect bilateral relations because of that factor. Indeed, it had little effect on relations between Italy and the western powers. This was despite the fact that the Italian regime was amplifying Italy's revisionist aspirations, and despite the fact that the regime attempted to spread revolution abroad. The fascists did not solicit direct comparisons to the Comintern, and Mussolini would claim that fascism was not for export when he

---

[174] Eberhard Kolb, *The Weimar Republic*, trans. P. S. Falla and R. J. Park, 2nd ed. (New York: Routledge, 2005), 162–63.

[175] Prince Max of Baden, *The Memoirs of Prince Max of Baden*, trans. W. M. Calder and C. W. H. Sutton, vol. 2 (London: Constable & Co., 1928), 312.

[176] Harry Harmer, *Friedrich Ebert* (London: Haus Publishing, 2008), 143.

[177] Charles Williams, *Adenauer: The Father of the New Germany* (London: Little, Brown and Company, 2000), 196–97. Many of his fellow Catholics were just as hostile toward the communists, if not more so, and thus in favor of aligning with Nazis. See Klaus Große Kracht, "Campaigning Against Bolshevism: Catholic Action in Late Weimar Germany," *Journal of Contemporary History* 53 no. 3 (2018): 550–73.

had an interest in appearing as a good European. But he made increasingly clear that he regarded his movement as a transnational phenomenon. He eventually aided fascist movements in France and Britain, but because these movements were not regarded as significant, there were no contagion concerns in those states. The Soviet Union had no fear of fascist contagion and, after a fitful start, pursued a policy of attempting to ingratiate itself with Italy to try to break out of its isolation.

In Germany, though, there was a robust fascist movement, yet there were no significant fears of contagion, contrary to my theory. Likewise, Weimar foreign policy was not notably affected by the fear of contagion. It is the one instance in the book where there was a significant revolutionary movement and there does not seem to be a significant fear of contagion, despite the fact that revolutionary movements were emboldened by the Italian fascists. The reasons are peculiar to this era, when there were two revolutionary movements in the Weimar Republic. Many elites were not committed to the existing regime, and even if they were, they thought the Nazis and other right-wing revolutionaries were not the threat that the leftist revolutionaries were, and were even a useful tool against them.

The Italian ambassador in London advised the British fascists to take advantage of the support of conservatives and then get rid of them. He pointed to the Italian example: "The reactionaries believed they could use us to defeat socialism and democracies and then be in charge themselves; when they realized the threat of socialism was a joke compared with the Revolution which you were preparing, they were alarmed and tried to withdraw, but it was too late."[178] Conservatives were usually not that gullible. They recognized that while they shared some goals with fascists, they differed from them, too. Hitler had said, "The problem of defeating Bolshevism is that of the fascisisation of all the European states."[179] Conservatives, however, disagreed. They usually preferred their own. They would reach out to and cooperate with fascists at home and abroad only when they felt they did not have better options.[180] Despite the upheavals of World War I, economic depression, and revolutions, elites in the non-Soviet regimes were good at reconstituting their power.[181] Those who were pressured to deal with the fascists and thought they could control them were ultimately mistaken. But their beliefs were not entirely unreasonable. Even the fascist regimes had a hard

---

[178] Dorril, *Blackshirt*, 273.

[179] Morgan, *Fascism in Europe*, 161.

[180] For example, despite claims to the contrary, the conservative force of German big business did not prefer to aid the Nazi Party. Nazis were "the last hope rather than the first choice" of capitalists, as Kershaw says. Henry Ashby Turner, *German Big Business and the Rise of Hitler* (New York: Oxford University Press, 1985); Ian Kershaw, *The Nazi Dictatorship*, 4th ed. (New York: Oxford University Press, 2000), 48. For a larger discussion of the relationship between the conservatives and the fascists, see Martin Blinkhorn, *Fascism and the Right in Europe 1919–1945* (Harlow: Pearson Education, 2000); Blinkhorn, *Fascists and Conservatives* (London: Unwin Hyman, 1990).

[181] Charles S. Maier, *Recasting Bourgeois Europe* (Princeton: Princeton University Press, 1975).

time implementing a social revolution given their necessary compromises with conservatives and other institutions. It would take war for them to achieve their full aims.[182]

Conclusion

This book has a simple theory: leaders would fear contagion effects of revolutions when they had opposition movements of a similar type, and this fear of contagion would be relatively independent of the policies of the revolutionary state attempting to promote revolution abroad. This fear of contagion would, in turn, prompt hostility toward the revolutionary state and cooperation among states with similar movements and thus fears of contagion. How well does this model explain the reaction to the Russian and Italian revolutions?

This chapter shows the power of the theory. There was usually fear of contagion when there were significant revolutionary movements, although in the German response to the Italian Revolution this was not the case. This fear of contagion, and its corresponding international effects, existed independently of revolutionary states acting as platforms to spread revolution abroad. Russia certainly attempted to spread revolution abroad, though the fears of contagion and international reaction predated much of this activity. Italy also attempted to spread revolution abroad by aiding insignificant fascist movements that did not have a significant effect on the host country's behavior. There were limitations to the theory, though. The lack of German contagion fears of fascism is not what the domestic contagion effects theory would predict.

Paired with the fascist case, the lack of similar fears of contagion regarding Italy and corresponding lack of an effect on international politics draws into relief the contrast with how Russia was handled. Keith Neilson has noted that there were two revisionist powers in interwar Europe, Germany and Italy, and two status quo powers, Britain and France. The other great power, Russia, was revolutionary but not necessarily revisionist.[183] That is, the Soviets were committed in the long run to overturning the capitalist order, but rather than trying to overthrow the territorial order, they were in the interim just trying to survive, and were more than willing to play balance-of-power politics with the West. The Bolsheviks were very aware that divisions among the capitalists were the

---

[182] MacGregor Knox, *Common Destiny: Dictatorship, Foreign Policy, and War in Fascist Italy and Nazi Germany* (New York: Cambridge University Press, 2000).

[183] Keith Neilson, *Britain, Soviet Russia, and the Collapse of the Versailles Order 1919–1939* (Cambridge: Cambridge University Press, 2006), 5.

only reason they survived, and thus they were willing to cut deals with capitalist states.[184] Why the western powers did not align with the Soviet Union against Germany is one of the great puzzles of realist balance-of-power theory. The attention to this puzzle usually focuses on the 1930s and especially the immediate run-up to the outbreak of war, but the basic pattern was laid down before then.[185]

The Soviet Union, as Neilson says, became a somewhat status quo player internationally but was a threat to other states' domestic order. It was thus ostracized. In contrast, Italy was a revisionist player internationally but mostly not a threat to states' domestic order, and it was embraced. One can argue about whether fascism is more ideologically distant than communism from liberalism. It is not obvious what the answer to that question is. But what explains the different responses to these movements is not the amount of ideological distance but the perceived threat one was to the political and social order compared to the other. The western powers pulled Mussolini into the community of powers and minimized the revolutionary danger, to some extent because he was seen as a bulwark against Bolshevism. The ideological danger of fascism was not so much its possible contagion but the fact that it motivated these fascist states to engage in expansionist behavior. This was deemed manageable when the "least of the great powers," Italy, was fascist. When the most powerful state in Europe, Germany, succumbed, that was a bigger problem. Even then, Germany was a threat the western powers thought they could manage, and they seemed to think it was less of a problem than the communist threat. Even Churchill, who is credited with an appreciation of the Nazi threat that exceeded that of his Conservative colleagues, was hesitant to take an anti-German/pro-Soviet line until the late 1930s, and he might have gone the other way if the Spanish Civil War had resulted in a victory for leftist forces.[186]

The reaction to these revolutions was not as straightforward as the simple theory of this book. Germany's policy toward the Russian Revolution was at times exactly the opposite of what the theory would expect. There were many factors affecting great-power relations of the period beyond the fear of contagion.

---

[184] Debo, *Survival and Consolidation*, 311–14; Stephen Kotkin, *Stalin: Paradoxes of Power, 1878–1928* (New York: Penguin Press, 2014), 556–58.

[185] For examinations of the 1930s from this perspective, see Mark L. Haas, "Ideology and Alliances: British and French External Balancing Decisions in the 1930s," *Security Studies* 12, no. 4 (2003): 34–79; Michael Jabara Carley, *1939: The Alliance That Never Was and the Coming of World War II* (Chicago: Ivan R. Dee, 1999); Sandra Halperin, "The Politics of Appeasement: The Rise of the Left and European International Relations During the Interwar Period," in *Contested Social Orders*, ed. David Skidmore, 128–64 (Nashville: Vanderbilt University Press, 1997); Alexander Anievas, "The International Political Economy of Appeasement: The Social Sources of British Foreign Policy During the 1930s," *Review of International Studies* 37 (2011): 601–29.

[186] David Carlton, *Churchill and the Soviet Union* (Manchester: Manchester University Press, 2000), 210.

But what is surprising is how much of international politics is illuminated by the theory, especially in the extraordinary context of a world war and its aftermath. Indeed, it is impossible to explain the relations among the great powers in this critical period without understanding how the powers would react to the communist threat.

6

The Islamic Revolution and the Middle East

In 1979, the Iranian Revolution replaced the Persian monarchy with an Islamic republic and scrambled the politics of the entire region. In the aftermath of the revolution, there was a complete reversal of Middle Eastern alliances, including Saudi Arabia newly aligning with Iraq, giving support to the very military machine that would threaten it only a few years later. Iraq, meanwhile, invaded Iran, starting a war that ended in the antebellum status quo after becoming the bloodiest and costliest in modern Middle Eastern history. What explains these outcomes? I will argue, based in part on an investigation into primary sources, that fears that the Iranian Revolution might spread in good part explain the large and sometimes puzzling effects the revolution had on the international politics of the region.

The domestic contagion effects theory asserts that leaders will fear the contagion of revolutions when there are significant opposition movements of a similar type within their own country. Moreover, this fear of contagion will be independent of whether the revolutionary state attempts to promote revolution abroad. The Iranian Revolution was a potential boost to political Islam across the region. The basic goal of the Islamist movements was to displace regimes of insufficient religiosity with those that would make Islamic law the basis of legitimacy and conduct. I find a significant Islamist revolutionary movement prior to the Iranian Revolution in all the major regional powers, with the exception of Saudi Arabia. However, the Saudis got a significant Islamist opposition movement in November 1979, and, as expected, Saudi fear of contagion arose immediately, as did the Saudis' hostility toward Iran, *before* Iran attempted to act as a platform in spreading revolution.

My theory also predicts that anticipation of contagion will prompt hostility toward the revolutionary state and cooperation among states with similar revolutionary movements. The Saudis' cooperation with Iraq is consistent with this theory, although anomalous for balance-of-power theory. The theory correctly predicts Iraqi-Saudi reconciliation with Egypt in the context of a shared ideological threat. It also predicts the hostility of Egypt, Syria, and Iraq toward Iran. I show that the fear of contagion was critical in explaining Iraqi hostility

Revolutionary Contagion and International Politics. Chad E. Nelson, Oxford University Press. © Oxford University Press 2022. DOI: 10.1093/oso/9780197601921.003.0006

toward Iran. To be sure, I also find that the fear of Iran acting as a platform was decisive in explaining the actual outbreak of the Iran-Iraq War. Egypt was hostile toward Iran for the model it gave Egypt's own Islamists, even though Iran did not act as a platform spreading revolution there. The theory would not predict the Syrian-Iranian alliance in the aftermath of the revolution, which shows that the theory highlights tendencies that are sometimes counteracted by other factors. Overall, one cannot explain the sea change of alliances in the aftermath of the revolution without taking into account the fear of contagion. Leaders saw attempts to blunt the Islamic wave by co-opting it as insufficient. Ruling-class strategies to deal with challengers at home clearly extended to foreign affairs.

As in previous chapters, I first assess the independent variables: (1) the extent to which the Iranian Revolution acted as a platform and a model to spread revolution, and (2) whether there was a significant Islamist revolutionary opposition movement in the major powers of the region—Iraq, Syria, Egypt, and Saudi Arabia. I then assess the international effects of the revolution by analyzing the policies of these powers toward the revolutionary state and toward each other before and after the revolution.

The Iranian Revolution

Within about a year, the Persian monarchy went from being perceived as very stable to completely collapsing. In early January 1979, the shah fled the country. Shortly thereafter, Ayatollah Khomeini, the symbol of the opposition, returned from exile, and the shah's caretaker government disbanded. What surprised observers further was the theocratic nature of the Islamic republic that was established. Islamic institutions played a crucial role in the mobilization against the shah's regime, and they helped legitimize revolutionary activity to a largely religious people. But there was certainly no consensus on the system of *velayat-e-faqih* (guardianship of the jurist), whereby clerics would exercise direct political power, that was eventually established by Khomeini. Uniting the various revolutionary groups—liberals, leftists, and Islamists—was their opposition to the shah. Many inside and outside the country assumed Khomeini was more of a charismatic figurehead. The ayatollah, however, proved to be much more than a figurehead, and from his return until 1983 he systematically removed all opposition. The most critical step was a clerical coup d'état or second revolution: in the aftermath of the takeover of the American embassy in November 1979, the moderate prime minister, Mehdi Bazargan, resigned. Khomeini used the charged atmosphere to get support for critical articles of the new constitution that granted the jurist—Khomeini—extensive powers.

Model

The Iranian Revolution served as a model of a people overthrowing the established order. It potentially had particular salience for the monarchical, pro-Western regimes of the Persian Gulf. In terms of what it was for, the revolution's purpose for the Islamists who ultimately triumphed was to bring Islam into politics. Different ideas existed in Iran as to what an Islamic republic consisted of, but the Islamic character of the new regime was undeniable. The particulars of the Iranian model, a product of Khomeini's idiosyncratic interpretation of Shi'ism, had limited appeal even among the Shia community in Iran, although the revolution would change that.[1]

If the Iranian Revolution was to serve as a broader model, which it did, it would be via the more general notion of what was wrong with Muslim societies and how to overcome that. Common to both Shia and Sunni radicals was the diagnosis that the Muslim world was in a state of apostasy given their infatuation with Western ideas and norms, and the prescription that the faithful must return to politics by overthrowing the existing regimes and enacting Islamic law. Khomeini was keen to emphasize the similarities and downplay the differences between Shia and Sunni. Iranian propaganda emphasized the commonalities, and Khomeini took steps to bridge the divide. For example, he prohibited the common Shia practice of criticizing Abu Bakr and Umar and praised prominent Sunni Islamists.[2] Today's highly sectarian Middle East should not obscure the fact that Iran was seen as a model for Islamists in general.

Platform

In Iran, the call to export the revolution was often portrayed as integral to the revolution itself. "The Iranian Revolution is not exclusively that of Iran," Khomeini insisted, "because Islam does not belong to any particular people.

[1] For an explication of the political theology of Shia religious authorities and critiques of Khomeini's concept of governance, see Hamid Mavani, *Religious Authority and Political Thought in Twelver Shi'ism: From Ali to Post-Khomeini* (New York: Routledge, 2013), 141–210; Hamid Mavani, "Ayatullah Khomeini's Concept of Governance (Wilayat Al-Faqih) and the Classical Shi'i Doctrine of Imamate," *Middle Eastern Studies* 47, no. 5 (2011): 807–24. Arjomand notes that the political revolution in Iran led to a religious revolution in Shia thought, whereby Khomeini's radical version of direct clerical rule gained ascendancy. Said Amir Arjomand, "Ideological Revolution in Shi'ism," in *Authority and Political Culture in Shi'ism*, ed. Said Amir Arjomand (Albany: State University of New York Press, 1988), 190–98.

[2] See Emmanuel Sivan, "Sunni Radicalism in the Middle East and the Iranian Revolution," *International Journal of Middle East Studies* 21, no. 1 (1989): 1–30; Wilfried Buchta, "The Failed Pan-Islamic Program of the Islamic Republic: Views of the Liberal Reformers of the Religious 'Semi-Opposition,'" in *Iran and the Surrounding World: Interactions in Culture and Cultural Politics*, eds. Nikki R. Keddie and Rudi Matthee (Seattle: University of Washington Press, 2002), 389–423.

Islam is revealed for mankind and the Muslims, not for Iran."[3] There was in Iran, as in other revolutionary states, a missionary motive for exporting the revolution. There was also a belief that if the revolution did not spread, it would be squelched. As Khomeini said in March 1980, "We should set aside the thought that we do not export our revolution, because Islam does not regard various Islamic countries differently and is the supporter of all the oppressed peoples of the world." He continued, echoing past revolutionaries, "If we remain in an enclosed environment we shall definitely face defeat."[4]

The particular targets for Khomeini's message were Muslims under the rule of tyrants in what were considered non-Islamic systems. Khomeini called for the unity of all Muslims and at times used language that suggested he rejected the nation-state system.[5] Nevertheless, he accepted the state system and insisted that Iran should help other states implement an Islamic government. In a widely distributed tract produced in exile, Khomeini had insisted, "It is our duty to remove from the life of Muslim society all traces of *kufr* [the rejection of divine guidance] and destroy them," but this was "a duty that all Muslims must fulfill, in every one of the Muslim countries, in order to achieve the triumphant political revolution of Islam."[6]

Khomeini and others felt that Iran's role in this process was chiefly as an example to Muslims in their own countries to rise up and depose their leaders just as Iranians had done with the shah. But they also were eager to use propaganda, or "sound advertising," to encourage emulation.[7] What became known

[3] Farhang Rajaee, *Islamic Values and World View: Khomeini on Man, the State, and International Politics* (Lanham: University Press of America, 1983), 82. Other overviews of Khomeini's foreign policy principles include R. K. Ramazani, "Khumayni's Islam in Iran's Foreign Policy," in *Islam in Foreign Policy*, ed. Adeed Dawisha (New York: Cambridge University Press, 1983); David Menashiri, "Khomeini's Vision: Nationalism or World Order?," in *The Iranian Revolution and the Muslim World*, ed. David Menashiri (Boulder: Westview Press, 1990), 9–32.

[4] R. K. Ramazani, *Revolutionary Iran: Challenge and Response in the Middle East* (Baltimore: The Johns Hopkins University Press, 1988), 24.

[5] The "boundaries drawn around the [territories of] the world to designate a country or homeland," he stated, "are the product of the deficient human mind." Rajaee, *Islamic Values and World View*, 77.

[6] Ruhollah Khomeini, *Islam and Revolution: Writings and Declarations of Imam Khomeini*, trans. Hamid Alger (Berkeley: Mizan Press, 1981), 48. It has been observed that despite his occasional rhetoric, Khomeini "both implicitly and explicitly accepted the existence of the territorial nation state" and often resorted to symbols of Iranian nationalism. Ervand Abrahamian, *Khomeinism: Essays on the Islamic Republic* (Berkeley: University of California Press, 1993), esp. 15. Khomeini utilized nationalism as a sense of patriotism, though he was against nationalism as an alternative to, or taking precedence over, Islam as a legitimating ideology. He saw the state as a means to furthering Islam. He did not explicitly acknowledge a possible tension between the Iranian state and revolutionary Islamic goals. James Piscatori notes that while Khomeini would suggest "that the goal of all present-day Muslims is to return to the medieval juristic hostility towards *dar al-harb* and to give primary political allegiance to the *umma*," this kind of thinking "coexists with nationalist thinking, and often in practice takes second place to it." James P. Piscatori, *Islam in a World of Nation-States* (New York: Cambridge University Press, 1986), 116.

[7] Rajaee, *Islamic Values and World View*, 83.

as the Ministry of Islamic Guidance invited Islamist groups to visit Iran, and it published and distributed works via student unions, activists, and cultural sections of Iranian embassies.[8] The revolutionaries also used the state-controlled media, such as radio stations broadcasting in Arabic, to spread their message.[9] One of the more visible means of exporting the revolution was the dissemination of propaganda via Iranian pilgrims on the Hajj to Mecca.[10] The new clerical regime also had a preexisting infrastructure of influence via the transnational network of Shia religious figures in Iraq, the Persian Gulf, and Lebanon.[11]

Beyond spreading the word abroad, some state organs gave direct aid to revolutionary opposition movements. The Office of Liberation Movements is one example, although the extent of its activities remains disputed.[12] The revolutionary regime aided Shia groups in Kuwait, Bahrain, Saudi Arabia, Iraq, and Lebanon. The form this aid took could be financial assistance, military training, or providing a refuge for a group's exiled leadership. The most notable example is the creation of Hezbollah in Lebanon with the help of the Iranian Revolutionary Guards.[13] The regime also hosted the Supreme Assembly for the Islamic Revolution in Iraq, created in November 1982. Iran was involved in supporting the Islamic Front for the Liberation of Bahrain, and it had ties with other Shia organizations, such as the Islamic Action Organization and the Islamic Revolution Organization in the Arabian Peninsula.[14]

Beyond subversion, Iran engaged in war to spread revolution. Iran's counter-invasion of Iraq in 1982 aimed to create an Islamist state in Iraq, which would, it was believed, be the first step in a chain reaction. If Saddam was deposed, Khomeini stated, the Iraqi people would establish an Islamist government, and

[8] Shireen T. Hunter, "Iran and the Spread of Revolutionary Islam," *Third World Quarterly* 10, no. 2 (1988): 743.

[9] Christian Marschall, *Iran's Persian Gulf Policy: From Khomeini to Khatami* (New York: Routledge Curzon, 2003), 28.

[10] Martin Kramer, "Khomeini's Messengers: The Disputed Pilgrimage of Islam," in *Religious Radicalism and Politics in the Middle East*, eds. Emmanuel Sivan and Menachem Friedman (Albany: State University of New York Press, 1990), 177–94.

[11] Laurence Louër, *Transnational Shia Politics: Religious and Political Networks in the Gulf* (New York: Columbia University Press, 2008).

[12] See Marschall, *Iran's Persian Gulf Policy*, 30–32.

[13] In November 1982, around fifteen hundred Revolutionary Guards, as well as clerics, set up shop in Lebanon's Beqaa Valley, providing military training and doctrinal guidance to what was then a loose coalition of Shia revolutionaries who wished to establish an Islamic state in Lebanon and resist the Israeli invasion. The loose coalition eventually hardened into a concrete organization under the name Hezbollah in the mid-1980s. See, e.g., Dominique Avon and Anaïs-Trissa Khatchadourian, *Hezbollah: A History of the "Party of God,"* trans. Jane Marie Todd (Cambridge, MA: Harvard University Press, 2012), 22–31.

[14] Hasan Tariq Alhasan, "The Role of Iran in the Failed Coup of 1981: The IFLB in Bahrain," *The Middle East Journal* 65, no. 4 (2011): 603–17; Toby Matthiesen, "Hizbullah Al-Hijaz: A History of the Most Radical Saudi Opposition Group," *The Middle East Journal* 64, no. 2 (2010): 182–83; Amatzia Baram, "Two Roads to Revolutionary Shi'ite Fundamentalism in Iraq," in *Accounting for Fundamentalisms: The Dynamic Character of Movements*, eds. Martin E. Marty and R. Scott Appleby (Chicago: The University of Chicago Press, 1994), 547–51.

"if Iran and Iraq unite and link up with one another, the other, smaller nations of the region will join them as well."[15]

In sum, revolutionary Iran acted as a model, but the degree to which it also acted as a platform varied over time and space. In 1979, domestic upheaval dominated Iranian leaders' concerns and moderates in foreign policy still held sway, limiting the export of revolution. Those outside the state initiated some of the most notable actions of Iran acting as a platform. Ayatollah Sadeq Rouhani called for Iran's annexation of Bahrain in August 1979, which the Iranian Foreign Ministry dismissed.[16] Ayatollah Mohammad Montazeri led volunteers to Lebanon in December 1979.[17] Shia Islamist exiles from the Persian Gulf set up radio stations to propagate their message, though with the help of Iran's Revolutionary Guard.[18] Iran's actions as a platform, particularly by the central government, picked up with the Iran-Iraq War, culminating with its invasion of Iraq in 1982. These actions, though, were limited to Shia communities, principally in Iraq but also in Saudi Arabia, Lebanon, and the Gulf states. Even then, the notion that Iran was orchestrating Shia groups across the region is exaggerated. The Iranian organizing and training of Iraqi and Saudi revolutionaries occurred after rather than before the uprisings inspired by the Iranian Revolution in these states. These uprisings were organic and relatively independent of Iran. There were extensive Iranian ties to Shia Islamists, and Iran eventually was acting as a platform in the most direct sense in Iraq—invading it for the purpose of establishing an Islamic regime. Iran had no direction over Sunni groups that had a similar Islamist message and did not act as a platform against Syria and Egypt.

Islamist Opposition in the Middle East

Were there significant revolutionary opposition movements in Egypt, Syria, Iraq, and Saudi Arabia of a similar character to the Islamic Revolution in Iran? The decade prior to the Iranian Revolution saw the rise of radical Islamist opposition movements across the region. The 1950s and 1960s was the apogee of leftist secular Arab nationalist ideologies—Nasserism and the Ba'th Party. In the aftermath of the spectacular failure of the Arab nationalist regimes in the 1967 Six-Day War with Israel, political Islamist movements emerged from the periphery to take a leading place in the opposition of the established regimes.

---

[15] Shaul Bakhash, *The Reign of the Ayatollahs: Iran and the Islamic Revolution* (New York: Basic Books, 1984), 232.

[16] Marschall, *Iran's Persian Gulf Policy*, 34–35.

[17] Mohammad Ataie, "Revolutionary Iran's 1979 Endeavor in Lebanon," *Middle East Policy* 20, no. 2 (2013): 137–57.

[18] Louër, *Transnational Shia Politics*, 181.

I argue in what follows that although the Islamic revival of the 1970s affected the entire Arab world, the political effects were not the same. Revolutionary Islamist organizations developed in the secular nationalist regimes of Egypt, Syria, and Iraq. In Saudi Arabia, however, the leadership did not perceive that there was a significant Islamist revolutionary movement. The closest case is the small group of Sunni messianic extremists, which seemed more isolationist than revolutionary. Among the Shia in Saudi Arabia, the Iranian Revolution would have a tremendous demonstration effect, transforming many individuals' worldviews from non-political to revolutionary. Elsewhere, the revolution emboldened pre-existing revolutionary movements.

Opposition in Egypt

Egypt had the region's most influential Islamist organization, the Muslim Brotherhood. It was only intermittently revolutionary, but its offshoots in the 1970s were. Gamal Abdel Nasser banned the Brotherhood after an assassination attempt against him in 1954. With many members and leaders in jail or exiled, the organization spent decades in the political wilderness.[19] Their opening emerged under Nasser's successor, Anwar Sadat, who reached out to Islamist groups as a counterweight to his leftist/Nasserist opposition. Sadat encouraged the Islamization of Egyptian society to act as a conservative force. He released hundreds of Brotherhood members from prison. The Brotherhood by the early 1970s eschewed violence. Its willingness to work within the political system disqualifies it as a revolutionary movement. Many Islamists, however, had radicalized during their period underground or in jail, following the lead of those such as Sayyid Qutb. Qutb had argued that Egypt was in a state of *jahiliyya*, or ignorance, and the implication was that the regime must be overthrown.[20]

Radicalized former members of the Brotherhood adopted Qutb's mantra, and some groups began to take direct action.[21] In April 1974, the Islamic Liberation

---

[19] Overviews of the Muslim Brotherhood include Richard P. Mitchell, *The Society of Muslim Brothers* (London: Oxford University Press, 1969); Carrie Rosefsky Wickham, *The Muslim Brotherhood: Evolution of an Islamist Movement* (Princeton: Princeton University Press, 2013).

[20] This analysis is in Qutb's *Signposts*, considered the Islamist equivalent of Lenin's *What Is to Be Done?* Not all the Islamist groups that were inspired by Qutb accepted his doctrine of jahiliyya; for many the problem was not Egyptian society as a whole but its anti-Islamic rulers. William E. Shepard, "Sayyid Qutb's Doctrine of 'Jajiliyya,'" *International Journal of Middle East Studies* 35, no. 4 (2003): 536. For an elaboration on Qutb and his impact, see John Calvert, *Sayyid Qutb and the Origins of Radical Islamism* (New York: Columbia University Press, 2010); James Toth, *Sayyid Qutb: The Life and Legacy of a Radical Islamic Intellectual* (New York: Oxford University Press, 2013).

[21] There are a variety of names by which these groups are referred to. The Islamic Liberation Organization, Munazzanat al-Tahir al-Islami, is also known as the Technical Military Academy group, or Jam'at al-Fanniyya al-'askariya. The Society of Muslims, Jama'at al-Muslimin, is known as Repentance and Holy Flight, or Takfir wa'l-Hijra. Overviews of radical Islamist groups in Egypt in this period include Gilles Kepel, *The Prophet and the Pharaoh: Muslim Extremism in Egypt*

Organization attempted a coup, which failed. In 1977, the Society of Muslims assassinated a former cabinet minister. Sadat's trip to Jerusalem to begin the peace process with Israel in November 1977 increased the ire of all Islamist groups. The Muslim Brotherhood publications and the Islamist student unions, which had effectively marginalized the leftists, lashed out against the regime. The regime's security forces confronted an organization called al-Jihad in 1978 that would go on to assassinate President Sadat in 1981. Egypt, then, had significant revolutionary groups that were part of a larger robust Islamist movement.

Opposition in Syria

Like Egypt, Syria had a secular regime and a robust revolutionary Islamist opposition movement. The Muslim Brotherhood in Syria was founded in 1945–46, inspired by, but independent of, the Muslim Brotherhood in Egypt.[22] For most of its history, it was not a revolutionary movement. Following the Syrian defeat in the 1967 Six-Day War, there were splits in the Brotherhood about whether they should prepare for jihad against the regime. In 1970, Hafez al-Assad came to power, the first Syrian leader of the Alawi sect, which many Islamists regarded as heretical. The Muslim Brotherhood, as in Egypt, was a Sunni organization, and a majority of Syrians were Sunni. The Alawis were the largest religious minority. In 1973, violent protests erupted when Assad promulgated a secular constitution. Assad responded by bolstering his Islamic credentials, such as including a provision in the constitution that the president of the republic had to be a Muslim, and he henceforth regularly attended Friday prayers. In 1976, a group called the Fighting Vanguard of the Mujahidin, a radical offshoot of the Muslim Brotherhood, began assassinating government officials, including Assad's nephew, and attacking regime institutions such as the police and the Ba'th Party.[23] By October 1979, the Muslim Brotherhood officially joined the

(Berkeley: University of California Press, 1985); Saad Eddin Ibrahim, "Anatomy of Egypt's Militant Islamic Groups: Methodological Note and Preliminary Findings," *International Journal of Middle East Studies* 12, no. 4 (1980): 423–53; Hamied N. Ansari, "The Islamic Militants in Egyptian Politics," *International Journal of Middle East Studies* 16, no. 1 (1984): 123–44.

[22] Joshua Teitelbaum, "The Muslim Brotherhood in Syria, 1945–1958: Founding, Social Origins, Ideology," *The Middle East Journal* 65, no. 2 (2011): 213–33.

[23] This group, sometimes referred to as just the Mujahidin, is often confused with the Brotherhood. Although many of its members retained ties with the Brotherhood, it was a distinct organization. Overviews of the Islamist opposition in Syria in this period include Raphaël Lefèvre, *Ashes of Hama: The Muslim Brotherhood in Syria* (London: C. Hurst & Co., 2013), 81–115; Line Khatib, *Islamic Revivalism in Syria: The Rise and Fall of Ba'thist Secularism* (New York: Routledge, 2011), 69–81; Nikolaos Van Dam, *The Struggle for Power in Syria: Politics and Society Under Asad and the Ba'th Party*, 4th ed. (London: I. B. Tauris, 2011), 89–117; Umar F. Abd-Allah, *The Islamic Struggle in Syria* (Berkeley: Mizan Press, 1983); Thomas Mayer, "The Islamic Opposition in Syria, 1961–1982,"

attempted revolution. Syria had a significant revolutionary movement that was beginning to launch an insurgency as the Iranian Revolution occurred.

Opposition in Iraq

In Iraq there was a brewing revolutionary movement among the Shia, the group that constituted a majority of Iraq's population.[24] Various Islamic organizations had sprouted up in the 1950s and 1960s among the Shia. The purpose of most of these was to combat communism and the perceived anti-religiousness of modern Iraqi society. The clandestine Islamic Da'wa Party, however, had the ambition of taking power and establishing an Islamic state in Iraq. Grand Ayatollah Muhammed Baqir al-Sadr, a high-ranking cleric, was instrumental in its formation and eventually became its leader. The Iranians, among others, would compare him to Khomeini, whom he was familiar with given Khomeini's thirteen years of exile in Najaf.

Da'wa and other Islamist groups such as the Islamic Action Organization grew in strength, numbers, and radicalization in the 1970s, especially from 1977 on.[25] The Ba'th Party's ascension to power in 1968 brought a totalitarian dislike of autonomous power, and they targeted even the accommodating clerics. This approach radicalized many Shia. In the mid-1970s, the Ba'th regime arrested and executed Shia figures, many of them Da'wa members. Most remarkable was the upheaval in Najaf and Karbala in 1977. Tens of thousands gathered and chanted slogans such as "Saddam take your hands off, neither our army nor our people want you."[26] The protests were eventually quelled after sixteen people were killed and thousands arrested, but they were an unprecedented challenge to the regime. The regime responded by increasing the surveillance and control of Shia

---

Orient 24, no. 4 (1983): 589–609; Hanna Batatu, "Syria's Muslim Brethren," *MERIP Reports* 110 (1982): 12–20.

[24] Among the Sunnis, there was a Muslim Brotherhood movement that was largely crushed by the regime in the early 1970s, and a branch of the Islamist party Hizb al-Tahrir, that was explicitly revolutionary. The Sunni groups were of relatively minor consequence compared to the Shia groups. Samuel Helfont, *Compulsion in Religion: Saddam Hussein, Islam, and the Roots of Insurgencies in Iraq* (New York: Oxford University Press, 2018), 22, 70–71.

[25] On the Shia political movements in Iraq during this period, see Faleh A. Jabar, *The Shi'ite Movement in Iraq* (London: Saqi, 2003), esp. 208–34; Baram, "Two Roads to Revolutionary Shi'ite Fundamentalism in Iraq"; T. M. Aziz, "The Role of Muhammad Baqir Al-Sadr in Shii Political Activism in Iraq from 1958 to 1980," *International Journal of Middle East Studies* 25, no. 2 (1993): 207–22; Joyce N. Wiley, *The Islamic Movement of Iraqi Shi'as* (Boulder: Lynne Rienner Publishers, 1992), esp. 45–60; Hanna Batatu, "Shi'i Organizations in Iraq: Al-Da'wah Al-Islamiyah and Al-Mujahidin," in *Shi'ism and Social Protest*, eds. Juan R. I. Cole and Nikki R. Keddie (New Haven: Yale University Press, 1986); Ofra Bengio, "Shi'is and Politics in Ba'thi Iraq," *Middle Eastern Studies* 21, no. 1 (1985): 1–14.

[26] Jabar, *The Shi'ite Movement in Iraq*, 213.

institutions and finances. It also incorporated more Shia into its leadership and burnished its religious credentials by such acts as declaring Imam Ali's birthday a national holiday. Like Egypt and Syria, Iraq had a significant revolutionary movement as the Iranian Revolution occurred.

Opposition in Saudi Arabia

Saudi Arabia was different from these other states, both in the nature of the regime and in the nature of the opposition. The basis of legitimacy of the Saudi state was not a secular nationalist ideology but Islam. There were tensions between the religious leaders and the Saud dynasty. But after putting down the Ikhwan revolt of 1929, the regime faced no religiously motivated revolutionary opposition until November 1979. Among the Sunni, there were two types of opposition.[27] The Islamic awakening, or Sahwa, was the more mainstream approach. It blended a traditional Wahhabi perspective on social issues with a Muslim Brotherhood approach to political issues. The political aim, however, was to "reform the state's policies without ever straightforwardly questioning the legitimacy of the state."[28] A smaller isolationist, "rejectionist" movement developed in the 1970s from which the movement around Juhayman al-'Utaybi, who would orchestrate the seizure of the Grand Mosque in Mecca in November 1979, would emerge. He regarded the regime as illegitimate, but admonished his followers to keep away from state institutions rather than advocating that they overthrow them. In other words, the movement seemed to be more millennialist, prone to withdraw into isolation rather than have a particular political, let alone revolutionary, agenda. The government showed some irritation at the radical nature of the religious interpretations of this movement, and arrested some of the members. But the government did not seem to regard the movement as a serious revolutionary threat.

The Shia in Saudi Arabia also did not exhibit signs of revolutionary behavior at first.[29] Concentrated in the Eastern Province, home to much of the country's

---

[27] This distinction is from Stéphane Lacroix, *Awakening Islam: The Politics of Religious Dissent in Contemporary Saudi Arabia*, trans. George Holoch (Cambridge, MA: Harvard University Press, 2011); Thomas Hegghammer and Stéphane Lacroix, *The Meccan Rebellion: The Story of Juhayman Al-'Utaybi Revisited* (Bristol: Amal Press, 2011).

[28] Thomas Hegghammer and Stéphane Lacroix, "Rejectionist Islamism in Saudi Arabia: The Story of Juhayman Al-'Utaybi," *International Journal of Middle East Studies* 39, no. 1 (2007): 105.

[29] Examinations of the Shia Islamist movements of the period include Toby Matthiesen, *The Other Saudis: Shiism, Dissent, and Sectarianism* (New York: Cambridge University Press, 2015), 91–113; Louër, *Transnational Shia Politics*, 82–102; Ibrahim, *The Shi'is of Saudi Arabia* (London: Saqi, 2006), 73–104.

oil production, the Shia had long been persecuted under Saudi rule, suffering not just de facto discrimination, as elsewhere in the Gulf, but also de jure discrimination.[30] An organization (more a network of Islamists) was founded in 1975, a branch of the Shia movement in Iraq called the Movement of Vanguards' Missionaries. It did not have revolutionary aims, but instead had the more modest goals of revitalizing Shia doctrine and encouraging a larger Shia political consciousness. It was the Iranian Revolution that radically changed the strategy of this organization as well as the consciousness of the Shia community at large. In the aftermath of the revolution and the unprecedented demonstrations against the regime in November 1979, the Saudi branch of the Movement of Vanguards' Missionaries was renamed the Islamic Revolution Organization in the Arabian Peninsula, signifying its new political mission.[31]

Thus, the Saudi regime was an outlier, perceiving no significant Islamist revolutionary movement at the outset of the Iranian Revolution. Historically, the possibility of leftists taking power via a military coup seemed the regime's greatest threat to power.[32] The Saudi leadership noticed religiously grounded critiques but still regarded their own religious credentials to be the source of legitimacy rather than of weakness. In 1979, the uprisings in the kingdom and the Iranian Revolution shocked the Saudi ruling classes and also warned other regimes in the region: if the Saudis could be challenged as insufficiently Islamist, then any regime could be.

Section Summary

The Islamic revival of the 1970s produced a significant revolutionary Islamist movement in the secular nationalist regimes of Egypt, Syria, and Iraq. In Saudi Arabia, however, there did not seem to be such a movement. The Iranian Revolution changed that.

---

[30] Most scholars estimate the proportion of the country's population who are Shia to be about 10–15 percent. See, for example, Toby Craig Jones, "Rebellion on the Saudi Periphery: Modernity, Marginalization, and the Shi'a Uprising of 1979," *International Journal of Middle East Studies* 38, no. 2 (2006): 231; Graham E. Fuller and Rend Rahim Francke, *The Arab Shi'a: The Forgotten Muslims* (London: Macmillan, 1999), 180; R. K. Ramazani, *The Gulf Cooperation Council: Record and Analysis* (Charlottesville: University Press of Virginia, 1988), 200.

[31] Matthiesen, *The Other Saudis*, 98.

[32] See Stephanie Cronin, "Tribes, Coups and Princes: Building a Modern Army in Saudi Arabia," *Middle Eastern Studies* 49, no. 1 (2013): 19–21; James Buchan, "Secular and Religious Opposition in Saudi Arabia," in *State, Society and Economy in Saudi Arabia*, ed. Tim Niblock (London: Croom Helm, 1982), 115.

International Relations of the Middle East Prior to the Iranian Revolution

To assess whether the Iranian Revolution affected patterns of international politics, I will first examine relations among the leading powers of the region prior to the revolution. I will show that Iran had reasonable relations with the other Arab powers, with the partial exception of Syria. The Egyptian peace with Israel shifted inter-Arab politics, and Iraq had reconciled with Saudi Arabia and Syria.

In inter-Arab politics, the division between "progressive" Egypt and "reactionary" states such as Saudi Arabia, characteristic of the "Arab Cold War" in the 1950s and 1960s, was transformed in the aftermath of the 1967 Six-Day War.[33] The rout discredited Nasserism and hurt the broader pan-Arab movement. It provided impetus for a more limited Egyptian policy centered on recovering Egyptian land from Israel. Nasser initiated rapprochement with Saudi Arabia, which Sadat, his successor, accelerated. Sadat also cooperated with Syrian president Hafez al-Assad and Saudi Arabia. The Cairo-Damascus-Riyadh alliance, or "Arab triangle," was a fragile institution, but it persisted for much of the 1970s. Saudi Arabia played broker between the other two states, which were often at odds with each other, as Assad became increasingly embittered by the Egyptian pursuit of an agreement that undermined Syria's bargaining position vis-à-vis Israel.

Egypt's decision to pursue a separate peace with Israel ultimately resulted in Syria breaking relations with Egypt. With Egypt removed from the Arab-Israeli dispute, Syria was in a much-weakened state vis-à-vis Israel. The Saudis were more sympathetic to Sadat's attempts to resolve the dispute. But they were hesitant about outright support for Sadat's initiatives, which would expose them to Arab criticism. They joined almost all Arab states and broke off relations with Egypt after the Camp David Accords.

Iraq had long rejected negotiations with Israel, though the bulk of its denunciations during this period were directed at Syria rather than Egypt. As late as 1978, Iraq maintained diplomatic relations with Egypt. Iraq was not threatened the way Syria was by the withdrawal of Egypt from the Arab-Israeli conflict. In fact, that withdrawal presented Saddam Hussein with an opportunity to seize the mantle of leader of the Arab states and push Syria into a subservient position. Iraq had several policy disagreements with Syria, but more fundamental to their antagonism was that both regimes were Ba'thist, and each saw the other as a rival for the leadership of the Ba'thist cause. They feared subversion from cliques

---

[33] The rivalry between and within Arab secular nationalist regimes and conservative monarchies is detailed in Malcolm H. Kerr, *The Arab Cold War: Gamal Abd Al-Nasir and His Rivals, 1958–1970* (London: Oxford University Press, 1971).

in their own party with ties to the other state.[34] Saddam said to his advisors in 1979, "Any relationship between Iraq and the system in Syria must take one of two directions—there is not a third direction—it is either collision or merger."[35] There was a brief attempt at some kind of unification in 1978–79. The Egyptian peace with Israel had left Syria exposed; its talks with Iraq were motivated by the need to balance against Israel. The reconciliation was initiated by Iraq. Iraq's stated motive was to shore up the Arab rejectionist front against Israel. Iraq led the charge in expelling Egypt from the Arab League. The attempted merger with Syria, however, was soon derailed, as discussed in what follows, and the relationship reverted to hostility.

In the Persian Gulf, the British decision to withdraw in 1971 created a power vacuum and the possibility of direct competition between the major littoral powers: Iraq, Saudi Arabia, and Iran. The shah's ambition was to assert Iranian primacy in the region, which had the backing of the United States.[36] The Saudis were somewhat wary of Iranian aspirations but soon came to a "spheres of influence" deal with Iran whereby Iran recognized the small Gulf states to be under Saudi protection, while Iran would control the Gulf waters.[37] Despite Iranian ambitions and power, the bigger threat from the Saudi perspective was Iraq. Iraq was a much weaker state, but it was a leftist revisionist power, routinely threatening and denouncing the Arab monarchies. Beyond the rhetoric, Iraq supported the leftist Dhofar rebellion against the sultan in Oman, as well as the leftist regime in South Yemen (which also supported the rebellion), and had border disputes with Kuwait and Saudi Arabia. The shah, on the other hand, was supportive of the conservative monarchs against leftist forces. He sent Iranian forces into Oman to help crush the Dhofar rebellion.[38] He was a balance against Iraq. He supported several coup attempts and gave critical aid to the Kurdish insurgency in Iraq.

---

[34] Eberhard Kienle, *Ba'th v. Ba'th: The Conflict Between Syria and Iraq 1968–1989* (London: I. B. Tauris & Co. Ltd., 1990); Baram, "Ideology and Power Politics in Syrian-Iraqi Relations, 1968–1984," in *Syria Under Assad*, eds. Moshe Ma'oz and Avner Yaniv (London: Croom Helm, 1986).

[35] CRRC SH-SHTP-A-000-911, "Discussion Between Saddam Hussein and Iraqi Officials About Iraq's Relationship with Syria," November 26, 1979. This document is from Iraqi records that were captured following the 2003 American invasion and were housed in the Conflict Records Research Center (CRRC) at National Defense University in Washington, DC.

[36] Roham Alvandi, *Nixon, Kissinger, and the Shah: The United States and Iran in the Cold War* (New York: Oxford University Press, 2014).

[37] Nadav Safran, *Saudi Arabia: The Ceaseless Quest for Security* (Ithaca: Cornell University Press, 1988), 134–38; Roham Alvandi, "Muhammad Reza Pahlavi and the Bahrain Question, 1968–1970," *British Journal of Middle Eastern Studies* 37, no. 2 (2010): 159–77; Faisal Salman al-Saud, *Iran, Saudi Arabia and the Gulf* (New York: I. B. Tauris, 2003), 29–56.

[38] J. E. Peterson, *Oman's Insurgencies: The Sultanate's Struggle for Supremacy* (London: Saqi, 2007), 329–31; Joseph A. Kechichian, *Oman and the World: The Emergence of an Independent Foreign Policy* (Santa Monica: RAND, 1995), 99–101.

Iraq and Iran eventually came to terms on the Kurdish issue, and relations in general, via a long-standing territorial dispute over the Shatt al-'Arab, the outlet into the Persian Gulf. The dispute concerned where exactly that border exists—whether it is in the median of the navigable channel or on the Iranian shore of the Shatt.[39] In the Algiers Accord of 1975, Saddam agreed to accept the middle of the channel as the border; in exchange, the shah ceased his support for the Iraqi Kurds in a rebellion that Saddam had thus far unsuccessfully attempted to tame. The insurrection promptly collapsed. The two sides promised not to intervene in the internal affairs of the other. This understanding became the basis of a relatively cooperative relationship from 1975 until the revolution.

Iraq's foreign policy toward not just Iran but also the other Gulf states exhibited a new pragmatism in this period. Iraq stopped supporting the leftist insurgency in Oman, ended its propaganda against Saudi Arabia, and ended several border disputes with the Saudis.[40] The reduced threat from Iraq prompted Saudi Arabia to more evenly balance between Iran and Iraq.

Regarding the Egyptian-Iranian relationship, the shah and Nasser had been on opposite sides of the leftist/pro-Soviet and conservative/pro-Western divide. However, in the aftermath of the Six-Day War, Nasser reached out to Iran. In August 1970, a month before Nasser's death, Egypt and Iran resumed bilateral relations. The shah and Sadat had warm relations, particularly as Sadat moved to the conservative/pro-Western camp. Iran supported Egypt in the 1973 war and there was increased economic cooperation thereafter. Iran supported Egypt's outreach to Israel and pushed the Begin administration to negotiate with Sadat.[41]

Iran's relationship with Syria was strained mostly because of Ba'thist rule in Damascus. The shah did not appreciate Syria's backing of radical movements in the region, including the call to liberate "Arabistan," the Khuzestan province of Iran. He resisted attempts by Arab states to merge, which involved Syria. Nor did Iran look with favor on Syria's alliance with the Soviet Union. The Syrians did not like Iran's pro-American and pro-Israeli policies, or its support for pro-Western Arab regimes. In the mid-1970s, there was a thaw in the hostility when the shah cooperated with Syria and other Arab states during the 1973 war. In the war's aftermath, he even provided financial aid to Syria.[42] The shah's warm embrace

---

[39]   Richard N. Schofield, *Evolution of the Shatt Al-'Arab Boundary Dispute* (Cambridgeshire: Middle East and North African Studies Press, 1986).

[40]   Laurie Ann Mylroie, "Regional Security After Empire: Saudi Arabia and the Gulf" (PhD thesis, Harvard University, 1985), 148–49; F. Gregory Gause III, *The International Relations of the Persian Gulf* (New York: Cambridge University Press, 2010), 38.

[41]   This was a part of what Trita Parsi calls Iran's "Arab option," an effort to pull closer to the Arab position and pull back from the Israelis in an attempt to get Arab acceptance of Iranian hegemony. Trita Parsi, *Treacherous Alliance: The Secret Dealings of Israel, Iran, and the United States* (New Haven: Yale University Press, 2007), esp. 44.

[42]   Jubin M. Goodarzi, *Syria and Iran: Diplomatic Alliance and Power Politics in the Middle East* (London: Tauris Academic Studies, 2006), 16.

of Sadat's outreach toward Israel reversed this trend. Assad in fact provided a safe haven for Iranian Islamist opposition figures, including an offer of asylum to Khomeini.[43]

Thus, on the eve of revolution in Iran, Egypt was estranged from the Arab powers, but it still maintained relations with Iran. Iraq had cut ties with Egypt but had come to an accommodation with Saudi Arabia and Iran, and was briefly in an attempted merger with Syria. Saudi Arabia had reasonable relations not only with Iraq, but also with Iran and Syria, though it had severed ties with Egypt. Syria was cautiously undergoing a merger with Iraq and was cordial with Saudi Arabia, but acrimonious toward Egypt. Aside from troubles with Syria, the one state that had reasonable relations with all the others was the soon-to-be-revolutionary state: Iran.

Predictions

Given that there was a significant Islamist revolutionary movement in Iraq, Syria, Egypt, and (though not initially) Saudi Arabia, the theory predicts that these regimes would fear contagion, cooperate with each other, and be hostile toward the Iranian Revolution, reversing their previous stance (see Table 6.1).

Alternative theories have different expectations. Although traditionally Iran was much more powerful than Iraq, the chaos of the revolution meant that Iraq was for the first time probably the more powerful military actor.[44] From

---

[43] Christian Marschall, "Syria-Iran: A Strategic Alliance, 1979–1991," *Orient* 33, no. 3 (1992): 434–35; Patrick Seale, *Asad of Syria: The Struggle for the Middle East* (Berkeley: University of California Press, 1989), 352–53; Hussein J. Agha and Ahmad S. Khalidi, *Syria and Iran: Rivalry and Cooperation* (London: Pinter/The Royal Institute of International Affairs, 1995), 4. Assad also had ties to Lebanese Shia, particularly the Iranian-born Musa al-Sadr, for the purposes of legitimizing the Alawis as Shia Muslims. See Fouad Ajami, *The Vanished Imam: Musa Al Sadr and the Shia of Lebanon* (Ithaca: Cornell University Press, 1986), 174–75; Martin Kramer, "Syria's Alawis and Shi'ism," in *Shi'ism, Resistance, and Revolution*, ed. Martin Kramer (Boulder: Westview Press, 1987), 246–49.

[44] In both military and economic terms, the Iranian Revolution severely decreased Iran's capabilities. The shah had developed easily the most powerful military in the region, relying especially on arms imports from the United States. The military rapidly fell apart after the shah fled the country, and it faced purges from the revolutionary government. By the mid-1980s the total armed forces had surpassed pre-revolutionary levels due to the mobilization for the Iran-Iraq War. But the lack of training and equipment significantly affected their capabilities. The effect of the lack of arms imports was especially pernicious. Iraq, for example, from 1980 to 1987 imported 369 percent more arms than did Iran, and Iranian imports were often of poorer quality. Anthony H. Cordesman and Abraham R. Wagner, *The Lessons of Modern War*, vol. II, *The Iran-Iraq War* (Boulder: Westview Press, 1990), 48–53. Of course, Iran was also bogged down in a war with Iraq, and even with the war's conclusion, it was weaker vis-à-vis neighboring states than before the revolution. Iran's economy exhibited the same pattern. A recession beginning in 1977 escalated as the country tumbled into revolutionary chaos. The economy began to recover somewhat beginning in 1981, but by the end of the decade, Iran had still not reached the economic levels achieved in 1977. Jahangir Amuzegar, *Iran's Economy Under the Islamic Republic* (New York: I. B. Tauris and Co., 1993); Hooshang Amirahmadi, *Revolution and Economic Transition: The Iranian Experience* (Albany: State University of New York Press, 1990).

Table 6.1 Response to the Iranian Revolution

Regional Power	Stance Toward Iran Prior to Revolution	Significant Revolutionary Islamist Movement?	Prediction of Stance Toward Revolutionary Iran Given Revolutionary Movement	Outcome
Iraq	Amicable	Yes	Hostile	Hostile
Syria	Moderately hostile	Yes	Hostile	Aligned with Iran
Egypt	Aligned with	Yes	Hostile	Hostile
Saudi Arabia	Aligned with	Not at first, then yes	Not hostile initially, then hostile	Not hostile initially, then hostile

a balance-of-power perspective, Iraq's predominance might lead the other states—Saudi Arabia, Egypt, and Syria—to balance against Iraq. At a minimum, one would not expect them to switch their allegiance from Iran to Iraq. A realist perspective might expect hostility between Iran and Iraq, but the predicted motivation would be Iraq's attempt to prey on Iranian weakness rather than the mechanism posited by the domestic contagion effects theory. A theory of ideological distance has no decisive prediction in this case. The new Iranian regime explicitly used religion to justify its rule, which would attract Saudi Arabia and repel the secular regimes. Meanwhile, Iran's move from a monarchy to a republic should repel Saudi Arabia and attract the Arab republics. Beyond these general theories, there are expectations driven by the particular historical conditions. My theory supposes that there will be cooperation between Egypt and other Arab states, but one might not expect this given that the Arab states had just severed relations with Egypt because of the Egyptian-Israeli peace deal. Regarding the Syrian-Iranian relationship, one might expect cooperation rather than the hostility my theory expects given that Iran was against its two main enemies, Israel and Iraq.

We will see that the predictions of other theories do not fit the facts well. Instead, there was a complete reversal of relations with the onset of the revolution, driven in large measure by leaders' fear of contagion from the Iranian Revolution to the various Islamist movements in their states. In short, the theory of this book better explains how states responded to the Iranian Revolution than the theories just mentioned. The exception is Syria, which aligned with Iran despite the presence of a revolutionary Islamist movement. This important exception reminds us of the probabilistic nature of the theory and that while the mechanisms theorized here are clearly visible in the Iran-Syria dyad, they can be overwhelmed by other factors in certain conditions.

International Relations of the Iranian Revolution, 1979–88

Iraqi Reaction to the Iranian Revolution

After the Iranian Revolution, relations between Iran and Iraq deteriorated to the point of war because of the fear of contagion from the Iranian Revolution. Many have argued that the Iraqi invasion of Iran was largely or exclusively driven by Iraqi opportunism—striking Iran while it was weak, with the aim of making geopolitical gains.[45] However, I argue that Iraq's fear of revolution spreading was paramount. The deterioration of relations between Iran and Iraq corresponds with, and was caused by, Iraqi domestic turmoil and not the weakening of Iran.[46] The Iranian model served as a demonstration effect for an Islamist uprising in Iraq. The uprisings began with relatively minimal Iranian involvement in spreading revolution. But the shadow of Iran potentially acting as a platform loomed. Iran's role as a platform explains the outbreak of war.

As discussed, the Ba'thist regime had come to an accommodation with the shah of Iran, and as he became consumed with domestic problems, Saddam showed no signs of attempting to take advantage of Iranian weakness. His response to the Iranian Revolution was initially one of cautious optimism. Geopolitically, the fact that the new regime had an anti-Western and anti-Israel perspective was a welcome change from the shah. Saddam made clear that he was willing to work with the new regime provided the Iranians respected Iraqi sovereignty and did not intervene in Iraqi affairs.[47] This was the basis of the Iran-Iraq rapprochement of 1975.

---

[45] See, for example, Michael Axworthy, *Revolutionary Iran: A History of the Islamic Republic* (New York: Oxford University Press, 2013), 188–89; Andrew T. Parasiliti, "The Causes and Timing of Iraq's Wars: A Power Cycle Assessment," *International Political Science Review* 24, no. 1 (2003): 183–84; Kanan Makiya, *Republic of Fear: The Politics of Modern Iraq* (Berkeley: University of California Press, 1998), 262–76; Phebe Marr, *The Modern History of Iraq*, 2nd ed. (Boulder: Westview Press, 2004), 182–83. Many accounts stress opportunism as well as the fear of revolutionary spillover. See Hal Brands, "Why Did Saddam Invade Iran? New Evidence on Motives, Complexity, and the Israel Factor," *The Journal of Military History* 75, no. 3 (2011): 861–85; Shaul Bakhash, "The Troubled Relationship: Iran and Iraq, 1930–1980," in *Iran, Iraq, and the Legacies of War*, eds. Lawrence G. Potter and Gary G. Sick (New York: Palgrave Macmillan, 2004), 21–22; Cordesman and Wagner, *The Lessons of Modern War*, 31–33; Ramazani, *Revolutionary Iran*, 62–69.

[46] My account below is elaborated in Chad E. Nelson, "Revolution and War: Saddam's Decision to Invade Iran," *The Middle East Journal* 72, no. 2 (2018): 246–66.

[47] See his public and private statements in Iraq News Agency, "Saddam Husayn on Relations with Iran, United States," February 14, 1979, Foreign Broadcast Information System (hereafter FBIS), Daily Report: Middle East and Africa collection (hereafter MEA), vol. V, no. 033, p. E1; CRRC

In the early days of the revolution, there were uncertainties as to the character of the regime that would emerge. Iraqi leaders dismissed Khomeini as an old man who would have a largely ceremonial role in the new regime. Iraq welcomed the new government of Prime Minister Mehdi Bazargan, particularly after Iran's withdrawal from the Western-aligned Central Treaty Organization (CENTO), and invited him to visit Iraq in order to improve relations between the two countries.[48] But this honeymoon was to be short-lived. While Hussein drew a distinction between the Bazargan government and clerical forces, the former did not control the latter.[49] After an initial period of dual sovereignty, the Bazargan government was increasingly marginalized from the spring of 1979 onward.

At the same time, the Iranian Revolution was emboldening Iraqi Islamists. As a result, relations with Iran deteriorated. A key turning point was late spring/early summer 1979. Ever since Khomeini's return to Iran in February 1979, there had been a smattering of protests in Iraq. Grand Ayatollah Muhammad Baqir al-Sadr in Iraq, a high-ranking cleric and leader of the Da'wa Party in Iraq, was soon the focus of attention from both the opposition and the regime. Word of his communications with Khomeini prompted demonstrations in support of both Sadr and Khomeini in Najaf and elsewhere. Khomeini sent a message to Sadr, urging him to stay in Iraq.[50] In June, Sadr issued a fatwa forbidding Muslims from joining the ruling Arab Socialist Ba'th Party. He was arrested, which prompted riots in several cities that were put down by force. Sadr was released, but subsequently put under house arrest. Shia groups within Iraq formed an umbrella organization called the Islamic Liberation Movement with the goal of overthrowing the Ba'th regime.[51] Also at this time, key figures from an earlier Kurdish insurgency crossed into Iran and received aid.[52]

These events had a clear effect on Iraqi-Iranian ties. At the time of a meeting between Saddam and his advisors in the late spring of 1979, relations with Iran were already clearly tense. However, the group ruled out war with Iran and considered the possibility that Iran was beginning to fragment in such a way that

SH-SHTP-A-000-851, "Meeting Between Saddam Hussein and Military Officials Regarding al-Khomeini, Iranian Kurdistan, and Iranian Forces with Iraqi Diplomats," February 20, 1979.

[48] Ramazani, *Revolutionary Iran*, 58; Majid Khadduri, *The Gulf War: The Origins and Implications of the Iraq-Iran Conflict* (New York: Oxford University Press, 1988), 81.
[49] Iraqi foreign minister Saddoun Hamadi, in an October 1980 speech before the United Nations Security Council, detailed Iraqi efforts to reach out to the Bazargan government, only to be rebuked by the Khomeini faction that was actively working to undermine the Ba'th regime. See Tareq Ismael, *Iraq and Iran: Roots of Conflict* (Syracuse: Syracuse University Press, 1982), 203–12.
[50] Aziz, "The Role of Muhammad Baqir Al-Sadr," 216; Chibli Mallat, *The Renewal of Islamic Law: Muhammad Baqer as-Sadr, Najaf and the Shi'i International* (New York: Cambridge University Press, 1993), 51; Amatzia Baram, *Saddam Husayn and Islam, 1968–2003: Ba'thi Iraq from Secularism to Faith* (Baltimore: Johns Hopkins University Press, 2014), 140.
[51] Wiley, *The Islamic Movement of Iraqi Shi'as*, 54.
[52] Marr, *The Modern History of Iraq*, 182.

the country might break apart in the next several years.[53] The implication of the discussion was that, hopefully, the problems Iran was posing would solve themselves. Despite the consensus against war, the first military confrontation between the two countries occurred in early June when, in the context of ongoing protests in Iraq, Iraqi planes attacked several Iranian border villages, killing six people.[54] The attack presumably targeted Iraqi Kurdish guerillas but may have been an attempt to send a message to Iran. The Iraqi state newspaper *al-Thawra* warned Iran against "playing with fire."[55] Khomeini protested Sadr's arrest and the border incidents, praying for the "independence" of Islamic countries.[56] The Tehran International Service in Arabic was more explicit. It issued a call to rise up against the "Takriti gang," referring to the town that Saddam and much of the top Ba'th leadership hailed from.[57] *Al-Thawra* warned Iran of "the consequences of repeating the game played by the shah against Iraq," that is, interfering in the internal affairs of Iraq.[58]

Saddam responded to unrest among Shia with a carrot as well as a stick. He poured aid into the Shia-majority areas and began incorporating into his rhetoric Islamic symbols that cut across sectarian lines. He even resurrected the idea of a popularly elected national assembly (which would be Shia-dominated, given the Shia share of the population), mentioned in the 1970 constitution but never convened.[59] Tensions remained high, however, with more arrests, executions, and sporadic guerilla activity. Islamist groups received an influx of members and formed military wings, and a member of Da'wa's militant wing tried to assassinate Saddam.[60] Attempts by the Iraqi regime to coerce Grand Ayatollah Sadr into denouncing the Iranian Revolution failed. Instead, Sadr smuggled messages to his followers that called for a violent uprising against the regime.[61]

Relations between Iran and Iraq somewhat simmered after the border clashes in June 1979. However, Saddam solicited a meeting that the Non-Aligned Movement summit in Havana, Cuba, that September with Iranian foreign minister Ebrahim Yazdi, who told him that Iran's provisional government did not have the authority to ratify the Algiers Accord.[62] In October, Saddam began to

[53] CRRC SH-SHTP-A-001-404, "President Saddam Hussein Presiding Over a Meeting With the Iraqi Revolutionary Command Council to Discuss the Arabistan Crisis," April–May 1979.
[54] FBIS-MEA 79-111, June 7, 1979, R1.
[55] FBIS-MEA 79-115, June 13, 1979, E2
[56] FBIS-MEA 79-117, June 15, 1979, R3.
[57] FBIS-MEA 79-118, June 18, 1979, R13–R14; FBIS-MEA 79-119, June 19, 1979, R11–R12; FBIS-MEA 79-120, June 20, 1979, R13–R14.
[58] FBIS-MEA 79-117, June 15, 1979, R6; FBIS-MEA 79-122, June 22, 1979, R29–R31.
[59] Hiro, *The Longest War: The Iran-Iraq Military Conflict* (London: Grafton Books, 1989), 34–35.
[60] Wiley, *The Islamic Movement of Iraqi Shi'as*, 54–55.
[61] Aziz, "The Role of Muhammad Baqir Al-Sadr," 216–17; Baram, *Saddam Husayn and Islam*, 142.
[62] See the remarks of Mansour Farhang, who was in the meeting with Saddam and Yazdi, from Haleh Esfandiari et al., "The Iran-Iraq War: The View from Baghdad—Panel I: Origins of the Iran-Iraq War," conference, Wilson Center, Washington, DC, October 26, 2011; Mansur Farhang, " ملاقات با آیت الله خمینی و صدام پیش از آغاز جنگ" [The meeting with Ayatollah Khomeini and Saddam before

call the accord into question, complaining about territory that had not yet passed into Iraqi hands as per the agreement and demanding a renegotiation of the Shatt al-'Arab border.[63] Saddam was now demanding full sovereignty over the river, though he continued to abide by the agreement. In a token effort to gain support among Arab states, the Iraqi regime also called for the return to the United Arab Emirates of three disputed islands in the Strait of Hormuz that Iran had claimed in 1971.[64]

After the Bazargan government fell in November and clerical strength increased, the anti-Ba'th rhetoric in Iran heated up. By 1980, some Iranian government officials were again explicitly calling for the Ba'th regime's overthrow. In March, Iraq expelled the Iranian ambassador for interfering in the internal affairs of Iraq.[65] The Iraqi government passed a law on March 31, 1980, condemning all past and present members of Da'wa and its affiliates to death. A day later, a member of a Shia opposition group attempted to assassinate Deputy Prime Minister Tariq Aziz as he spoke at a university in Baghdad. During the funeral procession for those that were killed in the attempt against Aziz, a bomb was thrown, according to Iraqi reports, from the window of an "Iranian school."[66] The response from Iran was hardly conciliatory. Commentary on the Tehran International Service radio in Arabic noted that the assassination attempt "was not an isolated incident, but part of the general national struggle against imperialism and the criminal regime in power. It is not a bomb that missed its target, but part of a big explosion in Iraq these days that is bound to hit all its targets soon and uproot imperialism and that dictatorship."[67]

Saddam responded with the unprecedented step of executing a grand ayatollah, Muhammad Baqir al-Sadr, as well as his sister, Bint al-Huda. The regime began to expel from the country tens of thousands of Shia who were considered disloyal.[68] Gregory Gause notes that Hussein's rhetoric underwent an immediate

the start of the war], BBC, September 21, 2010, https://www.bbc.com/persian/iran/2010/09/100909_l55_war30th_khomeini_iraq.

[63] The territory he was referring to was the area of Zayn al-Qaws and Sayf Sa'd in Iraq's Diyala Governorate, near the middle of its border with Iran. According to the accord, Iran agreed to cede territory in exchange for the Shatt al-'Arab, but the commission delineating this border had disbanded due to the revolution before the changes could be implemented. See Hiro, The Longest War, 268.

[64] See, e.g., FBIS-MEA 79-193, October 3, 1979, E2; FBIS-MEA 79-199, October 12, 1979, E1. In the aforementioned late spring meeting, one of Saddam's advisors mentioned raising the issue of the Iranian claim on these islands as a means to convince other Arab states of the danger of the Iranian regime. See CRRC SH-SHTP-A-001-404.

[65] FBIS-MEA 5-48, March 10, 1980, E1.

[66] FBIS-MEA 5-68, April 7, 1980, E1–E2.

[67] FBIS South Asia collection (hereafter SAS) 8-68, April 7, 1980, I24.

[68] Ali Babakhan, "The Deportation of Shi'is During the Iran-Iraq War," in Ayatollahs, Sufis and Ideologues: State, Religion and Social Movements in Iraq, ed. Faleh Abdul-Jabar (London: Saqi Books, 2002), 192–200.

change, from warning the Iranians not to interfere in Iraqi internal affairs to verbally attacking the Iranian leadership and threatening war.[69] This was matched by a chorus of Iranian senior political and religious leadership, from Khomeini on down, calling on Iraqis and members of the Iraqi military to rise up against the regime, asserting that if they did so, they would receive Iranian assistance.[70] Iran's Ministry of Foreign Affairs, which had previously been the voice of relative moderation in the Islamic Republic, was no exception. In a statement confirming the martyrdom of Sadr, it declared: "We will not rest until the final overthrow of the criminal, imperialist and Zionist-agent regime of the treacherous Saddam Husayn. . . . [I]t is up to the Muslim nation of Iran to assist and render succor to the Muslim Iraqi nation with all its might."[71] Iranian radio was also broadcasting calls from Da'wa to rebel.[72]

This series of events seems to have convinced Saddam Hussein there was an orchestrated attempt to overthrow his regime and that he had to strike back. Most scholarship on the issue of the timing of the Iraqi decision to go to war with Iran places the decision in the aftermath of these events in April.[73] It was only at this stage that Saddam told the Iraqi military to start preparing for war.[74] This is

[69] F. Gregory Gause III, "Iraq's Decisions to Go to War, 1980 and 1990," *The Middle East Journal* 56, no. 1 (2002): 66. See also the official biography byFuad Matar, *Saddam Hussein: The Man, the Cause and the Future* (London: Third World Centre, 1981), 135.

[70] For Khomeini's call for revolution in Iraq, see FBIS-SAS-80-070, April 9, 1980, I6–I7; FBIS-SAS-80-078, April 21, 1980, I9.

[71] FBIS-SAS-80-080, April 23, 1980, I18. The Iranian foreign minister had declared earlier in the month that Iran was "determined to overthrow the Ba'thist regime of Iraq." FBIS-SAS-80-070, April 9, 1980, I6.

[72] See FBIS-SAS-8-71, April 10, 1980, I16–I17; FBIS-SAS-8-76, April 15, 1980, I16.

[73] See Williamson Murray and Kevin M. Woods, *The Iran-Iraq War: A Military and Strategic History* (New York: Cambridge University Press, 2014), 46–47; Amatzia Baram, "Saddam Husayn, the Ba'th Regime and the Iraqi Officer Corps," in *Armed Forces in the Middle East: Politics and Strategy*, eds. Barry Rubin and Thomas Keaney (London: Frank Cass, 2002), 214; Gause III, "Iraq's Decisions to Go to War," 67; Ofra Bengio, *Saddam's Word: Political Discourse in Iraq* (New York: Oxford University Press, 1998), 145; Hiro, *The Longest War*, 36; Chubin and Tripp, *Iran and Iraq at War* (London: I. B. Tauris & Co., 1988), 26. There is one significant source that puts Saddam's decision to invade much earlier. Americans met with Iranian officials in October 1979 and told them that Iraq was preparing to invade Iran. Although increasingly cited, this intelligence appears to have been fabricated by the American government and shared with the Iranians in an attempt to curry favor with them. See Nelson, "Revolution and War," 255–57.

[74] Iraqi generals report that they were notified in early July to plan for an invasion, although some were not aware of the decision for war until it broke out. See the interviews of several generals in Kevin M. Woods et al., *Saddam's Generals: Perspectives of the Iran-Iraq War* (Alexandria: Institute for Defense Analyses, 2011), 55, 115–16, 155, 190–91; Woods, Kevin M., Williamson Murray, and Thomas Holaday, *Saddam's War: An Iraqi Military Perspective of the Iran-Iraq War*, McNair Paper 70 (Washington, DC: National Defense University Press, 2009), 32; al-Hamdani, "Memoir," 2003, 22, Saddam Hussein Collection, Conflict Records Research Center. Edgar O'Ballance reports that General Jabbah al-Shemshah, Saddam's chief of staff, was ordered to plan for an invasion in May 1980, although he does not provide a citation. O'Ballance, Edgar, *The Gulf War* (London: Brassey's Defence Publishing, 1988), 48.

also when Saddam appears to have consulted with several Gulf countries about his intention to invade.[75]

From the spring of 1980 on, both Iran and Iraq called for the downfall of the other side, and engaged in a long string of border skirmishes and incursions into each other's airspace.[76] Iraq's domestic opposition continued, along with repression. In May 1980, Iraq notified the secretary-general of the United Nations that members of Da'wa had met with Iranian officials in the Iranian city of Qom, the center of the Islamic Republic's ascendant clerical leaders, and were plotting to overthrow the Iraqi regime. There was a smattering of attacks against government officials, including a June 1980 attempted assassination of Hussein by Iraqi airmen led by a Da'wa member.[77] Although Sunni Islamists were much smaller in number and less significant a threat, the regime also conducted a repression campaign against them, fearing that they supported the Iranian Revolution as well.[78] Iraq's director of intelligence declared that the government would deport any Iraqi who supported the Islamic revolution in Iran.[79] It was, however, not until September that Iraq unleashed a full-scale invasion, a delay attributed to the war-planning process and the wait to see whether the Nuzhih coup—an attempt by Iranian exiles in Iraq to overthrow the Iranian regime in July—would succeed.[80] Saddam actively backed this coup, in contrast to his caution toward Iran the previous year.

Again, when Saddam decided to invade Iran sheds light on his motives for initiating the war. In contrast to the opportunism argument, Hussein supported the shah until the end of his rule, showing no sign of taking advantage of the shah's increasingly deteriorating situation, and was at least initially on good terms with the weak provisional government.[81] Saddam's hostility toward Iran was caused by domestic upheaval in Iraq and not the weakening of the Iranian state. In addition, there is no evidence that Saddam was trying to annex the neighboring Iranian province of Khuzestan, a key aim for the opportunism argument. The

---

[75] Cordesman and Wagner, *The Lessons of Modern War*, 38–39nn25, 26; Ramazani, *Revolutionary Iran*, 60.

[76] Murray and Woods, *The Iran-Iraq War*, 90–92.

[77] Wiley, *The Islamic Movement of Iraqi Shi'as*, 57–58.

[78] Helfont, *Compulsion in Religion*, 77–78.

[79] Khalil Osman, *Sectarianism in Iraq: The Making of State and Nation Since 1920* (New York: Routledge, 2015), 233.

[80] The coup of course did not succeed, although the resulting purges perhaps further weakened the military. Mark J. Gasiorowski, "The Nuzhih Plot and Iranian Politics," *International Journal of Middle East Studies* 34 no. 4 (2002): 645–66.

[81] The chaos and the purges put Iraq in the unprecedented state of having a military advantage vis-à-vis Iran. One of the first actions of the revolutionary committee appointed by Khomeini was a purge of the armed forces. Accounts of the purges include Nikola B. Schahgaldian and Gina Barkhordarian, *The Iranian Military Under the Islamic Republic* (Santa Monica: Rand, 1987), 15–27; Sepehr Zabih, *The Iranian Military in Revolution and War* (New York: Routledge, 1998), 115–35. A detailed comparison of their forces and military advantage at the time is found in Cordesman and Wagner, *The Lessons of Modern War*, 56–70; Murray and Woods, *The Iran-Iraq War*, 65–84.

province had significant oil deposits and would provide Iraq with a less vulnerable access to the Gulf.[82]

Saddam probably wanted to restore the border of the Shatt al-'Arab to its pre-1975 position. But the benefits of moving the border from the middle of the channel to the Iranian shore would not significantly alter the strategic balance between Iran and Iraq. However, the border was not primarily about geopolitics. It was symbolic, a means to send a signal to Iran to stop meddling in Iraqi affairs.[83] Saddam had a domestic political interest in making the conflict about Iraqi rights to territory rather than the domestic threat that Iran posed. Saddam said "we will force their heads into the mud to enforce our political will on them, which can only happen militarily."[84] At a minimum, he was sending a message to Iran not to interfere in Iraqi affairs. But the limited invasion had a greater goal— the collapse of the revolutionary government, perhaps by politically discrediting the regime with an Iraqi victory.

Some scholars have argued that the fear of revolutionary contagion destabilizing the Ba'thist regime was not a motivation for Saddam's invasion. Their strongest argument is that by the time Saddam had invaded Iran, the contagion threat had been averted. Subversion by Da'wa and other Shia groups had already been dealt with, proven by the fact that Iraqi Shia largely remained loyal (or at least not openly subversive) for the entirety of the Iran-Iraq War.[85] The problem with this argument is hindsight bias. It assumes Saddam knew that the threat had passed. Based on Da'wa's own admissions, Amatzia Baram has noted that the Ba'thist regime had indeed at least temporarily suppressed the opposition, so street protests were not viable, as evidenced by the lack of demonstrations following the April 1980 execution of Grand Ayatollah Sadr.[86] However, clandestine opposition continued, such as the assassination attempt mentioned

---

[82] The captured Iraqi documents evince no aim of annexing Khuzestan. See CRRC SH-SHTP-A-001-404; CRRC SH-GMID-D-000-620, "General Military Intelligence Directorate Regarding the People of Arabistan (Arabs in Southern Iran) in Al Ahwaz Area Calling for Independence," various dates, 1979; CRRC SH-SHTP-D-000-559, "Meeting Between Saddam Hussein and Iraqi Officials Regarding Relations with Europe, Russia, China, the Gulf Countries, and the United States," November 1979. For elaboration of this claim, see Nelson, "Revolution and War," 260–65.

[83] For the argument that the significance of the Shatt al-'Arab was not the territory but the symbolic value used for other political goals, see Will D. Swearingen, "Geopolitical Origins of the Iran-Iraq War," *Geographical Review* 78, no. 4 (1988).

[84] CRRC SH-SHTP-A-000-835, "Meeting Between Saddam Hussein, the National Command, and the Revolutionary Command Council Discussing the Iran-Iraq War," September 16, 1980.

[85] Makiya, *Republic of Fear*, 265. The extent of Shia loyalty can be overstated. Beyond the assassination attempts, one indicator of the disloyalty is that as many as thirty thousand deserters from the military were hiding in the southern Iraqi marshes. Lisa Blaydes, *State of Repression: Iraq Under Saddam Hussein* (Princeton: Princeton University Press, 2018), 277.

[86] Amazia Baram, "The Impact of Khomeini's Revolution on the Radical Shi'i Movement of Iraq," in *The Iranian Revolution and the Muslim World*, ed. David Menashiri (Boulder: Westview Press, 1990), 144; Baram, *Saddam Husayn and Islam*, 143–45.

earlier and others.[87] The regime could not be confident that these covert attempts would not be successful and that more overt, large-scale demonstrations would not reemerge. Their continued concern is evident in the fact that it was after the events of early April 1980—the assassination attempt against Aziz and subsequent execution of Baqir al-Sadr—that the regime began to deport tens of thousands of Iraqis deemed disloyal. In speeches in February and June, Saddam even raised the possibility that Iraq could split apart.[88] As Baram states, "The Shi'i opposition in Iraq had burned out, but with Khomeini as a source of inspiration"—and, one might add, direct Iranian aid—"it could rise from the ashes."[89]

The Iran-Iraq War was a protracted conflict that Saddam did not expect. Given Iran's weakness, Saddam thought the Iranians would have to succumb to Iraqi superiority, but Iran did not comply. Khomeini rejected a possible ceasefire, claiming that Iran "will not rest until the downfall of the decadent Iraqi Ba'thist regime."[90] Iran was committed to not only expelling Iraq from Iranian territory but also overthrowing the Iraqi regime and establishing an Islamic state. They accomplished the former by 1982, and established the Supreme Assembly for the Islamic Revolution in Iraq, with the Iraqi cleric Muhammad Baqir al-Hakim at its head.[91] Fortunately for Iraq, it had better allies than Iran, and the increasing international support for Iraq would enable Saddam to hold on and eventually fight Iran to a draw. Domestically, Saddam used both carrots and sticks to control the opposition, and he tilted more toward religion to legitimize his rule.[92] He was using all the tools at his disposal to preserve his regime.

Iraqi hostility toward Iran was not driven by opportunism or abstract ideological differences. It was a response to the emboldening effects Iran had on social forces that were a threat to the Iraqi regime. The fear of contagion from the Iranian Revolution is why Iraq reacted with increasing hostility toward Iran, eventually escalating to war. Iran had little involvement at first in what was

[87] There were unconfirmed reports of aborted coups, and a network of senior Shia officers was uncovered that was said to be responsible for five attempts on Saddam's life. Twelve officers and two hundred others were executed by firing squad. See Colin Legum, Haim Shaked, and Daniel Dishon, eds., *Middle East Contemporary Survey*, vol. 5, 1980–81 (New York: Holmes & Meier Publishers, Inc., 1982), 585.

[88] See Efraim Karsh and Inari Rautsi, *Saddam Hussein: A Political Biography* (New York: The Free Press, 1991), 148. Ofra Bengio noted in 1985 "That the regime's fears of al-Dawa have not subsided [since the 1980 crackdown] is evident from the discussions during the Baath party's Ninth Congress held in June 1982 which concentrated on this party and attacked it ferociously." Bengio, "Shi'is and Politics in Ba'thi Iraq," 6. The intensity of the crackdown on internal opposition during the period in 1980 may be seen as the opposition's impotence, but it also revealed the fears of the leadership that the threat of the opposition was to be taken very seriously.

[89] Baram, *Saddam Husayn and Islam*, 152.

[90] Colin Legum, Haim Shaked, and Daniel Dishon, eds., *Middle East Contemporary Survey*, vol. 4, 1979–80 (New York: Holmes & Meier Publishers, Inc., 1981), 21.

[91] A brief overview of SAIRI is given in Baram, "Two Roads to Revolutionary Shi'ite Fundamentalism in Iraq," 547–51.

[92] Helfont, *Compulsion in Religion*; Baram, *Saddam Husayn and Islam*.

largely an indigenous revolt sparked by the Iranian Revolution. But clearly Iran's actions, and the anticipation of further actions, explain the outbreak of war, if not hostility.

The counterfactual of what Saddam would have done if an Islamist regime had come to power that was not able to act as a significant platform—a state that was not a powerful neighbor with extensive ties to the religious leaders of the majority of its population—is partially answered by his policy toward other Islamists. Saddam was not above supporting Sunni Islamist groups, particularly the Muslim Brotherhood in Syria, to bleed the Syrian regime, and to learn about their networks so that the Iraqis could better fight them at home.[93] But his regime did not want Islamist forces coming to power in the region. A revealing recording of the deliberations among Iraqi leaders over their policy toward Islamists in Sudan in 1986 indicates their position. Saddam's advisors expressed reservations about Sudan's Islamists. There was the fear that they would embolden the Egyptian Brotherhood and other groups. The Iraqis noted the emboldening effect of the Iranian Revolution in convincing other Islamists that seizing power was possible, despite the sectarian differences. They resolved that although they would utilize such groups for their own purposes, "if the Muslim Brotherhood is about to come to power, this becomes a national battle and we ally with anyone who prevents this danger."[94] Although Iran's actions as a platform were important, it was a potent model as well.

Syrian Reaction to Iranian Revolution

The Syrian reaction to the Iranian Revolution shows that sometimes leaders know the political risks of policies that are contrary to what the domestic contagion effects theory would predict but have compelling reasons to carry out those policies anyway. Like Iraq, Syria had a robust Islamist opposition movement. The movement was bordering on revolt at the time of the Iranian Revolution, which further emboldened it. This incentivized Syrian hostility toward Iran, as the theory predicts, but the need for allies overshadowed this. The Syrians reached out to the Iranian regime, first because of the need for an ally against Israel in the context of the post–Camp David Middle East and second because of a need for an ally against Iraq when Syrian-Iraqi relations deteriorated. It is clear that Assad

---

[93] Lefèvre, Ashes of Hama, 133; Abu Mus'ab al-Suri, Lessons Learned from the Jihad Ordeal in Syria, https://www.ctc.usma.edu/harmony-program/lessons-learned-from-the-jihad-ordeal-in-syria-original-language-2.

[94] CRRC SH-SHTP-A-001-167, "Meeting Between Saddam Hussein and Ba'ath Party Members Regarding the Status of the Party in the Arab World and Exploitation of the Muslim Brotherhood as an Ally," July 24, 1986.

was trying to minimize the Islamist threat at home, but, as was the case with the Germans reaching out to the Bolsheviks, geopolitical factors trumped contagion concerns. In addition, the concern that Iran would have an emboldening effect on Syria's Islamist opposition was blunted by the fact that Iran did not act as a platform by aiding Syria's Islamist opposition. It spurned the Islamists and embraced the regime. This considerably weakened the power of the model of the Iranian Revolution in the eyes of the Islamists. If Iran and Iraq had made different policy choices, though, the Syrian-Iranian alliance might not have developed.

Twelve days after Khomeini returned to Iran, Assad sent him a telegram congratulating him for a revolution that "is inspired by the great principles of Islam."[95] Syria was the first Arab country to recognize the new regime. In March, Assad sent his information minister to Iran to develop ties, and the minister met with Khomeini. What motivated Assad to draw close to Iran was the same impulse that drove him to pursue unity talks with Iraq. The Egyptian-Israeli peace had left him dangerously vulnerable vis-à-vis Israel. He needed allies. His relations with the shah had progressively deteriorated the more the shah had supported Egypt making peace with Israel. The new Iranian regime was everything the shah was not in such matters. Its ideological position was much like the Syrians'—against the peace process, anti-Israeli, and anti-American. Thus, there was an opportunity to start relations anew and bolster the rejectionist front.

Whether an alliance between Iran and Syria would develop, however, was not at all clear. One possible factor pushing against the relationship was that as the revolution was radicalizing in Iran, a revolution was also brewing in Syria. In June 1979, the members of the Fighting Vanguard attacked the Military Academy at Aleppo, killing eighty-three cadets (mostly Alawis) and wounding many more. This was the beginning of a low-level civil war between the regime and Islamist groups. The Islamists' strategy seemed to be to provoke the regime into a confrontation, with the hopes that the regular army when called up would buckle given the predominance of Sunnis within its ranks.[96] Another aim was to prompt the Syrian Muslim Brotherhood to join the confrontation, which was successful.[97] The Assad regime dramatically increased the repression of the Muslim Brotherhood, which radicalized in response. In October 1979, the Brotherhood officially endorsed the use of violence against the regime.

The Muslim Brotherhood and other Sunni Islamists strongly supported the Iranian Revolution and saw it as a source of inspiration. They did not dwell on the particularities of the Iranian regime. For them, the revolution was victory for Islam over un-Islamic leaders. They suggested that Assad would soon share

[95] FBIS-MEA-79-30, February 12, 1979, H1.
[96] Van Dam, *The Struggle for Power in Syria*, 98.
[97] Lefèvre, *Ashes of Hama*, 102.

the fate of the shah. The Muslim Brotherhood called on the ulema to play a key role in mobilizing the masses against the regime in Syria, as it had in Iran.[98] In the aftermath of the Iranian Revolution, the Syrian regime drew closer to the symbols of Islam by, for example, requiring that all state declarations bear the Islamic date as well as the Christian date.[99] Assad took the Islamist threat very seriously. Islamists nearly killed him in an assassination attempt in June 1980. In response, Assad had hundreds of Islamists in prison executed and made membership in the Muslim Brotherhood punishable by death.[100] In October 1980, Islamist groups united under the Syrian Islamic Front in order to combat the regime. An indication of the regime's sense of insecurity is that Assad reportedly had a security entourage of twelve thousand soldiers, and the three generals heading the state security services had sixty soldiers each.[101]

Assad's Islamist uprising could have cooled his enthusiasm toward the new Iranian regime because of the negative example it set at home, but by the summer of 1979 Syria also needed an ally against Iraq. Unity talks with Iraq collapsed then, probably because Saddam heard that factions within the Iraqi Ba'th Party planned to use the federation and Syrian help as a means to constrain him. Saddam accused the Syrians of orchestrating a coup against him. The Syrians strenuously denied any connection, but the merger deteriorated into acrimony.[102] Amid the invective, it was clear that Assad was now in an even more dangerous position.

The rapprochement with Iran that developed was both a cause and a consequence of the further deterioration of relations with Iraq. A month after the negotiations between Syria and Iraq ended, the Syrian foreign minister went to Iran to explore expanding relations. This was followed by visits from the Iranian foreign minister in September and the deputy prime minister in October 1979. Syria strongly supported Iran in the hostage crisis, seemingly undeterred by the radicalization going on within Iran. Further talks led to tangible results. In the spring of 1980, as relations between Iraq and Iran were reaching new lows, Syria began transferring Soviet-made arms to Iran to replace its depleted stock. Iraq

---

[98] Abd-Allah, *The Islamic Struggle*, 184–85.

[99] Hans Günter Lobmeyer, *Opposition und Widerstand in Syrien* (Hamburg: Deutsches Orient-Institut, 1995), 270.

[100] Thomas Pierret, *Religion and State in Syria: The Sunni Ulama from Coup to Revolution* (New York: Cambridge University Press, 2013), 66.

[101] Gerard Michaud, "The Importance of Bodyguards," *MERIP Reports* 110 (1982): 29.

[102] One possible reason for the unraveling of the merger was that the Syrians were not willing to accept a junior role in the merger, and Iraq pushed them further than they wanted to go, hoping to entrap them. Mufti, however, argues that the affair was principally for Saddam Hussein to purge Ba'thist officers and consolidate his rule by exposing those who were not fully loyal to him. Malik Mufti, *Sovereign Creations: Pan-Arabism and Political Order in Syria and Iraq* (Ithaca: Cornell University Press, 1996), 209–20.

harshly criticized Syria for doing so, and in August, Iraq expelled the Syrian ambassador in protest.

Beyond cultivating ties with Iran as an ally against Iraq and Israel, Assad may have reached out to the Iranians in an effort to make sure the Iranians did not aid his Islamist opposition as well as to discredit the Iranian example by virtue of their very ties with him. There is no evidence whether or not this was a motive of Assad's outreach to Iran, but it is what happened.[103] The more he reached out to Iran and Iran responded, the more illegitimate the Iranian example became for his domestic opposition. Islamists initially expressed bewilderment at the growing Syrian-Iranian rapprochement. Their own efforts to reach out to the Iranians were to no avail.[104] Syrian radio in April 1980 aired a statement by an Iranian official praising Assad and denouncing the Islamists as gangs carrying out the Camp David conspiracy, which prompted criticism within Iran and Syria.[105] The Iranian prime minister made a similar statement in December.[106] By the fall of 1980, the Syrian Muslim Brotherhood had ceased making public statements about the Iranian Revolution. Their manifesto of revolution produced in November 1980, despite having a section on foreign affairs, curiously does not mention the Iranian Revolution, a glaring omission.[107]

Upon the outbreak of war between Iran and Iraq in September 1980, Syria was silent for the first two weeks, seemingly waiting to see whether the Iranian regime would survive. Assad was soon denouncing Iraq for starting the wrong war against the wrong enemy at the wrong time.[108] To Assad, the real enemy was of course Israel. A quick Iraqi victory would also embolden his other enemy, Iraq. Syria increasingly notched up its aid to Iran. It leveraged its new treaty with the Soviet Union to continue the delivery of Soviet weapons to Iran. In October, Iraq broke relations with Syria. In the spring of 1981, Assad consented to Iranians using Syrian airspace to attack Iraq. In December, though, he traveled to the Gulf states, seeking aid given the Israeli threat (Israel having just annexed the Golan Heights) and his Islamist opposition. They informed him that any aid was conditional on him abandoning his pro-Iranian position. As a response, he declared that it was now time that Iran and Iraq stop fighting so that energies could be turned toward Israel. But his attempt to mediate a ceasefire was rejected by Iran.

---

[103] Also, drawing near to Iran enabled Assad to link the Alawis with Shias, mainstreaming what many considered a heretical sect. Khatib, *Islamic Revivalism in Syria*, 93.

[104] Brynjar Lia, "The Islamist Uprising in Syria, 1976–82: The History and Legacy of a Failed Revolt," *British Journal of Middle Eastern Studies* 43, no. 4 (2016): 550; Lobmeyer, *Opposition und Widerstand in Syrien*, 271; Batatu, "Syria's Muslim Brethren," 13; Abd-Allah, *The Islamic Struggle*, 186–87.

[105] Abd-Allah, *The Islamic Struggle*, 183–84.

[106] Goodarzi, *Syria and Iran*, 43.

[107] The manifesto is reproduced in Abd-Allah, *The Islamic Struggle*, 201–67.

[108] Seale, *Asad of Syria*, 357.

By this time, the Syrian Islamists' silence regarding the Iranian Revolution had turned to hostility. Iran continued to back Assad's regime in its contest with the Islamists. The leader of the Islamic Republican Party in Iran explicitly said that the party could not condone the uprising when Assad was confronting imperialist agents such as Israel and Egypt and, not incidentally, supporting the Iranian Revolution.[109] In the context of such lack of support, a Syrian Islamist leader, in an interview with a German newspaper, made clear that if they were victorious, their Islamic republic would differ greatly from Iran's: "We do not wish to replace one dictatorship with another."[110] The Islamists, however, were not victorious. The insurgency culminated in an uprising in Hama in February 1982 that Assad decisively crushed, killing thousands in the process.

Syria and Iran deepened their ties in the spring and summer of 1982. In the spring, they signed a trade and oil deal. Most significantly, Syria cut off Iraqi access to the trans-Syrian pipeline, halving Iraqi exports and costing Syria $17 million a day.[111] At the same time, Assad was aiding Kurdish insurgents who were sabotaging Iraq's other pipeline and tying down troops. The tightening of the Syrian-Iranian relationship was driven by Assad's push to rid Iraq of Saddam Hussein. Assad had just survived a severe insurgency to some extent backed by Iraq, and saw an opportunity to finish Saddam off given the momentum swinging in Iran's favor. The Syrian press called on the Iraqis to bring down his regime.[112]

The Syria-Iranian relationship was further bolstered by Israel's invasion of Lebanon in June 1982. Syria gave Iran permission to send a contingent of forces to Lebanon to mobilize the Lebanese and resist the Israelis.[113] This was the beginning of a long relationship between Iran, Syria, and Islamist groups in Lebanon, which came to symbolize the Syria-Iranian relationship.

The relationship was not without its tensions. By the mid-1980s, Hezbollah emerged as a concrete organization. Clearly inspired by and dependent on Iran, it had a tenuous relationship with the less militant Amal Party, which was close to the Syrian regime. Syria did not share Hezbollah and Iran's goal of making Lebanon an Islamic republic, but Assad allowed the groups to operate given their ability to mobilize the Shia against Israel. There was little chance of establishing such a regime in a state with a significant Christian community, among others, who rejected an Islamic republic.[114]

[109] FBIS-SAS-81-077, April 22, 1981, I6.
[110] Abd-Allah, *The Islamic Struggle*, 283.
[111] Chubin and Tripp, *Iran and Iraq at War*, 179–80.
[112] Legum, Shaked, and Dishon, eds., *Middle East Contemporary Survey*, vol. 6, 1981–82 (New York: Holmes & Meier Publishers, Inc., 1984), 866.
[113] Goodarzi, *Syria and Iran*, 64–72.
[114] Anoushiravan Ehteshami and Raymond A. Hinnebusch, *Syria and Iran: Middle Powers in a Penetrated Regional System* (New York: Routledge, 1997), 125.

The issue of an Islamic state in Iraq was a more salient threat to Iran-Syria ties. Assad wanted Saddam deposed but wanted a secular regime to take his place. Iran wanted an Islamic republic modeled after its own. Syria had made clear before the Iranian invasion of Iraq that Syria would not support such a move and threatened to reevaluate its stance on the Iran-Iraq War. The Syrians "vigorously" opposed Iran's announcement early in 1982 of a four-stage plan to establish an Islamic republic in Iraq.[115] Syria did not reevaluate its alignment, given the context of the Israeli invasion of Lebanon. The potential of an Islamist regime in Iraq remained, though, a major potential source of conflict in 1982–83, with Syria favoring a Ba'thist colonel as Saddam's replacement, and Iran favoring an Iraqi cleric. Iraq's successful resistance of the Iranian invasion dissipated Syrian concerns. Syria's alignment with Iran would persist through the Iran-Iraq War and beyond.

The relationship between Syria and Iran, sometimes rocky, was not inevitable. Had relations with Iraq not deteriorated, it might not have even developed, especially if, as the revolution radicalized in Iran, Iran had not supported Assad against his opposition. The choice by the revolutionary regime in Iran to stand with the Syrian regime had important implications for its broader appeal, and is insufficiently studied by scholars of Iranian foreign policy. The decision was not just a dilemma of power politics versus ideology. Courting Syria gave the Iranians an ally not just against Iraq but also against Israel. It furthered the Iranians' message that the revolution was not just a narrow sectarian matter; it was about anti-imperialism and liberating the oppressed. And the alignment would weaken the ability of Arab states to construct a narrative of a united Arab front against the Persians. But the alignment also undercut Iranian attempts to appeal to Sunni Islamist groups who had the same basic program as the Iranian Revolution and expressed sympathy toward it. As one partisan stated, "No miscalculation of the Iranian Islamic Revolution could have given greater gratification to its enemies than its ties to the Asad regime, and sincere Sunni supporters of the Islamic Republic could only stand back in disbelief."[116] This was a chance to put into practice Khomeini's ecumenical rhetoric. In contrast, backing the Alawi regime against the Sunni Islamists emphasized the sectarian nature of the revolution. There is some evidence that Iranians appreciated the dilemma they were in, but they clearly felt the benefits outweighed the disadvantages.[117]

---

[115] Yair Hirschfield, "The Odd Couple: Ba'thist Syria and Khomeini's Iran," in *Syria Under Assad*, eds. Moshe Ma'oz and Avner Yaniv (London: Croom Helm, 1986), 113; Shireen T. Hunter, *Iran and the World: Continuity in a Revolutionary Decade* (Bloomington: Indiana University Press, 1990), 221n79.

[116] Abd-Allah, *The Islamic Struggle*, 182.

[117] There are reports of a divide within the government on the policy toward Syria. In an interview with Jubin Goodarzi, former president Bani Sadr claimed that there was no serious consideration of backing the Syrian Muslim Brotherhood because its links with Jordan and Iraq had compromised its Islamic credentials. An alternative version is that the Islamic Republic compromised its credentials

Syrian policy was born out of desperation to protect itself against Israel and then Iraq. This overshadowed possible qualms about aligning with Iran, a source of inspiration for the regime's Islamist opposition. Those qualms further dissipated as Iran reached out to the regime and was thus discredited in the eyes of the opposition. The Iranian regime was supporting Assad against its enemies, both those at home and those abroad. Given that kind of support, Assad seems to have assessed that despite the impact Iran might have as a model for his Islamist opposition, it was worth siding with Iran.

Egyptian Reaction to the Iranian Revolution

Iran did not act as a platform in spreading revolution to Egypt, but it was a model that emboldened Egyptian rebels, despite the sectarian divide. Egyptian Islamists rejected notions that the revolution was specifically Shia and put it in the broad context of a victory of Islamic forces against anti-Islamic ones. This emboldening effect was one of the reasons for the deterioration of relations between Iran and Egypt. The revolution had also removed a leader staunchly in the American camp and put in place a regime that would clearly not be in the American orbit. Egypt's peace deal with Israel rankled Iranian leaders, and that was the official reason Iran broke diplomatic relations with Egypt. The other Arab states also disagreed with Egypt's treaty with Israel, and yet shared their concerns about Iran that would lead to a reconciliation of Egypt with Iraq and Saudi Arabia.

Sadat at least initially did not seem concerned about the effects of the Iranian Revolution. The Egyptians promptly recognized the new regime. But this would soon change. Sadat explained, "Egypt has always been eager to be friends with Iran under the principles of noninterference in the state's domestic affairs and respect of the will of the peoples and their right to a free choice without foreign interference."[118] In January 1979, a journalist close to Sadat told acting Foreign Minister Boutros-Ghali that the Iranian Revolution would not prompt Sadat to crack down on Islamist groups like the Brotherhood: "Half the people present imagine that the shah will return victorious, and the other half think that the

---

by reaching out to Syria, and in doing so forced the Syrian Islamist opposition to turn to Iraq, which in turn caused defections within the Islamists' ranks. The Iranians were at least aware of the negative impact their policy could have at home. News of the Islamist uprising in Syria was for the most part blacked out by Iranian state news agencies to save the Iranians the embarrassment of backing the Syrian regime against an Islamist opposition. Yosef Olmert, "Iranian-Syrian Relations: Between Islam and Realpolitik," in *The Iranian Revolution and the Muslim World*, ed. David Menashiri (Boulder: Westview Press, 1990), 173; Goodarzi, *Syria and Iran*, 301–3nn94, 105, 109; 'Izz al-Din al-Faris, *Iranian-Syrian Relations: The Myth and the Reality* (Berkeley: Concerned Muslims of Northern California, [1982]).

[118] FBIS-MEA-79-032, February 14, 1979, D1.

[Muslim Brotherhood] can never take over Egypt. Sadat himself still thinks that the real danger comes from communism."[119]

The shah, however, did not return victorious, and the revolution buoyed radical Islamists in Egypt.[120] The enthusiasm for the revolution grew despite the fact that, prior to the revolution, there was very little awareness of or interaction with Iranian Islamist thought among Sunni radicals in Egypt, despite the similarities in their basic message.[121] The Muslim Brotherhood, though, was careful to avoid direct comparisons between the shah and Sadat in its still legal publications.[122] Sit-ins and campus demonstrations from Islamist student groups seemed to mimic the beginning of the Iranian Revolution.

Sadat took care to rein in Islamist forces. In a series of speeches, he attacked religious interference in Egyptian politics, and the Muslim Brotherhood in particular for changing from a religious organization to an underground terrorist organization. He temporarily suspended the Brotherhood's primary publication, al-Da'wa, and cracked down on Islamists in student unions.[123] The state-controlled newspapers, meanwhile, provided theological critiques of the Islamic Republic.[124] At the same time, in the aftermath of the Iranian Revolution, Sadat increased his efforts to use Islam to legitimate his regime. For example, he proposed a constitutional amendment to make sharia law the main source of legislation.[125] There are reports that several of his senior advisors repeatedly warned Sadat that he must take further action against Islamist organizations. At a meeting toward the end of 1979, an advisor supposedly said, "We ought to crack

[119] Boutros Boutros-Ghali, *Egypt's Road to Jerusalem: A Diplomat's Story of the Struggle for Peace in the Middle East* (New York: Random House, 1997), 182. Interestingly, American observers begged to differ. As early as 1975, US ambassador Eilts cabled, "We continue to believe that the religious right has vastly more potential disruptive power in Egypt than does the left, and for the [regime] to connive deliberately at [a] Muslim Brotherhood renaissance is playing with fire." Cited in Paul Chamberlin, "A World Restored: Religion, Counterrevolution, and the Search for Order in the Middle East," *Diplomatic History* 32, no. 3 (2008): 465.

[120] Ibrahim reports that the success of the Iranian Revolution gave radical Islamist groups "a tremendous boost." "At the time our interviews [of radical Islamists in Egyptian prisons] were stopped by the government [in February 1979, when Khomeini returned to Iran and an Islamic Republic was declared] the morale of [the Islamist groups] was soaring high. When we drew their attention to the significant doctrinal differences between the Shi'is and the Sunnis, both dismissed them as inconsequential." Ibrahim, "Anatomy of Egypt's Militant Islamic Groups," 443.

[121] Sivan, "Sunni Radicalism in the Middle East and the Iranian Revolution."

[122] Rudi Matthee, "The Egyptian Opposition on the Iranian Revolution," in *Shi'ism and Social Protest*, eds. Juan R. I. Cole and Nikki R. Keddie (New Haven: Yale University Press, 1986), 247–74. See also Shahrough Akhavi, "The Impact of the Iranian Revolution on Egypt," in *The Iranian Revolution: Its Global Impact*, ed. John L. Esposito (Miami: Florida International University Press, 1990), 138–56; Walid M. Abdelnasser, "Islamic Organizations in Egypt and the Iranian Revolution of 1979: The Experience of the First Few Years," *Arab Studies Quarterly* 19, no. 2 (1997): 25–39.

[123] Kepel, *The Prophet and the Pharaoh*, 156.

[124] Nader Entessar, "The Lion and the Sphinx: Iranian-Egyptian Relations in Perspective," in *Iran and the Arab World*, eds. Hooshang Amirahmadi and Nader Entessar (New York: St. Martin's Press, 1993), 168.

[125] Kirk J. Beattie, *Egypt During the Sadat Years* (New York: Palgrave, 2000), 259, 262.

down before it's too late. Otherwise, they will have us all shot at the first opportunity." An aide sympathetic to the Muslim Brotherhood responded, "Would you prefer, perhaps, the communists?" Sadat angrily replied, "I am not the Shah of Iran and our Muslims are not Khomeinists."[126] He would crack down on radicals, but he still seemed to have regarded religious forces as something he could largely control: most of them would support his rule, and the radicals could be contained.[127] But as the revolution continued to radicalize and embolden Sadat's internal opposition, he shifted toward a harder line against both his Islamist opposition and the Iranian Revolution.

Iran, following the lead of other Arab states, broke off diplomatic relations with Egypt in April 1979 because of the Camp David Accords. Egypt responded by severing relations on the same day. Sadat added a denunciation of Khomeini, which became more virulent thereafter. In a December 1979 interview, he castigated Khomeini as a lunatic who was full of hate. He was "sad for the Islamic nation, because Khomeini's fever is beginning to catch onto some Moslem leaders. But I will not hesitate to fight this disease if it tries to creep into some souls here."[128] Sadat strained to portray the Islam of the Iranian Revolution as a perversion of Islam. His press emphasized the differences between Sunni and Shia. He denounced Iran's taking American embassy officials hostage as un-Islamic. Sadat had approved of an American request for a leader of the Muslim Brotherhood to act as a mediator in the hostage crisis. But after hearing Khomeini praise the Muslim Brotherhood and declare himself a student of Hasan al-Banna, founder of the Brotherhood, he called the mission off to avoid "any contact or coordination" between the Brotherhood and the Iranian revolutionaries.[129] He supported

---

[126] Eric Rouleau, "Who Killed Sadat?," *MERIP Reports* 103 (1982): 5. In an interview with Kirk Beattie, Mustafa Khalil, the former prime minister and foreign minister under Sadat, said "Sadat didn't draw parallels between Iran and Egypt. The mullahs were much more powerful there; the shah had angered all the clergy, whereas here the clergy support the regime." Beattie notes that while perhaps Sadat in general did not make such comparisons, "one is well advised to recall Camelia Sadat's words about her father's admonition, 'Don't show you are weak.'" Beattie, *Egypt During the Sadat Years*, 267.

[127] The Egyptian military in 1981 even briefly trained a handful of Syrian Muslim Brotherhood members in guerilla tactics. It is unclear how high up the chain the decision was made to provide such training or what the motive was—perhaps to get back at Syria's castigation of Egypt, or learn more about Islamist networks. That the decision was a mistake from the Egyptian regime's perspective is clear from the gloating of Abu Mus'ab al-Suri, who worked as a trainer in the Arab-Afghan camps in Afghanistan: "The Egyptian military had trained me, and now, I have trained for them tens, perhaps hundreds of people, who are trainees and commanders in the *Egyptian Jihad Group* . . . and the *Islamic Group*." Brynjar Lia, *Architect of Global Jihad: The Life of Al-Qaida Strategist Abu Mus'ab Al-Suri* (New York: Columbia University Press, 2008), 45.

[128] Asef Bayat and Bahman Baktiari, "Revolutionary Iran and Egypt: Exporting Inspirations and Anxieties," in *Iran and the Surrounding World: Interactions in Culture and Cultural Politics*, eds. Nikki R. Keddie and Rudi Matthee (Seattle: University of Washington Press, 2002), 308.

[129] Abdullah Al-Arian, *Answering the Call: Popular Islamic Activism in Sadat's Egypt* (New York: Oxford University Press, 2014), 174.

American action against Iran in the hostage crisis.[130] Egypt's lack of support for the Islamic Republic prompted the Muslim Brotherhood publication, al-Da'wa, to go as far as saying that "many countries fear Iran because they themselves are ruled by oppressors," alluding to Sadat.[131]

The Iranian Revolution would transform the Iraqi-Egyptian relationship from hostility to amity and draw Egypt closer to the Gulf states. Even before the Iran-Iraq War, Sadat offered Egyptian support to Gulf states threatened by Iran. That conflict would be a barometer of the Egyptian leader's stance toward the Iranian Revolution. Iraq had not previously endeared itself to Egypt. It had led the rejectionist camp against Egypt, convening summits in the fall of 1978 and spring of 1979 to orchestrate the severance of connection between Egypt and Arab states. Upon the invasion of Iran by Iraq, Sadat expressed neutrality and condemned both parties.[132] But he said openly that he would like to see anyone instead of Khomeini ruling Iran and suggested that the time was ripe for a military coup.[133]

Sadat's hostility toward Iraq faded, despite Iraq's previous anti-Egyptian actions. In early 1981, Egypt struck an arms deal with Iraq.[134] Iraq, for its part, did not want to renew its relationship with Egypt publicly, but it needed the weapons. There are several reasons Sadat reached out to his former enemy—he may have wanted to use aid to Iraq as a means to tout his credentials of defending the Arab nation, as a vehicle to reintegrate with the Arab states, and he saw that Egypt could benefit economically from selling military equipment and increasing economic ties with Iraq. But supporting Iraq also provided a means to contain the Iranian Revolution.

At home, Sadat ordered a harsh suppression of opposition movements, including Islamists, in the fall of 1981. He had built his legitimacy on greater democratization and his religious credentials, and so the crackdown strained support for his rule. Khomeini responded: "Today, with the widespread arrests of the Muslim Brothers in Egypt, Sadat has completed his service to Israel."[135] The crackdown directly prompted the assassination of Sadat by the Islamist group al-Jihad, news of which was welcomed in Tehran.

Sadat's successor, Hosni Mubarak, continued the policies initiated by Sadat: attempting to suppress as well as co-opt Islamist opposition and continuing to aid Iraq against Iran. The Mubarak regime attempted to isolate and

---

[130] Ramazani, Revolutionary Iran, 168–69. Sadat consistently supported the deposed shah. The shah had stayed briefly in Egypt after he left Iran, and Sadat repeatedly and publicly thereafter invited the shah to stay in Egypt. In March 1980, the shah accepted Sadat's invitation and lived in Egypt until his death in June, whereupon he was given a state funeral.

[131] Matthee, "The Egyptian Opposition on the Iranian Revolution," 259.

[132] FBIS-MEA- 80-214, November 3, 1980, D9.

[133] FBIS-MEA 80-191, September 30, 1980, D4.

[134] Legum, Shaked, and Dishon, Middle East Contemporary Survey, vol. 5, 258.

[135] Ewan Stein, Representing Israel in Modern Egypt: Ideas, Intellectuals and Foreign Policy from Nasser to Mubarak (New York: I. B. Tauris, 2012), 162.

punish the radicals and purge the armed forces of Islamist influence. Mubarak also tried to bolster the religious legitimacy of the regime by providing concessions to the Islamization of society, as well as increasing resources to the state-controlled religious institutions.[136] This did not satisfy the radicals. When Mubarak attempted to appease Islamists by selectively implementing Islamic law, the Egyptian Islamic Jihad demanded instead "an Islamic republic led by religious men, like Ayatollah Khomeini's government in Iran."[137] The Mubarak regime ensured that news of events in Iran rarely surfaced in print or on television. In 1985, while investigating an assassination attempt against a former interior minister, the Egyptian government claimed to uncover an Islamist movement connected to Iran. The only evidence provided was photographs of Khomeini discovered when security forces searched militants' homes. Nevertheless, Egypt expelled the two remaining Iranian diplomats in Cairo.[138]

Although not the only reason for Egyptian-Iranian estrangement, the Iranian model emboldening Egyptian Islamists was a significant cause of the deterioration of relations. This was despite the fact that Iran did not act as a platform in spreading revolution to Egypt. The Iranian revolutionary regime had its own reasons to reject Egypt because of Egypt's peace with Israel. But Egypt's anti-Iranian stance would lead it to reconcile with others that rejected Egypt's Israel policy.

Saudi Reaction to Iranian Revolution

The contagion effects from the Iranian Revolution did not initially alarm the Saudi regime. But they did by the end of 1979, when the Saudis perceived that revolutionary movements within their own state existed and were emboldened by the Iranian Revolution, independent of Iran acting as a platform. The fear of contagion prompted hostility toward Iran and cooperation with Iraq, their past and future enemy.

The Saudi regime had responded to upheaval in Iran by unconditionally backing the shah. They had expected the Americans to handle the situation and were upset at the Americans' willingness to abandon their ally.[139] As late as January 1979, Crown Prince Fahd was publicly supporting the shah and was expressing fear that communists would take advantage of the chaos in Iran.[140]

[136] For an elaboration of Mubarak's attempts, see Hesham al-Awadi, *In Pursuit of Legitimacy: The Muslim Brothers and Mubarak, 1982-2000* (New York: Tauris Academic Studies, 2004), 49-72.

[137] Ramazani, *Revolutionary Iran*, 173.

[138] Entessar, "The Lion and the Sphinx," 171. See also Nael Shama, *Egyptian Foreign Policy from Mubarak to Morsi: Against the National Interest* (New York: Routledge, 2014), 144.

[139] Safran, *Saudi Arabia*, 301-2.

[140] Legum, Shaked, and Dishon, *Middle East Contemporary Survey*, vol. 3, 1978-1979 (New York: Holmes & Meier Publishers, Inc., 1980), 749.

However, with the establishment of the new government, Saudi leaders sent messages of congratulations and emphasized their common Islamic roots.[141] Rather than seeing the Islamic Republic of Iran as a rival or threat, the Saudis, at least publicly, were conciliating the new regime, attempting to draw it in under the shared language of Islam.

The Saudi policy of appeasement, however, was soon strained. The Gulf states met to coordinate their policy toward the revolution. In July, they sent Shaykh Sabah, the longtime foreign minister of Kuwait, to confer with Iran. He found suitable interlocutors in the Bazargan government. They issued a joint communiqué affirming their commitment to the principles of "mutual respect and sovereignty, independence, and territorial integrity" and the need for "noninterference in other people's affairs."[142] But his meetings with the clerics, including Khomeini, were confrontational, and he provided a pessimistic assessment of the possibility of accommodation. Later in the summer of 1979, protests erupted among the Shia in Bahrain and Kuwait, rhetorically supported by senior Iranian clerics. Saudi Arabia dispatched two army brigades to Bahrain at Bahrain's request.[143]

The real impetus behind a change in Saudi policy, though, was the events of November 1979: revolutionary agitation in the Saudis' own realm alarmed them about the very real possibility of spillover from the Iranian Revolution, which was radicalizing at the same time. The takeover of the Grand Mosque in Mecca during the Hajj by a group of Islamist extremists was the first revolutionary upheaval by Sunni Islamists directed at the Saudi regime. Coupled with the shock of the uprising was the embarrassment that it took the security forces two weeks and foreign help (French special forces) to put down the uprising. The reliability of the National Guard came into question.[144]

While security forces were busy securing Mecca, unprecedented violent protests erupted among Shia in late November 1979 in the heart of the oil-producing region when some attempted to hold a religious procession that had previously been banned. Seven days of rioting ensued, leaving at least two dozen people dead and hundreds wounded. The Saudis rushed troops from Mecca and brutally crushed the rebellion before it could metastasize any further. The Shia uprising, like the Iranian Revolution, included a broader coalition than just those who approved of Khomeini's particular political model.[145] Nevertheless, the

---

[141] FBIS-MEA-79-032, February 14, 1979, C2; FBIS-MEA-79-081, April 25, 1979, C6.
[142] Mylroie, "Regional Security After Empire," 251–52.
[143] Legum, Shaked, and Dishon, *Middle East Contemporary Survey*, vol. 3, 441.
[144] Cronin, "Tribes, Coups and Princes," 22–23.
[145] Jones, "Rebellion on the Saudi Periphery."

rebellion was clearly inspired by the Iranian Revolution. Demonstrators held up pictures of Khomeini and took up his slogans, and Islamists led the protests.[146]

These violent protests clearly rattled Saudi officials. Although the Iranian Revolution did not directly inspire the Mecca incident, the siege of the Grand Mosque indicated a hitherto unsuspected level of rejection of the regime.[147] This rejection targeted the core of the regime's legitimacy—its religious credentials. The Shia disorder set an alarming precedent for what had been an ignored and supposedly apolitical population. The regime responded domestically with sticks and carrots. In both cases, not only were the perpetrators swiftly dealt with, but the regime also cast a dragnet looking for other possible connections. At the same time, the regime sought to ameliorate various groups' grievances. In the Shia community, part of the grievances stemmed from chronic underdevelopment; the kingdom therefore poured money into projects such as improving the infrastructure, though religious demands went largely unheeded. Saudi Shia Islamists who were clearly unsatisfied announced the creation of the Islamic Revolution Organization in the Arabian Peninsula. In a nod to Sunni Islamists' demands, authorities took such measures as tightening the alcohol ban, increasing religious control over the education system, and allocating significantly more resources to the construction of mosques and the support of other religious purposes.[148] Another large protest nevertheless occurred among the Shia on the anniversary of the Iranian Revolution in February.

The Saudis' attempt to shore up the regime had foreign policy consequences: their policy toward Iran began to change. The same month as the uprisings in Saudi Arabia brought the US hostage crisis and subsequent radicalization of the Iranian Revolution. Amid strident rhetoric from Iran denouncing the Saudi regime, the Saudis publicly played it cool.[149] In February 1980, in the aftermath of further Shia protests commemorating the Iranian Revolution, Crown Prince Fahd was asked about the possibility of contagion. He "wondered aloud on what basis the question was 'even asked.'" He explained that the Iranian revolutionaries had demanded rule based on Islamic principles, something that had existed in Saudi Arabia since its foundation.[150]

---

[146] Jacob Goldberg, "The Shi'i Minority in Saudi Arabia," in *Shi'ism and Social Protests*, eds. Juan R. I. Cole and Nikki R. Keddie (New Haven: Yale University Press, 1986), 240–41. Most scholars stress the lack of direct Iranian involvement in these revolts. Ibrahim, *The Shi'is of Saudi Arabia*, 121; Jones, "Rebellion on the Saudi Periphery," 215; Matthiesen, *The Other Saudis*, 181. See, though, Louër, *Transnational Shia Politics*, 165.

[147] The alleged Mahdi, Mohammed Abdullah, was supposedly asked during the siege whether the uprising was inspired by Iran, and he emphatically answered, "No!" Yaroslav Trofimov, *The Siege of Mecca: The 1979 Uprising at Islam's Holiest Shrine* (New York: Anchor Books, 2007), 70.

[148] Tim Niblock, *Saudi Arabia: Power, Legitimacy and Survival* (New York: Routledge, 2006), 83–84.

[149] Gerd Nonneman, *Iraq, the Gulf States and the War* (London: Ithaca Press, 1986), 21.

[150] Ramazani, *Revolutionary Iran*, 89.

Privately, the Saudis were reorienting their policy. They initially appeared to keep up their appeasement of Iran, letting the Americans and Iraqis lead the charge against the new regime in Tehran. But they increasingly showed an uncharacteristic willingness to assert themselves against Iran. In the context of increasing meetings between Saudi and Iraqi officials, Iraq seems to have shared with Saudi Arabia its plan to invade Iran in mid-1980, and the Saudis approved.[151] When Saddam Hussein formally abrogated the Algiers Accord in September, Iraqi envoys were sent to the Gulf states and returned home claiming to have gained their assent to the Iraqi action. Saudi Arabia did not deny the reports.[152] When war commenced a few days later, the Saudis gave permission to Iraqi warplanes to take shelter in the kingdom—despite the fact that Iran had threatened to attack Iraqi forces wherever they were—and they allowed their Red Sea ports to be used for the shipment of war supplies to Iraq.[153] They would continue to support Iraq throughout the war, especially through extensive loans.

Although Iran increasingly acted more directly as a platform in spreading revolution, Saudi hostility toward Iran developed when it was largely acting as a model. After the uprising among the Shia in 1979 and the subsequent repression, much of Saudi Arabia's Shia Islamist leadership fled to Iran. They received aid from the Iranians, although they tried to maintain their autonomy and resisted Iranian pressure for armed confrontation with the Saudi regime.[154] After a falling-out with the opposition movement, Iran in the later 1980s helped create an organization modeled after the Lebanon experience, Hizbullah Al-Hijaz.[155] The Saudis' most visible conflict with Iran involved the attempt by Iranian pilgrims at the Hajj, orchestrated by the Iranian government, to spread propaganda about the Iranian Revolution and against the Saudi regime. Iranian officials described these pilgrims as the ambassadors of the Iranian Revolution.[156] Conflict between Iranian pilgrims and the Saudi regime culminated in a confrontation at the 1987 Hajj in which around four hundred Iranians were killed and thousands injured. Iranian officials responded with calls to liberate Mecca.

The fear of contagion effects from the Iranian Revolution convinced the Saudis to support their former enemies, the Iraqis, whom they had previously

---

[151] Marschall, *Iran's Persian Gulf Policy*, 68; Henner Fürtig, *Iran's Rivalry with Saudi Arabia Between the Gulf Wars* (Reading: Ithaca Press, 2002), 62; Safran, *Saudi Arabia*, 361–62; Nonneman, *Iraq*, 22–23.

[152] Safran, *Saudi Arabia*, 364. In fact, Crown Prince Fahd may have told Saddam that President Carter gave him a green light in order to push Hussein to war. See Baram, *Saddam Husayn and Islam*, 152. It is doubtful, however, that the United States told him to convey this message. See Hal Brands, "Saddam Hussein, the United States, and the Invasion of Iran: Was There a Green Light?," *Cold War History* 12, no. 2 (2012): 319–43.

[153] Gause III, *The International Relations of the Persian Gulf*, 72.

[154] Matthiesen, *The Other Saudis*, 117–19.

[155] Matthiesen, "Hizbullah Al-Hijaz."

[156] FBIS-SAS-83-165, August 24, 1983, I2.

considered an ideological and geopolitical threat. The fact that the Iraqis were a potential geopolitical threat was illustrated only a couple of years after the Iran-Iraq War, when the Iraqi military, bolstered by Saudi finance, threatened to invade Saudi Arabia.

Cooperation Among Counterrevolutionaries

I have shown states' direct response to the Iranian Revolution in terms of their policy toward Iran, but there is also the indirect response in terms of how the revolution affected relations between other states. The domestic contagion effects theory argues there will be cooperation among states that have similar contagion fears. Because each state eventually perceived a significant Islamist movement in its midst and thus feared contagion, my argument predicts contagion fears to be a powerful source of cooperation between Iraq, Syria, Saudi Arabia, and Egypt. Even though Syria does not conform to this prediction, the cooperation between Saudi Arabia, Egypt, and Iraq is notable, particularly because there are strong reasons to suppose this kind of cooperation would not happen.

From a balance-of-power perspective, one might not expect Saudi Arabia in particular to side with Iraq precisely when Iran was weakened and Iraq was in a position of superiority. Yet the Saudis gave Iraq substantial support. Precise figures are not known, but it is estimated that by the end of 1982, Saudi Arabia had lent its former enemy about $20 billion in the fight against Iran.[157] An unusually outspoken Saudi prince declared in December 1981 that Saudi Arabia "totally supports the Iraqi position in the war" and that Iraq was doing a service by protecting the entire Arab nation.[158] Typically, the Saudis were somewhat more coy in their public statements, but they unquestionably supported Iraq against Iran throughout the war. As a result, the Saudis earned the enmity of Iran, which called for the regime's overthrow.[159] The Saudis also assisted their former ideological enemy in organizing "Popular Islamic Conferences" in an attempt to bolster Iraq's Islamic credentials and discredit Iran's participation in the war.[160]

---

[157] Nonneman, *Iraq*, 97. Rangwala estimates the Saudis ended up loaning Iraq $35 billion over the course of the war. Glen Rangwala, "The Finances of War: Iraq, Credit and Conflict, September 1980 to August 1990," in *The Iran-Iraq War: New International Perspectives*, eds. Nigel Ashton and Bryan Gibson (New York Routledge, 2013), 97.

[158] Legum, Shaked, and Dishon, *Middle East Contemporary Survey*, vol. 6, 787.

[159] Beyond supporting Iraq financially and diplomatically against Iran, Saudi Arabia attempted to undermine the stability of Iran's revolutionary regime by glutting the market so that Iran's meager exports would be worth less. Hooshang Amirahmadi, "Iranian-Saudi Arabian Relations Since the Revolution," in *Iran and the Arab World*, eds. Hooshang Amirahmadi and Nader Entessar (New York: St. Martin's Press, 1993), 141–44.

[160] Samuel Helfont, "Islam in Saudi Foreign Policy: The Case of Ma'ruf Al-Dawalibi," *The International History Review* 42, no. 3 (2020): 8.

Besides their support for Iraq, the Saudis also shored up their relations with the five smaller Persian Gulf states. In 1981, Saudi Arabia formed the Gulf Cooperation Council (GCC) with those states. Talk of such a regional organization predated the Iranian Revolution, but it had not previously been realized because there was a fear of Saudi Arabia using the organization to dominate the smaller states. The GCC was a direct consequence of the Iranian Revolution— the primary purpose of the organization (though not mentioned in the founding charter) was to coordinate resources in order to fend off an internal political threat, their Islamist opposition, inspired by the Iranian Revolution.[161] Agreements were particularly forthcoming in the wake of an attempted coup in Bahrain in 1981. One of the first areas of cooperation among members involved the sharing of intelligence concerning possible dissidents. Shortly thereafter, the countries signed various bilateral agreements concerning extradition, deportation, border crossing, and the exchange of equipment and information.[162] While these states still feared Saudi domination, their interest in protection, given their perceived internal threat environment, outweighed the risks, just as it had done for the Italian states that had welcomed Austrian protection in the face of liberal revolutions (Chapter 4).

One reason to suppose that there would not be reconciliation between Iraq and Egypt is simply their previous history, described earlier, where Iraq was leading the rejectionist front in isolating Egypt from Arab politics. But Sadat and Saddam began cooperating over their shared interest in combating Iran, a trend that continued under Mubarak. The Iranian push into Iraq in 1982 further increased Iraqi efforts to secure Egyptian aid, which was forthcoming. Egypt provided war matériel and military advisors. An estimated $1 billion in war matériel made its way to Iraq in 1982, and in 1985 there was a $2 billion deal.[163] Egypt provided pilots for the Iraqi air force, in addition to other soldiers.[164] Iraq was increasingly willing to publicly embrace Egypt. In 1983, the foreign ministers of Egypt and Iraq visited each other's states and lifted trade sanctions. In 1984, Iraq led an effort to get Egypt back into the Islamic Conference Organization. This process culminated with the resumption of diplomatic relations between Egypt and Iraq in 1987 and Iraq's support of Egypt's unconditional rehabilitation in the Arab world. The principal reason Iraq was able to fend off an Iranian invasion

---

[161] See e.g., Matteo Legrenzi, *The GCC and the International Relations of the Gulf* (London: I. B. Tauris, 2011).

[162] Ramazani, *The Gulf Cooperation Council*, 35–38. Another aspect of the GCC was its efforts toward economic cooperation, which would particularly benefit the Shia. Scott Cooper, "State-Centric Balance-of-Threat Theory: Explaining the Misunderstood Gulf Cooperation Council," *Security Studies* 13, no. 2 (2003): 336–38.

[163] Ralph King, *The Iran-Iraq War: The Political Implications*, Adelphi Papers (London: The International Institute for Strategic Studies, 1987), 43.

[164] Entessar, "The Lion and the Sphinx," 172.

and fight Iran to a standstill is that Iraq had access to allies that Iran did not have. Iran's only significant regional ally was Syria. Besides American support, Iraq had the support of most other Arab states, most importantly the Gulf states, who financed the war.

Conclusion

The domestic contagion effects theory asserts that leaders fear the spread of revolutionary contagion when there are significant revolutionary movements within their own borders. This was the case among the Arab states assessed here. In Iraq, Egypt, and Syria, the Iranian Revolution emboldened radical Islamists, which led to an increased crackdown on such movements. In Saudi Arabia, their fear of contagion developed exactly as the theory would expect. The kingdom initially perceived that it had no significant Islamist revolutionary opposition, unlike other states, and thus did not at first exhibit any particular alarm over the possible contagion from the Iranian Revolution. However, the takeover of the Grand Mosque and the Shia riots in late 1979 changed the Saudis' perception of their domestic opposition, and their fear of the contagion of the Iranian Revolution became evident.

The theory also claims that states' fear of contagion will primarily be driven by characteristics of the host rather than the activities of the infecting agent. This is not to say that states are indifferent to other states acting as a platform; rather, the existence of opposition movements is a necessary condition for states to fear the revolutionary contagion abroad. There is evidence for this thesis in the international impact of the Iranian Revolution. What caused Saudi Arabia to worry about the contagion of the Iranian Revolution was the domestic upheaval in the kingdom in November 1979, events in which Iran had no direct involvement. In Egypt, there was alarm at the possibility that the revolution would embolden Islamists, which it indeed did, even though Iran never had any significant ties with these Sunni opposition movements.

However, the Iraqi response to the Iranian Revolution shows the strong effect that a revolutionary state acting as a platform can have on another state's response to the revolution. Iraq was clearly alarmed by the radicalization of the Iranian Revolution in Islamist terms, which could act as a model to Iraq's domestic opposition. Although the Ba'thist regime preferred to cast the Shia insurrection as the work of outsiders rather than admit it had an indigenous insurrection spurred by the example of the Iranian Revolution, the latter was certainly the case. Prior to the Iran-Iraq War, Iran's aid to the Iraqi opposition was largely symbolic. But Iran was engaging in propaganda and the ties that the revolutionary regime had with the Iraqi opposition, and its ability to mobilize them, was obvious. The two major turning points in the deterioration of Iran-Iraq relations, June 1979 and April 1980, were directly tied to Iranian interference in Iraqi affairs. When Khomeini broadcasted a message to Sadr telling him to remain in Iraq despite persecution by the Iraqi government and Sadr responded, it set off a wave of protests in Iraqi cities in support of Sadr and Khomeini. What pushed Hussein over the edge toward initiating war with Iran was the attempted assassination of Aziz, which was deemed to have Iranian fingerprints.

This is an ideal case for the influence of a country acting as a platform: a much bigger next-door neighbor that has extensive ties with a community that is the majority of the target's population. Saddam probably reasoned that it would be hard enough for him to contain his opposition when Iran was serving as a model. The more Iran served as a platform, directly aiding Saddam's domestic opposition, the more difficult (if not impossible) it would be to suppress that opposition. He had had a hard enough time with the Kurds when they received aid from the shah. Saddam had said in 1975 that the greatest strategic threat to Iraq was when an external power was backed by a "local power," that is, a group within Iraq.[165] The fear of contagion was not dependent on the revolutionary state acting as a platform, but that was certainly an amplifier of fear.

Iranian attempts to export revolution were initially quite modest in Iraq and Saudi Arabia (and nonexistent in Egypt) when these states hardened their stance toward Iran. An American intelligence report on Iran's attempts to export revolution in March 1980 seems to have been correct in its assessment that "Iran so far has provided mostly rhetoric and propaganda to other revolutionaries, safe haven for foreign dissidents, and a meeting place for radicals."[166] Iran's relatively light touch was not just because its leaders were consumed with domestic problems. Their position seemed to have been that they would set the example and perhaps provide some propaganda, and others could go and do likewise. It obviously did not work out. After the war started, Khomeini publicly expressed his puzzlement that the Iraqis had not risen up.[167] Iran ended up providing more direct means of aid, including invading Iraq. But the basic pattern of hostility had already been stepped up before the more direct aid began.

My theory also argues that the fear of contagion would have a decisive effect on international affairs—there would be cooperation among states with similar revolutionary opposition and conflict with the revolutionary state. That is, taking

[165] CRRC SH-MISC-D-000-508, "Seminar Attended by President Saddam Hussein and Iraqi Officials Regarding Study of the Kurdish Case," June 1975.

[166] "Iran: Exporting the Revolution," https://www.cia.gov/library/readingroom/document/cia-rdp81b00401r000500100001-8.

[167] FBIS-SAS-80-190, September 29, 1980, I2; Baram, "The Impact of Khomeini's Revolution on the Radical Shi'i Movement of Iraq," 144. He seemed to believe the claim of Ayatollah Shirazi, a prominent Iraqi cleric in exile in Iran, that the Ba'thists were "rootless twigs which we can easily blow over." FBIS-SAS-80-073, April 14, 1980, I31.

domestic measures would not be enough. Their regime preservation strategies would extend into foreign policy, and this pattern of cooperation and conflict would exist sometimes in contrast to geopolitical pressures. All of the regimes, including the secular nationalist regimes, tried to use a variety of carrots and sticks to deal with their Islamist opposition, including attempts to increase their own legitimacy by appealing to Islam. But three of the four regimes deemed domestic measures insufficient.

Syria's policy toward Iran, however, is clearly inconsistent with the theory's prediction. The Ba'thist regime undoubtedly had a significant revolutionary Islamist opposition movement, which was emboldened by the Iranian Revolution. Assad nevertheless reached out to Iran and remained bitter enemies with Iraq and, to lesser extents, Egypt and then Saudi Arabia. Syria's potential fear of contagion from the Iranian Revolution was simply overwhelmed by its need for an ally against Israel and Iraq.

In today's Middle East, where sectarianism looms large, ancient sectarian hatreds are often given as an explanation for the animosity between Sunni Arab states and Shia Iran. Of course, the sectarian perspective does not explain why most of the Arab states, minus Syria, were allied with Iran prior to the revolution. Likewise, why many rulers were against Iran in the aftermath of the revolution should not be explained in purely sectarian terms. As I have shown, the Iranian Revolution inspired Islamists across the Shia-Sunni divide, and that threatened these rulers. They were against revolutionary Islamists, whether Shia or Sunni. Iran's foreign policy of abandoning the Muslim Brotherhood in Syria, though, would give the conflict a more sectarian dimension.

Besides Syria, the pattern of conflict and cooperation predicted in the theory finds support in the alignments among states after the Iranian Revolution. The revolution brought about a dramatic change of alignments that is difficult to explain using realist explanations, which focus on the distribution of material power. Iran was unquestionably more powerful before the revolution, and yet Egypt, Saudi Arabia, and Iraq had friendly relations with Iran. The revolution dramatically weakened Iranian power, but these states balanced against Iran.[168] The Iran-Iraq War, in contrast, had little effect on alignments in the region, suggesting that the change in patterns of conflict and cooperation was not just a function of states' responses to Iranian aggression. Saudi Arabia and Egypt aided Iraq against Iran well before Iran continued into Iraq. That is, the threat was not just about Iran's ability to project power, or even its willingness to do so. One cannot explain the realignment of the Middle East after the Iranian Revolution by referencing the balance of power, or even Iranian intentions. One must take

---

[168] Gregory Gause III, "Balancing What? Threat Perception and Alliance Choice in the Gulf," *Security Studies* 13, no. 2 (2003): 273–305.

into account the fear that a wave of revolutionary political Islam was sweeping through the system.[169] This explains the Saudis arming Iraq, which would go on to threaten it a few years later. It explains why relations with Iraq and Iran broke down. And it explains why other Arab states were open to reintegrating Egypt back into their fold.

---

[169] On the ideational threat Iran posed to Egypt and Saudi Arabia, see Lawrence Rubin, *Islam in the Balance: Ideational Threats in Arab Politics* (Stanford: Stanford University Press, 2014), 41–60.

7

Conclusions, Extensions, and Implications

This book tests a straightforward theory: the presence of significant revolutionary movements determines whether leaders fear revolutionary contagion. When there are contagion concerns, there is conflict with the revolutionary state and cooperation with states that have similar fears. This simple explanation for the most part helped make sense of a diverse array of cases in this book. This includes cases that are otherwise puzzling from an ideological perspective, such as the French monarchy supporting democratic revolutions in other states only a few years before the French Revolution and the Soviets being relatively amicable to fascist Italy, and cases that are otherwise puzzling from a realist perspective, such as the lack of a Franco-Russian alliance against the German powers in Europe of the 1820s and the lack of a Franco-Russian alliance against Germany in the 1920s.

The response to democratic revolutions during the ancien régime, detailed in Chapter 3, was largely a confirmation of the theory. The lack of a significant democratic revolutionary movement in their own countries meant there was no significant fear of contagion, even in soon-to-be-revolutionary France, despite claims to the contrary. In contrast to the ideological theory, the French monarchy clasped hands with revolutionary democrats in American and the Netherlands. While some radicals and conservatives wondered about the wisdom of French policy, the extent to which French leaders were concerned about their alliance partner being a democracy was about the partner's reliability rather than the emboldening effect it would have on critics of the regime.

The response to liberal revolutions during the Concert of Europe in Chapter 4 was largely a confirmation of the theory. The revolts discussed in this chapter were like the ones described in the previous chapter—in weak states not acting as platforms—but the domestic context was much different. There were significant revolutionary movements in the great powers and a corresponding fear of contagion, which led to conflict with the revolutions and cooperation among the great powers. This chapter paired with the previous one shows what the great powers were not doing—exploiting these revolutions for geopolitical gain. The fear of revolution as a cause of restraint in this era has been dismissed by some of the leading scholars, but the great powers' actual policies toward revolutions show how central it was, as expected by the theory.

Revolutionary Contagion and International Politics. Chad E. Nelson, Oxford University Press. © Oxford University Press 2022. DOI: 10.1093/oso/9780197601921.003.0007

The response to communism and fascism, discussed in Chapter 5, supported the predictions of the domestic contagion effects theory, though not entirely. The hostility toward the communist revolution that my theory highlights is sometimes played down, but it was essential in explaining both Allied intervention in the Russian Revolution and the entire structure of interwar European politics, exhibited in the continued existence of Poland. That system was fragile precisely because there was no reconstitution of a Russian-Western alliance to check Germany. The West's hostility toward communism due to contagion concerns is key to that outcome. There was obviously a great deal going on in international relations during and after World War I, and sometimes geopolitical factors overwhelmed the effect of the fear of contagion. The fear of contagion did not cause rivalries to end. Notably, the German reaction to the Russian Revolution at times contradicted the theory. Also, the Weimar government's reaction to fascism was not as expected, because leaders were more concerned with the communist threat.[1] The other states' reaction to fascism was as expected. The ostracism of the Soviets contrasts with the treatment of the Italian fascists.

In the Middle East (Chapter 6), my theory predicted, for the most part, hostility toward Iran because of fears of contagion. Using primary sources, I made a revisionist argument about how the origins of the Iran-Iraq War were due to this factor. In addition, Saudi hostility toward Iran was driven by the Saudis' new perception of a revolutionary movement within their own borders. Egyptian reconciliation with Arab states was also driven by the shared ideological threat. The fact that Sunni Islamist movements initially saw the Iranian Revolution as a model to be emulated is something that is often forgotten, despite the international effects the revolution had. The exception is Syria, where geopolitical pressures trumped the concerns my theory emphasizes.

I have proposed a simple and strong argument. My theory does not capture some of the nuances at play in the international response to revolutions, and even some of the bigger issues—for example, how states might agree on opposing a revolution but have profound disagreements on the correct counterrevolutionary strategy. The argument that the fear of contagion in these particular circumstances would be the basis of their foreign policies, dictating patterns of cooperation and conflict, is a strong one. It assumes the fear of contagion will overwhelm other factors that may compete with it, most notably geopolitical pressures. And it assumes that policy substitutions—simply ramping up repression while carrying on a traditional foreign policy—will not be considered sufficient. This argument, and the assumptions embedded in it, was not always

---

[1] Post–World War I Europe was a relatively unique environment that had two revolutionary movements. My domestic contagion effects theory, like the ideological theory, does not handle multiple revolutionary threats well. Mark Haas provides a more dynamic approach to these issues in Mark L. Haas, *Frenemies: When Do Ideological Enemies Ally?* (Ithaca: Cornell University Press, 2022).

correct. Syria's policy of accommodating Iran is exactly what the theory would not predict, as was Germany's encouragement of revolution in Russia. But what is more notable is how much of international politics is illuminated by the theory. To use the same analogy as John Mearsheimer does, it is like a flashlight in a dark room, not illuminating all the details, but providing the general shapes and usually effective at helping one navigate through the darkness.[2]

Applying the theory to these cases allows us to see the international politics of these periods in a new light, and the cases illuminate the theory. Together, these cases more often than not lend support for the hypotheses of this book. The first set of hypotheses was about when leaders would fear contagion. I claimed that leaders anticipate revolutionary contagion infecting their own regime when they perceive there is a significant revolutionary movement in their state of the same character as the revolution, and that this fear was irrespective of the policy of the revolutionary state. The revolutions in the 1820s prompted a fear of contagion, whereas the American Revolution and the Dutch Patriot Revolt did not, because there were significant revolutionary movements in Europe in the 1820s and there were not in the 1780s. In the twentieth century, the revolutionary states of Iran, Italy, and Russia all acted as a platform, though not uniformly. In some cases, the revolutionary state did not act as a platform, such as in the Iranian-Egyptian dyad, and yet prompted contagion concerns. The fear of contagion was not contingent on the revolutionary state acting as a platform, even when it did. The fears of socialist/communist contagion, for example, were most extensive when Russia was weak and not acting as much of a platform. In Saudi Arabia, the fear of contagion was not immediate because the regime did not perceive a significant revolutionary movement, but there was that fear after those perceptions changed with the uprisings of fall 1979, and before Iran was significantly involved with the Saudi Shia opposition. Fascist Italy aided revolutionary movements in Britain and France that were insignificant, and thus their meddling was not a cause of concern. The contrast between the contagion fears of communism and the lack thereof with fascism was particularly revealing. Even in a state that had a significant fascist movement, Germany, the fears of the left overwhelmed the concerns about the revolutionary right. Both Russia and Iran were in some ways unlikely models—states on the periphery of their systems whose revolutions brought forth an idiosyncratic version of revolutionary socialism and political Islam. They nevertheless both inspired a broader movement and prompted corresponding contagion concerns.

The second set of hypotheses was about the international effect of the fear of contagion. My theory supposed that such fears would lead to hostility toward

---

[2] John J. Mearsheimer, *The Tragedy of Great Power Politics* (New York: W. W. Norton and Company, 2001), 11.

the revolutionary state when contagion fears were present and to cooperation with states that shared similar fears. This was not always borne out, as discussed. But in most cases the pattern of conflict and cooperation was what my theory predicted, sometimes in contrast to geopolitical pressures and realist theory, and sometimes in contrast to the ideological thesis. One of the notable findings is the extent of cooperation between states that share the fear of revolution, and this was observed from the cooperation in the Concert of Europe to the Saudis' support of Iraq.

Another notable finding is the extent to which a state simply acting as a model can generate a hostile response. Certainly, the extent to which states act as platforms affects leaders' reaction to them, especially when the state is powerful. One might add an addendum to the theory: the greater the power of the state, the more the platform factor outweighs concerns about the model, assuming there is a significant revolutionary movement in the host state. But the fact that leaders are concerned about powerful states attempting to spread revolution abroad is not unexpected. What is more interesting is that leaders fear states acting as models, even when those states are peripheral ones. Given how neglected this issue has been and the fact that the mechanism is so indirect, the extent of its causal weight is surprising. It would have been relatively unsurprising if leaders responded negatively when other states attempted to overthrow them. But fears of contagion and thus leaders' international reaction is not conditioned on such policies.

Extensions of the Theory

The theory of this book could be applied to other cases, including more contemporary events such as the Arab Spring. For example, Saudi concern about the contagion of revolutionary movements is not the only factor that explains Saudi foreign policy since the Arab uprisings in 2011, but one would be hard-pressed to explain Saudi policy without recourse to this factor. A perspective that emphasizes ideological distance would expect that the Saudis would welcome the fall of Hosni Mubarak and the transition of the Egyptian regime away from a secular nationalist regime and eventually toward the Muslim Brotherhood, which assumed the presidency in 2012. But a Muslim Brotherhood regime in Egypt "could offer an alternative model for the relationship between Islam and the state," and indeed, "when Islamist governments came to power throughout the region, the Saudi regime's main worry was that its own Islamists would feel emboldened."[3] The Saudi regime had an enormous amount of carrots, as well as sticks, to use with their actual and potential opposition, and they did this in

---

[3] Oz Hassan, "Undermining the Transatlantic Democracy Agenda? The Arab Spring and Saudi Arabia's Counteracting Democracy Strategy," *Democratization* 22, no. 3 (2015): 483; Stéphane

the aftermath of the Arab Spring. King Abdullah announced in the immediate aftermath of the Egyptian Revolution a $130 billion spending initiative that included salary raises for government workers, tens of thousands of new jobs, and housing loans.[4] But this was not considered sufficient. Ruling-class strategies extended into foreign affairs. The Saudis supported the Mubarak regime in the throes of revolution, and they were hostile toward the Muslim Brotherhood regime that emerged. In Muslim Brotherhood leader and Egyptian president Mohamed Morsi's inaugural address, he declared "We are not exporting the revolution . . . we do not interfere in anyone's affairs. Meanwhile, we do not allow anyone to interfere in our affairs."[5] His first trip abroad was to Saudi Arabia to reassure it. Nevertheless, the Saudis could not be reassured, because the issue was not Egyptian behavior but the very existence of the Muslim Brotherhood regime. The Saudis encouraged the coup against Morsi and supported the subsequent Abdel Fattah el-Sisi regime. The Saudis' hostility toward the Muslim Brotherhood—in contrast to the secular regime—does not conform to the ideological school's theory, which posits that similar ideologies will attract and different ideologies will repel. But the model of a Muslim Brotherhood regime posed a threat to Saudi domestic rule, while the secular Sisi regime did not.

Saudi Arabia's foreign policy in the Arab Spring more generally exhibited contagion concerns. The Saudis' major foreign policy goal in the aftermath of the American invasion of Iraq and prior to the Arab Spring was the containment of Iranian influence in the region, especially salient now that the Saudis had lost Iraq as a balancer. This goal coincided with the aim of containing revolution in the case of Bahrain, where Saudi troops helped crush that uprising, and where a successful revolution would not only provide a model for Saudi opposition movements, but also bring to power a Shia majority thought to favor Iran. This was to some degree also a concern about the Muslim Brotherhood in Egypt, although Morsi insisted he was not realigning with Iran, exhibited by the fact that he called for the ouster of Bashir al-Assad of Syria, Iran's principal ally. The revolt in Syria, however, pitted the Saudis' geopolitical and domestic concerns against each other. A revolt overthrowing Assad would rid the region of Iran's ally, but it also might bring to power Islamists who would provide a model and

---

Lacroix, "Saudi Arabia's Muslim Brotherhood Predicament," https://pomeps.org/saudi-arabias-mus lim-brotherhood-predicament. See also Toby Matthiesen, "The Domestic Sources of Saudi Foreign Policy: Islamists and the State In the Wake of the Arab Uprisings," in *Rethinking Political Islam Series* (Washington, DC: Brookings Institution, 2015); Raphaël Lefèvre, "Saudi Arabia and the Syrian Brotherhood," Middle East Institute, https://www.mei.edu/publications/saudi-arabia-and-syrian-brotherhood.

[4] Lin Noueihed and Alex Warren, *The Battle for the Arab Spring: Revolution, Counter-Revolution and the Making of a New Era* (New Haven: Yale University Press, 2012), 254.
[5] Mohamed Morsi, "President Mohamed Morsi's Speech at Cairo University, Saturday, June 30, After Taking Oath of Office," http://www.ikhwanweb.com/article.php?id=30156.

a platform for Saudi Arabia's dissidents. Saudi policy from the beginning of the uprising in Syria has exhibited both these factors. The Saudis have aided opposition movements to overthrow Assad, but they have increasingly been concerned about controlling who gets their patronage so that the wrong people do not come to power. They have also prohibited their own citizens from fighting in the conflict.[6] Thus, while not the only factor in Saudi foreign policy, the fear of contagion is a critical one. It is necessary to understand Saudi policy, which is not merely the product of geopolitical pressures or ideological differences.

In addition, the concern of revolutionary contagion can help us make sense of contemporary great-power politics. On Russia's western flank, it has been hostile toward revolutions in Ukraine, first in 2004 and then in 2013–14. Especially given the democratic protests in Russia beginning in 2011, Vladimir Putin was not anxious to see a similar figure toppled in neighboring Ukraine. The same holds true for the democratic protests erupting in Belarus beginning in 2020. Of course, there are also other motives for Putin to be hostile toward these pro-Western democratic movements. The West is a fused geopolitical and domestic ideological threat to Putin's regime. International relations scholars, though, often place too much emphasis on geopolitical factors. There is a large debate about how NATO expansion has antagonized Russia, and not enough emphasis on how revolutions and Western democracy promotion—what Putin perceives as attempts to spread revolution—have led to the deterioration of Western-Russian relations.[7] Russia's "sovereign democracy" will feel threatened by uprisings in its neighborhood, and Western attempts to lay the groundwork for or aid those revolts will be a major source of friction.

The same goes for China's autocratic regime. The regime's suppression of the Hong Kong 2019–20 democratic protests exhibits its fears. China advocates sovereignty and nonintervention in internal affairs as international relations principles, and emphasizes the "civilizational differences" between itself and the liberal Western world.[8] Both regimes seek to discredit the model of liberal democracy to their domestic population. China and Russia increasingly feel threatened by

[6] See, for example, Angus McDowall, "Islamist Threat at Home Forces Saudi Rethink on Syria," Reuters, February 11, 2014.

[7] For works that emphasize this domestic threat, see, for example, Michael McFaul, "Putin, Putinism, and the Domestic Determinants of Russian Foreign Policy," International Security 45, no. 2 (2020): 95–139; Brian D. Taylor, The Code of Putinism (New York: Oxford University Press, 2018), esp. 179; Mette Skak, "Russian Strategic Culture: The Role of Today's Chekisty," Contemporary Politics 22, no. 3 (2016): 324–41; Paul D'Anieri, "Democracy and Geopolitics: Understanding Ukraine's Threat to Russia," in Ukraine and Russia: People, Politics, Propaganda and Perspectives, eds. Agnieszka Pikulicka-Wilczewska and Richard Sakwa (Bristol: E-International Relations Publishing, 2015), 233–41; Vladimir Shlapentokh, "Perceptions of Foreign Threats to the Regime: From Lenin to Putin," Communist and Post-Communist Studies 42, no. 3 (2009): 305–24.

[8] See, for example, Andrew J. Nathan, "China's Challenge," Journal of Democracy 26, no. 1 (2015): 156–70.

the "liberal" international order. Concern about preserving their regime is essential to explaining their outlook, and policy prescriptions solely focused on geopolitics will miss the mark.

The domestic contagion effects theory could be applied to more cases, but another way to extend the subject is to widen the focus. This book is largely about when the fear of revolutionary contagion is not salient and how it becomes so. What remains to be examined is how that fear dissipates as the larger ideological wave diminishes. One view is that contests between a revolutionary state and its rivals only come to a close with a convergence on one type of regime, usually the elimination of the revolutionary regime.[9] This is the implication of the ideological perspective in international relations. But it is not necessary for all regimes to converge on one type for the contest to end. For example, the ideological rivalry between the leftist pan-Arab revolutionary regimes and conservative monarchical regimes came to a close without the region converging on one regime type. Instead, the pan-Arab revolutionary ideology was discredited and lost much of its salience for international politics.

One of the reasons ideological rivalries can settle is that contagion effects diminish. While this book focuses on the fears of contagion in the aftermath of a revolution, how the decline of these transnational ideological contests is played out could be investigated further.[10] The focus of attention here has been on potential counterrevolutionary states, which have received less attention than revolutionary states. However, there is still work to be done to understand the process by which revolutionary states come to an accommodation with their neighbors, which involves both the revolutionary state and its neighbors.

The domestic contagion effects theory focuses on the domestic politics of the host state as an explanation for when leaders fear revolutionary contagion—in particular, whether there is a significant revolutionary movement of the same character as the revolution. One area to further investigate is how counterrevolutionary states stabilize their domestic instability.[11] I have said that just because a ruler has temporarily dealt with her or his revolutionary opposition does not mean that the fear of contagion will disappear. There is a good degree of uncertainty, and what seems to be a crushed revolutionary opposition movement could reconstitute itself. Indeed, a good example of this is Saddam Hussein's fear

---

[9] See John M. Owen, *The Clash of Ideas in World Politics: Transnational Networks, States, and Regime Change, 1510–2010* (Princeton: Princeton University Press, 2010), chap. 3.

[10] See, though, David Armstrong, *Revolution and World Order: The Revolutionary State in International Society* (New York: Oxford University Press, 1993); Chad E. Nelson and Arthur A. Stein, "The Attenuation of Revolutionary Foreign Policy," *International Politics* 52, no. 5 (2015): 626–36.

[11] See, though, F. Gregory Gause III, "Revolutionary Fevers and Regional Contagion: Domestic Structures and the Export of Revolution in the Middle East," *Journal of South Asian and Middle Eastern Studies* 14, no. 2 (1991): 273–305; Kurt Weyland, "Crafting Counterrevolution: How Reactionaries Learned to Combat Change in 1848," *American Political Science Review* 110, no. 2 (2016): 215–31.

that his Islamist opposition could rise from the ashes, as discussed. But if time goes on without any sign of a reconstitution of an opposition movement, leaders will probably increasingly gain confidence that they are out of the danger zone, and fears of contagion effects will begin to attenuate.

Contagion effects, as I have shown, are often independent of the policy of revolutionary states. Still, how those contagion effects attenuate can involve not just the characteristics of the host, but also those of the infecting agent. In other words, domestic developments in the host country can coincide with the actions of the revolutionary state that reinforce a diminishment of contagion concerns. First of all, the foreign policy of the revolutionary state may diminish its appeal in the eyes of co-partisans, as we saw was the case for Islamists in Syria when Iran allied with the Syrian regime over them. Even by acting as a platform to spread revolution, the revolutionary state can diminish its appeal among some as it sides with certain groups and not others. This was the case with the Bolsheviks, who often targeted much of their ire toward rivals on the left. Second, the domestic politics of the revolutionary state can reduce the attractiveness of the model. During the 1930s, massive failures in collectivization, the Stalinist purges, and so forth did a good deal to discredit the Soviet Union in the eyes of many on the left. But the process by which contagion effects settle down and revolutionary states cease to be revolutionary is by no means straightforward or linear. There are dangers contagion can flare up again, as occurred in the aftermath of World War II, when the Soviet victory renewed faith in its model.[12]

When does a revolutionary state cease to be a revolutionary state? An answer to that question could focus on the domestic politics of the revolutionary state. When does it cease to engage in revolutionary transformation at home?[13] In terms of the international effects of revolutions, the question involves both when the revolutionary state ceases to act as a platform—when it ceases to attempt to export revolution—and when it ceases to be a model, which, as noted, involves the characteristics of the host as well as the infecting agent. There has been some discussion of the patterns of revolutionary foreign policy,[14] and of when revolutionary states give up their revolutionary goals. Regarding the latter, scholars range from neorealists who argue that revolutionary states rapidly give up their revolutionary goals given the pressures of the international system to those who

---

[12] Seva Gunitsky, *Aftershocks: Great Powers and Domestic Reforms in the Twentieth Century* (Princeton: Princeton University Press, 2017), 161–66.

[13] This is often a difficult question to answer. Bailey Stone notes that the notion of "Thermidor" "has probably occasioned more conceptual heartburn for [comparative analysts of revolution] than almost any other term in their lexicon." The problem is not so much determining when reigns of terror end and the Thermidor begins, but when the Thermidor, and the revolution, unambiguously ends and politics as usual begins. Bailey Stone, *The Anatomy of Revolution Revisited: A Comparative Analysis of England, France, and Russia* (New York: Cambridge University Press, 2014), 394.

[14] See, for example, Fred Halliday, *Revolution and World Politics: The Rise and Fall of the Sixth Great Power* (Durham: Duke University Press, 1999), 133–57.

CONCLUSIONS, EXTENSIONS, AND IMPLICATIONS   225

argue that the revolutionary states never give up their revolutionary goals—revolutionary foreign policy ends when the regime is replaced.[15] Revolutionary foreign policy, however, is more complicated than that. Further analysis of the process by which revolutionary states give up their goals and how they and their neighbors come to an accommodation is warranted.

Implications of the Theory

My findings have implications for four literatures. Most directly, they contribute to the study of the international effects of revolutions. The mechanism elaborated here does not exhaust the ways in which revolutions can affect international politics.[16] But it is an important one. Most of the literature in this area examines how revolutions often lead to interstate war.[17] One of the main mechanisms posited for how revolutions can prompt interstate conflict is that the weakness of the revolutionary state prompts neighboring states to opportunistically invade.[18] This is a plausible mechanism that can explain some cases. An example is Somalia's invasion of Ethiopia in 1977, taking advantage of Ethiopian weakness in the aftermath of its revolution to gain the long-coveted Ogaden region.[19] But there are reasons to doubt that a mere fluctuation in power is usually a sufficient explanation for conflict, such as the finding that civil wars do not often prompt opportunistic wars, which should not be functionally different from revolutions in terms of power fluctuations.[20] The cases examined here were

[15] For the former, see Kenneth Waltz, *Theory of International Politics* (Reading: Addison-Wesley, 1979), 127–28; Mearsheimer, *The Tragedy of Great Power Politics*, 191. For the latter, see Maximilian Terhalle, "Revolutionary Power and Socialization: Explaining the Persistence of Revolutionary Zeal in Iran's Foreign Policy," *Security Studies* 18, no. 3 (2009): 557–86.

[16] For example, Bukovansky explains how the American and French Revolutions shifted the parameters of political legitimacy in international political culture "from dynastically legitimated monarchical sovereignty to popularly legitimated national sovereignty." Mlada Bukovansky, *Legitimacy and Power Politics: The American and French Revolutions in International Political Culture* (Princeton: Princeton University Press, 2002), 2.

[17] See Jeff Colgan and Jessica L. P. Weeks, "Revolution, Personalist Dictatorships, and International Conflict," *International Organization* 69, no. 1 (2015): 163–94; Jeff Colgan, "Domestic Revolutionary Leaders and International Conflict," *World Politics* 65, no. 4 (2013): 656–90; Paul Ewenstein, *Realism and Revolution: Why (Some) Revolutionary States Go to War* (New York: Peter Lang, 2020); Stephen M. Walt, *Revolution and War* (Ithaca: Cornell University Press, 1996); Patrick Conge, *From Revolution to War: State Relations in a World of Change* (Ann Arbor: University of Michigan Press, 1996); Kyung-Won Kim, *Revolution and the International System* (New York: New York University Press, 1970).

[18] Ewenstein, *Realism and Revolution*; Walt, *Revolution and War*, 32.

[19] Gebru Tareke, "The Ethiopia-Somalia War of 1977 Revisited," *International Journal of African Historical Studies* 33, no. 3 (2000): 635–67.

[20] Civil wars increase the likelihood of outside intervention, but it is for the purposes of affecting the outcome in the civil war rather than opportunism. Kristian Skrede Gleditsch, Idean Salehyan, and Kenneth A. Schultz, "Fighting at Home, Fighting Abroad: How Civil Wars Lead to International Disputes," *Journal of Conflict Resolution* 52, no. 4 (2008): 479–506. See also Kenneth A. Schultz and

often in weak states where power did not dissuade neighbors from intervening before or after revolutions. It is a plausible explanation for Iraq's invasion of Iran, which is seen as an exemplar of this thesis, but I have shown how Iraqi hostility toward Iran corresponds not with Iranian weakness but with the radicalization of the revolution in Iran and the corresponding emboldening effects it was having in Iraq. The weakening of Iran was a necessary but not sufficient condition for war. This is probably representative of other cases—usually there are also other factors leading to war besides the mere weakening of the power of the revolutionary state, and it often involves the ideological change brought about by the revolution.

Another principal mechanism by which revolutions can lead to war, which involves the ideological change resulting from a revolution, is through misperceptions of intention. States misperceive the intentions of others because, in the absence of information, they view the other through the prism of their ideology. This leads to "spirals of suspicion," in which each side perceives the other as hostile.[21] The claim that misperception causes conflict assumes that both sides have benign intentions but cannot effectively communicate those intentions.[22] The alternative is that when there is conflict the players correctly perceive the hostility of one side or the other, or both. My theory assumes that under certain circumstances there are counterrevolutionaries that are not benign—they want to crush the new regime.[23] There are certainly other pathways to conflict besides the mechanism I describe in this book.[24] There is not one single explanation for why revolutions can sometimes increase the security competition between states. But

Henk E. Goemans, "Aims, Claims, and the Bargaining Model of War," *International Theory* 11, no. 3 (2019): 344–74.

[21] Kim, *Revolution and the International System*; Walt, *Revolution and War*, 33–37.

[22] Arthur A. Stein, *Why Nations Cooperate: Circumstance and Choice in International Relations* (Ithaca: Cornell University Press, 1990), 55–56.

[23] Perhaps the most plausible case where misperception can be said to have been a cause of revolution leading to war is the onset of the French Revolutionary Wars. Some argue that French revolutionaries misperceived the hostile intentions of Austria and Prussia. But even in this case, to what extent this was a misperception and whether this was the primary cause of the war are debatable. For example, Kaiser takes issue with the notion of a benign Austria, and Blanning emphasizes French domestic politics, along with miscalculations of power. Thomas E. Kaiser, "La fin du renversement des alliances: La France, l'Autriche et la déclaration de guerre du 20 avril 1792," *Annales historiques de la Révolution française*, no. 351 (2008): 77–98; T. C. W. Blanning, *The Origins of the French Revolutionary Wars* (New York: Longman, 1986).

[24] For example, another way that relations can deteriorate between revolutionary states and others is when revolutionaries see conflict as a means to consolidate their revolution, as seen in the French case, noted previously, as well as others. Snyder argues that Third World revolutionaries during the Cold War would initiate hostilities with the United States as a means to sideline their domestic liberal rivals. Robert S. Snyder, "The U.S. and Third World Revolutionary States: Understanding the Breakdown in Relations." *International Studies Quarterly* 43, no. 2 (1999): 265–90. Another means to conflict is when the revolutionary states have expansionist aims, as was the case with the fascist regimes.

there are good reasons to suppose that the contagion mechanism is one of the main ways that revolutions can lead to a deterioration of relations between states.

Much of the focus has been on how revolutions can lead to international conflict. But it is important to highlight how revolutions can lead to international cooperation. A notable finding of the book is how the fear of contagion can lead to an unusual degree of cooperation among states with similar movements. This finding is a contribution not only to the study of the international effects of revolution, but also to the literature on the relationship between internal instability and foreign policy. The relationship between domestic instability and international conflict in the international relations literature is almost exclusively examined through the lens of the diversionary theory—the notion that leaders initiate external conflict to solve their internal problems. The evidence in this book is in many ways the opposite of the diversionary theory—instability often leads to cooperation rather than conflict, and conflict is targeted at a source of the problem rather than a diversion.

The fact that domestic instability can lead to cooperation rather than conflict is underappreciated. Many studies, taking their cue from the diversionary theory, have attempted to find a relationship between internal instability and external conflict, but there has been no conclusive finding.[25] There are several possible reasons for this. Scholars have often ignored the scope conditions of the conflict probability mechanism of the diversionary thesis[26] or other narrower mechanisms,[27] the need to take into account policy substitution effects,[28] or the effects of strategic interaction: states with internal conflict will be expected by potential target states to behave more aggressively, and thus the target state will be more willing to avoid disputes.[29] While these are valid critiques, the issue is not just delimiting the narrow conditions under which leaders will reach for diversion as a solution. There needs to be more emphasis on how internal instability will make states want to be more cooperative in the international realm.

[25] Because of the lack of a general finding between internal instability and external conflict, studies have alternatively suggested that particular regime types (mature democracies, autocracies, transitioning or ethnically fragmenting regimes) lead to war.

[26] Arthur A. Stein, "Conflict and Cohesion: A Review of the Literature," *The Journal of Conflict Resolution* 20, no. 1 (1976): 145; Jack S. Levy, "Domestic Politics and War," *Journal of Interdisciplinary History* 18, no. 4 (1988): 640.

[27] Jaroslav Tir, "Territorial Diversion: Diversionary Theory of War and Territorial Conflict," *The Journal of Politics* 72, no. 2 (2010): 413–25; Kyle Haynes, "Diversionary Conflict: Demonizing Enemies or Demonstrating Competence?," *Conflict Management and Peace Science* 34, no. 4 (2017): 337–58.

[28] Amy Oakes, *Diversionary War: Domestic Unrest and International Conflict* (Stanford: Stanford University Press, 2012).

[29] Alastair Smith, "Diversionary Foreign Policy in Democratic Systems," *International Studies Quarterly* 40, no. 1 (1996): 133–53; Brett Ashley Leeds and David R. Davis, "Domestic Political Vulnerability and International Disputes," *Journal of Conflict Resolution* 41, no. 6 (1997): 814–34; Ahmer Tarar, "Diversionary Incentives and the Bargaining Approach to War," *International Studies Quarterly* 50, no. 1 (2006): 169–88.

In addition to enhancing our understanding of the international effects of revolutions and how domestic instability can affect international politics, this book helps us unpack the international effects of ideological differences between states. I began this book with one of the long-standing questions in the study of international politics that nevertheless gets short shrift: whether ideological differences between states affect international politics. I asserted that this question was too blunt. It needs to be further specified: when are ideological differences salient, why, and how much? What we need are mechanisms that vary, because clearly ideological differences matter at some times and not others. Instead, most of the work in political science focuses on the distinctions between democracies and autocracies, which misses many other ways of ordering regimes that people have fought over, and does not get at why the salience of ideological differences varies over time and space. I have elaborated one compelling mechanism, whereby a revolution under certain conditions inspires a fear of contagion in other states and correspondingly affects their foreign policy. This does not exhaust how ideology can affect international politics. But it is a main mechanism. The contest over regime types, the great debate over which ideology should reign, has not just had domestic effects. It has had a profound effect on international politics, despite its neglect by international relations scholars, and the mechanism I examine is a principal way in which this effect works.

While I have shown that ideological differences among states can have profound effects on relations between them, I have also shown that sometimes they do not. It is important that ideological differences not be exaggerated. The domestic contagion effects theory asserts particular conditions under which ideological differences between states become salient for international politics. There can be other ways in which ideological differences between states affect international politics. But often international politics carries on with little or no reference to the internal characteristics of regimes, even in cases where it might be expected that there would be fear of revolutionary contagion. Part of the reason ideological differences between states and the great ideological struggle over regime types have been ignored in the study of international politics is that these things matter in certain times and places but not others, and so we need theories that account for that variation, such as the theory in this book.

Another contribution this book makes is to the burgeoning literature on diffusion and demonstration effects in world politics. Scholars have increasingly noted how such indirect international factors affect domestic political outcomes. This book extends their findings by showing that leaders are aware of how protests and regime change can diffuse, and are trying to prevent that diffusion from occurring. They have second-image-reversed-driven foreign policy. They recognize that the international system can affect their own domestic politics, so they attempt to shape it in a way that preserves their rule.

Kenneth Waltz rhetorically asked in his *Theory of International Politics*, "Which is more precarious: the life of a state among states, or of a government in relation to its subjects? The answer varies with time and place."[30] His point was to establish that, because of this variation, the use of force or the constant fear of it cannot be used to distinguish between international and domestic affairs. But if the life of a government in relation to its subjects was more precarious than the life of a state among states, could this not have an effect on how states interact with each other? His assumption that states want to survive helps lead to the conclusion that what drives international politics is distribution of capabilities. However, if it is not the survival of states but the survival of regimes, social orders, or leaders that is salient, very different factors may be relevant, including ideological factors. Ideology in international relations is often considered as the opposite of realpolitik perspectives and, at times, the opposite of rationalist perspectives. But this is unwarranted. Ideological factors can be tightly bound with a regime's survival.

[30] Waltz, *Theory of International Politics*, 103.

Bibliography

Abd-Allah, Umar F. *The Islamic Struggle in Syria*. Berkeley: Mizan Press, 1983.

Abdelnasser, Walid M. "Islamic Organizations in Egypt and the Iranian Revolution of 1979: The Experience of the First Few Years." *Arab Studies Quarterly* 19, no. 2 (Spring 1997): 25–39.

Abrahamian, Ervand. *Khomeinism: Essays on the Islamic Republic*. Berkeley: University of California Press, 1993.

Acomb, Francis. *Anglophobia in France, 1763–1789*. Durham: Duke University Press, 1950.

Adams, Henry M. *Prussian-American Relations, 1775–1871*. Cleveland: The Press of Western Reserve University, 1960.

Adams, Willi Paul. "German Translations of the American Declaration of Independence." *The Journal of American History* 85, no. 4 (1999): 1325–49.

Agha, Hussein J., and Ahmad S. Khalidi. *Syria and Iran: Rivalry and Cooperation*. London: Pinter/The Royal Institute of International Affairs, 1995.

Ajami, Fouad. *The Vanished Imam: Musa Al Sadr and the Shia of Lebanon*. Ithaca: Cornell University Press, 1986.

Akhavi, Shahrough. "The Impact of the Iranian Revolution on Egypt." In *The Iranian Revolution: Its Global Impact*, edited by John L. Esposito, 138–56. Miami: Florida International University Press, 1990.

Al-Arian, Abdullah. *Answering the Call: Popular Islamic Activism in Sadat's Egypt*. New York: Oxford University Press, 2014.

al-Awadi, Hesham. *In Pursuit of Legitimacy: The Muslim Brothers and Mubarak, 1982–2000*. New York: Tauris Academic Studies, 2004.

al-Faris, 'Izz al-Din. *Iranian-Syrian Relations: The Myth and the Reality*. Berkeley: Concerned Muslims of Northern California, [1982].

al-Hamdani, Raad Majid. "Memoir." Conflict Records Research Center archives. 2003.

al-Suri, Abu Mus'ab. *Lessons Learned from the Jihad Ordeal in Syria*. https://www.ctc. usma.edu/harmony-program/lessons-learned-from-the-jihad-ordeal-in-syria-origi nal-language-2.

Alexander, R. S. *Bonapartism and Revolutionary Tradition in France: The Fédérés of 1815*. New York: Cambridge University Press, 1991.

Alhasan, Hasan Tariq. "The Role of Iran in the Failed Coup of 1981: The IFLB in Bahrain." *The Middle East Journal* 65, no. 4 (Autumn 2011): 603–17.

Alvandi, Roham. "Muhammad Reza Pahlavi and the Bahrain Question, 1968–1970." *British Journal of Middle Eastern Studies* 37, no. 2 (2010): 159–77.

Alvandi, Roham. *Nixon, Kissinger, and the Shah: The United States and Iran in the Cold War*. New York: Oxford University Press, 2014.

Amirahmadi, Hooshang. "Iranian-Saudi Arabian Relations Since the Revolution." In *Iran and the Arab World*, edited by Hooshang Amirahmadi and Nader Entessar, 139–60. New York: St. Martin's Press, 1993.

Amirahmadi, Hooshang. *Revolution and Economic Transition: The Iranian Experience.* Albany: State University of New York Press, 1990.

Amuzegar, Jahangir. *Iran's Economy Under the Islamic Republic.* New York: I. B. Tauris and Co., 1993.

Anderson, M. S. *The Eastern Question, 1774–1923.* New York: St. Martin's Press, 1966.

Andreski, Stanislav. "On the Peaceful Disposition of Military Dictatorships." *Journal of Strategic Studies* 3, no. 3 (1980): 3–10.

Angress, Werner T. *Stillborn Revolution: The Communist Bid for Power in Germany, 1921–1923.* Princeton: Princeton University Press, 1963.

Anievas, Alexander. "The International Political Economy of Appeasement: The Social Sources of British Foreign Policy During the 1930s." *Review of International Studies* 37 (2011): 601–29.

Ansari, Hamied N. "The Islamic Militants in Egyptian Politics." *International Journal of Middle East Studies* 16, no. 1 (March 1984): 123–44.

Appleby, Joyce. "America as a Model for the Radical French Reformers of 1789." *The William and Mary Quarterly* 28, no. 2 (April 1971): 267–86.

Archives parlementaires de 1787 à 1860. Deuxième série. Vol. 30. Paris: Librairie Administrative de Paul Dupont, 1875.

Arjomand, Said Amir. "Ideological Revolution in Shi'ism." In *Authority and Political Culture in Shi'ism,* edited by Said Amir Arjomand, 178–209. Albany: State University of New York Press, 1988.

Armitage, David. *The Declaration of Independence: A Global History.* Cambridge, MA: Harvard University Press, 2007.

Armstrong, David. *Revolution and World Order: The Revolutionary State in International Society.* New York: Oxford University Press, 1993.

Aron, Raymond. *Peace and War: A Theory of International Relations.* Translated by Richard Howard and Annette Baker. Garden City: Fox, Doubleday and Company, Inc., 1966.

Ascoli, Peter. "American Propaganda in the French Language Press During the American Revolution." In *La révolution américaine et l'Europe.* Paris: Centre National de la Recherche Scientifique, 1979.

Ataie, Mohammad. "Revolutionary Iran's 1979 Endeavor in Lebanon." *Middle East Policy* 20, no. 2 (2013): 137–57.

Avon, Dominique, and Anaïs-Trissa Khatchadourian. *Hezbollah: A History of the "Party of God."* Translated by Jane Marie Todd. Cambridge, MA: Harvard University Press, 2012.

Axworthy, Michael. *Revolutionary Iran: A History of the Islamic Republic.* New York: Oxford University Press, 2013.

Aziz, T. M. "The Role of Muhammad Baqir Al-Sadr in Shii Political Activism in Iraq from 1958 to 1980." *International Journal of Middle East Studies* 25, no. 2 (May 1993): 207–22.

Baack, Lawrence J. *Christian Bernstorff and Prussia: Diplomacy and Reform Conservatism, 1818–1832.* New Brunswick: Rutgers University Press, 1980.

Babakhan, Ali. "The Deportation of Shi'is During the Iran-Iraq War." In *Ayatollahs, Sufis and Ideologues: State, Religion and Social Movements in Iraq,* edited by Faleh Abdul-Jabar, 183–210. London: Saqi Books, 2002.

Baden, Prince Max. *The Memoirs of Prince Max of Baden.* Translated by W. M. Calder and C. W. H. Sutton. Vol. 2. London: Constable & Co., 1928.

Bagot, Josceline, ed. *George Canning and His Friends: Containing Hitherto Unpublished Letters, Jeux d'Esprit, Etc.* Vol. II. London: John Murray, 1909.

Bakhash, Shaul. *The Reign of the Ayatollahs: Iran and the Islamic Revolution*. New York: Basic Books, 1984.

Bakhash, Shaul. "The Troubled Relationship: Iran and Iraq, 1930–1980." In *Iran, Iraq, and the Legacies of War*, edited by Lawrence G. Potter and Gary G. Sick, 11–27. New York: Palgrave Macmillan, 2004.

Baldoli, Claudia. "Anglo-Italian Fascist Solidarity? The Shift from Italophilia to Naziphilia in the BUF." In *The Culture of Fascism: Visions of the Far Right in Britain*, edited by Julie V. Gottlieb and Thomas P. Linehan, 147–61. London: I. B. Tauris, 2004.

Bancroft, George. *History of the United States of America, from the Discovery of the Continent*. Vol. V. New York: D. Appleton and Company, 1888.

Baram, Amatzia. "Ideology and Power Politics in Syrian-Iraqi Relations, 1968–1984." In *Syria Under Assad*, edited by Moshe Maʾoz and Avner Yaniv, 125–39. London: Croom Helm, 1986.

Baram, Amatzia. "Saddam Husayn, the Baʾth Regime and the Iraqi Officer Corps." In *Armed Forces in the Middle East: Politics and Strategy*, edited by Barry Rubin and Thomas A. Keaney, 206–30. London: Frank Cass, 2002.

Baram, Amatzia. *Saddam Husayn and Islam, 1968–2003: Baʾthi Iraq from Secularism to Faith*. Baltimore: Johns Hopkins University Press, 2014.

Baram, Amatzia. "Two Roads to Revolutionary Shiʾite Fundamentalism in Iraq." In *Accounting for Fundamentalisms: The Dynamic Character of Movements*, edited by Martin E. Marty and R. Scott Appleby, 531–88. Chicago: The University of Chicago Press, 1994.

Baram, Amazia. "The Impact of Khomeini's Revolution on the Radical Shiʾi Movement of Iraq." In *The Iranian Revolution and the Muslim World*, edited by David Menashiri, 131–51. Boulder: Westview Press, 1990.

Barker, Rodney. *Political Legitimacy and the State*. New York: Oxford University Press, 1990.

Bartlett, C. J. *Castlereagh*. London: Macmillan, 1966.

Bartley, Russell H. *Imperial Russia and the Struggle for Latin American Independence, 1808–1828*. Austin: University of Texas Press, 1978.

Barton, H. A. "Sweden and the War of American Independence." *The William and Mary Quarterly* 23, no. 3 (July 1966): 408–30.

Batatu, Hanna. "Shiʾi Organizations in Iraq: Al-Daʾwah Al-Islamiyah and Al-Mujahidin." In *Shiʾism and Social Protest*, edited by Juan R. I. Cole and Nikki R. Keddie, 179–200. New Haven: Yale University Press, 1986.

Batatu, Hanna. "Syria's Muslim Brethren." *MERIP Reports* 110 (November–December 1982): 12–20.

Bauerkämper, Arnd. "Transnational Fascism: Cross-Border Relations Between Regimes and Movements in Europe 1922–1939." *East Central Europe* 37, nos. 2/3 (2010): 214–46.

Bayat, Asef, and Bahman Baktiari. "Revolutionary Iran and Egypt: Exporting Inspirations and Anxieties." In *Iran and the Surrounding World: Interactions in Culture and Cultural Politics*, edited by Nikki R. Keddie and Rudi Matthee, 305–26. Seattle: University of Washington Press, 2002.

Beales, Derek. *Joseph II*, vol. 1, *In the Shadow of Maria Theresa, 1741–1780*. New York: Cambridge University Press, 1987.

Beales, Derek. *Joseph II*, vol. 2, *Against the World, 1780–1790*. New York: Cambridge University Press, 2009.

Beattie, Kirk J. *Egypt During the Sadat Years*. New York: Palgrave, 2000.

Beissinger, Mark R. "Structure and Example in Modular Political Phenomena: The Diffusion of Bulldozer/Rose/Orange/Tulip Revolutions." *Perspectives on Politics* 5, no. 2 (2007): 259–76.

Belchem, John. *"Orator" Hunt: Henry Hunt and English Working-Class Radicalism*. New York: Oxford University Press, 1985.

Bemis, Samuel Flagg. *The Diplomacy of the American Revolution*. Bloomington: Indiana University Press, 1967.

Bengio, Ofra. *Saddam's Word: Political Discourse in Iraq*. New York: Oxford University Press, 1998.

Bengio, Ofra. "Shi'is and Politics in Ba'thi Iraq." *Middle Eastern Studies* 21, no. 1 (January 1985): 1–14.

Bennett, Andrew, and Jeffrey T. Checkel, eds. *Process Tracing: From Metaphor to Analytic Tool*. New York: Cambridge University Press, 2015.

Bennett, G. H. *British Foreign Policy During the Curzon Period, 1919–1924*. London: St. Martin's Press, 1995.

Berejikian, Jeffrey. "Revolutionary Collective Action and the Agent-Structure Problem." *American Political Science Review* 86, no. 3 (1992): 647–57.

Bernard, Philippe, and Henri Dubeif. *The Decline of the Third Republic, 1914–1938*. Translated by Anthony Forster. New York: Cambridge University Press, 1985.

Bertier de Sauvigny, Guillaume de. *The Bourbon Restoration*. Translated by Lynn M. Case. Philadelphia: The University of Pennsylvania Press, 1966.

Bertier de Sauvigny, Guillaume de. *France and the European Alliance, 1816–1821: The Private Correspondence of Metternich and Richelieu*. Notre Dame: University of Notre Dame Press, 1958.

Bertier de Sauvigny, Guillaume de. *Metternich et la France après le Congrès de Vienne*. Vol. 2. Paris: Hachette, 1970.

Bertrand, Charles Lloyd. "Revolutionary Syndicalism in Italy, 1912–1922." PhD thesis, University of Wisconsin, 1969.

Bew, John. *Castlereagh: A Life*. New York: Oxford University Press, 2012.

Billinger, Robert D., Jr. *Metternich and the German Question: States' Rights and the Federal Duties, 1820–1834*. Newark: University of Delaware Press, 1991.

Bisley, Nick. "Counter-Revolution, Order and International Politics." *Review of International Studies* 30, no. 1 (2004): 49–69.

Black, Jeremy. *British Foreign Policy in an Age of Revolutions, 1783–1793*. New York: Cambridge University Press, 1994.

Black, Jeremy. "Sir Robert Ainslie: His Majesty's Agent-Provocateur? British Foreign Policy and the International Crisis of 1787." *European History Quarterly* 14, no. 3 (July 1984): 253–83.

Blanning, T. C. W. "Paul W. Schroeder's Concert of Europe." *The International History Review* 16, no. 4 (November 1994): 701–14.

Blanning, T. C. W. *The Origins of the French Revolutionary Wars*. New York: Longman, 1986.

Blatt, Joel Richard. "French Reaction to Italy, Italian Fascism and Mussolini, 1919–1925: The Views from Paris and the Palazzo Farnese." PhD thesis, University of Rochester, 1976.

Blatt, Joel. "Relatives and Rivals: The Responses of the Action Française to Italian Fascism, 1919–1926." *European Studies Review* 11, no. 3 (1981): 263–92.

Blaydes, Lisa. *State of Repression: Iraq Under Saddam Hussein*. Princeton: Princeton University Press, 2018.

Blinkhorn, Martin. *Fascism and the Right in Europe 1919–1945*. Harlow: Pearson Education, 2000.

Blinkhorn, Martin. *Fascists and Conservatives*. London: Unwin Hyman, 1990.

Bolkhovitinov, Nikolai N. *The Beginnings of Russian-American Relations, 1775–1815*. Translated by Elena Levin. Cambridge, MA: Harvard University Press, 1975.

Bolkhovitinov, Nikolai N. *Russia and the American Revolution*. Translated by C. Jay Smith. Tallahassee: The Diplomatic Press, 1976.

Borzecki, Jerzy. *The Soviet-Polish Peace of 1921 and the Creation of Interwar Europe*. New Haven: Yale University Press, 2008.

Bosworth, R. J. B. "The British Press, the Conservatives, and Mussolini, 1920–1934." *Journal of Contemporary History* 5, no. 2 (1970): 163–82.

Boutros-Ghali, Boutros. *Egypt's Road to Jerusalem: A Diplomat's Story of the Struggle for Peace in the Middle East*. New York: Random House, 1997.

Brady, Joseph H. *Rome and the Neapolitan Revolution of 1820–1821: A Study of Papal Neutrality*. New York: Columbia University Press, 1937.

Brands, Hal. "Saddam Hussein, the United States, and the Invasion of Iran: Was There a Green Light?" *Cold War History* 12, no. 2 (May 2012): 319–43.

Brands, Hal. "Why Did Saddam Invade Iran? New Evidence on Motives, Complexity, and the Israel Factor." *The Journal of Military History* 75, no. 3 (July 2011): 861–85.

Braunthal, Julius. *History of the International*. Vol. 1. New York: Frederick A. Praeger, 1967.

Brewer, John. *Party Ideology and Popular Politics at the Accession of George III*. New York: Cambridge University Press, 1976.

Brook-Shepherd, Gordon. *Iron Maze: The Western Secret Service and the Bolsheviks*. London: Macmillan, 1998.

Broué, Pierre. *The German Revolution, 1917–1923*. Translated by John Archer. Leiden: Brill, 2005.

Buchan, James. "Secular and Religious Opposition in Saudi Arabia." In *State, Society and Economy in Saudi Arabia*, edited by Tim Niblock, 106–24. London: Croom Helm, 1982.

Buchta, Wilfried. "The Failed Pan-Islamic Program of the Islamic Republic: Views of the Liberal Reformers of the Religious 'Semi-Opposition.'" In *Iran and the Surrounding World: Interactions in Culture and Cultural Politics*, edited by Nikki R. Keddie and Rudi Matthee, 281–304. Seattle: University of Washington Press, 2002.

Bueno de Mesquita, Bruce, Alastair Smith, Randolph M. Siverson, and James D. Morrow. *The Logic of Political Survival*. Cambridge, MA: MIT Press, 2003.

Bukovansky, Mlada. *Legitimacy and Power Politics: The American and French Revolutions in International Political Culture*. Princeton: Princeton University Press, 2002.

Burgwyn, H. James. *The Legend of the Mutilated Victory*. Westport: Greenwood Press, 1993.

Burke, Edmund. *Letters on a Regicide Peace*. Indianapolis: Liberty Fund, 1999 [1796].

Calvert, John. *Sayyid Qutb and the Origins of Radical Islamism*. New York: Columbia University Press, 2010.

Cameron, J. David. "Carl Graap and the Formation of Weimar Foreign Policy Toward Soviet Russia from 1919 until Rapallo." *Diplomacy and Statecraft* 13, no. 4 (2002): 75–95.

Cameron, J. David. "To Transform the Revolution into an Evolution: Underlying Assumptions of German Foreign Policy Toward Soviet Russia 1919–1927." *Journal of Contemporary History* 40, no. 1 (2005): 7–24.

Carley, Michael Jabara. *1939: The Alliance That Never Was and the Coming of World War II*. Chicago: Ivan R. Dee, 1999.

Carley, Michael Jabara. "Anti-Bolshevism in French Foreign Policy." *The International History Review* 2, no. 3 (1980): 410–31.

Carley, Michael Jabara. "The Origins of the French Intervention in the Russian Civil War, January–May 1918: A Reappraisal." *The Journal of Modern History* 48, no. 3 (1976): 413–39.

Carley, Michael Jabara. "The Politics of Anti-Bolshevism: The French Government and the Russo-Polish War, December 1919 to May 1920." *The Historical Journal* 19, no. 1 (1976): 163–89.

Carley, Michael Jabara. "Prelude to Defeat: Franco-Soviet Relations, 1919–39." *Historical Reflections* 22, no. 1 (Winter 1996): 159–88.

Carley, Michael Jabara. *Revolution and Intervention: The French Government and the Russian Civil War*. Kingston: McGill-Queen's University Press, 1983.

Carley, Michael Jabara. *Silent Conflict: A Hidden History of Early Soviet-Western Relations*. Lanham: Rowman & Littlefield, 2014.

Carlton, David. *Churchill and the Soviet Union*. Manchester: Manchester University Press, 2000.

Carr, Edward Hallett. *The Bolshevik Revolution 1917–1923*. Vol. 3. Baltimore: Penguin Books, 1953.

Carsten, F. L. *Reichswehr and Politics: 1918 to 1933*. Oxford: Oxford University Press, 1966.

Carsten, F. L. *Revolution in Central Europe 1918–1919*. Berkeley: University of California Press, 1972.

Cassels, Alan. *Mussolini's Early Diplomacy*. Princeton: Princeton University Press, 1970.

Cassels, Alan. "Mussolini and German Nationalism, 1922–1925." *The Journal of Modern History* 35, no. 2 (1963): 137–57.

Caughey, John Walton. *Bernardo de Gálvez in Louisiana, 1776–1783*. Berkeley: University of California Press, 1934.

Censer, Jack R. *The French Press in the Age of Enlightenment*. New York: Routledge, 1994.

Chamberlin, Paul. "A World Restored: Religion, Counterrevolution, and the Search for Order in the Middle East." *Diplomatic History* 32, no. 3 (June 2008): 441–68.

Chateaubriand, M. de. *The Congress of Verona: Comprising a Portion of Memoirs of His Own Times*. Vol. II. London: Richard Bentley, 1838.

Chávez, Thomas E. *Spain and the Independence of the United States: An Intrinsic Gift*. Albuquerque: University of New Mexico Press, 2002.

Chernev, Borislav. *Twilight of Empire: The Brest-Litovsk Conference and the Remaking of East-Central Europe, 1917–1918*. Toronto: University of Toronto Press, 2017.

Chiozza, Giacomo, and H. E. Goemans. *Leaders and International Conflict*. New York: Cambridge University Press, 2011.

Chubin, Shahram, and Charles Tripp. *Iran and Iraq at War*. London: I. B. Tauris & Co., 1988.

Claudin, Fernando. *The Communist Movement*. Vol. 1. New York: Monthly Review Press, 1975.

Clemens, Detlev. "The 'Bavarian Mussolini' and His 'Beerhall Putsch': British Images of Adolf Hitler, 1920–24." *The English Historical Review* 114, no. 455 (1999): 64–84.

Cobban, Alfred. *Ambassadors and Secret Agents: The Diplomacy of the First Earl of Malmesbury at the Hague*. London: Jonathan Cape, 1954.

Colenbrander, H. T. *De patriottentijd*. Vol. 3. The Hague: Martinus Nijhoff, 1897–1899.

Colgan, Jeff, and Jessica L. P. Weeks. "Revolution, Personalist Dictatorships, and International Conflict." *International Organization* 69, no. 1 (Winter 2015): 163–94.

Colgan, Jeff. "Domestic Revolutionary Leaders and International Conflict." *World Politics* 65, no. 4 (October 2013): 656–90.

Collins, Irene. *Government and Society in France, 1814–1848*. New York: St. Martin's Press, 1970.

Conge, Patrick. *From Revolution to War: State Relations in a World of Change*. Ann Arbor: University of Michigan Press, 1996.

Conley, Timothy K., and Melissa Brewer-Anderson. "Franklin and Ingenhousz: A Correspondence of Interests." *Proceedings of the American Philosophical Society* 141, no. 3 (1997): 276–96.

Cook, Chris, and John Paxton. *European Political Facts, 1900–1996*. New York: St. Martins Press, 1998.

Cooper, Scott. "State-Centric Balance-of-Threat Theory: Explaining the Misunderstood Gulf Cooperation Council." *Security Studies* 13, no. 2 (Winter 2003): 306–49.

Cordesman, Anthony H., and Abraham R. Wagner. *The Lessons of Modern War*, Volume II, *The Iran-Iraq War*. Boulder: Westview Press, 1990.

Corwin, Edward S. *French Policy and the American Alliance of 1778*. Princeton: Princeton University Press, 1916.

Coxe, William. *History of the House of Austria from the Foundation of the Monarchy by Rhodolph of Hapsburgh to the Death of Leopold the Second*. Vol. 2. London: Luke Hansard and Sons, 1807.

Craeybeckx, J. "The Brabant Revolution: A Conservative Revolt in a Backward Country?" In *Revolutions in the Western World, 1775–1825*, edited by Jeremy Black, 389–423. New York: Routledge, 2016.

Cronin, Stephanie. "Tribes, Coups and Princes: Building a Modern Army in Saudi Arabia." *Middle Eastern Studies* 49, no. 1 (January 2013): 2–28.

Cuarto, Federico, ed. *Le relazioni diplomatiche fra la Gran Bretagna e il Regno di Sardegna, I Serie: 1814–1830*. Vol. I. Rome: Istituto Storico Italiano, 1972.

D'Anieri, Paul. "Democracy and Geopolitics: Understanding Ukraine's Threat to Russia." In *Ukraine and Russia: People, Politics, Propaganda and Perspectives*, edited by Agnieszka Pikulicka-Wilczewska and Richard Sakwa, 233–41. Bristol: E-International Relations Publishing, 2015.

Dakin, Douglas. "The Formation of the Greek State, 1821–33." In *The Struggle for Greek Independence*, edited by Richard Clogg, 156–81. New York: Macmillan, 1973.

Dallin, Alexander, Merritt Abrash, Gifford D. Malone, Michael Boro Petrovich, James M. Potts, and Alfred J. Rieber. *Russian Diplomacy and Eastern Europe 1914–1917*. New York: King's Crown Press, 1963.

Danneman, Nathan, and Emily Hencken Ritter. "Contagious Rebellion and Preemptive Repression." *Journal of Conflict Resolution* 58, no. 2 (2014): 254–79.

Davis, John A. *Naples and Napoleon: Southern Italy and the European Revolutions (1760–1860)*. New York: Oxford University Press, 2006.

Debo, Richard K. *Revolution and Survival: The Foreign Policy of Soviet Russia 1917–1918*. Toronto: University of Toronto, 1979.

Debo, Richard K. *Survival and Consolidation: The Foreign Policy of Soviet Russia 1918–1921*. Montreal: McGill-Queen's University Press, 1992.

de Caprariis, Luca. "'Fascism for Export'? The Rise and Eclipse of the Fasci Italiani all'Estero." *Journal of Contemporary History* 35, no. 2 (2000): 151–83.

de Graaf, Beatrice. *Fighting Terror After Napoleon: How Europe Became Secure After 1815*. New York: Cambridge University Press, 2020.

De Grand, Alexander. *The Italian Left in the Twentieth Century: A History of the Socialist and Communist Parties*. Bloomington: Indiana University Press, 1989.

Deniel, Alain. *Bucard et le Francisme*. Paris: Jean Picollec, 1979.

Dickinson, H. T. "Radicals and Reformers in the Age of Wilkes and Wyvill." In *British Politics and Society from Walpole to Pitt, 1742–1789*, edited by Jeremy Black, 123–46. London: Macmillan, 1990.

Diehl, James M. *Paramilitary Politics in Weimar Germany*. Bloomington: Indiana University Press, 1977.

Dippel, Horst. *Germany and the American Revolution, 1770–1800*. Translated by Bernhard A. Uhlendorf. Wiesbaden: Franz Steiner Verlag GMBH, 1978.

Dippel, Horst. "Prussia's English Policy After the Seven Years' War." *Central European History* 4, no. 3 (1971): 195–214.

Dorril, Stephen. *Blackshirt: Sir Oswald Mosley and British Fascism*. New York: Penguin Books, 2006.

Douglas, Allen. *From Fascism to Libertarian Communism: Georges Valois Against the Third Republic*. Berkeley: University of California Press, 1992.

Doyle, William. *Aristocracy and Its Enemies in the Age of Revolution*. New York: Oxford University Press, 2009.

Doyle, William. *Origins of the French Revolution*. New York: Oxford University Press, 1988.

Duesenberry, James. *Income, Saving and the Theory of Consumer Behavior*. Cambridge, MA: Harvard University Press, 1949.

Dull, Jonathan R. *Benjamin Franklin and the American Revolution*. Lincoln: University of Nebraska Press, 2010.

Dull, Jonathan R. "Benjamin Franklin and the Nature of American Diplomacy." *The International History Review* 5, no. 3 (1983): 346–63.

Dull, Jonathan R. *A Diplomatic History of the American Revolution*. New Haven, CT: Yale University Press, 1985.

Dull, Jonathan R. "Franklin the Diplomat: The French Mission." *Transactions of the American Philosophical Society* 72, no. 1 (1982): 1–76.

Dull, Jonathan R. *The French Navy and American Independence: A Study of Arms and Diplomacy, 1774–1787*. Princeton: Princeton University Press, 1975.

Eatwell, Roger. *Fascism: A History*. New York: Penguin, 1995.

Eatwell, Roger. "On Defining the 'Fascist Minimum': The Centrality of Ideology." *Journal of Political Ideologies* 1, no. 3 (1996): 303–19.

Echeverria, Durand. "Condorcet's *The Influence of the American Revolution on Europe*." *The William and Mary Quarterly* 25, no. 1 (January 1968): 85–108.

Echeverria, Durand. *Mirage in the West: A History of the French Image of American Society to 1815*. Princeton: Princeton University Press, 1968.

Edwards, P. G. "The Foreign Office and Fascism 1924–1929." *Journal of Contemporary History* 5, no. 2 (1970): 153–61.

Edwards, Peter. "The Austen Chamberlain-Mussolini Meetings." *The Historical Journal* 14, no. 1 (1971): 153–64.

Egret, Jean. *The French Prerevolution*. Translated by Westley D. Camp. Chicago: The University of Chicago Press, 1977.

Ehrman, John. *The Younger Pitt: The Years of Acclaim*. London: Constable, 1969.

Ehteshami, Anoushiravan, and Raymond A. Hinnebusch. *Syria and Iran: Middle Powers in a Penetrated Regional System*. New York: Routledge, 1997.

Elkins, Zachary, and Beth Simmons. "On Waves, Clusters, and Diffusion: A Conceptual Framework." *The Annals of the American Academy of Political and Social Science* 598, no. 1 (2005): 33–51.

Ellis, P. Berresford, and Seumas Mac A'Ghobhainn. *The Scottish Insurrection of 1820.* London: Pluto Press, 1989.

Elman, Colin. "Explanatory Typologies in Qualitative Studies of International Politics." *International Organization* 59, no. 2 (2005): 293–326.

Emerson, Donald E. *Metternich and the Political Police: Security and Subversion in the Hapsburg Monarchy (1815–1830).* The Hague: Martinus Nijhoff, 1968.

Entessar, Nader. "The Lion and the Sphinx: Iranian-Egyptian Relations in Perspective." In *Iran and the Arab World*, edited by Hooshang Amirahmadi and Nader Entessar, 161–89. New York: St. Martin's Press, 1993.

Evans, Richard J. *The Coming of the Third Reich.* New York: Penguin Books, 2005.

Ewenstein, Paul. *Realism and Revolution: Why (Some) Revolutionary States Go to War.* New York: Peter Lang, 2020.

Fäy, Bernard. *The Revolutionary Spirit in France and America.* New York: Harcourt, Brace and Company, 1927.

Ferreiro, Larrie D. *Brothers at Arms: American Independence and the Men of France and Spain Who Saved It.* New York: Alfred A. Knopf, 2016.

Fiddick, Thomas C. *Russia's Retreat from Poland, 1920.* London: Macmillan, 1990.

Fischer, Fritz. *Germany's Aims in the First World War.* New York: W. W. Norton and Company, 1967.

Fohlen, Claude. "The Impact of the American Revolution on France." In *The Impact of the American Revolution Abroad.* Washington, DC: Library of Congress, 1976.

Freund, Gerald. *Unholy Alliance.* London: Chatto and Windus, 1957.

Fuller, Graham E., and Rend Rahim Francke. *The Arab Shi'a: The Forgotten Muslims.* London: Macmillan, 1999.

Fürtig, Henner. *Iran's Rivalry with Saudi Arabia Between the Gulf Wars.* Reading: Ithaca Press, 2002.

Gardner, Lloyd C. *Safe for Democracy.* Oxford: Oxford University Press, 1984.

Gartzke, Erik, and Alex Weisiger. "Fading Friendships: Alliances, Affinities and the Activation of International Identities." *British Journal of Political Science* 43, no. 1 (January 2013): 25–52.

Gasiorowski, Mark J. "The Nuzhih Plot and Iranian Politics." *International Journal of Middle East Studies* 34, no. 4 (November 2002): 645–66.

Gatzke, Hans W. *European Diplomacy Between Two Wars, 1919–1939.* Chicago: Quadrangle Books, 1972.

Gatzke, Hans W. "Von Rapallo nach Berlin Stresemann und die Deutsche Rußlandpolitik." *Vierteljahrshefte für Zeitgeschichte* 4, no. 1 (1956): 1–29.

Gause, F. Gregory, III. "Balancing What? Threat Perception and Alliance Choice in the Gulf." *Security Studies* 13, no. 2 (Winter 2003): 273–305.

Gause, F. Gregory, III. *The International Relations of the Persian Gulf.* New York: Cambridge University Press, 2010.

Gause, F. Gregory, III. "Iraq's Decisions to Go to War, 1980 and 1990." *The Middle East Journal* 56, no. 1 (Winter 2002): 47–70.

Gause, F. Gregory, III. "Revolutionary Fevers and Regional Contagion: Domestic Structures and the Export of Revolution in the Middle East." *Journal of South Asian and Middle Eastern Studies* 14, no. 2 (1991): 11–31.

Gay, Peter. *The Dilemma of Democratic Socialism: Edward Bernstein's Challenge to Marx.* New York: Columbia University Press, 1952.

Gerson, Louis L. *Woodrow Wilson and the Rebirth of Poland, 1914–1920.* New Haven: Yale University Press, 1953.

Gibler, Douglas M., and Scott Wolford. "Alliances, Then Democracy: An Examination of the Relationship Between Regime Type and Alliance Formation." *Journal of Conflict Resolution* 50, no. 1 (2006): 129–53.

Gilbert, George. *The Radical Right in Late Imperial Russia: Dreams of a True Fatherland?* New York: Routledge, 2016.

Gilley, Bruce. *The Right to Rule: How States Win and Lose Legitimacy.* New York: Columbia University Press, 2009.

Glad, Betty, and Charles Taber. "Images, Learning and the Decision to Use Force: The Domino Theory of the United States." In *Psychological Dimensions of War*, edited by Betty Glad, 56–81. Newbury Park: Sage, 1990.

Gleditsch, Kristian Skrede, Idean Salehyan, and Kenneth Schultz. "Fighting at Home, Fighting Abroad: How Civil Wars Lead to International Disputes." *Journal of Conflict Resolution* 52, no. 4 (August 2008): 479–506.

Goeschel, Christian. *Mussolini and Hitler: The Forging of the Fascist Alliance.* New Haven: Yale University Press, 2018.

Goldberg, Jacob. "The Shi'i Minority in Saudi Arabia." In *Shi'ism and Social Protests*, edited by Juan R. I. Cole and Nikki R. Keddie, 230–46. New Haven: Yale University Press, 1986.

Golder, Frank A. "Catherine II and the American Revolution." *The American Historical Review* 21, no. 1 (1915): 92–96.

Goldstein, Robert Justin, ed. *The Frightful Stage: Political Censorship of the Theatre in Nineteenth-Century Europe.* New York: Berghahn Books 2009.

Goldstein, Robert Justin. *Political Censorship of the Arts and the Press in Nineteenth-Century Europe.* New York: St. Martin's Press, 1989.

Goldstein, Robert Justin. *Political Repression in 19th Century Europe.* Totowa: Barnes & Noble Books, 1983.

Goldstein, Robert Justin, ed. *The War for the Public Mind: Political Censorship in Nineteenth-Century Europe.* Westport: Praeger, 2000.

Goldstone, Jack A. "Toward a Fourth Generation of Revolutionary Theory." *Annual Review of Political Science* 1 (2001): 139–87.

Goodarzi, Jubin M. *Syria and Iran: Diplomatic Alliance and Power Politics in the Middle East.* London: Tauris Academic Studies, 2006.

Gooding, John. "The Liberalism of Michael Speransky." *The Slavonic and East European Review* 64, no. 3 (July 1986): 401–24.

Gooding, John. "Speransky and Baten'kov." *The Slavonic and East European Review* 66, no. 3 (July 1988): 400–25.

Goodwin, Jeff. *No Other Way Out: States and Revolutionary Movements, 1945–1991* New York: Cambridge University Press, 2001.

Gordon, Harold J. *Hitler and the Beer Hall Putsch.* Princeton: Princeton University Press, 1972.

Gorman, Thomas K. *America and Belgium: A Study of the Influence of the United States upon the Belgian Revolution of 1789–1790.* London: T. Fisher Unwin Ltd., 1925.

Gourevitch, Peter. "The Second Image Reversed: International Sources of Domestic Politics." *International Organization* 32, no. 4 (1978): 881–912.

Graham, Erin R., Charles R. Shipan, and Craig Volden. "The Diffusion of Policy Diffusion Research in Political Science." *British Journal of Political Science* 43, no. 3 (2013): 673–701.

Grathwol, Robert P. *Stresemann and the DNVP: Reconciliation or Revenge in German Foreign Policy, 1924–1928.* Lawrence: The Regents Press of Kansas, 1980.

Griffin, Roger. *The Nature of Fascism.* New York: Routledge, 1991.

Griffiths, David M. "American Commercial Diplomacy in Russia, 1780 to 1783." *The William and Mary Quarterly* 27, no. 3 (1970): 379–410.

Griffiths, David M. "Catherine the Great, the British Opposition, and the American Revolution." In *The American Revolution and "a Candid World,"* edited by Lawrence S. Kaplan, 85–110. Kent: Kent State University Press, 1977.

Griffiths, David M. "Nikita Panin, Russian Diplomacy, and the American Revolution." *Slavic Review* 28, no. 1 (1969): 1–24.

Griffiths, David M. "Soviet Views of Early Russian-American Relations." *Proceedings of the American Philosophical Society* 116, no. 2 (1972): 148–56.

Grimsted, Patricia Kennedy. *The Foreign Ministers of Alexander I: Political Attitudes and the Conduct of Russian Diplomacy, 1801–1825.* Berkeley: University of California Press, 1969.

Große Kracht, Klaus. "Campaigning Against Bolshevism: Catholic Action in Late Weimar Germany." *Journal of Contemporary History* 53, no. 3 (2018): 550–73.

Guettel, Jens-Uwe. "Reform, Revolution, and the 'Original Catastrophe': Political Change in Prussia and Germany on the Eve of the First World War." *The Journal of Modern History* 91, no. 2 (2019): 311–40.

Guillon, E. *Les complots militaires sous la restauration, d'après les documents des archives.* Paris: E. Plon, Nourrit et Cie, 1895.

Guizot, M., and Madame Guizot de Witt. *The History of France from the Earliest of Times to 1848.* Translated by Robert Black. Vol. 5. Boston: Aldine Book Publishing Co., n.d.

Gunitsky, Seva. *Aftershocks: Great Powers and Domestic Reforms in the Twentieth Century.* Princeton: Princeton University Press, 2017.

Haas, Mark L. "Ideology and Alliances: British and French External Balancing Decisions in the 1930s." *Security Studies* 12, no. 4 (2003): 34–79.

Haas, Mark L. *Frenemies: When Do Ideological Enemies Ally?* Ithaca: Cornell University Press, 2022.

Haas, Mark L. *The Ideological Origins of Great Power Politics, 1789–1989.* Ithaca: Cornell University Press, 2005.

Hale, Henry E. "Regime Change Cascades: What We Have Learned from the 1848 Revolutions to the 2011 Arab Uprisings." *Annual Review of Political Science* 16 (2013): 331–53.

Halévy, Élie. *England in 1815.* London: Ernest Benn Limited, 1964.

Halévy, Élie. *A History of the English People in the Nineteenth Century.* Vol. 6, Book II. New York: Peter Smith, 1952.

Halliday, Fred. "International Society as Homogeneity: Burke, Marx, Fukuyama." *Millennium: Journal of International Studies* 21, no. 3 (1992): 435–61.

Halliday, Fred. *Revolution and World Politics: The Rise and Fall of the Sixth Great Power.* Durham: Duke University Press, 1999.

Halperin, Sandra. "The Politics of Appeasement: The Rise of the Left and European International Relations During the Interwar Period." In *Contested Social Orders*, edited by David Skidmore, 128–64. Nashville: Vanderbilt University Press, 1997.

Hamnett, Brian R. "Process and Pattern: A Re-Examination of the Ibero-American Independence Movements, 1808–1826." *Journal of Latin American Studies* 29, no. 2 (1977): 279–328.

Handler, Edward. *America and Europe in the Political Thought of John Adams*. Cambridge, MA: Harvard University Press, 1964.

Hardman, John. *The Life of Louis XVI*. New Haven: Yale University Press, 2016.

Hardman, John. *Louis XVI*. New Haven: Yale University Press, 1993.

Hardman, John, and Munro Price, eds. *Louis XVI and the Comte de Vergennes: Correspondence 1774–1787*. Studies on Voltaire and the Eighteenth Century Vol. 364. Oxford: Voltaire Foundation, 1998.

Harmer, Harry. *Friedrich Ebert*. London: Haus Publishing, 2008.

Harris, Robert D. "French Finances and the American War, 1777–1783." *The Journal of Modern History* 48, no. 2 (June 1976): 233–58.

Hartley, Janet M. "The 'Constitutions' of Finland and Poland in the Reign of Alexander I: Blueprints for Reform in Russia?" In *Finland and Poland in the Russian Empire: A Comparative Study*, edited by Michael Branch, Janet Hartley and Antoni Mączark, 41–61. London: University of London, 1995.

Hassan, Oz. "Undermining the Transatlantic Democracy Agenda? The Arab Spring and Saudi Arabia's Counteracting Democracy Strategy." *Democratization* 22, no. 3 (2015): 479–95.

Haworth, Paul Leland. "Frederick the Great and the American Revolution." *The American Historical Review* 9, no. 3 (1904): 460–78.

Haynes, Kyle. "Diversionary Conflict: Demonizing Enemies or Demonstrating Competence?" *Conflict Management and Peace Science* 34, no. 4 (2017): 337–58.

Hegghammer, Thomas, and Stéphane Lacroix. *The Meccan Rebellion: The Story of Juhayman Al-'Utaybi Revisited*. Bristol: Amal Press, 2011.

Hegghammer, Thomas, and Stéphane Lacroix. "Rejectionist Islamism in Saudi Arabia: The Story of Juhayman Al-'Utaybi." *International Journal of Middle East Studies* 39, no. 1 (February 2007): 103–22.

Helfont, Samuel. *Compulsion in Religion: Saddam Hussein, Islam, and the Roots of Insurgencies in Iraq*. New York: Oxford University Press, 2018.

Helfont, Samuel. "Islam in Saudi Foreign Policy: The Case of Ma'ruf Al-Dawalibi." *The International History Review* 42, no. 3 (2020): 449–64.

Herr, Richard. *Eighteenth-Century Revolution in Spain*. Princeton: Princeton University Press, 1958.

Heydemann, Günther. "The Vienna System Between 1815 and 1848 and the Disputed Anti-Revolutionary Strategy: Repression, Reforms, or Constitutions?" In *"The Transformation of European Politics, 1763–1848": Episode or Model in Modern History?*, edited by Peter Krüger and Paul W. Schroeder, 187–203. New York: Palgrave Macmillan, 2002.

Hiden, John. *Germany and Europe 1919–1939*. London: Longman, 1993.

Himmer, Robert. "Soviet Policy Toward Germany During the Russo-Polish War, 1920." *Slavic Review* 35, no. 4 (1976): 665–82.

Hiro, Dilip. *The Longest War: The Iran-Iraq Military Conflict*. London: Grafton Books, 1989.

Hirschfield, Yair. "The Odd Couple: Ba'thist Syria and Khomeini's Iran." In *Syria Under Assad*, edited by Moshe Ma'oz and Avner Yaniv, 187–203. London: Croom Helm, 1986.

History of the Internal Affairs of the United Provinces, from the Year 1780 to the Commencement of Hostilities in June 1787. London: G. G. J. and J. Robinson, 1787.

Hitler, Adolf. *Hitler's Table Talk, 1941–1944*. Translated by Norman Cameron and R. H. Stevens. New York: Enigma Books, 2000.

Hohler, Susanne. *Fascism in Manchuria: The Soviet-China Encounter in the 1930s*. London: I. B. Tauris, 2017.

Hohler, Susanne. "Russian Fascism in Exile: A Historical and Phenomenological Perspective on Transnational Fascism." *Fascism* 2, no. 2 (2013): 121–40.

Holroyd, Richard. "The Bourbon Army, 1815–1830." *The Historical Journal* 14, no. 3 (1971): 529–52.

Hone, J. Ann. *For the Cause of Truth: Radicalism in London, 1796–1821*. New York: Oxford University Press, 1982.

Hull, Anthony H. *Charles III and the Revival of Spain*. Washington, DC: University Press of America, 1980.

Hunter, Shireen T. "Iran and the Spread of Revolutionary Islam." *Third World Quarterly* 10, no. 2 (April 1988): 730–49.

Hunter, Shireen T. *Iran and the World: Continuity in a Revolutionary Decade*. Bloomington: Indiana University Press, 1990.

Hutson, James H. *John Adams and the Diplomacy of the American Revolution*. Lexington: University Press of Kentucky, 1980.

Ibrahim, Fouad. *The Shi'is of Saudi Arabia*. London: Saqi, 2006.

Ibrahim, Saad Eddin. "Anatomy of Egypt's Militant Islamic Groups: Methodological Note and Preliminary Findings." *International Journal of Middle East Studies* 12, no. 4 (December 1980): 423–53.

Ismael, Tareq. *Iraq and Iran: Roots of Conflict*. Syracuse: Syracuse University Press, 1982.

Israel, Jonathan. *Democratic Enlightenment: Philosophy, Revolution, and Human Rights, 1750–1790*. New York: Oxford University Press, 2011.

Israel, Jonathan I. *The Expanding Blaze: How the American Revolution Ignited the World, 1775–1848*. Princeton: Princeton University Press, 2017.

Israel, Jonathan. *A Revolution of the Mind: Radical Enlightenment and the Intellectual Origins of Modern Democracy*. Princeton: Princeton University Press, 2010.

Jabar, Faleh A. *The Shi'ite Movement in Iraq*. London: Saqi, 2003.

Jackisch, Barry A. *The Pan-German League and Radical Nationalist Politics in Interwar Germany, 1918–1939*. Burlington: Ashgate, 2012.

Jacob, Margaret C. *Living the Enlightenment: Freemasonry and Politics in Eighteenth-Century Europe*. New York: Oxford University Press, 1991.

Jacobson, Jon. "On the Historiography of Soviet Foreign Relations in the 1920s." *The International History Review* 18, no. 2 (1996): 336–57.

Jacobson, Jon. *When the Soviet Union Entered World Politics*. Berkeley: University of California Press, 1994.

Jarausch, Konrad H. "Cooperation or Intervention? Kurt Riezler and the Failure of German Ostpolitik 1918." *Slavic Review* 31, no. 2 (1972): 381–98.

Jarrett, Mark. *The Congress of Vienna and Its Legacy: War and Great Power Diplomacy After Napoleon*. New York: I. B. Tauris, 2013.

Jászi, Oszkár. *Revolution and Counterrevolution in Hungary*. New York: H. Fertig, 1969.

Jervis, Robert, and Jack L. Snyder. *Dominoes and Bandwagons: Strategic Beliefs and Great Power Competition in Eurasian Rimland*. New York: Oxford University Press, 1991.

Jervis, Robert. *System Effects: Complexity in Political and Social Life*. Princeton: Princeton University Press, 1997.

Joll, James. *The Second International 1889–1914*. London: Weidenfeld and Nicolson, 1955.

Jones, Toby Craig. "Rebellion on the Saudi Periphery: Modernity, Marginalization, and the Shi'a Uprising of 1979." *International Journal of Middle East Studies* 38, no. 2 (May 2006): 213–33.

Jost, John T. "The End of the End of Ideology." *American Psychologist* 61, no. 7 (2006): 651–70.

Journals of the Continental Congress, 1774–1789. Vol. 5. Washington, DC: Government Printing Office, 1906.

Kagan, Korina. "The Myth of the European Concert: The Realist-Institutionalist Debate and Great Power Behavior in the Eastern Question, 1821–1841." *Security Studies* 7, no. 2 (Winter 1997/98): 1–57.

Kahng, Gyoohyoung. "Intervention and Coexistence: The Comintern's Revolutionary Propaganda in Great Britain and Anglo-Soviet Relations, 1920–1927." PhD thesis, Ohio University, 1998.

Kaiser, Thomas E. "La fin du renversement des alliances: La France, l'Autriche et la déclaration de guerre du 20 avril 1792." *Annales historiques de la Révolution française*, no. 351 (January–March 2008): 77–98.

Kaplan, Lawrence S. *Colonies into Nation: American Diplomacy, 1763–1801*. New York: The Macmillan Company, 1972.

Karsh, Efraim, and Inari Rautsi. *Saddam Hussein: A Political Biography*. New York: The Free Press, 1991.

Katz, Mark N. *Revolutions and Revolutionary Waves*. New York: St. Martin's Press, 1997.

Kautsky, John H. *Karl Kautsky: Marxism, Revolution and Democracy*. New Brunswick: Transaction Publishers, 1994.

Kechichian, Joseph A. *Oman and the World: The Emergence of an Independent Foreign Policy*. Santa Monica: RAND, 1995.

Kellogg, Michael. *The Russian Roots of Nazism: White Émigrés and the Making of National Socialism, 1917–1945*. New York: Cambridge University Press, 2005.

Kendall, Walter. *The Revolutionary Movement in Britain, 1900–21: The Origins of British Communism*. London: Weidenfeld & Nicolson, 1969.

Kennedy, Sean. "The End of Immunity? Recent Work on the Far Right in Interwar France." *Historical Reflections* 34, no. 2 (2008): 25–45.

Kepel, Gilles. *The Prophet and the Pharaoh: Muslim Extremism in Egypt*. Berkeley: University of California Press, 1985.

Kerr, Malcolm H. *The Arab Cold War: Gamal Abd Al-Nasir and His Rivals, 1958–1970*. London: Oxford University Press, 1971.

Kershaw, Ian. *Hitler: 1889–1936 Hubris*. New York: W. W. Norton & Company, 1998.

Kershaw, Ian. *The Nazi Dictatorship*. 4th ed. New York: Oxford University Press, 2000.

Kettle, Michael. *The Allies and the Russian Collapse: March 1917–March 1918*. Minneapolis: University of Minnesota Press, 1981.

Khadduri, Majid. *The Gulf War: The Origins and Implications of the Iraq-Iran Conflict*. New York: Oxford University Press, 1988.

Khatib, Line. *Islamic Revivalism in Syria: The Rise and Fall of Ba'thist Secularism*. New York: Routledge, 2011.

Khomeini, Ruhollah. *Islam and Revolution: Writings and Declarations of Imam Khomeini*. Translated by Hamid Alger. Berkeley: Mizan Press, 1981.

Kienle, Eberhard. *Ba'th v. Ba'th: The Conflict Between Syria and Iraq 1968-1989*. London: I. B. Tauris & Co. Ltd., 1990.

Kim, Kyung-Won. *Revolution and the International System*. New York: New York University Press, 1970.

King, Ralph. *The Iran-Iraq War: The Political Implications*. Adelphi Papers. London: The International Institute for Strategic Studies, 1987.

Kissinger, Henry A. *A World Restored: Metternich, Castlereagh and the Problems of Peace, 1812-1822*. Boston: Houghton Mifflin, 1957.

Kitchen, Martin. *The Silent Dictatorship: The Politics of the German High Command Under Hindenburg and Ludendorff, 1916-1918*. New York: Holmes & Meier Publishers, 1976.

Klein, Fritz. "Between Compiègne and Versailles: The Germans on the Way from a Misunderstood Defeat to an Unwanted Peace." In *The Treaty of Versailles: A Reassessment After 75 Years*, edited by Manfred F. Boemeke, Gerald D. Feldman, and Elisabeth Glaser, 203-20. Cambridge: Cambridge University Press, 1998.

Klippel, Diethelm. "The True Concept of Liberty: Political Theory in Germany in the Second Half of the Eighteenth Century." In *The Transformation of Political Culture: England and Germany in the Late Eighteenth Century*, edited by Eckhart Hellmuth, 447-66. New York: Oxford University Press, 1990.

Knox, MacGregor. *Common Destiny: Dictatorship, Foreign Policy, and War in Fascist Italy and Nazi Germany*. New York: Cambridge University Press, 2000.

Kolb, Eberhard. *The Weimar Republic*. Translated by P. S. Falla and R. J. Park. 2nd ed. New York: Routledge, 2005.

Koesel, Karrie J. and Bunce, Valerie J. "Diffusion-Proofing: Russian and Chinese Responses to Waves of Popular Mobilizations Against Authoritarian Rulers." *Perspectives on Politics* 11, no. 3 (2013): 753-68.

Kotkin, Stephen. *Stalin: Paradoxes of Power, 1878-1928*. New York: Penguin Press, 2014.

Kozlovski, Piotr. *Diorama social de Paris*. Paris: Honoré Champion, 1997.

Kraehe, Enno E. "Austria, Russia and the German Confederation, 1813-1820." In *Deutscher Bund und Deutsche Frage 1815-1866*, edited by Helmut Rumpler, 264-80. Munich: Verlag, 1990.

Kramer, Martin. "Khomeini's Messengers: The Disputed Pilgrimage of Islam." In *Religious Radicalism and Politics in the Middle East*, edited by Emmanuel Sivan and Menachem Friedman, 177-94. Albany: State University of New York Press, 1990.

Kramer, Martin. "Syria's Alawis and Shi'ism." In *Shi'ism, Resistance, and Revolution*, edited by Martin Kramer, 237-54. Boulder: Westview Press, 1987.

Krieger, Leonard. *An Essay on the Theory of Enlightened Despotism*. Chicago: University of Chicago Press, 1975.

Krieger, Leonard. *The German Idea of Freedom: History of a Political Tradition*. Boston: Beacon Press, 1957.

Krüger, Peter, and Paul W. Schroder, eds. *"The Transformation of European Politics, 1763-1848": Episode or Model in Modern History?* New York: Palgrave Macmillan, 2002.

Kuran, Timur. "Now Out of Never: The Element of Surprise in the East European Revolution of 1989." *World Politics* 44, no. 1 (1991): 7-48.

Kurzman, Charles. "Structural Opportunity and Perceived Opportunity in Social-Movement Theory." *American Sociological Review* 61, no. 1 (February 1996): 153-70.

Lacroix, Stéphane. "Saudi Arabia's Muslim Brotherhood Predicament." https://pomeps. org/saudi-arabias-muslim-brotherhood-predicament.

Lacroix, Stéphane. *Awakening Islam: The Politics of Religious Dissent in Contemporary Saudi Arabia*. Translated by George Holoch. Cambridge, MA: Harvard University Press, 2011.

Lai, Brian, and Dan Reiter. "Democracy, Political Similarity, and International Alliances, 1816–1992." *Journal of Conflict Resolution* 44, no. 2 (2000): 203–27.

Lang, David Marshall. *The First Russian Radical: Alexander Radischev, 1749–1802*. London: George Allen and Unwin, 1959.

Laven, David. "Austria's Italian Policy Reconsidered: Revolution and Reform in Restoration Italy." *Modern Italy* 2 (1997): 3–33.

Laybourn, Keith, and Dylan Murphy. *Under the Red Flag*. Thrupp: Sutton Publishing, 1999.

Lazitch, Branko, and Milorad M. Drachkovitch. *Lenin and the Comintern*. Vol. 1. Stanford: Hoover Institution Press, 1972.

Ledeen, Michael. *Universal Fascism: The Theory and Practice of the Fascist International, 1928–1936*. New York: Howard Fertig, 1972.

Leeds, Brett Ashley, and David R. Davis. "Domestic Political Vulnerability and International Disputes." *Journal of Conflict Resolution* 41, no. 6 (1997): 814–34.

Lefèvre, Raphaël. *Ashes of Hama: The Muslim Brotherhood in Syria*. London: C. Hurst & Co., 2013.

Lefèvre, Raphaël. "Saudi Arabia and the Syrian Brotherhood." Middle East Institute, 2013. https://www.mei.edu/publications/saudi-arabia-and-the-syrian-brotherhood.

Legrenzi, Matteo. *The GCC and the International Relations of the Gulf*. London: I. B. Tauris, 2011.

Legum, Colin, Haim Shaked, and Daniel Dishon, eds. *Middle East Contemporary Survey*, Vol. 3, *1978–79*. New York: Holmes & Meier Publishers, Inc., 1980.

Legum, Colin, Haim Shaked, and Daniel Dishon, eds. *Middle East Contemporary Survey*, Vol. 4, *1979–80*. New York: Holmes & Meier Publishers, Inc., 1981.

Legum, Colin, Haim Shaked, and Daniel Dishon, eds. *Middle East Contemporary Survey*, Vol. 5, *1980–81*. New York: Holmes & Meier Publishers, Inc., 1982.

Legum, Colin, Haim Shaked, and Daniel Dishon, eds. *Middle East Contemporary Survey*, Vol. 6, *1981–82*. New York: Holmes & Meier Publishers, Inc., 1984.

Lemke, Douglas, and William Reed. "The Relevance of Politically Relevant Dyads." *Journal of Conflict Resolution* 45, no. 1 (2001): 126–44.

Lenin, V. I. *Collected Works*. Vol. 31. Moscow: Progress Publishers, 1965.

Lerner, Marc H. "Radical Elements and Attempted Revolutions in Late 18th-Century Republics." In *The Republican Alternative: The Netherlands and Switzerland Compared*, edited by André Holenstein, Thomas Maissen, and Maarten Prak, 301–20. Amsterdam: Amsterdam University Press, 2008.

Lerner, Warren. "Attempting a Revolution from Without: Poland in 1920." In *The Anatomy of Communist Takeovers*, edited by Thomas T. Hammond, 94–106. New Haven: Yale University Press, 1975.

Levey, Jules. "George Calois and the Faisceau: The Making and Breaking of a Fascist." *French Historical Studies* 8, no. 2 (1973): 279–304.

Levy, Carl. "Fascism, National Socialism, and Conservatives in Europe, 1914–1945: Issues for Comparativists." *Contemporary European History* 8, no. 1 (1999): 97–126.

Levy, Carl. "Italian Anarchism, 1870–1926." In *For Anarchism: History, Theory, and Practice*, edited by David Goodway, 25–78. New York: Routledge, 1989.

Levy, Jack S. "Domestic Politics and War." *Journal of Interdisciplinary History* 18, no. 4 (1988): 653–73.

Levinger, Matthew. *Enlightened Nationalism: The Transformation of Prussian Political Culture, 1806–1848.* New York: Oxford University Press, 2000.

Levinger, Matthew. "Hardenberg, Wittgenstein, and the Constitutional Question in Prussia, 1815–22." *German History* 8, no. 3 (October 1990): 257–77.

Lia, Brynjar. *Architect of Global Jihad: The Life of Al-Qaida Strategist Abu Mus'ab Al-Suri.* New York: Columbia University Press, 2008.

Lia, Brynjar. "The Islamist Uprising in Syria, 1976–82: The History and Legacy of a Failed Revolt." *British Journal of Middle Eastern Studies* 43, no. 4 (2016): 541–59.

Lindemann, Albert S. *A History of European Socialism.* New Haven: Yale University Press, 1983.

Lindemann, Albert S. *The "Red Years": European Socialism Versus Bolshevism 1919–1921.* Berkeley: University of California Press, 1974.

Linehan, Thomas. *British Fascism 1918–1939: Parties, Ideology, and Culture.* Manchester: Manchester University Press, 2000.

Linz, Juan J. "Some Notes Toward a Comparative Study of Fascism in Sociological Historical Perspective." In *Fascism: A Reader's Guide*, edited by Walter Laqueur, 3–121. Berkeley: University of California Press, 1976.

Liss, Peggy K. *Atlantic Empires: The Network of Trade and Revolution, 1713–1826.* Baltimore: The Johns Hopkins University Press, 1983.

Livingston, Luther S. *Franklin and His Press at Passy.* New York: The Grolier Club, 1914.

Lobmeyer, Hans Günter. *Opposition und Widerstand in Syrien.* Hamburg: Deutsches Orient-Institut, 1995.

Lockhart, R. H. Bruce. *Memoirs of a British Agent.* London: Putnam, 1934.

Lodge, Richard. *Great Britain and Prussia in the Eighteenth Century.* Oxford: Clarendon Press, 1923.

Long, John W. "Searching for Sidney Reilly: The Lockhart Plot in Revolutionary Russia, 1918." *Europe-Asia Studies* 47, no. 7 (1995): 1225–41.

Lopez, Claude A., ed. *The Papers of Benjamin Franklin*, Volume 27, *July 1 Through October 31, 1778.* New Haven: Yale University Press, 1988.

Louër, Laurence. *Transnational Shia Politics: Religious and Political Networks in the Gulf.* New York: Columbia University Press, 2008.

Love, Gary. "'What's the Big Idea?': Oswald Mosley, the British Union of Fascists and Generic Fascism." *Journal of Contemporary History* 42, no. 3 (2007): 447–68.

Lundgreen-Nielsen, Kay. "The Mayer Thesis Reconsidered: The Poles and the Paris Peace Conference, 1919." *The International History Review* 7, no. 1 (1985): 68–102.

Lundgreen-Nielsen, Kay. *The Polish Problem at the Paris Peace Conference.* Translated by Alison Borch-Johansen. Odense: Odense University Press, 1979.

Lyandres, Semion. *The Bolsheviks' "German Gold" Revisited: An Inquiry into the 1917 Accusations.* Pittsburg: University of Pittsburg Press, 1995.

Macaulay, Neill. *Dom Pedro: The Struggle for Liberty in Brazil and Portugal, 1798–1834.* Durham: Duke University Press, 1986.

Macfarlane, L. J. "Hands Off Russia: British Labour and the Russo-Polish War, 1920." *Past and Present* 38 (1967): 126–52.

Madariaga, Isabel de. *Britain, Russia, and the Armed Neutrality of 1780.* New Haven: Yale University Press, 1962.

Madariaga, Isabel de. *Russia in the Age of Catherine the Great.* London: Weidenfeld and Nicolson, 1981.

Madariaga, Isabel de. "Spain and the Decembrists." *European History Quarterly* 3, no. 2 (April 1973): 141–56.

Mahoney, James, and Gary Goertz. "The Possibility Principle: Choosing Negative Cases in Comparative Research." *American Political Science Review* 98, no. 4 (November 2004): 653–69.

Mahoney, James. "Process Tracing and Historical Explanation." *Security Studies* 24, no. 4 (2015): 200–218.

Maier, Charles S. *Recasting Bourgeois Europe*. Princeton: Princeton University Press, 1975.

Maier, Pauline. *American Scripture: Making the Declaration of Independence*. New York: Alfred A. Knopf, 1997.

Makiya, Kanan. *Republic of Fear: The Politics of Modern Iraq*. Berkeley: University of California Press, 1998.

Mallat, Chibli. *The Renewal of Islamic Law: Muhammad Baqer as-Sadr, Najaf and the Shi'i International*. New York: Cambridge University Press, 1993.

Malmesbury, James Harris. *Diaries and Correspondence of the Earl of Malmesbury*. Vol. 2. London: Richard Bentley, 1844.

Manceron, Claude. *The French Revolution*, Vol. 2, *The Wind from America*. Translated by Nancy Amphoux. New York: Alfred A. Knopf, 1978.

Mann, Michael. *Fascists*. New York: Cambridge University Press, 2004.

Mann, Michael. *The Sources of Social Power*. Vol. 2. New York: Cambridge University Press, 1993.

Manning, A. F. "Reports of the British Embassy in Rome on the Rise of Fascism." *Risorgimento* 1 (1980): 33–45.

Marks, Sally. "Mistakes and Myths: The Allies, Germany, and the Versailles Treaty 1918–1921." *The Journal of Modern History* 85, no. 3 (2013): 632–59.

Marks, Sally. "The Myth of Reparations." *Central European History* 11, no. 3 (1978): 231–55.

Marr, Phebe. *The Modern History of Iraq*. 2nd ed. Boulder, CO: Westview Press, 2004.

Marsella, Mauro. "Assessing European Fascism: The View from Mussolini's Italy." PhD thesis, McMaster University, 2006.

Marschall, Christian. *Iran's Persian Gulf Policy: From Khomeini to Khatami*. New York: Routledge Curzon, 2003.

Marschall, Christian. "Syria-Iran: A Strategic Alliance, 1979–1991." *Orient* 33, no. 3 (September 1992): 433–46.

Marshall, Peter H. *William Godwin*. New Haven: Yale University Press, 1984.

Matar, Fuad. *Saddam Hussein: The Man, the Cause and the Future*. London: Third World Centre, 1981.

Matthee, Rudi. "The Egyptian Opposition on the Iranian Revolution." In *Shi'ism and Social Protest*, edited by Juan R. I. Cole and Nikki R. Keddie, 247–74. New Haven: Yale University Press, 1986.

Matthiesen, Toby. "The Domestic Sources of Saudi Foreign Policy: Islamists and the State in the Wake of the Arab Uprisings." In *Rethinking Political Islam Series*. Washington, DC: Brookings Institution, August 2015.

Matthiesen, Toby. "Hizbullah Al-Hijaz: A History of the Most Radical Saudi Opposition Group." *The Middle East Journal* 64, no. 2 (Spring 2010): 179–97.

Matthiesen, Toby. *The Other Saudis: Shiism, Dissent, and Sectarianism*. New York: Cambridge University Press, 2015.

Mavani, Hamid. "Ayatullah Khomeini's Concept of Governance (Wilayat al-Faqih) and the Classical Shi'i Doctrine of Imamate." *Middle Eastern Studies* 47, no. 5 (September 2011): 807–24.

Mavani, Hamid. *Religious Authority and Political Thought in Twelver Shi'ism: From Ali to Post-Khomeini.* New York: Routledge, 2013.

Mayer, Arno J. *Politics and Diplomacy of Peacemaking: Containment and Counterrevolution at Versailles, 1918–1919.* New York: Alfred A. Knopf, 1967.

Mayer, Thomas. "The Islamic Opposition in Syria, 1961–1982." *Orient* 24, no. 4 (1983): 589–609.

Mazour, Anatole G. *The First Russian Revolution, 1825.* Stanford: Stanford University Press, 1962.

McCalman, Iain. *Radical Underworld: Prophets, Revolutionaries and Pornographers in London, 1795–1840.* New York: Cambridge University Press, 1988.

McCary, Ben C. *The Causes of the French Intervention in the American Revolution.* Toulouse: Édouard Privat, 1928.

McDermott, Kevin, and Jeremy Agnew. *The Comintern: A History of International Communism from Lenin to Stalin.* London: Macmillan, 1996.

McDowall, Angus. "Islamist Threat at Home Forces Saudi Rethink on Syria." Reuters, February 11 2014.

McFarlane, Anthony. "The American Revolution and the Spanish Monarchy." In *Europe's American Revolution,* edited by Simon P. Newman, 26–50. New York: Palgrave Macmillan, 2006.

McFarlane, Anthony. "Civil Disorders and Popular Protests in Late Colonial New Granada." *The Hispanic American Historical Review* 64, no. 1 (1984): 17–54.

McFarlane, Anthony. "Rebellions in Late Colonial Spanish America: A Comparative Perspective." *Bulletin of Latin American Research* 14, no. 3 (1995): 313–38.

McFaul, Michael. "Putin, Putinism, and the Domestic Determinants of Russian Foreign Policy." *International Security* 45, no. 2 (2020): 95–139.

McMeekin, Sean. *The Russian Revolution: A New History.* New York: Basic Books, 2017.

Mearsheimer, John J. *The Tragedy of Great Power Politics.* New York: W. W. Norton and Company, 2001.

Melograni, Piero. *Lenin and the Myth of World Revolution.* Atlantic Highlands: Humanities Press International, Inc., 1989.

Menashiri, David. "Khomeini's Vision: Nationalism or World Order?" In *The Iranian Revolution and the Muslim World,* edited by David Menashiri, 40–57. Boulder: Westview Press, 1990.

Metternich, Richard, ed. *Memoirs of Prince Metternich, 1815–1829.* Vol. III. London: Richard Bentley & Son, 1881.

Michaud, Gerard. "The Importance of Bodyguards." *MERIP Reports* 110 (November–December 1982).

Mitchell, Richard P. *The Society of Muslim Brothers.* London: Oxford University Press, 1969.

Mitzen, Jennifer. *Power in Concert: The Nineteenth-Century Origins of Global Governance.* Chicago: The University of Chicago Press, 2013.

Mitzen, Jennifer. "Reading Habermas in Anarchy: Multilateral Diplomacy and Global Public Spheres." *American Political Science Review* 99, no. 3 (August 2005): 401–17.

Moffat, Ian C. D. *The Allied Intervention in Russia, 1918–1920.* New York: Palgrave Macmillan, 2015.

Morgan, David W. *The Socialist Left and the German Revolution*. Ithaca: Cornell University Press, 1975.

Morgan, Philip. *Fascism in Europe, 1919–1945*. London: Routledge, 2003.

Morris, Richard B. *The Peacemakers: The Great Powers and American Independence*. New York: Harper & Row, 1965.

Morsi, Mohamed. "President Mohamed Morsi's Speech at Cairo University, Saturday, June 30, After Taking Oath of Office." http://www.ikhwanweb.com/article.php?id=30156.

Mosse, George L. *The Fascist Revolution: Toward a General Theory of Fascism*. New York: H. Fertig, 1999.

Mufti, Malik. *Sovereign Creations: Pan-Arabism and Political Order in Syria and Iraq*. Ithaca: Cornell University Press, 1996.

Murphy, Orville T. *Charles Gravier, Comte de Vergennes: French Diplomacy in the Age of Revolution, 1719–1787*. Albany: State University of New York Press, 1982.

Murphy, Orville T. *The Diplomatic Retreat of France and Public Opinion on the Eve of the French Revolution, 1783–1789*. Washington, DC: The Catholic University of America, 1998.

Murray, Williamson, and Kevin M. Woods. *The Iran-Iraq War: A Military and Strategic History*. New York: Cambridge University Press, 2014.

Mylroie, Laurie Ann. "Regional Security After Empire: Saudi Arabia and the Gulf." PhD thesis, Harvard University, 1985.

Nada, Narciso. *Le relazioni diplomatiche fra l'Austria e il Regno di Sardegna, I Serie: 1814–1830*. Vol. 2. Rome: Istituto Storico Italiano, 1970.

Nahas, Maridi. "State-Systems and Revolutionary Challenge: Nasser, Khomeini, and the Middle East." *International Journal of Middle East Studies* 17, no. 4 (1985): 507–27.

Nathan, Andrew J. "China's Challenge." *Journal of Democracy* 25, no. 1 (2015): 156–70.

Neely, Sylvia. *Lafayette and the Liberal Ideal, 1814–1824: Politics and Conspiracy in an Age of Reaction*. Carbondale: Southern Illinois University Press, 1991.

Neilson, Keith. *Britain, Soviet Russia, and the Collapse of the Versailles Order 1919–1939*. Cambridge: Cambridge University Press, 2006.

Nekrich, Aleksandr M. *Pariahs, Partners, Predators: German-Soviet Relations 1922–1941*. New York: Columbia University Press, 1997.

Nelson, Chad E. "Revolution and War: Saddam's Decision to Invade Iran." *The Middle East Journal* 72, no. 2 (2018): 246–66.

Nelson, Chad E., and Arthur A. Stein. "The Attenuation of Revolutionary Foreign Policy." *International Politics* 52, no. 5 (2015): 626–36.

Niblock, Tim. *Saudi Arabia: Power, Legitimacy and Survival*. New York: Routledge, 2006.

Nichols, Irby C., Jr. *The European Pentarchy and the Congress of Verona, 1822*. The Hague: Martinus Nijhoff, 1971.

Nicolaisen, Peter. "John Adams, Thomas Jefferson, and the Dutch Patriots." In *Old World, New World: America and Europe in the Age of Jefferson*, edited by Leonard J. Sandosky, Peter Nicolaisen, Peter S. Onuf, and Andrew J. O'Shaughnessy, 105–30. Charlottesville: University of Virginia Press, 2010.

Nitti, Francesco S. *Peaceless Europe*. London: Cassel and Company, 1922.

Nolte, Ernst. *Three Faces of Fascism*. New York: Mentor, 1969.

Nonneman, Gerd. *Iraq, the Gulf States and the War*. London: Ithaca Press, 1986.

Noueihed, Lin, and Alex Warren. *The Battle for the Arab Spring: Revolution, Counter-Revolution and the Making of a New Era*. New Haven: Yale University Press, 2012.

O'Ballance, Edgar. *The Gulf War*. London: Brassey's Defence Publishing, 1988.

O'Meara, Patrick. *The Decembrist Pavel Pestel: Russia's First Republican.* New York: Palgrave Macmillan, 2003.

O'Neill, Barry. *Honor, Symbols, and War.* Ann Arbor: The University of Michigan Press, 1999.

Oakes, Amy. *Diversionary War: Domestic Unrest and International Conflict.* Stanford: Stanford University Press, 2012.

Oberlander, Erwin. "The All-Russian Fascist Party." *Journal of Contemporary History* 1, no. 1 (1966): 158–73.

Olmert, Yosef. "Iranian-Syrian Relations: Between Islam and Realpolitik." In *The Iranian Revolution and the Muslim World*, edited by David Menashiri, 171–88. Boulder: Westview Press, 1990.

Orlow, Dietrich. *The History of the Nazi Party: 1919–1933.* Pittsburgh: The University of Pittsburgh Press, 1969.

Orr, Andrew. "The Myth of the Black Sea Mutiny: Communist Propaganda, Soviet Influence and the Re-Remembering of the Mutiny." *French History* 32, no. 1 (2018): 86–105.

Osman, Khalil. *Sectarianism in Iraq: The Making of State and Nation Since 1920.* New York: Routledge, 2015.

Owen IV., John M. "When Do Ideologies Produce Alliances? The Holy Roman Empire, 1517–1555." *International Studies Quarterly* 49, no. 1 (March 2005): 73–99.

Owen, John M. *The Clash of Ideas in World Politics: Transnational Networks, States, and Regime Change, 1510–2010.* Princeton: Princeton University Press, 2010.

Palmer, R. R. *The Age of the Democratic Revolution.* Princeton: Princeton University Press, 1959.

Palmer, R. R. "The Dubious Democrat: Thomas Jefferson in Bourbon France." *Political Science Quarterly* 72, no. 3 (1957): 388–404.

Paquette, Gabriel. "The Brazilian Origins of the 1826 Portuguese Constitution." *European History Quarterly* 41, no. 3 (July 2011): 444–71.

Parasiliti, Andrew T. "The Causes and Timing of Iraq's Wars: A Power Cycle Assessment." *International Political Science Review* 24, no. 1 (January 2003): 151–65.

Parsi, Trita. *Treacherous Alliance: The Secret Dealings of Israel, Iran, and the United States.* New Haven: Yale University Press, 2007.

Parssinen, T. M. "The Revolutionary Party in London, 1816–20." *Bulletin of the Institute of Historical Research* 45, no. 111 (May 1972): 266–82.

Patterson, A. Temple. *The Other Armada: The Franco-Spanish Attempt to Invade Britain in 1779.* Manchester: Manchester University Press, 1960.

Payne, Stanley G. *Civil War in Europe, 1905–1949.* New York: Cambridge University Press, 2011.

Payne, Stanley G. *A History of Fascism, 1914–1945.* Madison: The University of Wisconsin Press, 1995.

Payne, Stanley G. "Soviet Anti-Fascism: Theory and Practice, 1921–1945." *Totalitarian Movements and Political Religions* 4, no. 2 (2003): 1–62.

Pearce, Brian. *How Haig Saved Lenin.* London: Macmillan, 1987.

Pearlman, Wendy. "Emotions and the Microfoundations of the Arab Uprisings." *Perspectives on Politics* 11, no. 2 (June 2013): 387–409.

Peterson, J. E. *Oman's Insurgencies: The Sultanate's Struggle for Supremacy.* London: Saqi, 2007.

Pettrachi, Giorgio. *La Russia rivoluzionaria nella politica italiana: Le relazioni italo-sovietiche, 1917–1925.* Rome: Gius. Laterza & Figli, 1982.

Phelps, Reginald H. "'Before Hitler Came': Thule Society and Germanen Orden." *The Journal of Modern History* 35, no. 3 (1963): 245–61.

Pierret, Thomas. *Religion and State in Syria: The Sunni Ulama from Coup to Revolution.* New York: Cambridge University Press, 2013.

Pierson, Stanley. *Marxism and the Origins of British Socialism.* Ithaca: Cornell University Press, 1973.

Pilbeam, Pamela M. *Republicanism in Nineteenth-Century France, 1814–1871.* London: Macmillan, 1995.

Pinto, António Costa, and Aristotle Kallis. *Rethinking Fascism and Dictatorship in Europe.* New York: Palgrave Macmillan, 2014.

Piscatori, James P. *Islam in a World of Nation-States.* New York: Cambridge University Press, 1986.

Polasky, Janet L. *Revolution in Brussels.* Hanover: University Press of New England, 1987.

Polasky, Janet L. *Revolutions Without Borders: The Call to Liberty in the Atlantic World.* New Haven: Yale University Press, 2015.

Pons, Silvio. *The Global Revolution: A History of International Communism, 1917–1991.* New York: Oxford University Press, 2014.

Poole, Robert. *Peterloo: The English Uprising.* New York: Oxford University Press, 2019.

Popkin, Jeremy D. "Dutch Patriots, French Journalists, and the Declarations of Rights: The *Leidse Ontwerp* of 1785 and Its Diffusion in France." *The Historical Journal* 38, no. 3 (September 1995): 553–65.

Popkin, Jeremy D. "Print Culture in the Netherlands on the Eve of the Revolution." In *The Dutch Republic in the Eighteenth Century: Decline, Enlightenment, and Revolution,* edited by Margaret C. Jacob and Wijnand Mijnhardt, 273–91. Ithaca: Cornell University Press, 1992.

Potthoff, Heinrich, and Susanne Miller. *The Social Democratic Party of Germany.* Translated by Martin Kane. Bonn: Dietz, 2006.

Price, Munro. "The Dutch Affair and the Fall of the Ancien Régime, 1784–1787." *The Historical Journal* 38, no. 4 (1995): 875–905.

Price, Munro. *Preserving the Monarchy: The Comte de Vergennes, 1774–1787.* New York: Cambridge University Press, 1995.

Prousis, Theophilus C. *Russian Society and the Greek Revolution.* DeKalb: Northern Illinois University Press, 1994.

Quennell, Peter, ed. *The Private Letters of Princess Lieven to Prince Metternich, 1820–1826.* New York: E.P. Dutton, 1938.

Raeff, Marc. *Plans for Political Reform in Imperial Russia, 1730–1905.* Englewood Cliffs: Prentice Hall, 1966.

Rainbolt, John C. "Americans' Initial View of Their Revolution's Significance for Other Peoples, 1776–1788." *The Historian* 35, no. 3 (1973): 418–33.

Rajaee, Farhang. *Islamic Values and World View: Khomeini on Man, the State, and International Politics.* Lanham: University Press of America, 1983.

Rangwala, Glen. "The Finances of War: Iraq, Credit and Conflict, September 1980 to August 1990," in *The Iran-Iraq War: New International Perspectives,* eds. Nigel Ashton and Bryan Gibson, 92–105. New York Routledge, 2013.

Ramazani, R. K. *The Gulf Cooperation Council: Record and Analysis.* Charlottesville: University Press of Virginia, 1988.

Ramazani, R. K. "Khumayni's Islam in Iran's Foreign Policy." In *Islam in Foreign Policy,* edited by Adeed Dawisha, 9–32. New York: Cambridge University Press, 1983.

Ramazani, R. K. *Revolutionary Iran: Challenge and Response in the Middle East.* Baltimore: The Johns Hopkins University Press, 1988.

Rath, R. John. *The Provisional Austrian Regime in Lombardy-Venetia.* Austin: University of Texas Press, 1969.

Reed, John. *Ten Days That Shook the World.* New York: Boni and Liveright, 1919.

Rees, Tim, and Andrew Thorpe. *International Communism and the Communist International.* Manchester: Manchester University Press, 1998.

Regan, Patrick M. *Civil Wars and Foreign Powers: Outside Intervention in Intrastate Conflict.* Ann Arbor: University of Michigan Press, 2000.

Reinerman, Alan. "Metternich and the Papal Condemnation of the 'Carbonari,' 1821." *The Catholic Historical Review* 54, no. 1 (April 1968): 55–69.

Reinerman, Alan J. *Austria and the Papacy in the Age of Metternich: Between Conflict and Cooperation, 1809–1830.* Vol. I. Washington, D.C.: The Catholic University Press of America, 1979.

Reinerman, Alan J. "Metternich, Alexander I, and the Russian Challenge in Italy, 1815–20." *The Journal of Modern History* 46, no. 2 (June 1974): 262–76.

Reinerman, Alan J. "Metternich, the Papacy, and the Greek Revolution." *East European Quarterly* 12, no. 2 (Summer 1978): 177–88.

Rendall, Matthew. "Russia, the Concert of Europe, and Greece, 1821–29: A Test of Hypotheses About the Vienna System." *Security Studies* 9, no. 4 (Summer 2000): 52–90.

Resnick, Daniel Phillip. *The White Terror and the Political Reaction After Waterloo.* Cambridge, MA: Harvard University Press, 1966.

Riddell, John. *Founding the Communist International: Proceedings and Documents of the First Congress, March 1919.* New York: Pathfinder Book, 1987.

Rodríguez, Mario. "The Presence of the American Revolution in the Contemporaneous Spanish World." *Proceedings of the Pacific Coast Council on Latin American Studies* 6 (1977–79): 15–24.

Rogger, Hans. "Was There a Russian Fascism? The Union of Russian People." *The Journal of Modern History* 36, no. 4 (1964): 398–415.

Romani, George T. *The Neapolitan Revolution of 1820–1821.* Evanston: Northwestern University Press, 1950.

Rosenbaum, Kurt. *Community of Fate: German-Soviet Diplomatic Relations 1922–1928.* Syracuse: Syracuse University Press, 1965.

Rouleau, Eric. "Who Killed Sadat?" *MERIP Reports* 103 (February 1982): 3–5.

Royle, Edward, and James Walvin. *English Radicals and Reformers, 1760–1848.* Lexington: The University Press of Kentucky, 1982.

Royle, Edward. *Revolutionary Britannia? Reflections on the Threat of Revolution in Britain.* Manchester: Manchester University Press, 2000.

Rubin, Lawrence. *Islam in the Balance: Ideational Threats in Arab Politics.* Stanford: Stanford University Press, 2014.

Safran, Nadav. *Saudi Arabia: The Ceaseless Quest for Security.* Ithaca: Cornell University Press, 1988.

Salisbury, Christopher G. "For Your Freedom and Ours: The Polish Question in Wilson's Peace Initiatives, 1916–1917." *Australian Journal of Politics and History* 49, no. 4 (2003): 481–500.

Salman al-Saud, Faisal. *Iran, Saudi Arabia and the Gulf.* New York: I. B. Tauris, 2003.

Sambanis, Nicholas. "Do Ethnic and Non-Ethnic Civil Wars Have the Same Causes? A Theoretical and Empirical Inquiry (Part 1)." *Journal of Conflict Resolution* 45, no. 3 (2001): 259–82.

Sassoon, Donald. *One Hundred Years of Socialism: The West European Left in the Twentieth Century*. New York: I. B. Tauris, 1996.

Savigear, P. "Carbonarism and the French Army, 1815–1824." *History* 54, no. 181 (June 1969): 198–211.

Schahgaldian, Nikola B., and Gina Barkhordarian. *The Iranian Military Under the Islamic Republic*. Santa Monica: Rand, 1987.

Schama, Simon. *Patriots and Liberators: Revolution in the Netherlands, 1780–1813*. New York: Alfred A Knopf, 1977.

Schapiro, J. Salwyn. *Condorcet and the Rise of Liberalism*. New York: Harcourt, Brace and Company, 1934.

Schelling, Thomas C. *The Strategy of Conflict*. Cambridge, MA: Harvard University Press, 1960.

Schinness, Roger. "The Conservative Party and Anglo-Soviet Relations." *European Studies Review* 7, no. 4 (1977): 393–407.

Schneer, Jonathan. *The Lockhart Plot: Love, Betrayal, Assassination and Counterrevolution in Lenin's Russia*. New York: Oxford University Press, 2020.

Schofield, Richard N. *Evolution of the Shatt Al-'Arab Boundary Dispute*. Cambridgeshire: Middle East and North African Studies Press, 1986.

Schorske, Carl E. *German Social Democracy, 1905–1917: The Development of the Great Schism*. Cambridge, MA: Harvard University Press, 1955.

Schroeder, Paul W. "Containment Nineteenth Century Style: How Russia Was Restrained." *The South Atlantic Quarterly* 82, no. 1 (1983): 1–18.

Schroeder, Paul W. "Did the Vienna Settlement Rest on a Balance of Power?" *The American Historical Review* 97, no. 3 (1992): 683–706.

Schroeder, Paul W. *Metternich's Diplomacy at Its Zenith, 1820–1823*. Austin: University of Texas Press, 1962.

Schroeder, Paul W. *The Transformation of European Politics, 1763–1848*. New York: Oxford University Press, 1994.

Schulte Nordholt, J. W. "The Impact of the American Revolution on the Dutch Republic." In *The Impact of the American Revolution Abroad*, 41–63. Washington, DC: Library of Congress, 1976.

Schulte Nordholt, Jan Willem. *The Dutch Republic and American Independence*. Translated by Herbert H. Rowen. Chapel Hill: University of North Carolina Press, 1982.

Schultz, Kenneth A., and Henk E. Goemans. "Aims, Claims, and the Bargaining Model of War." *International Theory* 11, no. 3 (2019): 344–74.

Scott, H. M. *British Foreign Policy in the Age of the American Revolution*. Oxford: Clarendon Press, 1990.

Scott, H. M. "Sir Joseph Yorke, Dutch Politics and the Origins of the Fourth Anglo-Dutch War." *The Historical Journal* 31, no. 3 (1988): 571–89.

Seale, Patrick. *Asad of Syria: The Struggle for the Middle East*. Berkeley: University of California Press, 1989.

Service, Robert. *Lenin: A Political Life*. Vol. 3. Bloomington: Indiana University Press, 1995.

Service, Robert. *Spies and Commissars*. New York: Public Affairs, 2012.

Shama, Nael. *Egyptian Foreign Policy from Mubarak to Morsi: Against the National Interest.* New York: Routledge, 2014.

Shepard, William E. "Sayyid Qutb's Doctrine of 'Jajiliyya.'" *International Journal of Middle East Studies* 35, no. 4 (November 2003): 521–45.

Shlapentokh, Vladimir. "Perceptions of Foreign Threats to the Regime: From Lenin to Putin." *Communist and Post-Communist Studies* 42, no. 3 (2009): 305–24.

Shorrock, William I. *From Ally to Enemy: The Enigma of Fascist Italy in French Diplomacy.* Kent: Kent State University Press, 1988.

Siemann, Wolfram. *Metternich: Strategist and Visionary.* Translated by Daniel Steuer. Cambridge, MA: Harvard University Press, 2019.

Simmons, Beth A., and Zachary Elkins. "The Globalization of Liberalization: Policy Diffusion in the International Political Economy." *American Political Science Review* 98, no. 1 (2004): 171–89.

Simmons, Beth A., Frank Dobbin, and Geoffrey Garrett. "Introduction: The International Diffusion of Liberalism." *International Organization* 60, no. 4 (2006): 781–810.

Simon, Michael W., and Erik Gartzke. "Political System Similarity and the Choice of Allies: Do Democracies Flock Together, or Do Opposites Attract?" *Journal of Conflict Resolution* 40, no. 4 (1996): 617–35.

Simon, Walter M. *The Failure of the Prussian Reform Movement, 1807–1819.* Ithaca: Cornell University Press, 1955.

Sivan, Emmanuel. "Sunni Radicalism in the Middle East and the Iranian Revolution." *International Journal of Middle East Studies* 21, no. 1 (February 1989): 1–30.

Skak, Mette. "Russian Strategic Culture: The Role of Today's *Chekisty.*" *Contemporary Politics* 22, no. 3 (2016): 324–41.

Skidmore, David, ed. *Contested Social Orders and International Politics.* Nashville: Vanderbilt University Press, 1997.

Skocpol, Theda. *States and Social Revolutions: A Comparative Analysis of France, Russia, and China.* New York: Cambridge University Press, 1979.

Skuy, David. *Assassination, Politics and Miracles: France and the Royalist Reaction of 1820.* Montreal: McGill-Queen's University Press, 2003.

Slater, Jerome. "The Domino Theory and International Politics: The Case of Vietnam." *Security Studies* 3, no. 2 (1993): 186–224.

Slater, Jerome. "Dominos in Central America: Will They Fall? Does It Matter?" *International Security* 12, no. 2 (1987): 105–34.

Smele, Jonathan D. *The "Russian" Civil Wars, 1916–1926.* London: Hurst & Company, 2015.

Smith, Alastair. "Diversionary Foreign Policy in Democratic Systems." *International Studies Quarterly* 40, no. 1 (1996): 133–53.

Smith, Page. *John Adams,* Volume I, *1735–1784.* Garden City: Doubleday & Company, 1962.

Smyth, Gillespie, ed. *Memoirs and Correspondence (Official and Familiar) of Sir Robert Murray Keith.* Vol. 2. London: Henry Colburn, 1849.

Snyder, Robert S. "The U.S. and Third World Revolutionary States: Understanding the Breakdown in Relations." *International Studies Quarterly* 43, no. 2 (1999): 265–90.

Sorel, Albert. *Europe and the French Revolution: The Political Traditions of the Old Regime.* Translated by Alfred Cobban and J. W. Hunt. London: Collins, 1969 [1885].

Soucy, Robert. *French Fascism: The First Wave, 1924–1933.* New Haven: Yale University Press, 1986.

Soucy, Robert. *French Fascism: The Second Wave, 1933–1939*. New Haven: Yale University Press, 1995.

Soucy, Robert. "Problematising the Immunity Thesis." In *France in the Era of Fascism: Essays on the French Authoritarian Right*, edited by Brian Jenkins, 65–104. New York: Berghahn Books, 2005.

Soulavie, John Lewis. *Historical and Political Memoirs of the Reign of Lewis XVI*. Vol. V. London: G. and J. Robinson, 1802.

Spellanzon, Cesare. *Storia del risorgimento e dell'unità d'Italia*. Vol. 1. Milan: Rizzoli, 1933.

Spitzer, Alan B. *Old Hatreds and Young Hopes: The French Carbonari Against the Bourbon Restoration*. Cambridge, MA: Harvard University Press, 1971.

St. Clair, William. *That Greece Might Still Be Free: The Philhellenes in the War of Independence*. London: Oxford University Press, 1972.

Steenson, Gary P. *"Not One Man! Not One Penny!": German Social Democracy, 1863–1914*. Pittsburgh: University of Pittsburgh Press, 1981.

Stein, Arthur A. "Conflict and Cohesion: A Review of the Literature." *The Journal of Conflict Resolution* 20, no. 1 (1976): 143–72.

Stein, Arthur A. *Why Nations Cooperate: Circumstance and Choice in International Relations*. Ithaca: Cornell University Press, 1990.

Stein, Ewan. *Representing Israel in Modern Egypt: Ideas, Intellectuals and Foreign Policy from Nasser to Mubarak*. New York: I. B. Tauris, 2012.

Steiner, Zara. *The Lights That Failed: European International History 1919–1933*. New York: Oxford University Press, 2005.

Stephan, John J. *The Russian Fascists: Tragedy and Farce in Exile, 1925–1945*. New York: Harper & Row, 1978.

Sternhell, Zeev. *Neither Right nor Left: Fascist Ideology in France*. Translated by David Maisel. Berkeley: University of California Press, 1986.

Sternhell, Zeev, with Mario Sznajder and Maia Asheri. *The Birth of Fascist Ideology*. Translated by David Maisel. Princeton: Princeton University Press, 1994.

Stevens, John. *England's Last Revolution: Pentrich, 1817*. Buxton: Moorland Publishing Company, 1977.

Stevenson, David. "The Failure of Peace by Negotiation in 1917." *The Historical Journal* 34, no. 1 (March 1991): 65–86.

Stites, Richard. "Decembrists with a Spanish Accent." *Kritika: Explorations in Russian and Eurasian History* 12, no. 1 (Winter 2011): 5–23.

Stites, Richard. *The Four Horsemen: Riding to Liberty in Post-Napoleonic Europe*. New York: Oxford University Press, 2014.

Stocker, Paul. "Importing Fascism: Reappraising the British Fascisti, 1923–1926." *Contemporary British History* 30, no. 3 (2016): 326–48.

Stone, Bailey. *The Anatomy of Revolution Revisited: A Comparative Analysis of England, France, and Russia*. New York: Cambridge University Press, 2014.

Strang, David. "Adding Social Structure to Diffusion Models: An Event History Framework." *Sociological Methods and Research* 19, no. 3 (1991): 324–53.

Swearingen, Will D. "Geopolitical Origins of the Iran-Iraq War." *Geographical Review* 78, no. 4 (October 1988): 405–16.

Sweet, Paul R. *Friedrich von Gentz: Defender of the Old Order*. Madison: University of Wisconsin Press, 1941.

Sweets, John F. "Hold That Pendulum! Redefining Fascism, Collaborationism and Resistance in France." *French Historical Studies* 15, no. 4 (1988): 731–58.

Tannenbaum, Edward R. *The Action Française: Die-Hard Reactionaries in Twentieth Century France*. New York: John Wiley & Sons, 1962.

Tarar, Ahmer. "Diversionary Incentives and the Bargaining Approach to War." *International Studies Quarterly* 50, no. 1 (2006): 169–88.

Tareke, Gebru. "The Ethiopia-Somalia War of 1977 Revisited." *International Journal of African Historical Studies* 33, no. 3 (2000): 635–67.

Taylor, Brian D. *The Code of Putinism*. New York: Oxford University Press, 2018.

Te Brake, Wayne P. "Provincial Histories and National Revolution in the Dutch Republic." In *The Dutch Republic in the Eighteenth Century: Decline, Enlightenment, and Revolution*, edited by Margaret C. Jacob and Wijnand Mijnhardt, 60–90. Ithaca: Cornell University Press, 1992.

Teitelbaum, Joshua. "The Muslim Brotherhood in Syria, 1945–1958: Founding, Social Origins, Ideology." *The Middle East Journal* 65, no. 2 (Spring 2011): 213–33.

Temperley, Harold, and Lillian M. Penson. *Foundations of British Foreign Policy from Pitt to Salisbury: Documents Old and New*. London: Cambridge University Press, 1938.

Temperley, Harold. *The Foreign Policy of Canning, 1822–1827*. London: Archon Books, 1966.

Terhalle, Maximilian. "Revolutionary Power and Socialization: Explaining the Persistence of Revolutionary Zeal in Iran's Foreign Policy." *Security Studies* 18, no. 3 (2009): 557–86.

Thackeray, Frank W. *Antecedents of Revolution: Alexander I and the Polish Kingdom, 1815–1825*. New York: Columbia University Press, 1980.

Therry, R., ed. *The Speeches of the Right Honourable George Canning*. Vol. 6. London: James Ridgway & Sons, 1836.

Thomis, Malcom I., and Peter Holt. *Threats of Revolution in Britain, 1789–1848*. London: The Macmillan Press, 1977.

Thompson, Wayne C. "Voyage on Uncharted Seas: Kurt Riezler and German Policy Towards Russia, 1914–1918." *East European Quarterly* 12, no. 2 (1980): 171–88.

Thurlow, Richard. *Fascism in Britain*. London: I. B. Tauris, 1998.

Thurlow, Richard. "Passive and Active Anti-Fascism: The State and National Security, 1923–45." In *Varieties of Anti-Fascism: Britain in the Inter-War Period*, edited by Nigel Copsey and Andrzej Olechnowicz, 162–80. London: Palgrave Macmillan, 2010.

Tilly, Charles. *European Revolutions, 1492–1992*. Cambridge: Wiley-Blackwell, 1996.

Tir, Jaroslav. "Territorial Diversion: Diversionary Theory of War and Territorial Conflict." *The Journal of Politics* 72, no. 2 (2010): 413–25.

Tooze, Adam. *The Deluge: The Great War, America, and the Remaking of the Global Order, 1916–1931*. New York: Penguin Books, 2014.

Torunsky, Vera. *Entente der Revisionisten? Mussolini und Stresemann 1922–1929*. Keulen-Wenen: Böhlau, 1986.

Toth, James. *Sayyid Qutb: The Life and Legacy of a Radical Islamic Intellectual*. New York: Oxford University Press, 2013.

Trachtenberg, Marc. *Reparations in World Politics: France and European Economic Diplomacy, 1916–1923*. New York: Columbia University Press, 1980.

Trachtenberg, Marc. "Versailles Revisited." *Security Studies* 9, no. 3 (2007): 191–205.

Trofimov, Yaroslav. *The Siege of Mecca: The 1979 Uprising at Islam's Holiest Shrine*. New York: Anchor Books, 2007.

Trotsky, Leon. *Problems of Civil War*. New York: Pathfinder Press, 1970.

Turner, Henry Ashby, Jr. *German Big Business and the Rise of Hitler*. New York: Oxford University Press, 1985.

Turner, R. T. "Europe and the Belgian Revolution, 1789–90." PhD thesis, University of California, Los Angeles, 1944.

Ulam, Adam B. *Expansion and Coexistence*. New York: Praeger Publishers, 1968.

Uldricks, Teddy J. *Diplomacy and Ideology*. London: Sage Publications Ltd., 1979.

Ullman, Richard H. *The Anglo-Soviet Accord*. Princeton: Princeton University Press, 1972.

Van Dam, Nikolaos. *The Struggle for Power in Syria: Politics and Society Under Asad and the Ba'th Party*. 4th ed. London: I. B. Tauris, 2011.

Van Tyne, C. H. "French Aid Before the Alliance of 1778." *The American Historical Review* 31, no. 1 (1925): 20–40.

Vanderhill, Rachel. "Active Resistance to Democratic Diffusion." *Communist and Post-Communist Studies* 50, no. 1 (2017): 41–51.

Vane, Charles William, Third Marquess of Londonderry, ed. *Correspondence, Despatches, and Other Papers, of Viscount Castlereagh, Second Marquess of Londonderry*. Vol. 12. London: John Murray, 1853.

Venturi, Franco. *The End of the Old Regime in Europe, 1776–1789*. Translated by R. Burr Litchfield. Vol. 2. Princeton: Princeton University Press, 1991.

Vernadsky, George. "Reforms Under Czar Alexander I: French and American Influences." *The Review of Politics* 9, no. 1 (January 1947): 47–64.

Von Riekhoff, Harald. *German-Polish Relations, 1918–1933*. Baltimore: Johns Hopkins University Press, 1971.

Wade, Rex A. *The Russian Search for Peace*. Stanford: Stanford University Press, 1969.

Waite, Robert G. L. *Vanguard of Nazism*. Cambridge, MA: Harvard University Press, 1952.

Walldorf, C. William, Jr. *To Shape Our World for Good: Master Narratives and Regime Change in U.S. Foreign Policy, 1900–2001*. Ithaca: Cornell University Press, 2019.

Walt, Stephen M. *The Origins of Alliances*. Ithaca: Cornell University Press, 1987.

Walt, Stephen M. *Revolution and War*. Ithaca: Cornell University Press, 1996.

Walt, Stephen M. "Why the Tunisian Revolution Won't Spread." *Foreign Policy*, January 16 2011.

Waltz, Kenneth. *Theory of International Politics*. Reading: Addison-Wesley, 1979.

Wandycz, Piotr S. *France and Her Eastern Allies, 1919–1925*. Minneapolis: University of Minnesota Press, 1962.

Ward, A. W., and G. P. Gooch, eds. *The Cambridge History of British Foreign Policy, 1783–1919*, Vol. II, *1815–1866*. New York: Macmillan, 1923.

Webster, C. K. *The Congress of Vienna, 1814–1815*. London: G. Bell & Sons, 1934.

Webster, Charles. *The Foreign Policy of Castlereagh, 1815–1822*. London: G. Bell and Sons, 1947.

Weis, Eberhard. "Enlightenment and Absolutism in the Holy Roman Empire: Thoughts on Enlightened Absolutism in Germany." *The Journal of Modern History* 58 (1986): S181–S197.

Werner, Suzanne, and Douglas Lemke. "Opposites Do Not Attract: The Impact of Domestic Institutions, Power, and Prior Commitments on Alignment Choices." *International Studies Quarterly* 41 (1997): 529–46.

Weyland, Kurt. "The Arab Spring: Why the Surprising Similarities with the Revolutionary Wave of 1848?" *Perspectives on Politics* 10, no. 4 (December 2012): 917–34.

Weyland, Kurt. "Crafting Counterrevolution: How Reactionaries Learned to Combat Change in 1848." *American Political Science Review* 110, no. 2 (2016): 215–31.

Weyland, Kurt. "The Diffusion of Revolution: '1848' in Europe and Latin America." *International Organization* 63, no. 2 (2009): 391–423.

Weyland, Kurt. *Making Waves: Democratic Contention in Europe and Latin America Since the Revolutions of 1848*. New York: Cambridge University Press, 2014.

Wharton, Francis. *The Revolutionary Diplomatic Correspondence of the United States*. Vol. 2. Washington, DC: Government Printing Office, 1889.

Whatmore, Richard. *Against War and Empire: Geneva, Britain, and France in the Eighteenth Century*. New Haven: Yale University Press, 2012.

Wheeler-Bennett, John W. *Brest-Litovsk, the Forgotten Peace, March 1918*. London: Macmillan & Co., 1963.

Whitaker, Arthur P. "The Pseudo-Aranda Memoir of 1783." *The Hispanic American Historical Review* 17, no. 3 (1937): 287–313.

White, Eugene Nelson. "Was There a Solution to the Ancien Régime's Financial Dilemma?" *The Journal of Economic History* 49, no. 3 (September 1989): 545–68.

White, Stephen. *Britain and the Bolshevik Revolution: A Study in the Politics of Diplomacy, 1920–1924*. New York: Holmes & Meier, 1979.

White, Stephen. "Soviets in Britain: The Leeds Convention of 1917." *International Review of Social History* 19, no. 2 (1974): 165–93.

Whitehead, Laurence. *The International Dimensions of Democratization: Europe and the Americas*. New York: Oxford University Press, 2001.

Whiteman, Jeremy J. *Reform, Revolution and French Global Policy, 1787–1791*. Burlington: Ashgate, 2003.

Wickham, Carrie Rosefsky. *The Muslim Brotherhood: Evolution of an Islamist Movement*. Princeton: Princeton University Press, 2013.

Wieczynski, Joseph L. "The Mutiny of the Semenovsky Regiment in 1820." *Russian Review* 29, no. 2 (April 1970): 167–80.

Wiley, Joyce N. *The Islamic Movement of Iraqi Shi'as*. Boulder: Lynne Rienner Publishers, 1992.

Williams, Charles. *Adenauer: The Father of the New Germany*. London: Little, Brown and Company, 2000.

Williamson, Philip. "The Conservative Party, Fascism and Anti-Fascism 1918–1939." In *Varieties of Anti-Fascism: Britain in the Inter-War Period*, edited by Nigel Copsey and Andrzej Olechnowicz, 73–97. New York: Palgrave Macmillan, 2010.

Witt, Pierre de. *Une invasion prussienne en Hollande en 1787*. Paris: E. Plon, Nourrit et Cie, 1886.

Wohl, Robert. *French Communism in the Making, 1914–1924*. Stanford: Stanford University Press, 1966.

Woodhouse, C. M. *Capodistria: The Founder of Greek Independence*. London: Oxford University Press, 1973.

Woodhouse, C. M. *The Philhellenes*. London: Hodder and Stoughton, 1969.

Woods, Kevin M., Williamson Murray, and Thomas Holaday. *Saddam's War: An Iraqi Military Perspective of the Iran-Iraq War*. McNair Paper 70. Washington, DC: National Defense University Press, 2009.

Woods, Kevin M., Williamson Murray, Elizabeth A. Nathan, Laila Sabara, and Ana M. Venegas. *Saddam's Generals: Perspectives of the Iran-Iraq War*. Alexandria: Institute for Defense Analyses, 2011.

Worrall, David. *Radical Culture: Discourse, Resistance and Surveillance, 1790–1820*. Detroit: Wayne State University Press, 1992.

Wright, Almon R. "The Aranda Memorial: Genuine or Forged?" *The Hispanic American Historical Review* 17, no. 3 (1938): 445–60.

Wright, Gordon. *France in Modern Times.* New York: W. W. Norton & Company, 1995.

Wright, Jonathan. *Gustav Stresemann: Weimar's Greatest Statesman.* Oxford: Oxford University Press, 2002.

Yamada, Norihito. "George Canning and the Spanish Question, September 1822 to March 1823." *The Historical Journal* 52, no. 2 (June 2009): 343–62.

Yonge, Charles Duke, ed. *Life and Administration of Robert Banks, Second Earl of Liverpool, K.G., Late First Lord of the Treasury: Compiled from Original Documents.* Vol. II. London: Macmillan and Co., 1868.

Zabih, Sepehr. *The Iranian Military in Revolution and War.* New York: Routledge, 1998.

Zaretsky, Robert D. "Neither Left, nor Right, nor Straight Ahead: Recent Books on Fascism in France." *The Journal of Modern History* 73, no. 1 (2011): 118–32.

Zeman, Z. A. B. *Germany and the Revolution in Russia, 1915–1918.* London: Oxford University Press, 1958.

Zeman, Z. A. B., and W. B. Scharlau. *The Merchant of Revolution.* London: Oxford University Press, 1965.

Ziegler, Philip. *Addington: A Life of Henry Addington, First Viscount Sidmouth.* London: Collins, 1965.

Index

Abu Bakr, 175
Action Committees for Roman Universality (CAUR), 150–51
Action Française, 155–56, 161
Adams, John, 35–36
Addington, Henry (Lord Sidmouth), 90
Adenauer, Konrad, 168
Affaires de l'Angleterre et de l'Amérique, 50
Aggelopoulos, Georgios (Patriarch of Constantinople Gregory V), 105
al-Jihad, 180, 206
al-Saud, Abdullah bin Abdulaziz (King Abdullah), 221
al-Saud, Fahd bin Abdulaziz (Crown Prince Fahd), 207, 209, 210n152
al-'Utaybi, Juhayman, 182
al-Assad, Bashir, 221–22
al-Assad, Hafez, 180, 184, 187, 187n43, 197–203, 200n103, 215
al-Banna, Hasan, 205
al-Hakim, Muhammad Baqir, 196
al-Huda, Bint, 192
al-Sadr, Grand Ayatollah Muhammad Baqir, 181, 190–93, 195–96, 214
al-Suri, Abu Mus'ab, 205
Albert, Charles, 79
Alexander I (Emperor of Russia), 83–84, 92, 94, 97, 100–9, 116
Algiers Accord, 186, 189, 191–92, 210
All-Russian Fascist Party, 154
Amal Party, 201
American embassy takeover (1979), 174
American Revolution, 7, 28–29, 32–33, 38, 39, 57, 78, 95, 113, 225n16
   American goals, 34, 36n10
   American propaganda, 34–35
   Austrian policy toward, 28, 55–57
   British policy toward, 33n3, 34
   French policy toward, 7, 28–29, 32–33, 33n5, 44–51, 57–58, 75–76, 217
   French propaganda, 50
   effect on French Revolution, 75n138
   as a model, 33–34, 36, 56, 59n85, 113
   as a platform, 33–36, 113
   Prussian policy toward, 28, 54–55
   Spanish policy toward, 28–29, 32, 33n5, 34, 34n4, 46–52, 57–58
   Russian policy toward, 28, 52–54

Anglo-Dutch War (1780–84), 59, 61–62
Antoinette, Marie, 85
Arab Cold War, 1, 184, 223
Arab Spring, 220–21
Arab triangle, 184
Aranda, Pedro, 47, 47n38, 51, 55
Aron, Raymond, 1
Arouet, François-Marie (Voltaire), 37
Assembly of Notables (France), 67, 73n112
Austrian Netherlands, 39, 56, 64, 68, 72n132, 73n134, 74, 74n137, 77
Aziz, Tariq, 192, 196, 214

Balance of power, 2n3, 4–5, 16, 45, 51, 63, 64n90, 106n89, 118, 126–27, 132, 137–39, 141, 147, 157, 163, 170–71, 173, 185, 188, 195, 211, 215, 221, 229, *see also* geopolitics/ geopolitical advantage, realism, realpolitik, spheres of influence
Balfour, James (Lord Balfour), 138
Baram, Amatzia, 195
Bastianini, Giuseppe, 150
Batavus, Willem (William V, Prince of Orange), 35–36, 58–59, 61–62, 65–68, 70–72, 75
Ba'th Party/Ba'th regime, Iraq, 181, 189–92, 190n49, 193n71, 195–96, 199, 199n102, 202, 213, 214n167
Ba'th Party/Ba'th regime, Syria, 178, 180, 186, 215
Ba'thist rivalry, Iraq and Syria, 184–85, 199
Bavarian Soviet Republic, 135
Bazargan, Mehdi, 174, 190, 192, 194, 208
Beer Hall Putsch, 153, 165
Belarusian democratic protests (2020), 222
Belgium, revolt in (1789–90), 72–73, *see also* Austrian Netherlands
Bernstein, Edward, 122n11
Bismarck, Otto von, 123, 125
Blanketeers, 89
Bolshevism, 119–20, 122n11, 128, 128n25, 131, 142, *see also* communism/socialism, Russian Revolution, socialism
   aims, 119–20
   Bolshevik propaganda, 135–36, 142, 146, 224
   foreign policy, 120, 130–31
   as an ideological threat, 30, 171
Bonapartism, 87
Bourbon Restoration (France), 87, 88n33, 92
Boutros-Ghali, Boutros, 203

de Brienne, Loménie, 70
British Communist Party, 152
British Fascisti, 153, 153n123
British Union of Fascists (BUF), 151, 153,
    162–63
Bucard, Marcel 155
Bukharin, Nikolai, 130
burghers (Dutch Republic), 59
Burke, Edmund, 15n10
Byron, George Gordon (Lord Byron), 80n2
Byzantine Empire, 93

Camp David Accords, 200, 205
Canning, George, 108–9, 108n101, 110–12, 114
Carbonari, 79, 81, 88, 94, 105n86
Carley, Michael, 14.
Carlsbad Decrees, 85, 94, 98
Cartel of the Left, 155, 161
Cassels, Alan, 161
Castries, Charles Eugène Gabriel de La Croix de
    (marquis de Castries), 70
Catherine the Great (Empress of Russia), 37, 39,
    52–54, 61, 72, 93, 104
    Greek Project, 53
Cato Street Conspiracy, 89, 90, 113
Cecil, Robert, 131, 135
Center Party (Germany), 168
Central Treaty Organization (CENTO), 190
Chamberlain, Austen, 160
Charbonnerie, 88, 107
Charles III (King of Spain), 40, 45–47,
    47n38, 51
Charter of 1814, 87
Chateaubriand, François-René de, 109, 114
Chiaramonti, Barnaba Niccolò Maria Luigi,
    (Pope Pius VII), 105, 105n86
Churchill, Winston, 135, 160, 171
Cobbet, William, 88
Cold War, 1, 5n9, 19, 121
collective action problem, 10
colonial revolts, 39n21, 40–42, 51, 57–58
Comintern, 30, 120–21, 144, 146, 164, 168
Committee for Organizing a Provisional
    Government (Britain), 89
communism/socialism, 7, 14, 19, 27, 29–30,
    120, 124, 126, 142, 146, 162–63, 172, 181,
    204, 218
    American fear of, 5n9
    definition of, 122n11
    development of, 122
    versus fascism, 21, 30, 118, 149, 165, 167, 218
Comunero Rebellion, 40
Condorcet, Nicholas de, 38, 75

Congress of Vienna system, 92, 94, 117n125,
    217, 220
Consalvi, Ercole (Cardinal Consalvi), 100n66
cordon sanitaire, 136, 139
Corfu incident, 160–61
Cortes (Spanish legislature), 110–11
counterrevolutionary strategies, 140–41, 218
    censorship, 22, 50, 86–87, 91, 102
    co-option, 15, 87, 174, 182, 191, 206, 209
    covert activities, 22, 91, 114, 132–34, 132n42
    repression, 10, 14, 22, 22n19, 85, 87, 91, 100,
        114, 116n122, 141, 153, 194, 198, 206,
        210, 218
Croix de Feu, 155–56, 155n132
Curzon, George, 160
Curzon Line, 140

Danubian Principalities, 79, 105, see also Greek
    Revolution
Dawes Plan, 147
Declaration of Independence, 33, 34, 36, 36n12
Declaration of Rights of Man, 75
democracy, 2–3, 5–6, 19, 22, 27–29, 32, 34,
    36–37, 59, 69–70, 73, 82, 94, 113, see also
    liberalism
democratic peace theory, 2
demonstration effect, 10, 10n1, 26, 32–33, 43,
    46, 57, 69, 129, 132, 179, 189, 228, see also
    diffusion, revolutions as models
Dhofar rebellion, 185, 186
Dickenson, John, 49n44
Diderot, Denis, 37, 38n18, 49n44
diffusion, 6, 10, 10n1, 228 see also demonstration
    effect, revolutions as models
Diplomatic Revolution, 43, 56
diversionary theory, 7, 227
Dmowski, Roman, 138–39
Dom Miguel I (King of Portugal), 110–11
Dom Pedro I (King of Portugal), 111, 111n110
domestic contagion effects theory, 5, 7, 14, 16–
    17, 20, 32, 57, 62, 93, 125–26, 134, 136, 145,
    147, 159, 170, 173, 188, 197, 213, 217–20,
    218n1, 223, 228
    case selection strategy, 20, 27–28, 119
    cooperation and conflict predictions, 95, 98,
        104, 116, 118, 211, 214–15, 217–20
    empirical support, 53, 55, 74, 78, 95, 98, 104,
        113, 136, 142, 159, 164, 168, 211, 217–20
    epidemiological analogy, 4, 9, 12, 26, 113,
        162, 213, 224
    theoretical typology, 16–17
domestic repression, 91, 141
domino theory, 5n9, 14

Dual Alliance, 125
Duesenberry, James, 10n1
Dutch Patriot Revolt (Dutch Democratic
    Revolution), 7, 28–29, 32, 58–60, 66, 68,
    70, 78, 95
    Austrian policy toward, 28, 64, 72–73
    British policy toward, 28, 50, 65–68, 71, 75
    contemporary perspectives, 73–74
    foreign policy prior to Revolt, 61
    French policy toward, 7, 28–29, 63–64,
        66–71, 74, 75, 217
    as a model, 60, 75, 113
    as a platform, 60, 113
    Prussian policy toward, 7, 28, 59, 65–68,
        75 see also Batavus, Willem (William V,
        Prince of Orange)
    recognition of America, 35
    Russian policy toward, 28, 72

Ebert, Friedrich, 168
Egyptian Islamic Jihad, 207, see also al-Jihad
Egyptian Revolution (1952), see Free Officers' coup
Egyptian Revolution (2011), 221
    Saudi response to, 221
Egyptian Islamic Jihad, see al-Jihad
Egyptian-Israeli peace, 180, 184–88, 197–98,
    203, 207
el-Sisi, Abdel Fattah, 221
Enlightenment, 37–40, 82, see also Radical
    Enlightenment
    political thought of 37, 42
    Russian Enlightenment, 39
Entente Cordial, 125

Falange, 151
Family Compact, 42
Fasci all'Estero, 150
fascism, 7, 20–21, 27, 29–30, 118, 152, 155–56,
    155n132, 158, 167, 171, 226n24
    definition of, 149n103
    contrast to liberalism and communism/
        socialism, 148–49, 158, 168, 171
    as a revolutionary movement, 148–49, 167
    as a transnational movement, 149–50, 156, 169
Fascist International, 150
Favier, Jean Louis, 49
February Revolution (Russia), 119, see also
    Provisional Government, Russian
    Revolution
Felix, Charles (King of Piedmont), 79
Ferdinand I (King of Naples), 79, 93, 102
Ferdinand VII (King of Spain), 79, 98, 107–9,
    109n105, 115

Ferdinand, Charles (duc de Berri), 87, 107, 113
Fighting Vanguard of the Mujahidin, 180,
    180n23, 198
Finnish Civil War, 131
focal points, 10, 10n1
Foch, Ferdinand, 135
Francis II (Emperor of Austria), 85–86, 86n27
Francistes, 154–55
Franklin, Benjamin, 35, 35n5, 55n74
Frederick the Great (King of Prussia), 37, 39,
    54–55, 61, 63–66
Frederick William II (King of Prussia), 66–68,
    71–72
Frederick William III (King of Prussia), 84
freemasonry, 37, 37n15
Free Officers' coup, 3n5, 13
Freikorps, 152, 168
French Revolution (1789), 7, 20, 32, 36n11,
    37–38, 38n18, 50, 56, 60, 69, 73–76,
    75n138, 90n46, 93, 146, 217, 225n16
    ideological effects of, 82, 91
    relationship to Enlightenment, 37
French Revolution (1830), 28n30, 108n99
French Revolution (1848), 28n30
French Revolutionary Wars, 1, 12, 18, 83, 92–93,
    146, 226n23
French Section of the Worker's International
    (SFIO), 122–23
Fürstenbund, 64n94

de Gálvez, Bernardo, 46
Gause III, F. Gregory, 192
General Confederation of Labor (CGT), 123
Geneva Revolution 35, 76–77
von Gentz, Friedrich, 101n71
Geopolitics/geopolitical advantage, 4–7, 5n9,
    14, 16, 18, 25, 29–30, 32, 54, 56, 63, 75–78,
    92–95, 97, 99, 102, 104, 106, 108, 112–13,
    115, 117, 119, 126–27, 140, 144, 189, 195,
    198, 211, 215, 217–18, 220–23 see also
    balance of power, realism, realpolitik,
    spheres of influence
George III (King of Britain), 33, 64n94, 67, 71, 88
George IV (King of Britain), 88
German Confederation, 85–86, 91–92, 100n68,
    see also Carlsbad Decrees
German Socialist Party, 152
German Nationalist Protection and Defiance
    Federation, 152
German National People's Party (DNVP), 153
German Völkisch Freedom Party (DVFP), 152
German unification, 125
Gibraltar, 42, 48–49, 52

Godwin, William, 71n125
Goebbels, Joseph, 163n156
Goldstone, Jack, 3n5
Goodarzi, Jubin, 202n117
Grand Mosque, seizure of, 182–83, 208–9
Gravier, Charles (comte de Vergennes), 44–48,
    51, 63–64, 64n90, 66–67, 69–70, 69n112,
    76, 76n148
Greek Revolution, 7, 28–29, 78, 79–80, 104–5
    Austrian policy toward, 105
    British policy toward, 106
    French policy toward, 105
    as a model, 80, 113
    as a platform, 81, 113
    Russian policy toward, 78, 104–6, 115–16
    nationalism as motivating force, 80
Grimaldi, Jerónimo, 46, 47n38, 51
Gulf Cooperation Council (GCC), 100n66, 212
Gunitsky, Seva, 5
Gustav III (King of Sweden), 76, 76n148,
    76n149

Haas, Mark, (*Ideological Origins of Great Power
    Politics*), 1–2, 26
von Hardenberg, Karl August, 85, 97
Harmsworth, Esmond (Lord Rothermere), 153
Harris, James (1st Earl of Malmesbury), 65,
    67–68, 71
Helphand, Alexander, 128
Hezbollah, 177, 177n13, 201
Hitler, Adolf, 147, 152, 163n156, 164–69
Hizb al-Tahrir, 181n24
Hizbullah Al-Hijaz, 210
Holy Alliance, 94, 94n55, 101–2, 107, 110–12
Hong Kong democratic protests (2019–20), 222
Hottoman, François, 49
House of Commons (Britain), 41, 90
Hungarian Soviet Republic, 135
Hunt, Henry, 89
Hussein, Saddam, 177, 181, 184–86, 189–97,
    193n73, 199, 199n102, 201–2, 210, 212,
    214, 223–24

ideology, 13, 228–29
    definition of, 5
    as justification for rule, 1, 11
ideological contagion, 3–4, 9, 13–14, 24,
    32, 158
    applied to liberalism, 6
    attenuation of, 223–25
    as a force for cooperation, 4, 15–18, 24, 85,
    96, 118, 144–45, 158, 227
    horizontal versus vertical diffusion, 10n1

    leaders' fear of, 4–5, 8–9, 12–14, 16–19, 22–23,
    27, 29, 33, 49–50, 52–53, 57, 65, 68, 70–71,
    76–78, 95–97, 99–100, 113–116, 118, 124,
    127, 136, 139, 141, 144–48, 157–59, 162–65,
    167, 169–71, 173–74, 187–89, 195–96,
    209–21, 228
ideological differences/similarities (ideological
    distance), 1–5, 7, 9, 12–13, 15, 17–18, 24,
    26–27, 43, 56, 62, 74–75, 78, 82, 95, 131,
    133, 137, 143, 158, 164, 171, 188, 196, 198,
    211, 217, 220, 222–23, 228
    effect on conflict and cooperation, 2, 26–27,
    32, 78, 96, 133–34, 211
    Shia and Sunni, differences between, 175,
    205, 215
ideological theory, 2, 24, 32, 43, 62, 95, 158–59,
    163–64, 171, 188, 217–18, 218n1, 220, 223
Igenhousz, Jan, 55
Ikhwan revolt, 182
Imperial Fascist League, 153
Indépendants, 87
Independent Social Democratic Party (USPD), 129
Iran hostage crisis, 199, 209
Iran-Iraq War, 173, 177–78, 187n44, 189, 193–96,
    193n73, 193n74, 202, 206, 210–11, 214–15,
    218, 226
    Iranian goals, 196
    Iraqi fear of contagion, 30–31, 174
    opportunism argument, 194, 194n81
    Saudi support for Iraq, 220
Iranian Revolution, 7, 30–31, 173–75
    Egyptian policy toward, 30, 173–174, 203–7
    Iraqi policy toward, 30, 173–74, 189–97, 190n49
    Iranian propaganda, 176–77, 210, 213–14
    as a model, 174–76, 178, 189, 203, 210,
    218–19
    as a platform, 30–31, 173–78, 189, 197–98,
    203, 207, 209–10, 213–14, 219, 226
    policy toward Iraq, 190n49, 193n71
    policy toward Saudi Arabia, 208, 211, 219
    policy toward Syria, 202–3
    Saudi policy toward, 30, 207–11, 211n159,
    218, 220
    Syrian policy toward, 30, 197–203, 207–11,
    213, 215, 219
Iron Guard, 151
Islamic Action Organization, 177, 181
Islamic Conference Organization, 212
Islamic Da'wa Party, 181, 190–96
Islamic Front for the Liberation of Bahrain, 177
Islamic Liberation Movement, 190
Islamic Liberation Organization (Munazzanat
    al Tahir al-Islami), 179–180, 179n21

Islamic Republican Party, 201
Islamic Revolution Organization in the Arabian
    Peninsula, 177, 183, 209
Islamism/political Islam, 3, 27, 30–31, 173–75,
    178, 183, 198, 221–22
Israel, Jonathan, 38n18
Italian fascist revolution, 7, 29, 118, 148–49,
    154, 160–61
    British policy toward, 118, 159–63, 168
    fascist policies, 160–161, 163, 166–68
    French policy toward, 118, 159–63, 168
    German policy toward, 118, 164–70, 218
    as a model, 118, 149–50
    as a platform, 118, 150–52, 168–69, 219
    Soviet policy toward, 118, 163–64, 168–69, 217
Italian Socialist Party (PSI), 123–24

Jacobinism, 85, 106, 114n118
von Jagow, Gottlieb, 128
jahiliyya, 179, 179n20
Jay, John, 48
Jefferson, Thomas, 36n11
Jenkinson, Robert Banks (2nd Earl of
    Liverpool), 90n46
Jervis, Robert, 14
John VI (King of Portugal), 79, 110–11
Joseph II (Emperor of Austria), 37, 39, 55–56,
    61, 64–65, 72–74, 92–93

Kagan, Korina, 106n89
Kaplan, Lawrence, 57–58
Kapodistrias, Ioannis Antonios (Count
    Capodistria), 94, 101–2, 101n71, 106
Kapp Putsch, 140
von Kaunitz, Wenzel Anton, 55–56, 72
Keith, Robert Murray, 72
Keynes, John Maynard, 145
Khalil, Mustafa, 205n126
Khomeini, Ayatollah, 174–77, 175n1, 176n6,
    181, 187, 190–91, 193, 194n81, 196, 198,
    202, 205–08, 214
Kingdom of Sardinia, see Piedmont Revolution
Kingdom of the Two Sicilies, see Naples Revolution
Kissinger, Henry, 11
Klein, Fritz, 144
Kronstadt revolt, 142
Külmann, Richard von, 133–34
Kun, Béla, 135

Laibach, Congress of, 103–4
Lausanne Conference, 160
Le Faisceau, 151, 154–56, 161
League of Armed Neutrality, 52–53, 63, 72

League of Nations, 160
Lebanon War (1982), 201
legitimacy of rulers, 12, 26, 91, 106, 160, 173,
    182–83, 196, 204, 207, 209, 215
    as a concept, 11n5
Leidse Ontwerp, 75
Lenin, Vladimir, 119–21, 121n7, 122n11, 128,
    130, 131n35, 137, 140, 163, 179n20
liberalism, 6, 13, 19, 27, 50, 80–85, 87–88, 94,
    101–2, 110–12, 114, 148–49, 222, see also
    democracy
    contrast to radicalism, 82
Linguet, Simo-Nicholas Henri, 49n44
Lintorn-Orman, Rotha, 153
Litvinov, Maxim, 135
Lloyd George, David, 131–32, 135, 139–40, 145,
    145n97
Locarno conference, 147, 161
Louis XVI (King of France), 44–46, 64, 67, 69,
    70, 73n132, 75n138, 77
Louis XVIII (King of France), 87, 99, 109
Ludendorff, Erich, 133–34, 153
L'Union, 87
Luxemburg, Rosa, 123

Machiavell, Niccolò, 11
Maginot Line, 147
Maltzan, Ago, 142
Marc, Armand (comte de Montmorin), 70
March on Rome, 156–57, 163–65
Maria Theresa (Empress of Austria), 37, 39, 55, 61
Marxism, 120–24, 148–49, see also Bolshevism,
    communism/socialism, Russian
    Revolution, socialism
Marxist Russian Social Democratic Labor
    Party, 119
Mayer, Arno, 144
Mensheviks, 129
mercantilism, 45
von Metternich, Klemens, 85–86, 86n27, 93–95,
    97, 99–103, 105, 105n86, 108–9, 109n105,
    111–12, 114–117
Mexican Revolution, 13
Milyukov, Pavel 129
Ministry of Islamic Guidance, 177
Minorca, 42, 52
Mirabeau, Honoré, 35
Miracle of the Vistula, 141
Moñino y Redondo, José (Conde de
    Floridablanca), 47n38, 48
Montazeri, Ayatollah Mohammad, 178
de Montmorency, Mathieu Jean Felicité (duc de
    Montmorency-Laval), 109

Montreux conference, 151
Morsi, Mohamed, 221
Mosley, Oswald, 151, 153–54, 162
du Motier, Gilbert (Marquis de Lafayette), 88
Movement of Vanguards' Missionaries, 183. *See also* Islamic Revolution Organization in the Arabian Peninsula
Mubarak, Hosni, 206–7, 212, 220–21
Murat, Joachim, 93
Murphy, Orville, 68–69
Muslim Brotherhood
  in Egypt, 179–80, 182, 197, 203–6, 220–21
  in Iraq, 181n24, 197
  in Sudan, 197
  in Syria, 180, 180n23, 197–200, 202n117, 205n127, 215
Mussolini, Benito, 148–51, 153–54, 156, 158, 160–68

Naples Revolution (Kingdom of the Two Sicilies), 7, 28–29, 78–79
  Austrian policy toward, 99–103, 114
  British policy toward, 100, 103, 115
  French policy toward, 7, 29, 78, 95, 99–103, 115
  as a model, 80, 113
  as a platform, 81, 113
  Prussian policy toward, 100–1, 115
  Russian policy toward, 29, 78, 99–103, 115
Napoleonic Wars, effects of, 82, 91–93
Nasser, Gamal Abdel, 179, 184, 186
Nasserism, 1, 178, 184
National Fascist Party (PNF), 148
National Guard (Saudi Arabia), 208
National Socialist German Workers' Party (NSDAP), 147, 151–53, 163n156, 165, 167–68
nationalism, 1, 13, 80, 82, 128, 138, 148, 150–52, 155, 162, 176n6, 178
Nazi Party, *see* National Socialist German Workers' Party (NSDAP)
Neilson, Keith, 170–71
neorealism, *see* realism
Nicholas I (Emperor of Russia), 83n9
Non-Aligned Movement, 191
Northern System, 43
Novosl'stov, Nikolai, 83n12
Nuzhih coup, 194

October Revolution, *see* Russian Revolution
offense/defense balance theory, 25
Office of Liberation Movements, 177
Ogaden War (Ethio-Somali War), 225
Operation Schlusstein, 134n49

opposition groups, 4, 10–11, 13–14, 19–20, 22–23, 31, 33, 43, 57, 74, 78–80, 82, 113, 118, 177, 214, 219
  democrats in Austria, 39
  democrats in Britain, 41
  democrats in France, 38, 44
  democrats in Prussia, 39, 55
  democrats in Russia, 39
  democrats in Spain, 40–42, 44
  communists/socialists in Britain, 122, 124, 125
  communists/socialists in France, 122–23, 125
  communists/socialists in Germany, 122–23, 125, 159, 165, 167, 169
  communists/socialists in Italy, 122–23, 125
  definition of, 19
  fascists in Britain, 152–54, 159, 162, 168, 219
  fascists in France, 20, 152, 154–156, 158–59, 168, 219
  fascists in Germany, 29, 152–53, 156–57, 159, 169, 219
  fascists in Soviet Union, 152, 154, 164, 168–69
  Islamists in Egypt, 179–80, 183, 187, 204, 206, 213
  Islamists in Iraq, 179, 181–83, 187, 194, 196n88, 213–14, 224
  Islamists in Saudi Arabia, 173, 179, 182–83, 187, 203–7, 213, 219
  Islamists in Syria, 179–81, 183, 187, 197, 198–99, 213, 224
  leaders' subjective judgments of, 21
  liberals in Austria, 85–89
  liberals in Britain, 88–90
  liberals in France, 20, 86–88
  liberals in Prussia, 84–85
  liberals in Russia, 83–84
  organizational size, 19–20
  regimes' interest in deterring, 11
Osborne, Francis Godolphin (Marquess of Carmarthen), 71
Ottoman Empire, 43, 68, 73n134, 78–79, 93–95, 104, 106
Owen, John (*The Clash of Idea in World Politics*), 26

Pahlavi, Mohammad Reza (Shah of Iran), 174, 185–86, 187n44, 189, 194, 198, 204, 206n130, 207
Paine, Thomas 50, 50n46, 59
Pan-German League, 152
Panin, Nikita, 52–54
Papal States, 81, 100n66, *see also* Naples Revolution
Paris Peace Conference, *see* Treaty of Versailles

Parti Social Français, 155n131
Patriot party (Dutch Republic), 59–60, 63, 65–68, 70
People's Commissariat of Foreign Affairs (Narkomindel), 120–21
Pestel, Pavel, 84
Pétain, Henri Philippe Benoni Omer, 129
Peterloo Massacre, 89
philosophes, 37, 38n18, 49, 60
physiocrats, 37
Piedmont Revolution (Kingdom of Sardinia), 7, 28–29, 78–79
    Austrian policy toward, 103
    British policy toward, 103
    French policy toward, 7, 29, 78, 95, 103–4, 115
    as a model, 80, 113
    as a platform, 81, 113
    Prussian policy toward, 115
    Russian policy toward, 29, 78, 115
Pilsudski, Joseph, 138–39
Piscatori, James, 176n6
Pitt, William, 65–67
Poincaré, Raymond, 129–30, 155, 160, 162
Poland, independence of, 94, 137–42, 218
Poland, first partition of, 43
Polish Corridor, 141
Polish National Committee (KNP), 139–39
Polish Socialist Party, 138
Polish-Soviet War, 136, 139–41
Popular Islamic Conferences, 211
Portuguese Revolution, 7, 28, 78–79
    Austrian policy toward, 112
    British policy toward, 110–12, 115
    French policy toward, 78, 111–12
    as a model, 80, 113
    as a platform, 81, 113
    Russian policy toward, 112
    Spanish propaganda efforts, 81
Price, Munro, 69
Primo de Rivera, José Antonio, 151
process tracing, 19, 24
Provisional Government, 119, 128–29, 128n25, 138
public opinion, 98–99
Pugachev revolt, 39, 39n21
Putin, Vladimir, 222

Quadruple Alliance, 92, 95, 98
Qutb, Sayyid, 179, 179n20

Radical Enlightenment, 37–39, 74, see also Enlightenment
Radischev, Alexander, 53
von Ranke, Leopold, 57

Rassemblement National Populaire (RNP), 155n132
Raynal, Guillaume Thomas, 37, 38n18
Rayneval, Joseph Mathias Gérard de, 67, 69
realism, 2, 2n3, 75–76, 95, 147, 171, 188, 202, 215, 217, 220, 224, see also balance of power, geopolitics/geopolitical advantage, realpolitik, spheres of influence
realpolitik, 16–18, 25, 29, 32, 229, see also balance of power, geopolitics/geopolitical advantage, realism, realpolitik, spheres of influence
regents (Dutch Republic), 58, 60, 62, 66
Reinsurance Treaty, 125
rejectionist front, 198, 206, 212
Rendall, Matthew, 106
regime security, 6n10, 25, 114
Repentance and Holy Flight (Takfir wa'l-Hijra), see Society of Muslims (Jama'at al-Muslimin)
revolutionary foreign policy, 224–25
Revolutionary Guards (Iran), 177–78
revolutionary movements, see opposition groups
revolutionary waves, see ideological contagion
revolutions as models, 4, 9–13, 15–18, 23, 27, 220, 224
    mechanisms, 10–11, 10n1, 11n3, 26
revolutions as natural experiments, 3
revolutions as platforms, 4, 7, 9, 12, 15–18, 23, 27, 220, 224
    mechanisms, 12
    spatial and temporal patterns, 23, 25
revolutions, definition of, 3, 3n5, 19
Rey, Joseph, 87
Risorgimento, 157
Rouhani, Ayatollah Sadeq, 178
Rousseau, Jean-Jacques, 49
Ruhr, occupation of, 147, 157, 161
Russian Civil War, 132–36
Russian democratic protests (2011), 222
Russian Revolution, 7, 14, 29, 53, 118–20, 125, 127–30, 134–35, 137, 147
    Allied military intervention, 132–36, 142
    British policy toward, 118, 127, 130–31, 135–36, 138–40, 142, 144, 146
    French policy toward, 118, 127, 129–33, 135–36, 138–41, 144, 161
    German policy toward, 118, 127–30, 133–34, 137–38, 141–44, 146–47, 171, 198, 218–19
    Italian policy toward, 118, 127, 130, 132, 138, 144
    as a model, 118–20, 135, 146, 219
    as a platform, 118, 120–21, 130, 134–35, 142, 144, 146, 170, 219, 224
    Polish question, 137–142, 218

Russo-Turkish War (1768–74), 93
Russo-Turkish War (1787–92), 68, 72, 73

Sabah, Shaykh, 208
Sadr, Bani, 202n117
Sadat, Anwar, 179, 180, 184, 186, 203–6, 205n127, 206n130, 212
Schelling, Thomas, 10n1
Schroeder, Paul 78, 106, 109n105, 116
Sébastiani, Horace, 104
Second Continental Congress, 33, 53
second image reversed effect, 6–7, 228
Second International, 122, 124
Second Treaty of Paris, 92, 94, see also Congress of Vienna system
Seditious Meeting Act, 90
de Ségur, Philippe Henri (comte de Ségur), 50, 70
self-determination, 139
Semenovsky Revolt, 84, 102, 113, 259
Seven Years War, effects of, 33, 42–43, 54, 61
Shatt al-'Arab, 186, 192, 192n63, 195, 195n83
Skocpol, Theda, 3n5
Six Acts, 90, 98
Six-Day War, 178, 180, 184
Social Democratic Party of Germany (SPD), 122–23, 129, 168
social identity mechanism, 3, 26
socialism, 29, 118–24, 126, 129–31, 133, 136, 138, 149, 153, 159–60, 163–64, 168–69, 219, see also communism/socialism
Society of the Cincinnati, 35, 76n149
Society of Muslims (Jama'at al-Muslimin), 179n21, 180
Sorel, Albert, 77
Soucy, Robert 155–56
South Tyrol, 166–67
sovereignty, 32, 34, 60, 78, 80, 82
Spa Field riots, 90
Spanish Civil War, 171
Spanish Constitution of 1812, 79–80, 97, 97n56, 111
Spanish Revolution, 7, 28–29, 78–79
  Austrian policy toward, 97, 99, 108–9
  British policy toward, 97–99, 108–9, 108n101, 115
  French policy toward, 107, 109
  as a model, 80, 113
  as a platform, 81, 113
  Russian policy toward, 97, 108–9
  Prussian policy toward, 108–9
  Spanish propaganda efforts, 107
  spread to Naples, 99
Sparticus uprising, 135, 141

Spence, Thomas, 89
Spenceans, 89
Speransky, Michael, 83, 83n7
Spheres of influence, 92–93, 99, 103, 185 see also balance of power, geopolitics/geopolitical advantage, realism, realpolitik
spirals of suspicion model, 25, 226
stadtholder, see Batavus, Willem (William V, Prince of Orange)
Staglhelm (Steel Helments), 152
States General (Dutch Republic), 58, 68
Steiner, Zara 145, 159
Stewart, Robert (Lord Castlereagh), 81, 90, 93–95, 97–103, 97n58, 103n77, 108, 110
Stresemann, Gustav, 143, 165–66
Supreme Assembly for the Islamic Revolution in Iraq, 177, 196
Syrian Islamic Front, 199

Technical Military Academy (Jam'at al-Fanniyya al-'askariya), see Society of Muslims (Jama'at al-Muslimin)
Thermidorian Reaction, 224n13
Three Emperors' League, 1, 125
throne and alter, union of, 82, 105n86
Thule Society, 152
Tilly, Charles, 3n5
de la Tour du Pin-Gouvernet, Jean-Frédéric (Count La Tour du Pin), 103n77
transnational nationalism, 149, 169, see also nationalism
Treaty of Brest-Litovsk, 130–31, 134, 140, 145–46
Treaty of London, 126, 157
Treaty of Rapallo, 143
Triple Alliance, 125
Troppau, Congress of, 101–2
Trotsky, Leon, 120, 130, 131n35, 134, 137, 140
Tunisian Revolution, 14
Túpac Amaru II Rebellion, 40
Turgot, Anne Robert Jacques, 45, 75

Ukranian revolutions (2004 and 2013–14), 222
Ulam, Adam, 146
Union for Defense of the Motherland and Liberty, 132
Union of Salvation, 83

Valois, George, 151, 154
Verona, Congress of, 108–9
Versailles Treaty, 137, 139, 141–45, 147, 157, 162, 166
  reparations issue, 157
velayat-e-faqih (guardianship of the jurist), 174

Victor Emmanuel I (King of Sardinia), 79
Victor Emmanuel III (King of Italy), 148
de Vignerot du Plessis, Armand-Emmanuel
    (duc de Richelieu), 97, 101, 105–6, 117
Villéle, Joseph de, 105, 109
Volunteer Army, 132

Wahhabism, 182
Walldorf Jr., C. William, 27n25
Walt, Stephen (*Revolutions and War*), 14,
    25–26, 139
Waltz, Kenneth (*Theory of International
    Politics*), 229
War of Austrian Succession, 43

Washington, George, 46
Weimar Constitution, 168
Wellesley, Arthur (Duke of Wellington), 97,
    98n58, 100, 108
Weyland, Kurt, 13
Wilhelm II (German Emperor), 134
Wilhelmina, Frederika Sophia (Princess of
    Orange), 59, 61, 63, 65–68, 71–72, 72n129
Wilkes, John, 41n27
Wilson, Woodrow, 138–39

Yazdi, Ebrahim, 191
Yom Kippur War, 186
Ypsilantis, Alexander, 79, 104